ALRIGHT, LET'S CALL IT A DRAW

ALRIGHT, LET'S CALL IT A DRAW
The Life of John Pryor

by John & Rich Pryor

lanxnal
Delmar, New York

Alright, Let's Call It A Draw
Copyright © 2012 Richard J. Pryor

This is a book of narrative non-fiction. Every effort has been made to portray events and characters accurately based on memories of the author, writings and recordings of John Pryor, written correspondence and personal interviews. As in memoir, characters are combined, events are rearranged and imaginative prose used to fill gaps in the story. Despite these techniques, the author has endeavored to convey truth in regard to John Pryor's thoughts and actions.

Edited by Mary Jane Dittmar

Cover Design by Kelly Fahey
www.primeaufahey.com

Cover photograph © Ryan Donnell
www.ryandonnell.com

Published via CreateSpace
www.createspace.com

ISBN: 978-0-9857550-0-3
Library of Congress Control Number: 2012912549

Website: www.drjohnpryor.com
Correspondence: drjohnpryor@gmail.com

Printed in the United States of America

MEO FRATRI.
SI EGO DATVS ESSEM OPTIONEM,
MORTVVS ESSEM TECVM.

Only a life lived for others is a life worthwhile.
— Albert Einstein

Seek always to do some good, somewhere. Every man has
to seek in his own way to realize his true worth. You must
give some time to your fellow man. For remember, you don't
live in a world all your own. Your brothers are here too.
— Albert Schweitzer

I think of a hero as someone who understands the degree
of responsibility that comes with his freedom.
— Bob Dylan

Contents

Prologue

The journal is large, not like the little handbook Indiana Jones would use to map directions to a priceless artifact. The soft leather is warm and seems to breathe under my gentle hand. The corners are guarded by elaborate copper engravings and the fore edge is gold leaf, like an old bible. My fingers fall into the imprinted letters forming my name. An ornate hyphen spans the two dates.

I open the front cover. The title page bears my name, embossed in flowing calligraphy. The following page holds empty rows of expectant lines, thirsting for ink.

The pen is a Parker. I remember my brother gave me one like this. The matte black shaft cools my fingers. The cap has a gold clip shaped like an arrow—like the Order of the Arrow. I unsheathe the instrument and store the cap.

The nib hovers above cotton fiber. Time passes. I struggle to begin, where to start. Finally, I shrug and write ...

My name is John Pryor. I'm a surgeon. I'll be forty-three next month, and I just got killed.

I know, can you believe this shit?

I'm on call tonight. Omar's gonna have to cover for me. There's two dying in the ICU he doesn't know about. One needs to go back to the OR. I planned an in-service tomorrow with the corpsmen; it'll need to be rescheduled. God, there's so much shit to do—this can't be happening.

Carm's gonna be pissed. She's gonna be royally pissed. I told her—I said, "Carm, I have a bad feeling about this tour. I don't think I'm coming back alive." I don't know what it was, but I couldn't shake the feeling. She said I was being ridiculous.

But, I was right.

I can't believe it, but I was right. Now look at this—fucking dead.

I'm still not sure what happened. Christmas mass ended, and I headed for the barracks. A loud impact, like a metal container falling off a truck, stopped me. I should've hit the deck, but I hesitated. I stood frozen, eyes scanning the sky.

A deafening shriek, like a monster bottle rocket, shot toward me, and then... silence.

No boom. No pain. Nothing. I became numb. The barracks faded into a white cloud like fog rolling in from the coast. I felt my earthly footing dissolve away into a spiritual ether.

A dark figure appeared in the mist. As he approached, I recognized him.

"You're fucking kidding me, right?" I said.

I NEVER KID, *he said.*

His voice convinced me. I knew DEATH. *I battled him all my life, but I never heard him speak. Now, I couldn't deny he'd come for me.*

"What the hell happened?" I said. How could I be walking to the latrine one minute and dead the next? People don't die like this; they don't die instantly.

Prologue

He didn't answer. Instead he said, WHAT BROUGHT YOU TO IRAQ?

Isn't it obvious, I thought? I came to help the troops.

Then, I sensed a deeper meaning to his question. He wasn't asking why I was here, but what led me here. I thought of all the decisions and influences that culminated in Mosul, like Russian Matryoshka dolls, one set within another, marching backward in time.

"I'd have to tell you my whole life story," I said.

He handed me this journal and pen.

I'VE GOT TIME, *he said.*

Boy Scouts of America

July 1981. A rare breeze flutters the bed sheet disguising Camp Saratoga as Camp Toga. The gust delivers a mix of warm pine and creosote, forever reminding me of summer. Sizzling cicadas crescendo in the heat. On a birch-shaded hill, Scouts lash together a lookout tower. A waterfront whistle blows, arresting piranha-like turbulence; pairs of swimmers hold up dripping arms for a buddy check. A volley of .22 caliber popping corn echoes from the rifle range. A red-handled pitcher pump squeals icy water into open palms. Smiling campers exit the trading post, cheeks swollen with Swedish Fish, Charleston Chew and Snickers.

Meanwhile, I'm stealing a motorcycle.

It's my first attempt at grand larceny and, fortunately, I'm not alone. Encircling the motorcycle are my cohorts in crime, forming a huddle, like segments of a giant caterpillar. We're inching our way across a soggy field headed for the showers. The locked front wheel angles sharply to port; we lift it to move forward.

Slippery palms and trembling muscles force me to drop the wheel; our caterpillar pauses. Ankles sink into muddy sod. I wipe sweat from my forehead and survey the scene. I'm surrounded by my best friends; Scouts who have become my brothers.

Heaving the chrome handlebar with me is Paul Lonczak. Short and stocky, Paul was a starting linebacker and evoked images of John Belushi. During our fifty-mile canoe trip, Paul would portage a canoe with full pack while singing *I Want To Be An Airborne Ranger*. A year my senior, he possessed charisma and confidence that made him a natural leader.

When flustered, John Norris' mild stutter became debilitating. Once he was on stage giving a talk while we giggled our asses off in the front row. Hoff leaned up and whispered, "John, John... your fly is open!" John froze, mouth open, fighting the urge to look down or touch his crotch. His stuttering became incapacitating, and we cackled uncontrollably: His fly wasn't open.

Tim Hoff had a boisterous laugh and a huge gut to match. On rare occasions, he would treat us to a belly dance. Undulating waves of fat mesmerized his audience, especially after a few beers.

Joey Fox had to watch our burglary from the barn. A crooked, gimpy leg caused a severe limp. More an ambulatory impairment than handicap, Joe's leg slowed him down but never kept him out.

A few chromosomes shy of albinism, Shawn Brimhall could talk his way out of any indictment. The morning we rolled into camp, still drunk from the bars, Shawn took the lead when the camp director approached us.

"Where were you guys?" he asked with a scowl.

"We went to get the paper," Shawn said.

"Yeah? Where's the paper?"

"Oh," Shawn said without hesitation, "We read it and threw it away."

Art Crowe, Ed Davenport, and Dave Humphrey rounded out our band of thieves.

Then there's me, the white kid with an afro. Nearly six foot, not counting the hair, I was skinny as a toothpick. A spattering of freckles, summoned by the summer sun, contrasted against the green in my eyes. After wrestling a buck-toothed overbite into place, my braces had recently been removed, revealing a perfectly straight smile.

As you'd expect, you learn a lot in the Boy Scouts: tying knots, starting campfires, orienteering, swimming, the usual things. You wouldn't expect the other stuff: forging fake IDs, rolling a joint, picking locks and stealing motorcycles. To be fair, we weren't *stealing* the motorcycle; we were moving it without permission. It was a prank on the Admiral.

But the Admiral wasn't your typical camp counselor, and this wasn't your ordinary motorcycle.

The Admiral—no one knew his real rank or whether he was still in the Navy—was not to be fucked with. The first day at the archery range, he pulled a smoldering stogie from his teeth, wiped sweat from his scar and barked, "Where's Brockbank?"

Robbie Brockbank was a trouble magnet. If something was broke, stolen or crying, Brockbank was the first word to cross the leader's lips.

All eyes focused on Brockbank as he lowered a packet of Nestlé cocoa mix from his mouth. Dropping his clipboard, the Admiral was beside him in a blink. Brockbank flew off his seat and slammed into a pine with a resounding crunch. Fragments of bark splintered away as Brockbank gave out a groan. The Admiral dropped him to the ground with a thud.

"That's for doin nothin' wrong!" he said, pointing. "You fuck with me, Brockbank, and I'll have your balls. You understand?"

That was the Admiral.

The Harley was a 1939 fire engine red Knucklehead with leather saddle bags and whitewall tires. After months of restoration, the Admiral had delivered her to original condition. Evergreens rattled when the hog thundered into camp. He parked in the barn opposite the director's lodge without locking the doors; nobody was stupid enough to touch that machine.

"Hey," I asked no one in particular, "you know what would be really funny?" A bunch of us were lounging at the waterfront, soaking up the rays.

"What?" asked Norris, eyes squinting in my direction.

"If someone stole the Admiral's hog," I said with a mischievous smile.

An immediate outburst of laughter was mixed with "Yeah, right," "No way," and "Fucking suicide, man."

"No, listen," I said, "he keeps it in the barn. All we have to do is move it across the field to the showers. We won't do anything, just move it."

Among fellow fifteen-year-old boys, my reasoning was unassailable. "Yeah, but then what?" asked Hoff.

"Then nothing," I said. "We watch him freak out when he finds the barn empty. Eventually, someone will see it in the showers, and that will be it."

"That would be funny to see," said Lonczak, giving the idea some traction. If Paul was interested, then the plan was a go.

The next day, we convened near the trading post trying to act natural. Our mischief had taken many forms over the years: tying Brockbank to his cot, hoisting the leader's underwear, sneaking beers in our packs, breaking into the mess hall for a midnight snack. Stealing a motorcycle was on a whole new level.

My brother Rich and his friends suspected something and gathered around. We shared our plan, and they eagerly offered to help.

"Spaz," Paul said to the younger Scout, "we need a lookout."

"Sure," he said. "What do you want me to do?"

"Go halfway to the archery range," Paul said, "if you see the Admiral, you come running back and let us know."

"Got it!" Spaz took off to his post.

We turned our attention to the Knucklehead. It took two of us to push it off the kickstand. As Hoff and Norris started to push, it took a sharp left.

"Straighten out the wheel," Norris said.

"I can't—it's locked," I said. "Stop pushing for a sec."

Paul and I looked at each other.

"What'dya think?" he asked.

"Can we lift it?" I said.

Paul and I hoisted the front frame.

"Okay, push now," I said. Paul and I shuffled forward as the bike moved along.

On the dirt-packed driveway, we came to a stop. I eyed the distance to the showers and then glanced back into the barn.

"I think we can make it," I said. The others, not burdened with the front wheel, were more confident.

"C'mon, let's do it before Rooney sees us," Brimhall said.

It had rained the previous night. Most of the ground was dry, but our field to be crossed had a subtle dip. The pool of waterlogged grass and mud wasn't obvious until you were standing in it. Or trying to drag a four-hundred-pound motorbike through it.

It got worse.

Paul and I were getting fatigued, and the footing became precarious. Crowe was painted in mud after a fall. It took forever to move a few feet, and we were only halfway to the showers. It didn't help to see Spaz come running over the hill.

Wide-eyed and ashen, he seemed torn between warning us and running for his life. He settled on a shout as he ran by, "HE'S COMING!"

My heart started to pound; there was no time to think. The huddled group burst like a firecracker. Everyone fled except Paul and me. If we all ran, the bike would drop in the mud, and that would be a real problem. There was no way around it: *Someone would be left holding the motorcycle.*

I could see the Admiral coming in the distance; only a few seconds remained before we came into view. One of us still had time to escape.

Paul looked at me. "Go," he said, "I got it."

I hesitated. Then I started to run, and time seemed to freeze. Even now I can picture the scene in my head: Paul, the bike, the change in the Admiral's expression. As I ran, an icy chill fisted my gut.

What the hell am I doing? I thought.

In life, we are continually tested. Sometimes we learn the most about ourselves when we fail these tests. That day, I made a mistake. Children run. Cowards run. I shouldn't be running, I should be holding the handlebars with Paul, accepting responsibility for my actions.

I couldn't articulate it then, but, looking back, this was the day I became "somebody else" in "let somebody else take care of it." It set the tone for the rest of my life.

$\sim$

From the ages of eleven to sixteen, my free time was spent in the Scouts. Like any troop, we were a motley collection of kids staying out of trouble or getting into trouble, depending on your definition of trouble. Each Wednesday, the cafeteria tables at Okte Elementary were cleared, and we lined up by patrol. After reciting the pledge, Scout oath and law, bedlam reigned for the next hour.

Between shouts of laughter and horseplay, we planned trips, paid dues and played games. Parents took turns teaching merit badges about citizenship, emergency preparedness, personal management, Morse code, woodworking, astronomy, computers, and public speaking.

Controlling the chaos were our Scoutmasters.

MEL, initials for Michael E. Lonczak, was short with a round face and thinning hair. He descended from Polish ancestry and impressed us with tales of double shifts as a General Electric foreman. Once he showed up to a campout after working an overnight shift. I was amazed he could stay awake for so long.

Someone accidentally called Mr. Heffelfinger "Dad," and the nickname stuck. His personality was warm and comforting, like a father figure. George was a real outdoorsman who could navigate the Adirondacks without a map.

We called Mr. Burr "Jerry" behind his back. Lanky from years of cycling, he was the buzz-kill of the three, usually putting the brakes on our shenanigans before we got started. Whenever there was trouble, he would intercede saying, "Uhh, guys… I don't think that's such a good idea."

It became his mantra.

Once we pitched tents in a circle around the campfire. Mr. Burr came along and paced out the distance from tent to fire.

"Uhh, guys… you only have eight feet here; the book says the fire needs ten feet from the tents."

We looked around as if he were crazy.

"It's a *circle*, Mr. Burr; we'd have to move all the tents!"

It didn't matter. The book said ten feet. Jerry designed nuclear reactors for a living, so his fastidiousness could be excused, if not completely understood.

In the beginning, there were eight of us. As younger kids joined, we formed a leadership patrol and named it "The Wanderers."

Troop 30 quickly filled with characters: My little brother Rich, big hair and chipped front tooth; Mr. Burr's son, Dave, sporting coke bottle glasses; Mr. Heffelfinger's son, Darren, working on a moustache; Don Tozier, whose dad had the largest arms I've ever seen on a man. There were the Lacase brothers—Dane, Chad and little Beau, who made you wonder if his mom drank during her pregnancy. Paul Cupp, Pat Kelly, Mark Brazier and Kevin Hogan, who surprised us by not burning down camp while playing with matches. And Robbie Brockbank, who continued to get in trouble for a lifetime after leaving the troop.

Together we laughed, learned, explored and matured. We ventured in MEL's conversion van and Mr. Burr's "Yellow Submarine." Along the way, CB radios lit up the airways with farting noises and crude knock-knock jokes.

We toured Saratoga Battlefield, slept over at Plattsburgh Air Force Base and climbed Mt. Marcy. At Valley Forge, we learned of Washington's surprise attack against Hessian forces on Christmas 1776.

"Sneaky bastards," I said.

"Hey," Davenport said, "all's fair in love and war."

But the mainstay of our activities was the campout. There was the Spring Camporee, the Fall Camporee and, yes, the Winter Camporee. I spent a week at summer camp until I became a counselor; then it was five weeks. When I joined the Order of the Arrow, there were additional work weekends and conclaves.

We learned to pack a backpack, stay dry in the rain and pitch a tent in the dark. We learned to build campfires, cook meals, tie knots and use a compass. At summer camp, we learned to paddle a canoe, lash together a signal tower, survive in the wilderness and rescue a drowning victim.

In short, we learned to live up to our motto: Be Prepared.

Looking back, I learned more useful things in Scouts than in high school. I never used geometry much, but each Christmas I secured a tree using two half hitches MEL taught me. I can't recall the capital of South Dakota, but I remember how Mr. Heffelfinger built the campfire so that it would ignite with a single match. I can't remember the quadratic formula, but I can show you how Mr. Burr taught me to cook a meal in aluminum foil.

These and many more lessons shaped me as a young man.

❦

Summer 1982. Camp Saratoga. Crickets filled the midnight air like maracas, and remnants of campfire smoke wafted amidst the pines. Constellations festooned the heavens, the Pleiades, the Hyades and Orion visible through gaps in the forest canopy, but my attention was downward, dodging knotted roots and half-exposed rocks intent on tripping me.

"Stay with us, man!" Paul said, "Stay with us!"

I learned the two-man carry as a tenderfoot, but this was my first time applying it for real. Paul and I ran through the woods rescuing our wounded comrade.

"We're almost there, man; you're gonna make it!"

I couldn't stifle a laugh.

"It's not funny," Baker said between Paul and me, "shit fucking hurts."

A door burst open; the quiet slumber inside the Rabbit Hole exploded. Bright lights and shouts woke the counselors to instant chaos.

"What the fuck?" Rich said, eyes half open.

Paul and I shuffled in and dropped Baker into his bunk. In the light, I saw blood—my first time with a man's blood on my hands.

"What is it? What the hell happened?" The counselors in training stood shocked and frightened.

I tried to imagine what we looked like.

We were out on maneuvers—Lonczak, Hoff, Norris, Baker and me. Maneuvers was the act of donning combat fatigues, painting faces with camouflage grease and roaming the camp in the middle of the night. An adult might ask what in God's name we were doing out in the dark, to which we would reply, "Having fun, sir."

Fun, that is, until Baker landed his shin on the concrete dam. His scream should've woken the entire camp.

"Is it bad?" Baker started to sit up.

"Relax." Paul pushed him back down. "Let us take a look."

"I need scissors," I said, eyeing the bloody fatigues, "and get the first aid kit."

Norris offered Swiss army scissors, and Hoff threw me a towel; Brimhall focused a flashlight. The whites of their eyes gleamed like beacons in the green and brown camouflage. I cut the pant leg from the bottom; I stopped at the knee and parted the blood-soaked cloth.

There were gasps.

"What? What is it?" A half dozen hands stopped Baker from sitting up. "Does it need stitches?"

It needs fucking surgery, I thought.

The wound started below the knee and snaked down to the outside, edges gaped like a large mouth bass. Shin bone gave way to deep maroon of muscle. Yellow fat globules peeked from the margins, and blood drooled down his leg.

"Yeah," I sighed, packing it with gauze, "you're gonna need stitches."

"We hafta change and get cleaned up," Paul said, looking around, "then we'll get Rooney."

"What're we gonna tell him?" I asked.

"We'll think of something," said Paul.

After an hour of scrubbing, the grease paint was mostly gone. Stubborn spots remained, but we were clean enough to pass for campers. Norris summoned the camp director.

Ken Rooney grimaced, sucked in air and turned away. I replaced the gauze bandage before he went faint.

"You did this coming back from the latrine?" he asked, looking at the wall.

"Yeah," Baker said, "it must've been a sharp rock."

Mr. Rooney eyed the huddled Scouts. He didn't care that we were lying; he just wanted to resolve the problem.

"Who's coming to the hospital with me?" he sighed.

"I'll go," I said.

Saratoga Emergency Room was nearly empty. Mr. Rooney unfolded Baker's medical release form and handed it to a cute triage nurse with blonde hair and big tits. Baker and I exchanged smirks. I wondered if I looked as filthy.

I wheeled Baker past other patients: a mother consoling her crying infant, an old man gasping into a mask of white smoke, a sloven man smelling like piss. We arrived at our room, and Baker hobbled onto the stretcher.

Next to the gurney, Mr. Rooney sat and, despite his best efforts, began to nod off.

"Hey," Baker whispered, "see if you can grab his keys; we'll go out driving after I get stitched up."

I smiled at the thought.

"Yeah, right," I said, "I think he'd have us arrested."

A woman draped in a lab coat and stethoscope appeared. She flipped through the chart.

"Hello, Mr. Baker, my name is Dr. Pomeroy; it looks like you did a number on your leg. How'd this happen?"

Baker glanced at Rooney's slumped head, quietly snoring. I shrugged when our eyes met.

"I fell," he said. "We're at camp; I tripped going to the latrine. It musta been a sharp rock." A brunette nurse with nice legs wheeled over a towel-covered mayo stand. I liked the blonde better.

"Let's take a look," Dr. Pomeroy said. "Let me know if I'm hurting you."

She cut the dressing away, and the flesh flopped open.

"You *did* do a job, didn't you?" She glanced at me, "You okay watching?"

Okay, I have to tell you, looking at this wound in the bright lights of the ER was the coolest thing I'd ever seen. I was looking inside someone's leg! I could see veins and arteries and muscle. My gut fluttered; it felt as if I were on a roller coaster. I couldn't imagine anyone disturbed by something so…fascinating.

Dr. Pomeroy drew medication from a vial.

"What's that?" I asked.

"Lidocaine," she said giving me a sideways glance, "like novocaine when you go to the dentist." Baker twisted in agony as she injected the margins.

"It hurts going in," she said, "but then it'll be numb."

I was hooked. Every move was met with a question. What bone was that? How do you fix muscle? What are stitches made of? How long would it take to heal? How many stitches do you put? I was a real pain in the ass, but Dr. Pomeroy didn't seem to mind.

Finally, the wound was closed. A long caterpillar of sutures replaced what was once a gaping wound. Baker had fallen asleep. I was surprised Mr. Rooney hadn't fallen out of his chair. Despite the early morning hour, I wasn't tired.

"Well, that's it," Dr. Pomeroy said as she finished wrapping the leg, "thanks for keeping me company; usually, I have to tolerate some drunk swearing at me."

"No problem," I said, "it was totally excellent."

"Maybe you'll be a doctor someday," she offered.

A doctor? I thought.

The way she said it—like it was a real possibility—struck me. The exhilaration of watching the procedure and her suggestion were synergistic. At the time, I had no idea of what I would do with my life, but that night a seed had been planted.

I woke up Baker and gently shook Mr. Rooney's shoulder.

"We're done, Mr. Rooney," I said. "You want me to drive back to camp?"

Mid-yawn, he registered what I said.

"No thanks, John," he said. "I'm tired—not stupid."

☙

I ran for the foxhole, M-16 cradled in my arms. A slack chinstrap let my helmet flop forward, obscuring my view. I moved slowly despite running hard, like fighting a strong headwind. Soldiers' shouts filled the smoky battlefield. A scream of enemy fighter jets was the prelude to a shower of bombs. I ran with all my might, but it was like moving through molasses. I was nearly there, when, BOOM!

I awoke bolt upright, pulse pounding. My first dream of battle—so vivid. It really felt like I'd died. I slapped a mosquito buzzing my ear and curled up next to my tree. It's my Ordeal weekend. Tonight I'm out under the stars, alone in the woods with only crickets for company and a sleeping bag for shelter.

The Order of the Arrow (OA) is a separate organization within the Boy Scouts. Each year, the troop held elections to choose those Scouts who manifest the ideals of the brotherhood: service to others, Scout spirit, and leadership through example. Members of the OA were distinguished by a red arrow embroidered on a thin white sash.

Those elected must then pass the Ordeal work weekend. Candidates are forced to sleep under the stars and toil throughout the day with little food—all while remaining completely silent. A college fraternity performing the same ritual would have its charter revoked.

Earlier that day, I gathered with the other candidates in the mess hall. Davenport, Crowe and Hoff were also elected. We joked about the challenges ahead.

"I brought an umbrella in case it rains," I said.

"I'd like to see you hold an umbrella in your sleep," Davenport said.

"I'll train a squirrel to hold it," I said.

We fell silent as Chris Gimbrone walked to the front. He wore a plaid shirt; his arrow boasted a mid-shaft triangle denoting the vigil honor. A thick beard earned him his Indian name, Tooney, "bearded one."

"Welcome to the Ta-Oun-Ya-Wat-Ha Ordeal Weekend," he said with a smile. Chris discussed the ground rules and instructions for the next two days. When he was done, it was time to carve our arrows.

The wooden arrow distinguished candidates from Arrowmen, but also served to record violations in protocol. Any speaking or misconduct earned a notch in the arrow. Three notches, and you were out.

Outside the mess hall, we whittled maple branches into crude arrow shapes. When finished, mine looked more like a rocket than an arrow. Knotting a length of bailing twine, I draped it over my afro and stole a glance before letting it settle on my chest.

No notches, I promised.

We lined up in the fading twilight, a ragged crew dressed in T-shirts, zipper front sweatshirts, baseball caps and sneakers. Each had a sleeping bag tucked under one arm, and no one appeared prepared for the night alone.

Hiking along dwindling paths, I soon found myself bushwhacking through parts of camp I hadn't known existed. Periodically, the group would halt, and Chris would escort a candidate into the bush. Crunching of wooded detritus faded as the pair disappeared from view. A few minutes later, Chris reappeared alone and led the group onward.

Presently, it was my turn. Chris led me to a small clearing.

"This is your spot, John," he said, "I want you to reflect on why you're here. Why you were selected. If you complete your Ordeal, what responsibilities will you have to live up to?"

Later, I would get to know Chris pretty well, and this was uncharacteristic of him. He was usually a goof, smiling, giggling and having fun. But he took the principles of the OA seriously, and his dedication to the organization impressed me.

"Yes sir," I said, "I will."

The next morning, I was dead asleep, cocooned in my sleeping bag. A foot prodded me awake.

"Pryor. Wake up." It was Mike Shaver, one of the Arrowmen, trying to rouse me.

Buzzing mosquitoes had kept me awake all night, and I remained paralyzed with exhaustion.

The bottom of my bag abruptly yanked skyward, unceremoniously delivering me to the forest floor.

"He's up now," said Pete Anderson, an Arrowman with a more direct approach.

I pulled a rotting maple leaf from my fro and staggered toward the others, my bag trailing behind.

The monastic silence at breakfast was broken by an occasional cough or whisper of an Arrowman. I hungrily spooned my Cheerios and lifted the paper bowl for any remaining milk.

After collecting our utensils, we were handed small folds of colored paper. Inside was written:

> With the rising sun comes a new day.
> How will you handle the hardships to come?
> To join the Brotherhood of Cheerful Service,
> One must give of himself unselfishly.
> Ponder these words.

Outside, we were split up into small groups. One was sent to construct tent platforms, another to set up cots, a third went to cut grass and thin out the overgrowth. I grew increasingly anxious as the others received their tasks and departed. One chore was legendarily unpleasant, receiving sympathy from even the latrine detail.

I shifted my weight uncomfortably as the last group grabbed shovels and walked away. Only Hoff, Crowe and I remained.

"I guess the only thing left is… *muck the lake.*"

I bit my tongue trying not to swear.

Our "lake" was actually a dammed-up stream. During the year, silt, rocks and sticks would litter the swimming area. Now the dam was opened, and the lake drained. It was time to dredge up a year's worth of shit.

At the waterfront, Gimbrone gave mucking instructions.

"Take off your shoes and socks; they'll only get caught in the mud," he said. "Sticks and plants go here, garbage here, dead animals go here. We usually remove the muck in the shallow end. Fill up the wheelbarrow and dump it over there."

I entered the bog, my feet slowly sinking into the thick tar. It smelled dank and fetid like so many dead frogs scattered about. I pulled my trailing foot, but the mud resisted. I pulled harder, and it slowly rose with a slurping sound. I placed it quickly in front before losing balance. Just walking in this crap was a challenge.

The sun climbed, pushing the mercury close to 90 degrees. As we labored, the various piles started to gather mass. I lost my balance and fell face-first into the mire. My arms sank up to the elbows; for a moment, I thought I would suffocate before managing to get up on all fours. Hoff and Crowe couldn't contain their laughter as I wiped the mud out of my eyes and smiled in blackface. It smelled like shit, but I have to admit that it felt soothing in the intense heat of the day.

For lunch, we savored a few slices of bologna on Wonder bread, government surplus cheese and all the bug juice we could drink. Some of the others had notches in their arrows; one had two already. I wondered how many Scouts wouldn't make it through the weekend. After lunch, we were handed another piece of folded paper. This one read:

> A young scout left his gear in the rain.
> Who will help retrieve it?

Who will give of themselves,
So that others may be helped?
Ponder these words.

I spent the afternoon clearing rain-soaked ash, charred logs and bits of charcoal from the fire pits. When a fresh fire-lay stood on each platform, we returned to the parade field. Those done early were sent out to help others still working. I roamed with an increasingly larger gang, searching the camp for unfinished business. Finally, we had our full complement of candidates.

The work was done.

Our last meal was tomato soup and two slices of bread. I drank the bowl and used the bread to soak up any residue. My stomach continued to growl as I was given my final piece of paper to read:

The day is over, the work is done.
You have served your fellow man.
How does it make you feel?
This is your reward. Seek no other.
Each day brings new challenges.
Rise to meet them.
Ponder these words.

All I felt was hunger and fatigue. I pocketed the passage and followed the others outside. We lined up single file next to a long rope and were given blindfolds. An Arrowman checked that my blindfold was snug, and the rope was placed in my hand.

"Walk slowly," Chris said, "follow the rope; listen for directions."

The rope became taut in my grip, and I blindly lunged forward. After a few stumbles, I learned to lift my feet high and anticipate uneven ground. I felt the road briefly, but then we turned onto a wooded path. Despite my best efforts, I had no idea where we were.

In the distance, a drumbeat began. Boom bum bum bum, Boom bum bum bum, Boom bum bum bum... slow and steady. As I walked, the sound grew louder. The forest gave way to a grass field as we came upon the drumming. Flickering light penetrated my blindfold, and I smelled the campfires. The line stopped, and the rope went slack.

Boom bum bum bum, Boom bum bum bum, Boom Boom Boom Boom **BOOM!!**

The stunned silence was broken by crackling cinders.

"You may remove your blindfolds."

A line of candidates formed a semicircle around two large bonfires. Midway stood Allowat Sakima, an elaborate headdress reached for the stars before cascading behind. Two Indians in simple headbands flanked the chief holding long torches. Behind them an ornate, oversized bow floated horizontally with the string facing downward. Draped from end to end lay a neat row of starched white sashes; the embroidered red arrows danced in the flickering firelight.

The sight gave me goose bumps.

Arrowmen, dressed as Indians, stood dispersed around the ceremony. Some participated, others stood silent. One narrated the traditional lore while others acted various roles. Allowat Sakima stood motionless, arms folded, as the history and meaning of the brotherhood was revealed. The performance concluded; snapping, popping fire sounds filled the air again.

"Who brings these men to our sacred land?" the chief broke his silence.

An Indian standing with us responded.

"Have they demonstrated their willingness to serve others?"

"They have."

"Have they passed the Ordeal without flinching?"

"They have."

"Are they completely prepared to receive the obligation?

"They are."

"Let them hold up their right hand in the Scout sign and repeat the obligation."

I held up three fingers and repeated the obligation: I, John Pryor, do hereby promise on my honor as a scout that I will always faithfully observe and preserve the traditions of the Order of the Arrow, Wimachtendienk, Wingolauchsik, Witahemui. I will always regard the ties of Brotherhood in the Order of the Arrow as lasting and will seek to preserve a cheerful spirit even in the midst of irksome tasks and weighty responsibilities, and will endeavor, so far as my power lies, to be unselfish in service and devotion to the welfare of others.

Escorted by two Indians, the first Scout faced the chief. A sash from the great bow was draped across his chest. Allowat Sakima leaned close; the boy nodded and was led away.

I trembled when they came for me. I remember the chief's genial smile before he turned to select my arrow. Resting both hands on my shoulders, he whispered the admonition. I nodded and returned to the line.

Each year, thousands of scouts were inducted into the OA. Like me, they labored in silence and received an arrow. Like me, they raised their arms and repeated these words:

I will seek to preserve a cheerful spirit even in the midst of irksome tasks and weighty responsibilities, and will endeavor, so far as my power lies, to be unselfish in service and devotion to the welfare of others.

It was just a stupid club in the stupid Boy Scouts. It was all made up by some adult years ago hoping to steer young men toward a virtuous life. Most kids wouldn't retain the lesson beyond the weekend. For the rest, it would be abandoned with their youthful idealism.

But for me, something strange happened that weekend. The words settled in and found a place in my psyche.

The lesson stuck.

ℭℨ

Near the end of my scouting career, we embarked on the mother of all campouts. A weeklong journey by canoe and portage through wooded backcountry, It would qualify us for the Fifty Miler Afoot / Afloat award.

Days were spent paddling glacial lakes before lush Adirondack Mountains. Paddles gleamed in the sunlight before dipping and swinging back, splashing adjacent boats accidentally on purpose. The flotilla would beach for lunch, and we'd escape the noontime heat with a swim. Another league or portage, and we would pitch camp. After dinner, we exchanged stories by the campfire. In the morning, we packed up and followed Mr. Hefflefinger on to the next lake.

We arrived at Tupper Lake on the last day. In the evening, we would shampoo the smoke from our hair, don our least pungent shirts and head into "Town," but first we headed for *the cliff*. Darren told us about a sheer thirty-foot rock face the locals would jump off. It was right up our alley, and we paddled away from our campsite sans leaders.

The incline was steep and the footing precarious. I climbed slowly lest I slip and fall onto something that wasn't a lake. We gathered at the top and paused to appreciate the view. Robins, woodcocks and swallows dotted the sky as dragonflies darted through the thick air, heavy with the scent of pine. At the precipice, I spit over the edge and had to wait for it to hit the surface far below; doubts about jumping entered my mind.

We didn't notice Joe Fox was missing, still struggling in his ascent.

Ed Davenport had the balls to go first. Shouting "Bonzai!" he ran and leapt from the edge. He hung in midair for a time before deciding to hit the water. A few seconds later, his head broke the surface, and he beamed.

"That was awesome!" he yelled. "There's some rocks near the front. You really need to jump out to avoid them."

A few others went; then it was my turn. Heart racing, I ran toward the edge and jumped. A rush of air, tingling in my gut, disorientation, then slam. Hitting the water was like a punch to the head. Down, down I sank until the momentum stopped and I crawled back to the surface. Air! I took a breath.

Wow, I thought, *that was intense.*

I passed Joe as I climbed back up. Still close to the ground, he was undaunted in his pursuit to the top. While the others jumped and scampered up, each passing him on the way, Joe continued his dogged struggle; he would not be denied his turn.

We applauded when he finally reached the top. All smiles, Joe took in the view and waddled over to the edge. It was then we realized a problem. We were all running and jumping out to avoid rocks close to the edge. Joe had two modes of ambulating: hobbling, and vigorously hobbling without any noticeable difference in speed.

He couldn't run.

We sat, dripping in the afternoon sun, silently thinking of what to do. There was no way Joe could climb down the way he came. Paul pulled a leech from his leg and tossed it over the ledge.

"We could throw him," I said.

Paul looked up with surprise. "Yeah!" he said. "We could throw him!"

Our group became animated, muttering general agreement, "That'll work," "Yeah, sure," and "Why didn't I think of that?" Our confidence was lost on Joe as his expression changed from skepticism to panic.

"Uhh, guys.... I don't know..." he protested.

Paul and I grabbed him from either side and lifted. The group parted, forming a runway to the ledge. Joe was heavier than he looked, and we achieved, at most, half the normal velocity. Just before the edge, we stopped and heaved; I almost tumbled down after him.

Time slowed as Joe fell. He would clear the rocks, but his body pitched forward, heading for a thirty-foot face plant. We cringed as the wallop echoed across the lake, and Joe disappeared from sight.

"Holy shit!" Rich said.

Horrified faces surrounded me.

I just killed Joey Fox, I thought.

"What're we gonna tell his mom?" Hoff whispered.

Gentle undulations replaced the splash site; time passed.

Still nothing.

My actions, I realized, had consequences. If I threw Joe off a cliff and he broke his neck and drowned, I could reasonably be blamed. It was a horrible feeling.

Suddenly, Joe's face broke the surface. He let out a laugh and yelled, "Guys! That was G-R-E-A-T!"

I was never so relieved. We'd done lots of pranks over the years, but this was the first time I was genuinely scared we hurt someone. It would be years before I held another life in my hands, but the implications were no less profound.

Next time, I'd be more careful.

Shenendehowa

It was late afternoon when Burnt Hills kicked off against Shen. The spinning ball hung in the clouds before falling to earth. Sheridan caught it and ran strong until they felled him at the forty. A whistle blew, and the ref took the ball as special teams headed for the sidelines. I grabbed my helmet and trotted onto the freshly painted yard lines.

The scrimmage was my first game as a starting Freshman. Butterflies fluttered in my stomach, and my mind went blank. I reassured myself it was first down; as tight end, I'd have a few plays to warm up before they needed me.

Foam green *We're No. 1* hands peppered the bleachers, waving in the early autumn breeze. Leaping cheerleaders shook sparkling pompoms, struggling to fire up the lackluster crowd. Eddie O'Day nodded at coach's instructions and ran onto the field.

"Twenty-seven, cutback pass," Eddie said in the huddle.

"What!?" I blurted.

My heart jumped into my throat; a pass on first down, and the ball would come to me!

"I don't know," Eddied shrugged, "that's what Steuerwald wants."

I sucked in my mouthpiece and lined up. My face mask framed an enormous linebacker, but the cornerback was my real threat.

"Two! Twenty-four!"

My helmet muffled Eddie's yell, and I strained to hear the second hut.

"Hut!"

Here it comes...

"Hut!"

I exploded off the line. Muscles strained against the weight of my pads. Directly ahead, the cornerback advanced. Just before I reached him, the defensive line yelled, "Run!" Eddie and the team had fooled them, and the cornerback ignored me as I ran by.

Suddenly, I was wide open.

Pouring it on, my legs pumped like pistons, and I gasped for air around the suffocating mouthpiece. I glanced back at the receding cluster of battle. A ball launched from the mêlée.

My body took over; previous weeks of practice and routine kicked in. Maintaining my speed, I had to trust the ball would land *where I'm going to be*. I tracked it as my legs began to burn.

Then it was there, hanging right before me. I reached out and plucked it like an apple from the bough, surprised at how gently it landed in my hands. I pulled it close and turned away from the sideline. Wind whistled in my helmet as I sprinted for the goal. I stole one look back—no one even close—and pushed as hard as I could; all eyes were on me.

A cheer went up that belied the modest crowd. Spitting out the mouthpiece, I bent over to catch my breath. A loud whistle, the ref jogged toward me with both arms in the air. I tossed him the ball.

"Good job, son," he said.

Cheering crowds, leaping cheerleaders and my teammates pumping the air, it wasn't just a touchdown; crossing the goal was an induction. This was the day I let go of my individualism and became part of The Team.

❧

We moved to Clifton Park—a suburb of Albany, New York—when I was eight. My dad requested a transfer from the Department of Social Services when he realized Mt. Vernon wasn't a place to raise children. After unloading the moving van, Rich and I laid out on the front lawn, gazing at the ocean of stars, more spectacular than the New York City planetarium. Later, we were kept awake by the absolute silence. No traffic, no roaring motorcycles, no sirens, just the soft sounds of crickets.

Our school district was Shenendehowa, an Indian translation of "Great Plains," so we were called "The Plainsmen." Our mascot was a short, big-nosed Indian until ethnic mascots became politically incorrect.

My time was spent tackling Rich, playing CYO basketball, and camping with the Boy Scouts. Winters Rich and I sledded Boyack Hill until twilight; returning home, we peeled off soaking snowmobile suits and warmed up with hot cocoa. Summers we built tree forts and rode our mini bike through nearby sandlots. One year Rich and I attended basketball camp, but the rest of the summers were spent at Scout camp.

In elementary school, I was given a six-string Yamaha acoustic. I took lessons for a while but gave them up to learn songs on my own. An imitation Gibson Les Paul and Peavey amp soon followed. The house began to rattle as I belted chords from our den downstairs.

Middle school weekends were spent roller skating at Guptil's. Rich and I met friends to play foosball, skate or try to meet girls in the disco.

We called my paternal grandfather "Puppy," the nickname inherited from other grandchildren years ago. I was in the eighth grade when Puppy became a widower. At first he rented an apartment nearby, but soon he required more care and joined our nuclear family.

I entered the High School at the dawn of the '80s: MTV debuted on cable, VHS rental stores opened and I cruised the neighborhood, blasting *The Spirit of Radio* on my boom box. I spent increasingly more time with my friends, and Rich was demoted to "little-brother" status.

Then, I joined the ambulance corps.

In adolescence, our true character lies dormant, like a seed waiting to germinate. At sixteen, I heard a voice calling me to join the ambulance corps. Perhaps it was the ghost of my ancestor who served as a NYC fireman. Maybe I sought to be a hero, rescuing people from car accidents. Possibly, I was looking for excitement and adventure, eager to ride around with lights and sirens. But, I think, mostly I just wanted to help.

Whatever it was, I didn't ignore the voice.

Standing before a packed room of strangers, I raised my hand and pledged to uphold the rules and regulations, complete the requirements of membership and to represent the corps in a positive fashion. A brief applause welcomed me, and I shook hands with nearby members.

Dwight Pakan introduced me to the other members including Mike McEvoy and Kevin Krause. As the meeting broke up, he brought me into a supply room and fitted me with the basic gear of membership: white uniform shirt, red winter jacket, pager with charger, teardrop green light and a silver starburst badge.

Alone the next day, I pulled on a new pair of navy blue pants, slipped into the uniform shirt and pinned the silver badge. I posed in the bathroom mirror, examining myself in uniform. I couldn't wait to start riding—it would be so much fun.

I had no idea of what I was in for.

∽

I walked along the trench surrounded by mud. Wooden planks had been laid, but the mud consumed everything. It was twilight; the cold sank into my bones. In the distance, a whistle sounded, and I lined up with the others. I blew into my hands to warm them and held my Springfield close.

Suddenly, we were on the move. Troops climbed the makeshift ladders and began threading through gaps in the wire. I followed the coat before me and sloshed into the barren, crater marked battlefield.

Artillery began. First, the distant Pop! Pop! of cannons, small flashes of light like fireflies. My body tensed knowing the explosions were about to begin.

Boom! The deafening rounds shook the ground and splattered the mud. In the gray oncoming darkness, I could see the clouds forming.

"Gas! Gas! Gas!" Troops were shouting.

I dropped to one knee and turned to grab my gas mask, …It was gone.

Desperate, I searched the darkness—nothing but mud. The cloud engulfed me, gas stung my lips and burned my throat. I start coughing, gasping…

BEEP BEEP BEEP BEEP

The shrill pager shattered the midnight silence, jolting me awake. I flung off the sheets, jumped into my pants and threw on my shirt. The radio squelched, and a voice spoke, "EMS dispatch to Clifton Park–Halfmoon…" I fumbled to grab the pager while zipping up my fly, "… a 9-4, twenty-four Doherty Lane…" hopped along the upstairs hallway pulling on my sneakers, "…86 year old male, difficulty breathing…" nearly tumbled down the steps and burst out the front door.

I clipped the pager to the visor and fired up our Plymouth station wagon. The whirring motor reverberated on the metal roof, and the night swirled in waves of green light. The engine roared as I accelerated down Moe road.

"1975 to EMS dispatch," a voice crackled over the pager.

"1975," repeated the dispatcher.

"1975 en route to the scene."

"04:16."

My hands trembled, fighting the loose power steering as I sped through the night.

9-4, I thought, *is that a car accident?*

My heart pounded from adrenaline, but my brain was still half asleep. It took a while to mentally wake up.

No, 9-4, that's cardiac.

Terrain blurred as I pushed the pedal to 65. The spinning green landscape made me dizzy. I concentrated on the road ahead.

I feared I would be the last crewman to arrive, holding up the response. I pictured an elderly man struggling to breath, waiting for an ambulance that, in turn, was waiting for me.

I drove faster.

Pulling into the station, I skidded to a halt and jumped out, pager in one hand, my unbuttoned pants in the other. I ran to the back doors and climbed in.

"You in back there?" asked Dwight.

"Yeah, let's go!" I said buckling my belt. The acceleration dropped me to the bench. Pulsating red and white lights reflected in the bay doors. I finished buttoning my shirt and secured the pager to my belt.

Beth Newell, who routinely rode with Dwight, poked her head in the passageway to the front seats.

"Grab the ALS gear and put it on the stretcher," she tossed keys to the drug box cabinet.

I stood in a wide, low stance, fighting centrifugal forces of the speeding ambulance and gathered equipment: oxygen, cardiac monitor / defibrillator and drug box all piled onto the stretcher.

McEvoy's flashing green light marked the house as we approached. We parked and wheeled the equipment-laden gurney to the door. A gray-haired man in white T-shirt and striped pajama pants greeted us.

"This way," he sighed.

Every home tells a story—furnishings, pictures, smells. Entering a house is the first step in understanding the patient. Keen observation can reveal subtle secrets: a full ashtray, empty gin bottles, bloody clothes, empty pill bottles, medical equipment, clues that tell more than the patient is willing to admit. That first time in a stranger's home I felt like a voyeur. As the years passed, I never resolved the discomfort. I just got used to it.

On the edge of the bed an elderly man leaned forward, hands on knees, gasping for breath. An oxygen tube snaked from nose to portable cylinder. He stared straight ahead oblivious of the strangers in his bedroom. In the dim lamp light, sweat sparkled above cyanotic lips. Deep gurgling rattled with each respiration.

"He's really wet," Dwight removed a stethoscope. Beth started taking a blood pressure.

Wet? I thought.

"Yup," Mike said. He had responded wearing a Mickey Mouse T-shirt.

I remained clueless as the crew sprung into action. Even the patient and his son knew more than I did.

"Dad doesn't like taking his medications," the son said. "Do you, Dad?"

The man gave him a scowl before concentrating on his breathing again.

"Here, hold this," Beth thrust an IV bag in my hands. Grateful to finally have a role, I held it high. She spiked the bag, bled the line and tightened the clamp. Mike started the IV while Dwight rummaged in the drug box.

"Sixty?" asked Dwight.

"Eighty'd be better," Mike said

Dwight handed him the syringe. Mike injected the medication while Dwight pulled out the smallest medication bottle in the world.

"Sir, I want you to lift up your tongue…"

"Yeah. I've. Had. That. Before," he said. Dwight dropped the pill under his tongue.

Packed onto the stretcher, we extricated the patient to the ambulance. Beth jumped behind the wheel, and we headed for Ellis Hospital. Dwight opened the ALS radio and requested a medical control physician.

"John," he said, "can you grab another set of vital signs?"

I popped off the bench, plugged in my stethoscope and inflated the cuff. Listening for the pulse, I heard rumbling from the road. I reinflated the cuff and tried again; this time, I bled the cuff slower. I heard the first sound but couldn't make out the second. The patient gave me a worried look as I inflated the cuff a third time.

Dwight paused his report and looked at me for the blood pressure. I suddenly felt like I was on stage.

"160 on 90," *I think.*

Ellis' emergency department was deserted at 5 a.m.. Balling up the sheet tightly in my hands, we pulled the patient over to the hospital gurney. His breathing was easy, and his color had normalized.

Dwight disappeared to find supplies, and I helped Beth make up the stretcher. A physician approached me, asking questions.

"You'll want to ask that guy," I pointed to Mike, "he's the paramedic."

"The guy with the Mickey Mouse shirt?" he said.

"Yeah," I said, "that's him."

On the return home, Mike tutored me as I assailed him with questions. If I was going to survive this environment, I needed to learn a lot of things quickly.

"He had congestive heart failure, or CHF," he explained. "If the heart fails, blood backs up in the lungs. Fluid leaks into the alveoli and blocks the transfer of oxygen. So you basically drown in your own fluid."

Mike held a Ph.D. and several master's degrees as well as being a paramedic. Despite his credentials, he was humble, never giving the sense of superiority. He taught without condescension and managed to make me feel good about myself no matter how dumb I really was. I quickly realized I wanted to be like him.

We dropped Mike off at his car. He paused before closing the back doors.

"Good job tonight," he said.

Good job? I thought, *I held an IV bag and took a blood pressure! I was completely useless.*

"Thanks," I said.

"Stay out of trouble," he said and closed the door.

At the station, Beth and Dwight said goodbye and drove off together.

My first ambulance call was done. I was incompetent but, looking back, this day was a transition point. I had transformed from layperson to a health care provider. Admittedly, a naïve, ignorant and clueless provider, but one with potential; in the years to come, I would realize that potential.

Walking toward my car, panic gripped me as I reached for my keys. My pockets were empty.

Oh fuck, I thought, *where are my keys?*

They could be anywhere—the patient's house, the hospital, maybe the ambulance. Then, through the driver's window, I spied them dangling in the ignition.

The car was still running.

❧

A chill 70 mile per hour wind blows from the half-open window, venting carbon monoxide leaking from a cracked muffler. Chris Sheridan is riding shotgun, engaged in a futile attempt to find music on the AM dial. Poking between the front seats is Brian Mclintock, telling blonde jokes.

"A blonde was walking down the road with a healthy looking pig under her arm," McClintock says above the din of alien radio. "As she passed the bus stop, someone asked, 'Where did you get that?' And the pig says, 'I won her in a raffle!'"

I laugh, but Brian is pissed off.

"Pryor, what kind of person buys a car with only AM radio?" A Spanish preacher is cut off mid-prayer. "Fucking torture."

McClintock falls back and is replaced by Chris Gomes, who reaches forward and plugs in the green light.

"Woo-hoo! Let's go!" Gomes yells as Sheridan makes the sounds of a siren.

"Quit it," I said, unplugging the light, "you'll get me arrested."

Of all my friends, these were my best mates: Sheridan, McClintock and Gomes. Freshman through senior football, we played on and off the field, raided Saratoga, organized parties and planned road trips. The drinking age was eighteen back then, so a lot of what goes on at college today we did in high school.

Pulling off the Northway, we head up Route 9 into Saratoga Springs. Traffic slows on Broadway, and Gomes rolls down the window as we pass a cop on horseback.

"Hey," he yells, "shouldn't the dick be *under* the horse?"

Jesus Christ! I thought.

We burst out laughing as I accelerate around traffic, praying the cop didn't make out our plate number.

We pulled in to a municipal lot, and Sheridan climbed out the passenger window.

"You ever gonna fix that door?" Gomes asked.

"Hey," I said, "three out of four ain't bad."

Founded in 1691, Saratoga is home to the country's oldest thoroughbred track and holds the highest concentration of bars in the Capital District. Saturday night, we performed our weekly pub crawl.

"Barclays?" I asked.

"Where are the girls?" McClintock asked. We planned to meet our female complement tonight.

"Gaffney's," I said.

"Barclays it is then," said Gomes. "Let's warm up before we find them."

At Barclay's pub we drained a pitcher of Molson as patrons crowded the bar and the air filled with cigarette smoke. Fellow Shen students appeared, and together we heckled football players from other schools. Eventually, the girls found us.

"There you are!" Cindy gave me a kiss.

"Hey," I said, "we were waiting for you."

"You're such a liar," she said. "I told you we'd be at Gaffney's."

Cindy Siedel wasn't my first girlfriend, but she was different. Something about her eyes made her special. When I met her, I became spellbound, looking into her eyes. I tried to fight it, but our conversation would fade away and I would fall, helpless, into those sparkling eyes. It wasn't long before we started dating.

"Hey, Boo." Nancy said, and kissed Sheridan.

"Oh boo da bear da boo!" we chimed in, hounding Sheridan mercilessly about his pet name—Boo Bear.

Erin, Kristy, Becca and Jen completed our gang as we migrated to Desperate Annies, then Gaffney's and finally to Tin & Lint.

At one in the morning, I needed to go home. In a few hours, I would be on call for my Sunday shift on the ambulance. My announcement was met with fierce resistance from my inebriated mates.

"Wha?" Sheridan said. "Where you going? Iss shtill early."

"I'm on call in six hours," I said. "I gotta get some sleep."

"Les put it ta a vote," McClintock said. "Who wans ta go home?" There were no hands.

"No, it's not a vote," I said. "I'm going. Who wants to come with me?"

"An who wans ta stay," he said, ignoring me.

Hands waved, voting for last call at 4 a.m.

"The hans haf it," McClintock said. "You godda stay."

Torn between my friends and my responsibility, I remember feeling out of place. None of my friends had a commitment like the ambulance. Unlike retail, I couldn't show up at a call bleary eyed and hung-over. They didn't get it.

Fuck 'em, I thought.

I drove home alone and went to bed.

At 7:15 a.m., the tones woke me from a dead sleep. I threw on my clothes and grabbed the pager. A few steps out the front door, I stopped dead in my tracks, trying to understand the sight before me.

Naked axles rested on cinderblocks; a neat stack of tires towered on the lawn. Rich smiled from his Sunday paper bundle at the end of the driveway.

Holy shit! I thought.

"Did you do that?" I shouted.

"Are you high?" he said with a laugh. "Your *friends* did that!"

℘

With each ambulance call, I sucked a little less. The learning curve was steep for the basic stuff, and soon I was an asset to the crew. More formal training would occur when I started the Emergency Medical Technician (EMT) class, but until then I was learning by watching and doing.

I settled on the Friday night crew with Dwight and Beth. It was a sacrifice from social activities, but all the exciting stuff happened on Fridays.

Responding to the station was a blast. My green light was considered a courtesy light; it conferred no special authority, but a lot of motorists would pull over when they saw it. Riding the ambulance was a thrill even though I wasn't allowed to drive yet. Speeding to the scene of a car accident or heart attack, Dwight let me work the siren as he concentrated on traffic.

We stabilized heart attacks, revived unconscious diabetics and oxygenated the diff breathers. I was most useful on basic life support (BLS) calls: sports injuries, falls, general illness. The calls were diverse and unpredictable, and the fact that anything could happen at any minute kept me on edge.

The best calls were trauma. Mostly car accidents. There was the occasional shooting or stabbing. We ran hot to the trauma center as medics started IVs or inflated medical anti-shock trousers (MAST). A team of doctors, clad in surgical garb, would meet us in the trauma bay.

I remember watching the trauma dance for the first time, mesmerized at the sight. Organized chaos, nurses and doctors performed choreographed actions to stabilize the patient. Standing back, conducting this mayhem, stood Dr. John Fortune, trauma surgeon. Directing the staff, he projected calm, deliberate, leadership. The patient could be dying, the nurses confused, residents unsure, but Dr. Fortune was there, like a rock in the whirlwind, knowledgeable, confident, capable.

An impressive spectacle.

Dr. Fortune stood only a few steps away physically, but light years away professionally. At the time, I didn't want to be like him because he was so beyond my level I couldn't grasp the concept. I could sooner become a star or a god.

With increased competency and familiarity, I began to have fun. Dwight and Beth became good friends. I felt proud of helping people in need and transporting without charge. I settled into my new role as caregiver.

Then I got my ass kicked.

"Ems dispatch to Clifton Park–Halfmoon standby …"

It was Saturday. I was on with Kevin Kraus and Noreen Christopher. Kevin had the ambulance pulled out front while he washed his car in the bay. We climbed in the rig and called for information.

"Ems to Clifton Park–Half-moon, a 9-4, respiratory distress, ten-year-old with history of asthma…"

Asthma was pretty common, especially with kids. Usually the patient got better with aerosolized albuterol on the way to the hospital. Rarely, the paramedics would need to give IV medications. I smiled as we wove in and out of traffic, siren wailing. Asthma was a decent call—easy but not bullshit.

I followed Noreen through the door and will never forget the scene. An African American boy lay motionless on the carpet. Eyes bulged, fixed and frozen at the ceiling. Cyanotic lips, bluer than I'd ever seen before or since, outlined his gaping mouth, like he was frozen mid-scream. Instead of breathing, his chest spasmed with rhythmic hiccups. An older boy paced the room, crying, swearing, pleading with us to save his brother.

Blood drained from my face.

This isn't asthma, I thought, *they said it was a kid with asthma!*

Kevin broke the spell, thrusting keys into my hands. "Get the drug box." Noreen kneeled and took out the bag-valve-mask (BVM) I ran out to the ambulance.

In the rig, Kevin's nasal voice crackled from the portable radio, "EMS, portable 1951, tone out Clifton Park for additional manpower, ten year old cardiac arrest."

Arrest? I thought.

Keys rattled in my hands as I fumbled for the drug box. When I returned, Noreen was pumping his chest while Kevin squeezed the bag. I thought I was going to piss myself.

"Here, take this," Kevin said, handing off the BVM. Holding the mask against his face I squeezed the bag. Air farted out around the mask.

"Slowly," advised Noreen. "He's really tight."

Tight? I thought.

I repositioned the mask and tried again. This time, some air managed to go in.

Kevin readied the laryngoscope, and I pulled away. Inserting the blade, there was no movement or gag. Eyes fixed, lips blue and now throat bulging like a bull frog, I looked away, fighting a wave of nausea.

McEvoy showed up with other members. The medics started an IV and pushed meds while I squeezed the bag, now attached to the endotracheal tube (ET). It was no easier moving air, and frequently the safety valve would pop.

Why won't air go into this kid? I thought.

In the ambulance, Noreen and I switched tasks. I timidly pushed on his chest, trying not to hurt him. If I paused, the monitor went flatline except for artifact caused by bumps in the road.

I doubt anyone could be prepared for the scene in the ER, especially a naïve sixteen-year-old. The boy's mother waited for us. She was a nurse and knew the meaning of CPR. I can still hear her guttural, anguished scream. Nearly knocking me over, she fought us to get away, as if removing our efforts would restore his life. Staff gently restrained her, and she collapsed to the floor sobbing.

On the hospital stretcher, the ER staff took over. My knees buckled as I walked away leaving Kevin to explain our treatment. Later, I learned the details. The kid's asthma was getting worse, not responding to inhalers. Mom thought it would get better with epinephrine, so she gave him a shot and went to work. The brother came home to find him on the floor. The lesson burned into my brain years before I even approached medical school: Never treat your own family.

The bustle behind the curtain fell away to silence. A nurse appeared and retrieved the mother. She was slowly escorted back to the curtain, sobbing, legs giving out. Behind the curtain, she screamed again. I felt it in my spine. The father arrived, wild eyed, quick paced, urgently asking, "Where is he? Where is he?" He looked at us accusingly before being led to the curtain. I heard him, and it was too much.

I hid in an empty room, tears pouring out of me. I fell to my knees and clutched my gut. The grief was physical, palpable. I shook. I couldn't breathe. I never knew such pain.

I felt a hand on my shoulder. I looked up to see Kevin, tears in his eyes.

ᨶ

In the Shen cafeteria I sat despondent, observing my peers. *Children,* I thought.

Children eating lunch, smiling, laughing, tossing bits of food at each other. Some trying to read, others were telling stories as small groups listened. I wasn't one of them anymore. This is where I should be, enjoying high school, going out with friends, cheering on the basketball team.

The ambulance was a mistake. I thought it would be fun. I thought I could help. For two weeks, I couldn't get that kid out of my head. He invaded my dreams. In the middle of class, I saw his face. I heard his mother's cries. I was too young to be burdened with this shit.

A brown shopping bag containing a neatly folded uniform, pager and a green light sat in my room. I waited for the next meeting to turn it in.

ᨶ

The gang was glad to hear I would join them at the game on Friday. Shen had a hockey team but no rink, so all the games were away. Tonight they played in Schenectady, and I drove with Sheridan, Nancy, McClintock and Cindy. A cold front swept down from Canada, dropping the mercury to below zero.

"You got the beer?" I asked McClintock, my breath frozen in the night air.

"In the back," he said.

A few six-packs chilled in the trunk. Winter coats made it easy to conceal a few brewskies for the game.

It was a short walk to the rear of the rink. As we huddled our way along the frigid sidewalk, I saw someone laid out next to a retaining wall. My friends didn't notice. I tried to walk past, like the others, but then I had to stop.

Cindy noticed I wasn't keeping pace and looked back.

"What?" she asked.

The others stopped and turned as I approached the prostate figure.

"Hold on," I said, "just give me a second."

"C'mon, what are you doing?" McClintock protested. "John, I'm freezing my balls off!"

"Hey buddy," I asked. "You alright?"

Curled in a fetal position, facing the wall, his coat was filthy, his pants were ripped and he smelled of urine. As he turned his head up at me, I was relieved he wasn't dead.

"Fuck off," he managed before resuming his posture.

"John, c'mon," Sheridan said, now concerned. "He might be dangerous."

I squatted, closer.

"Hey, it's too damn cold to be out here tonight," I said. "Isn't there someplace warm you can go?"

He turned to me again. This time, there was a softness to his expression. Worn, tired eyes understood I was no threat, just some kid who didn't know shit.

"Thanks," he said more kindly. "Now fuck off."

Leaving the raucous cheering to my friends, I sat pensive as our team chased the puck around the ice. I thought about the kid who died. I thought about the homeless guy. What did I do? I walked right over, without thinking. Why? Why did I do that? I saw him and thought he was in trouble, possibly unconscious, that he might need help.

It was *in me* to do that. It was *in me* not to be afraid to help.

What's wrong with me? I thought.

That night, I returned home to my room. I quietly unpacked the brown paper bag and plugged in my pager.

◌

Two nights a week, I drove with Shawn Brimhall to Saratoga Hospital where Mike McEvoy was teaching an EMT course. The class was different from anything I'd ever learned in school because the material was directly applicable to my experience on the ambulance. Trigonometry was interesting and biology may be applicable *someday*, but tomorrow I might need to know how to insert an airway, apply a traction splint or place MAST pants.

Lectures came alive, either illuminating previous calls on or foreshadowing calls to come. The concrete applications impressed me and made medicine stand apart from other subjects.

The curriculum was extensive. Starting with the initial approach to the patient, obtaining a history and performing a physical exam, we learned to take vital signs, manage an airway and deliver oxygen. We learned to treat medical emergencies like cardiac failure and diabetes, trauma, abdominal complaints, psychiatric emergencies and precipitous childbirth. We learned to operate an ambulance safely, how to approach dangerous scenes, manage hazardous environments and perform rescue techniques. We learned to document a Pre-hospital Care Report and practiced radioing reports to the hospital. There was a lot to learn.

In the end, there was a final exam, both a multiple-choice test and a practical.

The practical struck fear in the hearts of EMT students. In front of a live evaluator, we were to demonstrate our medical abilities, knowledge and decision skills. There was no way to guess or hide behind an answer sheet.

Several stations tested a particular skill. One required me to secure a patient to a backboard, another would test an appropriate oxygen delivery device, at another a cervical injury required stabilization. Each was a bit nerve-racking, but each tested one simple skill or technique.

Then there was the trauma station.

Here, a mock patient lay on the ground, augmented with moulage (fake blood and injuries). The examinee would "come upon the scene" not knowing anything. He then asks the examiner questions to find out more information. The examiner answers questions but does not offer any information.

A list of required actions must be completed, or the examinee fails.

I stood next to the examiner, stethoscope draped around my neck, trauma shears tucked in my belt, wiping my palms against my pants. Mouth dry, I tried to slow my breathing.

Is the scene safe? Is the scene safe? I thought.

Countless students rushed in to secure the patient's c-spine only to have the examiner state they were electrocuted by a downed power line: Instant fail.

"You arrive at the scene of a car accident," the examiner said, "twenty-four-year-old male appears to have been ejected from one of the cars."

He looked down at the clipboard. It took me a moment to realize we'd begun.

"Uh-h," Physical effort held me back from jumping right to the patient's head. "Is the scene safe?" I said.

"The scene is safe." He made a checkmark on the clipboard.

I jumped to the patient's head.

"I would have an EMT hold cervical spine immobilization," I said.

"C-collar is applied and held by an EMT." Another check.

"I'm examining the airway; what do I see?" I asked.

"There is gurgling and broken teeth."

"I would remove the broken teeth and suction the airway," I said. "If needed, I would insert an oral airway."

Fear and anxiety dissolved away. My mind shifted, drawing on knowledge from class, practice for the test, but mostly from the experience I gained treating real patients. Almost subconsciously, I moved from one problem to the next, stabilizing the "patient."

Airway cleared, fractures splinted, arterial bleed bandaged. I even found the medic-alert bracelet declaring the patient a diabetic. I stood and announced I was done.

It's hard to convey the significance of this test, especially to those not in the medical field. It's not about treating a trauma patient. It's about demonstrating ability in front of a live examiner. The experience would serve me time and again in paramedic class, through medical school, and even during my oral examinations for surgery boards.

Whenever I performed a similar practical, I drew strength from that 18-year-old kid with sweaty palms; if he could do it then, I can do it now.

ଏ

"Ems dispatch to Clifton Park–Halfmoon, standby …"

I sat on the Plano box in the passage connecting the cab and the back of the ambulance. It was unsafe, but it offered a better view and made it easier to talk with Dwight and Beth. Dwight slowed the ambulance, waiting to see in which direction we would be headed.

"Ems dispatch to Clifton Park–Halfmoon, you have a 9-4, cardiac arrest, eighteen-month-old female drowning. Repeating for Clifton Park–Halfmoon, 9-4 cardiac arrest, eighteen-month-old drowning …"

The words shot down my spine, bristling the hair on the back of my neck. I pushed back into the cabin and began to throw equipment on the stretcher. My hands shook, and I had to forcibly slow my breathing.

An infant arrest was a nightmare. Emts and paramedics did their best to prepare for this horror, practicing on mannequins, memorizing algorithms, even preparing a special box just for pediatrics.

In the end, we pray it never happens.

The siren wailed continuously, punctuated by blasts of the airhorn. In the back, I tossed around like a rag doll as Dwight strained the diesel engine. Beth held the map book, directing the way. The radio erupted with additional help: 1971 en route, 1975 en route, 1973 en route. No one knew who was closest, so everyone available rushed to the scene.

The house was lit up with flashing lights. County Sheriff, State Trooper, fire first responder, 1971 and two green lights. Abandoning the stretcher, we ran with the als gear.

Inside, the scene was surreal. Silence belied a kitchen packed with strangers; only an occasional squelch of a radio broke the spell. Bubble bath filled the sink, a yellow ducky tucked into the foam. The mother stood in the corner; trembling hands prayed against her lips as tears streaked her mascara. The father tried to lay a reassuring hand on her shoulder, but she shrugged it off.

Most of the infant was obscured by the huddled paramedics. I could only see mottled, cyanotic legs bouncing rhythmically, pausing with the sound of the BVM. Mike opened the pediatric box, and Kevin rested the Datascope on the table. I was handed the oxygen tubing and dropped to the ground attaching it to the cylinder.

A draft, smelling of freshly fallen autumn leaves, blew into my face. I blinked and shook my head, but when my eyes opened He was still there.

At seven feet, he loomed over the proceedings. The heavy robe featured ornate, finely stitched patterns at the hem. The hood was large and draped forward, obscuring his face. Poking from the cuffs, his blanched, desiccated hands could easily be mistaken for bone. Leaning on the shaft of a large sickle, he focused on the resuscitation.

My eyes slowly scanned the room; no one else noticed DEATH.

Mike inserted the tube, Kevin pierced a vein and pushed epinephrine. They paused at the monitor, waveform settling to flatline. The paramedics glanced at each other with grim expressions. They had done all they could; it was time to pack up.

The ambulance ran hot to the ER, but it was futile. The paramedics were his only hope; the rest was psychological. The parents needed to know everything was done.

DEATH reappeared as the ER staff assumed care. After twenty minutes, DEATH raised a hand above the infant. He slowly lowered it and softly touched the baby's chest.

"Stop CPR," the doctor said.

The mother collapsed onto the lifeless body and sobbed. The husband rubbed her back and wept.

I didn't cry. Maybe it was too much to register. Maybe I was shocked at the sight of DEATH. Maybe I had toughened up since the asthma kid. Something inside me snapped. I went into a preservation mode, distancing myself emotionally.

This was the second time a patient had taken something from me. If I continued down this path, there was more to come. More encounters with DEATH, more patients stealing a chunk.

How long would I last before there was nothing left to take?

కొ

A flowing expanse of lawn runs downhill, swallowed whole by the gaping amphitheater. Stadium seats, accustomed to screaming concert-goers, held fidgeting graduates in silky white or green caps and gowns. Adoring parents searched the crowd, pointing, waving and flashing snapshots.

Commencement, 1984

Few transition points in life are more clearly defined. Like my peers, I was saddened to think it was over: football games, drinking in Saratoga, Sheridan and the gang, even the ambulance. I had done well, and I had no regrets.

But as the word implies, commencement is more a beginning than an ending, and I was eager to get started.

Started where and for what took the better part of my senior year to figure out. My dad pointed me toward State University of New York (SUNY) Binghamton. Initially, I was against it, but after a tour, I changed my mind and applied. Binghamton is one of the exclusive State University centers, more competitive than other SUNY colleges. I was accepted off the wait list.

I selected a major with medical school in mind but detested the idea of being labeled "Pre-Med." Biochemistry would prepare me just as well for medical school and also provide more options if I changed my mind.

My row stood, and we moved toward the stage. I scanned the audience searching for my parents. Perrotto, Pettit, Pigman, I slowly approached the stage, Platek, Poli…

"John Pryor."

Applause erupted as I walked to center stage. I accepted my diploma and smiled at the audience. I was on my way.

Binghamton

W hat's your major?" I shouted to be heard above the booming dance music. Behind her, the crowd lit up with flashes of color from spinning lights, and students gyrated, jumping, hands in the air. On the dance floor, a naked cowboy was doing push-ups. Beer flowed from keg taps like mini waterfalls.

This girl was hot—long dark hair, blazingly blue eyes and a smile that actually sparkled. She started talking, but all I heard was the booming dance music vibrating my loins.

I smiled, pretending to understand what she said and took another sip of beer. A few hours ago, this was the dining hall. It was freakin' awesome!

A week into college and already I had callous blisters from tennis, joined intramural lacrosse, and found a party each night. Meals were shared with dorm mates, and we found several pizza places that delivered. I remember calling Mom saying, "Thank you! Thank you for sending me here! This place is so much fun!"

"There you are!" I turned to see Cindy with her friends.

"Hey, what's up?" I said. The hot girl walked away.

Damn, I thought, *college is no place to have a girlfriend.*

ℰↃ

Situated just north of the Pennsylvania border, Binghamton, NY is one of the state's more isolated cities. Binghamton University began life as Harpur College before incorporation into the State University system in 1965. I arrived in the Fall of 1984.

Dad and I hauled my footlocker up three flights into my dorm. Mom sheeted the bed, and I plugged in a desk lamp. After lunch, we said our goodbyes, and Mom couldn't restrain her tears. As they drove off, I found myself on my own for the first time.

"College in the woods," a cluster of five dorms sequestered among the pines, was my new home. Each dorm took an Indian name; I lived in Seneca, a coed dorm segregated by floor.

The most anxiety-provoking aspect of freshman life is meeting your roommate. It's bizarre to think random pairing of complete strangers is an appropriate method for staffing dorms. I worried about whom I would be matched with and whether we would get along.

Todd Kesselman hailed from Rockland County, NY. A fellow Republican, we shared an enthusiasm for politics rarely seen on college campuses. He also introduced me to Bob Dylan and the Grateful Dead. We became fast friends.

Classes started, and I deciphered my schedule. Taking AP Biology in high school allowed my first semester to be light: Chemistry, Lab, Writing and Calculus. But, there was a hitch: calculus started at 8 a.m.

As far as I could remember it's been a struggle for me to get up in the morning. On Scout trips, the entire troop would be up and packed before I languidly crawled from my sleeping bag. Add a night of partying, and it was impossible for me to get up before noon. This had a deleterious effect on morning attendance.

I wasn't concerned. Honestly, there was so much more to college besides going to class.

ℰↃ

Mid-September the leaves around campus began to show a hint of color in the crisp morning air. Classes were in full swing, students had settled into college life and Rush Week began.

Of all the extracurricular activities, I was most excited about joining a fraternity. Investigating my options I found it difficult to find one that felt right. I tried to get Todd to help, but he wasn't into it.

"Why, not?" I asked. "It'll be great."

"Nah," he said, "I'm not interested in joining a Frat."

"Hey," I said, "don't call it a Frat. You wouldn't call your country a count, would you?"

Alpha Epsilon Pi, Sigma Alpha Mu, Zeta Beta Tau—it was all Greek to me. Then I heard about David Heyman. Dave was Sigma Nu from Carnegie Mellon looking to start a chapter in Binghamton. I liked the group he put together and wanted to be part of the founding brothers.

So I rushed Sigma Nu.

Pledging was a blast. A scavenger hunt had us relieving the university of various signs and library items. We held an ugliest date contest. I learned all sorts of drinking games and had to prove my mettle by chugging a beer in under ten seconds. In the end, I was presented with a inscribed paddle with coat of arms. It remained prominently displayed on a bookshelf throughout my future travels.

Lacking a fraternity house, we took turns hosting events. Most Wednesday nights, we had Purim, a weekly party named after the Jewish holiday. Organizing visits to Cornell and Syracuse earned me the nickname "Roadtrip." I also drove to Pennsylvania to purchase grain alcohol for the mixers.

At Purim and mixers, I pulled out the six string to lead singalongs. We sang Dylan and Pink Floyd, but the most requested were my originals including Why Did I Rush Sigma Nu? It went like this:

Why did I rush ZBT?
They ain't nothing like me,
They're not like the others,
They butt fuck their brothers !
Why did I rush ZBT?

Why did I rush AE PI ?
They said they were great,
That's a lie.

They're JAPS like the others,
Their dicks are fluorescent colors !
Why did I rush AE PI?

Why did I rush S A MU?
They're all losers too.
They joined a fraternity,
When they couldn't get into ZBT,
And that's why they joined S A MU.

Why did I rush Theta Tau?
They're all local anyhow,
They got some little sisters,
Suck so hard they give you blisters !
Why did I rush Theta Tau?

Why did I rush Sigma Nu?
They all call it Sigma Zoo,
They're not like the others,
They've got the coolest brothers !
That's why I rushed Sigma Nu.

Laughter erupted at each verse, with a generous applause at the end.

❧

Dirty sheets piled high in a corner, an open pizza box offered two-day old pepperoni slices and EMS magazines littered the end tables. Frozen burritos, heating in the microwave, competed with the smell of burned popcorn. Various posters, NYS memos and a large board with the call schedule covered the walls. On television, Tom Selleck drove his Ferrari around Oahu while the scanner crackled with voices from around the county.

It was a typical ambulance call room.

Harpur's Ferry, one of the few collegiate Advanced Life Support ambulances, served the Binghamton campus. Eager to continue my prehospital care experience, I joined mid semester and started taking call soon after. I imagined Harpur's Ferry would be just like Clifton Park: sick patients, cardiac arrests and trauma.

I imagined wrong.

The pristine ambulance and mint equipment were my first clues. Little used equipment meant little use, i.e., few calls. Splitting the call schedule among several dozen members allowed only a single four-hour shift per week. Do the math; several weeks could pass before I saw any action.

Then there was the "action."

Our population consisted of young, healthy students with a ten-mile-an-hour speed limit. Drunks, falls and menstrual cramps topped the list of common complaints. Interestingly, my most serious patient—an unconscious student at the bottom of the stairs, scalp split open and bleeding—was discovered while returning home from a party.

My time on Clifton Park had trained me well. I was more capable than the more highly trained but less experienced upperclassmen. I found myself in a leadership role for the first time, taking charge at calls and teaching other members.

Downtime spent in the call room or cruising around campus allowed me to get to know other members. Some I liked, some were annoying. A few of the medics were irremediably conceited. Then, one of the EMTs took a liking to me.

Kelly was a sophomore with a killer body but kind of plain looking. I noticed her name consistently appeared on the roster after I signed up. She sat uncomfortably close on the couch; more than once. I received unsolicited back rubs.

"Why can't I have problems like that?" Todd asked.

"You want her?" I said, "Call 911; maybe she'll hook up with you."

"Tell her you're not interested," said Todd.

"I told her I was going out with Cindy; she doesn't seem to care."

A week later, Kelly and I were alone, returning from a standby for a football game, when she turned down a secluded access road.

"Where are we going?" I asked.

She just smiled.

Parking the rig out of sight, Kelly proceeded to attack me. We wound up on the stretcher in the back.

Todd was astonished when I told him.

"Really?" he asked. "In the ambulance?"

"It was all her idea," I said. "I swear."

"I thought you didn't like her," he said.

"I don't."

"But you had sex with her," he argued.

"Yeah, *but I didn't kiss her!*" I insisted.

We broke down, laughing.

&

Thanksgiving break, I returned home eager to meet up with the old gang from Shen. I also plugged in my pager, starving for a call with real substance. On black Friday, I wasn't disappointed.

"Ems to Clifton Park, sixty-eight-year-old unconscious female ..."

Pulling on my ambulance jacket, I ran out to the car. While speeding to the station, the ambulance called en route, and I diverted directly to the scene. A man out front waved me down as I skidded to a stop. Grabbing my jump kit, I headed for the front door.

"She's in the living room ..."

"Stay here," I said. "The ambulance is on the way."

An extended family, called home for the holiday, crowded the living room. Worried faces parted, revealing a pale, cyanotic woman on the couch. DEATH held his hand above, lowering it slowly toward her chest.

Oh Jesus, I thought, *it's a code.*

I moved quickly, pulling the woman from DEATH's fingertips.

"Help me," I said, lowering her to the floor. "CPR doesn't work on the couch."

Trembling fingers searched for a pulse. For a second, I doubted myself: is there a pulse but I can't feel it?

No, I thought, *nobody looks this bad that has a pulse.*

Placing my palm on her sternum, my fist compression cracked like snapping twigs. One, two, three, four, I counted the rhythmic pumping. Pausing compressions I grabbed the BVM and fumbled for the mask to deliver ventilations. The mask wouldn't separate from the BVM.

Fuck it, I thought, tossing it aside.

I tilted her head back and delivered two mouth-to-mouth ventilations. Her lips were cold, and I tasted cranberry sauce.

I hate cranberry sauce, I thought, resuming compressions.

Mike dropped the Lifepak and gave me a quizzical look.

"Thought you were at school," he said, taking out the paddles.

"Home for break," I managed, trying to avoid banter in the shadow of DEATH.

Noreen ripped opened the woman's shirt and sliced her bra. I averted my gaze as breasts flopped apart. Mike applied the paddles, and we focused on the monitor. There was activity.

"V-tach," Mike said.

He thumbed the paddle switches, and a high pitch sounded as the charge accumulated.

"Okay, clear," he said, looking up and down the patient. There was a sudden, single convulsion as the shock delivered. All eyes returned to the monitor.

The waveform settled to flatline. Then a blip. Then another. Then a slow steady progression of normal looking blips. I checked the carotid again.

Holy shit! I thought.

"I got a pulse!" I said.

An icy sweat broke out as DEATH turned toward me. The faceless hood examined me for the first time, as though I had suddenly become worthy of his attention. A moment froze in time as we stared each other down. Finally, I blinked and DEATH was gone.

Mike hung a lidocaine drip, and we moved to the ambulance. En route, the woman started waking up and tried to talk. In the ER, she appeared to be stable.

After nearly two years on the ambulance, it was my first save. It was like scoring the winning touchdown in a championship game. It was like winning the lottery. It took a few days for the significance to sink in.

I defeated DEATH!

How cool was that?

&

Winter in Binghamton tended to be snowless and bleary. Icy rain from a leaden sky offered all the gloom and inconvenience of winter with none of the charm. Reports of a nor'easter rolling into New York's southern tier caused giddy anticipation of a good old fashioned snowstorm.

I returned to Seneca mid-afternoon, light fading as snow began to fall in earnest. Students returning from class stopped in the courtyard, mingling, talking. A snowball let loose, and it was like a cigarette tossed on a pile of oily rags. Snow started flying in every direction. Hordes of students rushed to join the mêlée.

"You want to get in on this?" Todd asked.

"Absolutely," I said tossing my bag against the wall.

Students congealed into teams alternately launching assaults and retreating. Snow flew everywhere, an occasional brave soul running forward for a better shot. Laughs and shouts echoed in the quad.

At the edge of the battlefield, eyeing the snowy ruckus with dubiety, stood a pizza man holding a stack of boxes. I decided to "help."

"HEY!" I yelled, running out with my hands up, "EVERYONE STOP FOR A MINUTE! THE PIZZA GUY'S GOTTA GET THROUGH!"

The mob held their fire. Snow silently blanketed the darkening quad as the delivery man started across the plaza. I headed back to my side and passed him on the way.

"Hey, thanks a lot," he said.

"No problem," I said, not believing anyone could be so stupid.

When the man reached midpoint, there was a distant shout, "Now!" A barrage of snowballs pummeled the man from every direction. Pizza boxes exploded in a cloud of powder. His hat was blown off, and the man quickly fell into a fetal position. A cheer went up, and the crowd redirected efforts on each other.

It was then I had my great idea.

Minutes later Todd, Adam and I, trembling with excitement, carried snowball-filled milk crates into the girl's lounge. From the third floor, we had the high ground, a strategic advantage in any battle. The open window was narrow, so we took turns firing on the unsuspecting crowd below. It didn't take long for them to figure out where the painful impacts were coming from. We forgot to turn out the lights.

"HEY! GET THEM UP THERE!"

Snowballs started flying at us. Some hit the outside wall or banged against the window, but many were flying into the lounge.

"Oh shit…" I said as snow splattered around the lounge, spraying furniture and covering the television. Heavy thuds rattled the window.

"Close the window!" Adam yelled, "Close it!"

Todd closed the window, but the assault intensified. Boom, Boom, Boom. Relentless snowballs pounded the window. We backed away. Suddenly the window exploded. A thousand fragments of glass mixed with splattering snow burst into the room. I flinched, raising my hand to protect my face.

A great cheer went up from outside, and the attack abated.

"Holy crap!" Todd said.

A frigid breeze swept through the room and ruffled papers pinned to the walls.

"Everyone okay?" I asked.

"Shit, what do we do now?" Adam said, surveying the jagged shards of broken window.

"I don't know," I said slowly, backing toward the exit, "but I'm glad this isn't *our* lounge!"

 confused

Standing under bright lights, I began to perspire under my surgical garb. The cap, mask, gown and gloves were a new experience for me.

I'll have to get used to it, I thought.

On the table lay all of the materials and instruments we needed for this delicate operation. It was my first attempt at such a case, and I approached the procedure with trepidation. Across the table stood Dr. Kesselman, similarly gowned and gloved. To his left sat Dr. Kaplan, acting anesthesiologist. The sounds of various medical devices beeped and chirped in the background.

"Nurse!" I barked.

"Yes, Dr. Pryor?" nurse Lee giggled.

"Would you mind wiping my forehead?" I said.

"Not at all, Dr. Pryor." Nurse Lee padded my forehead with a gauze.

"You gonna be okay?" asked Dr. Kesselman.

"The pressure... I just can't..." I squinted, fighting back the tears.

"Get a hold of yourself!" Dr. Kaplan said. "The patient needs you! You've got to be strong!"

I closed my eyes and took a deep breath. I gave a solemn nod.

"Let's proceed." I held out my hand. "Sterile water irrigation..."

Nurse Lee handed me the container of water.

"Steady the receiving basin," I said. Dr. Kesselman's gloved hands held the basin securely as I infused the solution.

"Good, Dr. Kesselman, confirm adequate levels please," I said.

Dr. Kesselman extended a tape measure.

"Twenty-two point five centimeters, well within parameters, doctor."

"Okay, let's have the vial of DSALF..." I said.

"DSALF?" asked nurse Lee.

"Desiccated suspended animation life forms, that packet right there..."

Nurse Lee lifted the packet with sterile forceps and carefully handed it to me.

I slowly infused the powder into the aqueous solution.

"Slowly!" shouted Dr. Kaplan.

"Dammit man, you want to kill them?" added Dr. Kesselman.

"I know what I'm doing!" I shouted. "You have *got* to trust me!" I gave them an intense look.

Dr. Kesselman and Dr. Kaplan exchanged a nervous glance. After a brief pause, Dr. Kesselman nodded. I continued to empty the container and handed the forceps back.

Everyone breathed a sigh of relief.

"Linear vinyl polymer agitator..." I held out my hand.

"What?"

"The cocktail stirrer..."

"Oh..."

I slowly agitated the solution. The room was silent. The tension was palpable. Thirty seconds, sixty seconds... two minutes.

Dr. Kaplan leaned closer. "Stop! Stop! I see something!"

I removed the agitator as we leaned closer. As the water settled, one could see tiny movements.

"Life!" I shouted. "We have created life!"

They all let out a huge cheer. The doctors proceeded to high five each other.

I removed my mask, revealing a broad smile. Nurse Lee couldn't control her laughter.

"I never thought Sea-Monkeys could be so much fun!" she said.

It was just another juvenile activity in a college dorm—a mock operation to make sea monkeys. I was dressed as a surgeon; it was a costume, all fake. I know this sounds crazy, but it had an effect on me. When I pulled off the gloves I looked at my hands, and a peculiar thought popped into my mind:

These are the hands of a surgeon, I thought.

Todd tapped me on the shoulder and handed me a beer.

"What?" asked Todd.

"Nothing," I said, "just a weird feeling."

❧

In the Spring, I completed my freshman year. I learned to function independently and made a lot of new friends. My grades weren't stellar, mostly Bs with a D in calculus. You know that nightmare of taking a final exam without going to class all semester? That was me in calculus.

My Grade Point Average (GPA) stood at 2.52.

❧

I returned sophomore year, falling back into my college routine: fraternity parties, lounge soirees, sleeping through class and psychologically torturing Cindy. It wasn't long before I was relieved of the latter.

Education in college goes well beyond the classroom. One of my greatest lessons was learned the day Cindy dumped me. It wasn't a spat, not a fight, no yelling or punches—just a cold resolve in those eyes I loved: I'm through with you.

I'm convinced that if we had met after college, we would've married. College, though, is a hard place to have relationships—lots of emotion, immaturity and testosterone. It's not surprising I screwed things up. I had my own insecurities and felt the more girls I could attract the more self-esteem I would gain. Piss poor excuses.

I knew Cindy loved me, and I took her for granted. I assumed she would always be there for me. I assumed she would always take me back after my transgressions. When she kicked me out of her life, I was devastated. The support, comfort, and sense of security she provided was gone, and I fell hard.

The only upside to our break-up was that I learned. I learned to appreciate the people in my life. If you don't, you'll lose them. It was too late to salvage the relationship with Cindy, but next time I would know better.

ↄ

It's dark in the makeshift hospital. Sandbag walls rise to the canvas ceiling, a string of bulbs fight to keep the darkness at bay.

I'm dressed like a surgeon in white scrubs trying to feel useful, but I don't know what to do. Wounded arrive, some screaming in pain, others unconscious. Nurses accost me, telling me I have to operate. I tell them to get ready for the OR, *and I'll be with them shortly.*

I see Hawkeye Pierce and approach him. Uncharacteristically sullen, he tends to the wounded. I tell him I'm new and would appreciate observing for a while before I try to operate on my own.

He tells me that there are too many patients. He needs me to start right away.

I begin to panic. I tell Hawk-eye there's been a mistake, I'm not a surgeon. I tell him I'm an EMT *and want to help, but I can't operate.*

He turns and hands me a scalpel. Try to do the best you can, he says.

An explosion shakes the hospital. I can feel the next mortar headed straight for me. I'm going to die, but I'm glad I won't have to operate. I hear the scream of an incoming rocket and close my eyes, bracing for impact …

"John, John." Todd was gently shaking me awake.

"Wha?" My head hurt, and I couldn't open my eyes.

"C'mon, wake up," he said; "don't you have a physics test?"

I parted my eyes enough to read the clock. 10:20 a.m.

Oh, fuck, I thought and pulled the pillow over my face.

"John?" Todd said.

"It started twenty minutes ago," I mumbled; "I'll have to make it up or something."

&

At three a.m. on a Wednesday, the floors of Seneca Hall are vacant and silent. In dorm 2U, two figures remain awake, huddled before the glow of a computer monitor. In the phosphorous light of the Macintosh, Todd carefully directed a "mouse" across the screen.

"Exemplary service," I suggested.

"That's good," Todd said as he inserted the adjective. "Should this be bold?"

"Yeah, can you do that?" I asked.

Todd highlighted the appropriate text and clicked Bold.

"That is so cool!" I said.

"Okay, let's print it out," Todd queried the laser printer. It was a gift from his uncle to further his studies.

Or commit fraud, I thought.

Well, it wasn't really fraud.

"The College Republicans of Binghamton University..." I proclaimed, "hereby present this Medal of Freedom Award to Senator Richard G. Lugar for his tireless efforts and exemplary service to the principles and ideals of the Republican Party."

"What do you think?" I asked.

"I think it's the biggest load of bullshit we've ever come up with," said Todd, "but it looks really good, and that's all that counts."

A few days earlier, I read Senator Luger was coming to Binghamton. Lugar, the Republican chairman of the Foreign Relations Committee, was to speak at a breakfast fund-raiser. Most college students wouldn't have raised an eyebrow, but for Todd and me, it was like Bob Dylan coming to town.

"We gotta go," I said.

"How much is it?" he asked.

"$250 a plate," I read. "Shit, that's a lot of beer money."

We thought for a while in silence.

"I got an idea," I said. Todd listened as I spelled it out. An hour later, I worked up the nerve to make the call.

"Ahh, yes, hello, my name is John Pryor, I'm the president of the Binghamton College Republicans." I paced nervously while trying to sound legitimate. "We understand Senator Lugar will be speaking to the University later this week ..."

Todd smiled and gave a thumbs up. I looked away before losing composure.

"Well, the members of our organization," *both of us,* "have voted to award him our highest honor, and we would appreciate the opportunity to present it to him in person ..."

I wondered if they would check my credentials. What would happen if I was caught lying to get close to a U.S. senator? I imagined the secret service interrogation: "So, Mr. Pryor, exactly what were you going to do to the Senator?"

I focused back on the conversation.

"Just two, myself and my co-president Todd Kesselman," I nodded at Todd. "Yes, thank you."

I hung up the phone and let out a woo-ho. Todd leapt from his bed, and we high-fived.

"They bought it!" I said. "We're in!"

We created a mock organization and finagled an invitation. Now we needed to procure an award, not an insignificant detail. We called several places to purchase a plaque or a medal, but nothing could be delivered on such short notice.

As the day wore on, we became increasingly desperate. It finally became clear that we would have to make something ourselves. We turned to the desktop publishing capabilities of the Macintosh.

I looked again at the printout and was impressed.

"We need a frame," I said.

Searching the room, Todd selected a picture from his desk. He pulled out the photo and tossed it over his shoulder. We inserted the print-out and surveyed our work.

"Probably need to do something about this," I said.

On the back, in flowery cursive, was written: *To Todd, I can always count on you to get me home after the party. Love, Stacy.*

The breakfast was held at a banquet hall off campus. Mercedes, BMWs and Cadillacs filled the parking lot. I felt out of place even before we entered the door. Inside we found our name tags on a large table. I pinned mine to the blazer on loan from Steve Drake along with the tie from Ed Schmidt and shoes from Dave Fellon. I came to college ill prepared for any formal event, much less a Republican fund-raiser.

The hall was big and bright. The circular tables were covered with delicate chinaware, fine crystal and ornate floral arrangements. Servants in tuxedo shirts bustled about delivering drinks and hors d'oeuvres. In the front, a podium was flanked by long tables.

"I bet the food doesn't suck," Todd said.

"I bet you're right," I agreed.

We made our way among the numbered tables filled with mostly older men in expensive looking suits. As we approached our table, Todd leaned close to me.

"That guy at our table looks familiar," he said.

"Yeah," I said, "where do we know him from?"

A little panic gripped me when I realized we would be seated next to the president of Binghamton University.

After introductions, Todd and I conversed easily while sipping mimosas and enjoying real eggs. The campus was predominantly Democratic, and the table was excited to see Republican students. We were the toast of the table.

Presently, the senator took the rostrum and spoke at length about Middle East politics and the U.S. support of Iraq in its war against Iran. I sipped some coffee and reflected on the meal.

"I could get used to this," I whispered to Todd; "when's the next senator coming?"

At the conclusion of the speech, some important looking people crowded around the senator. Dick Lugar smiled and spoke with businessmen. I shifted nervously and leaned over to Todd.

"What am I going to say?" I hadn't prepared any formal dialog.

"Relax," Todd said, "you'll think of something."

The senator turned his attention to us, and I shook his hand.

"John Pryor," I said. "This is Todd Kesselman."

"Well it's wonderful to see some young faces here today," Dick Lugar said with a bright smile.

"Thank you, senator," I swallowed, "Todd and I represent the College Republicans of Binghamton University. On behalf of the students, we would like to present you with this award for your service and dedication."

The senator graciously received the award from Todd and gave it a good look.

"This is just wonderful. Thank you. You know it is so important for students and young people like yourselves to take an active interest in politics. That's why I am so honored to receive this ..."

Politicians, it turns out, like to talk, and they are good at it. I learned that I didn't have to say much. Instead, we smiled and nodded as the senator went on about the future of the party and the need for more student activism. Then we all turned and smiled for the camera. A photographer snapped a few photos.

And that was it. We bullshitted our way into a fund-raiser, deceived the president of the university, and presented a mock award to a sitting u.s. senator. Now we could get back to college life.

Or so I thought.

The following day, the next domino fell. Our picture with the senator graced the front page of the local newspaper.

"No fucking way!" I said aloud looking at my smiling face next to Dick Lugar.

"Let me see that," Todd said, grabbing it from my hands.

"Holy crap, that's really us!"

We became instant celebrities; for the next few days, I was identified as "that guy with the Senator."

The following day, I was in my dorm room when the phone rang.

"Are you the student in the paper yesterday?" a voice asked.

My heart started to pound. Had I been found out? Was I in trouble?

"Yes," I admitted; "that's me."

The man claimed to be the chairman of the Broome County Republicans. He was glad to see students involved in politics and wanted to know if I was interested in helping out the county.

"Who is this really?" I said, wondering who was pranking me.

It was no joke.

At the county meetings, Todd and I met other prominent Republicans and made new contacts. The phone began to ring more often. The GOP gubernatorial candidate was coming to town—could we give him a tour of the campus? Could we pick up the comptroller? Would we be available to drive Jean Kirkpatrick to the airport? I even got to meet Bob Dole.

It got out of hand when the State Senate Majority leader asked us to help out with his campaign. We found ourselves in a sound studio recording radio commercials. Print and TV ads followed, and I frequently heard my voice broadcasted in the student center.

It got to the point where I had to choose between school and the Republicans. Once I agreed to run an errand without realizing I had a physics exam. I shouldn't have skipped the exam, but I felt I already made a commitment; people were counting on me.

It culminated with an invitation to the Republican State Convention. I recognized a committee member as the man who taught my Citizenship Merit Badge in Scouts. He promoted me from page to VIP, and I found myself on stage, leading the convention in the Pledge of Allegiance. Later, I sat in on meetings with Pat Robinson and eventually was introduced to Vice President George H. W. Bush.

My activities with the Republican party was a life lesson well beyond school. I participated in real-world politics with real-world leaders. While my fellow students were trapped in a fishbowl of the classroom, I dined with senators and conversed with the U.N. ambassador. In the short term, my grades suffered, but I was never one to let schoolwork get in the way of my education.

❧

I parked at the end of a row of cars across the street. Rich got out, and we started toward the muffled bass and raucous laughter emanating from the mixer. I gingerly placed my arm around my little brother's shoulder.

"Now listen," I said in a paternalistic tone, "these are my Sigma Nu brothers and Delta Phi Epsilon girls ..."

"Yeah," Rich said.

"I don't want you to embarrass me," I said, "so drink as much as you possibly can."

"Okay," he laughed, "I'll see what I can do."

My relationship with Rich began to change in college. We were always close, sharing a tent in Scouts, riding on the ambulance and playing guitar, but now we spent time together at bars and parties. He became less a little brother and more of a friend.

We filled our cups at the keg, and I introduced Rich to my fraternity. We mingled through the house scoping out the babes.

"Stay away from that one," I nodded to a bubbly blonde, "word is she's got crabs."

"They got a cure for that, don't they?" he said.

"True," I said.

After a while, we refilled our cups and settled in the kitchen.

"So how's it going in Syracuse?" I asked. Rich had abandoned college to enroll in a paramedic program at Upstate Medical University. He caught the EMS bug as bad as I did and planned on turning it into a career.

"Good," he said, "classes going well, learning to save lives.

"You're going to be a medic before me," I said. "You suck!"

"Dude, you're going to be a college graduate," he said; "I'll probably never finish college. Be happy with what you got."

Rich found a girl to talk to, and we separated. In the early morning hours, a few brothers and I circled the keg, passing around the tap, when the back door burst open.

"You're not gonna believe this; some kid just did a funnel of grain alcohol!"

What an idiot! I thought. *Who would be stupid enough to do a funnel of grain alcohol?*

We abandoned the keg to investigate.

Yup, it was Rich.

"What the hell were you thinking?" I asked him.

He gave me an incredulous, inebriated look. "I didn't know it was *grain alcohol!* They just handed it to me and said drink!"

Binghamton

❧

I finished my sophomore year with a GPA of 2.18, failing both physics I and II. The fraternity, ambulance and college Republican excursions had taken their toll.

My dad was deflated. He felt medical school was no longer an option, but I disagreed. He didn't understand the political contacts I made that year. With the right letter of recommendation, maybe from Senator Lugar, I was sure to get in.

❧

Junior year, my parents handed me the keys of emancipation, and I returned to campus driving a tan Nissan Stanza. The car allowed easy access to off-campus activities, and I wasted no time joining the city ambulance.

Union Ambulance served Endwell, West Endicott and Johnson City with a call volume of more than three thousand a year. The agency covered an urban area, busier than Clifton Park. With Union I would get even more experience than back home.

My schedule finally allowed electives and I registered for the pre-hospital advanced EMT course, but there was a snag: It wasn't a real paramedic class.

There are four levels of EMT in New York State: Basic, Intermediate, Critical Care and Paramedic. The difference between Critical Care Tech (CCT) and Paramedic was subtle but important. CCTs administered fewer medications and generally needed permission to do anything. Paramedics were more autonomous and could act on standing orders.

The county medics were critical care techs, not paramedics. Eager to work as an advanced EMT, I took what was offered.

❧

Halfway through my junior year, I began planning for life after college. I liked biochem and considered research or a graduate degree. Of course, the ambulance provided exposure to patient care, and the desire to become a physician grew stronger. I scheduled a meeting with Tom, the pre-health advisor.

During the interview, I fidgeted in the uncomfortable silence as Tom inspected my transcript.

He rubbed his forehead and looked up.

"To be brutally honest, John," he said, "it doesn't look good. You got a 'D' in calculus and failed both physics one and two. Even if we excuse these problems, the rest of your grades are only mediocre. Are you sure you want to pursue medical school?"

My face flushed with indignation. Who was this guy to tell me about getting into medical school? And what about my experience as an EMT? I was already treating patients while other applicants didn't know the working end of a stethoscope. Plus, he didn't know all the political connections I had made.

"Yes," I said, "I'm sure this is something I want to pursue."

"Okay, well, it's going to be an uphill battle. I mean a real struggle. I've learned that nothing is impossible, but right now there's little stopping Admissions from tossing out your application right off the bat. You'll have to repeat physics. If you take them in the summer, you can sit for the MCAT in the fall; that way, the physics will be fresh. You should probably retake calculus as well. Your only real hope is to perform well on the MCAT."

I missed the application cycle for admission following graduation. This meant I would need to find a job for a year regardless of my medical school plans.

⋐⋑

I matured as a prehospital provider during my junior year. Back on a municipal ambulance, I returned to real trauma, cardiac arrests, old patients struggling to breath, young kids with allergic reactions and crazy people trying to kill themselves.

Secrets of paramedic medicine were revealed to me. I learned to interpret the squiggly lines on the monitor. I memorized the medications and how they worked. I started IVs, learned to intubate, and used the paddles to defibrillate. As I learned something in class, I applied it on my next shift on the ambulance.

I practiced real medicine and loved every minute of it.

Jeff Gotro, the class instructor, also rode on Union. He became my preceptor and mentor. I found a common thread among Jeff, Dwight, Kevin and Mike. They had similar characteristics that made them great medics: authority, competency, intelligence and humor.

I emulated them as best I could.

Summer after my junior year, I redeemed myself in physics—A's in both I and II. Working three shifts a week, I completed my CCT internship. After a number of supervised calls, I was given my own number and allowed to function independently.

Now a Critical Care Tech, I functioned essentially as a paramedic.

During down time at the station, Jeff Groto and I discussed EMS as a profession. Despite the existence of EMTs and paramedics for over a decade, the public still perceived us as "ambulance drivers." We constantly encountered families that wanted us to "get them to the hospital" as quickly as possible. They didn't understand our ability to provide emergency treatment and that simply loading and speeding to the ER would actually delay care.

"We need a motto," I said to Jeff, "something to unify the profession and help us stand out."

"Like what?" Jeff asked.

"I don't know," I said. "You know, like the Boy Scouts have 'Be Prepared,' and New York City police and firefighters are known as the 'Finest and Bravest.' Seems like EMS needs something like that."

"I see what you're saying," Jeff said. "It's not a bad idea."

That night, I wrote down some ideas. Over the next few days, I fashioned an essay and showed it to Jeff.

"This is pretty good," he said. "You should submit it to JEMS."

JEMS was the Journal of Emergency Medical Services, the trade magazine for EMTs.

Why not? I thought.

I picked up a battered issue lying on the end table and found the address for submissions.

A month later, I received a letter from JEMS. They liked my article and would publish it. I received a half-dozen copies of the October issue. On the back page was my essay.

An EMS Motto
By John Pryor

The boy Scouts hail "Be Prepared," the Marines say, "Always Faithful." Both of these groups have found a way to summarize all their ideals and objectives in one phrase—a motto. One evening, I thought I would try to come up with a motto for EMS personnel, a phrase that would exemplify what the EMS system is striving for. What I came up with were three words: Prepared, Professional and Resourceful. All of the specific traits, characteristics and accomplishments of the ideal pre-hospital care provider are illustrated in these three simple words.

Prepared. The overwhelming majority of people in this country are not ready for, or have even thought about, the events that will take place on May 7, 1990. But because somewhere in this country someone will be critically traumatized on that day, we, as EMTs, will be ready for it. We are becoming ready by training ourselves and others, by implementing protocols and procedures, and by preparing and replacing equipment so it will be fully functional on May 7. On a smaller scale, all EMTs should prepare themselves for each shift. They should make sure their green lights work, check their personal equipment, and check the rig and all of its equipment; a full arrest is not the time to find an 02 tank with 100 pounds of pressure. All of these measures, large and small, will allow the EMT to handle a call professionally.

Professional. We are all aware of the tremendous growth and success of the EMS concept. Pre-hospital care no longer fills an accessory role in medicine but has become an integral part of it. With the expanded horizons of EMS, comes added, often grave, responsibilities. Dealing with human suffering and human life is not a task to be taken lightly; it must be dealt with in an accurate, intelligent and professional manner.

By professional, I do not refer to being compensated for services rendered; most people in this business are not. Instead, I refer to well-trained and educated EMTs who carry out their duties in the most effective manner possible. Professional EMTs adopt standards of practice that are shared by others in their field and strive to expand their knowledge of the practice through research (an area I feel is currently below standard within EMS).

Finally, professionals conduct themselves in a pleasant, informative and, above all, helpful manner to those outside the practice. The application of professionalism ranges from EMTs tucking in their shirts for those 3 a.m. calls to relaying concise and informative hospital reports to physicians.

Being prepared and professional are traits shared by many fields of practice and by many areas of medicine, but the EMT is set apart by resourcefulness, the third word of my motto.

Resourceful. There are many things that will happen in the field that cannot possibly be prepared for. Any EMS veteran will agree that anything can and will happen out there; and we are all destined to deal with an unfamiliar situation sooner or later. The ability to use resourcefulness is an important characteristic of a good EMT or EMT/A. All the protocols and procedures in the world won't help a bit when the EMT is faced with no-win situations, unforeseeable conditions, and problems with allocation of resources in the field. A professional follows accepted procedures whenever possible, but when an EMT needs a saw and all that is available is a hammer, the EMT makes it work, somehow saving a life.

As Dr. John Fortune of the Albany Trauma Center once said, "When your back is against the wall, the sky is the limit." How true this is; in the midst of all the confusion of a serious car accident, with what seems to be an impossible extrication, the EMT's ingenuity could save a life.

Although there is no way to learn resourcefulness, there are several ways to foster its growth. As always, keep cool. This is a trait often mastered by the EMT but one that can be easily lost in desperate situations. Be confident.

By virtue of their accomplishments and dedication in EMS, EMTs are capable of unimaginable feats. I recall an EMT who was faced with a severe pelvic incision that cut the femoral artery. The EMT quickly pinched off the ends of the artery with his own hands to stop the hemorrhage, thereby saving life and limb. EMTs should avoid kicking themselves for not thinking of something at the scene. Many ideas of how a situation could have been handled better will pop into the responder's head hours after a call; but no one, not even the EMT, should ever criticize a decision made under such pressure.

So there you have it, my suggestion for the EMT motto, "Prepared, Professional and Resourceful." With these words in mind, I invite you to examine your own conduct of service as I did; I am sure that you will find these three words helpful in becoming the best EMT and EMT/A possible.

John Pryor is a New York State AEMT-3 and rides with a Volunteer Emergency squad.

I held the magazine in my hands, smiling at the byline, captivated by my name in print. Still in college and already I had my first publication. How many medical school applicants were published? None, probably.

✧

Senior year, I moved off campus and shared an apartment with my friend Adam Kaplan. My first semester, I repeated calculus and finished up requirements for my major. In September, I sat for the Medical College Admission Test (MCAT).

The significance of this test cannot be overemphasized; it literally determined my fate. My academic record did not reflect my true ability, and a good MCAT score could prove it. A low score would sink me.

The MCAT has several sections that tested knowledge in biology, chemistry and physics but also problem solving and reading comprehension. Each section was graded on a scale from 0-16.

The results waited for me when I returned home on Thanksgiving. Alone in my room, I flipped the envelope over in my hands, trying to slow my breathing.

Those admitted to medical school obtain an average score of 10 in each category.

Holding a knife at the corner of the fold, I closed my eyes and sliced it open.

I scanned the page. It took a few minutes to register.

> Science Knowledge
> > Biology   10
> > Chemistry   09
> > Physics   10
> > Sci. Problems   09
> Skills Analysis
> > Reading   10
> > Quantitative   08

The scores were competitive and boosted my confidence. More importantly, I demonstrated to myself that I had ability—that if I put my mind to it, I could perform well academically.

I was still in the game.

❧

My last semester I spent more time on the ambulance than going out with friends. I honed my skills, worked codes, communicated with the ER docs and taught EMTs. Trauma was exciting, but I proved more useful on medical calls. Chest pain, heart failure, asthma, allergic reactions, diabetic coma, narcotic overdoses—with my treatment, these patients could be symptom free by the time we reached the ER.

I achieved a new level in patient care.

During this time, I met Dr. Paul Karmin. Paul was a physician who joined the ambulance to gain EMS experience. We worked many shifts together, and he provided a physician's insight to the medical field.

I shared my grades and discussed my concerns about getting into med school. Paul was very supportive and encouraged me to go for it.

"Never be afraid to try," he told me. "Someone's going to be accepted; it might as well be you."

His advice lingered for years. Whenever I felt disheartened or hopeless in my pursuit to get into medical school, I drew strength from Paul's words of encouragement.

&

In late May of 1988, sprouting tulips and dogwood blossoms rejuvenated the campus, fostering a sense of renewal, a fresh start, a new beginning. Cars, filled with parents and family, crammed the parking lots. Donning a cap and a silky black gown, I joined the class of 1988 for graduation.

Sitting in a sea of robes, I reflected on the past four years.

We learn more from our failures than our accomplishments, and I failed the most in college. I failed my relationship with Cindy. I failed to take responsibility on many occasions, but mostly I failed academically.

My ignominious GPA remained at 2.55, set for life like a botched tattoo.

Technically, I satisfied the requirements for graduation; emotionally, I felt like a fake. I had regrets, and they were bitter.

An epiphany occurred to me on that last day, just before I rose to receive a diploma I did not deserve. A final lesson from college: Live your life so there will be no regrets.

After the ceremony, I roamed the crowd of graduates and found Todd. It was hard to imagine our time together was over. We posed for a picture and promised to keep in touch.

Back at the apartment, a farewell party was in full swing. I mingled, meeting my friends' parents and being forced to answer the same question over and over: Where are you headed next?

New York City

August 1988. West 59th / Columbus Circle subway station. Gathering New Yorkers begin to crowd the platform, occasionally stretching a neck toward downtown or glancing at their watch. The sweltering subterranean air is suffocating; sweat beads my forehead. The crowd thickens, and I start to feel claustrophobic in my starched Oxford and strangling tie. The subway smell is both new and vaguely familiar; memories of childhood visits to the Museum of Natural History with my dad surface. Impulsively, I back away from the yellow line, paranoid some lunatic will push me onto the tracks. A garbled voice, not quite human, much less English, echoes along the mosaic tiles, prompting quizzical expressions at the ceiling.

Across the platform a southbound train lingers with its doors open. A conductor enters, yelling at a sleeping bum to get off the train.

"Fuck you!" the man barks.

Prodded with a boot, he falls off the seat and crawls toward the door. His feet are crippled; he can't walk.

The crowd parts as the man slithers to the closest bench and climbs up. I smell him from ten feet away.

8:20, and still no sign of the Uptown 1 train. I'll never make it to 168th in time.

Well, I thought, *welcome to New York.*

❦

Senior year in college is daunting, especially as the real world approaches like a river reaching the precipice of a waterfall. Regardless of my future medical school prospects, I needed a job. Hoping to use my degree, I applied to health departments, state police forensic labs and dozens of medical research labs for a tech position. But, I also enjoyed being a medic and looked into several professional ambulance services.

Eastern Ambulance served the city of Syracuse and its surrounding hinterland. A tour of the station revealed several Braun ambulances with medics dressed in deep blue uniforms preparing for their shift. I followed Dave Barnes, the paramedic supervisor, into his office.

"I see here that you're a level III," Dave said, "a critical care tech."

"Yeah, that's the highest level of training they offered in Binghamton," I said, "but at Union, the CCTs functioned essentially as paramedics."

"Well, they don't in this region," he said.

"It's okay," I assured him. "I have enough experience. I'm as good as any of *your* paramedics."

My arrogance surprised him.

Who is this college kid telling me how good my medics are? he thought.

"Like I said, in this region we don't recognize level IIIs," Dave continued. "If you worked for us, you would function as an EMT."

I was indignant.

"Are you serious?" I asked.

Dave smiled, happy to get a rise out of me.

"Yeah," he said, "would you be interested in working as a basic EMT?"

No fucking way! I thought.

"I'd have to think about that," I said.

At this point, the interview was over.

The same problem recurred elsewhere. No paid agencies recognized CCTs as paramedics; it was a serious disadvantage. I dropped the paramedic idea and focused on biochemistry.

My ulterior motive for applying to large medical centers was to make contacts that would help me in the future, either for medical or grad school. So I was excited to get an interview at Columbia University.

Dr. Richard Dekelbaum, an eminent researcher in the field of nutrition, recruited some of the most talented minds in nutritional research. I wondered what I was doing in his office. The interview was going well, however, and Dr. Dekelbaum hadn't even mentioned my GPA.

"What are your career goals, John?" Dr. Dekelbaum asked while looking at my résumé.

"I like organic chemistry and biochem," I answered; "I think I would prefer research that can benefit the medical community."

"Yes," he said, looking up, "but what I meant was, where do you see yourself five years from now?"

I have no idea, I thought.

"Right now, I'm not sure. I'm hoping to work for a while and see what interests me and then go from there. Once I find a field I'm interested in, then I might pursue grad school, maybe a Ph.D."

At the time I was being honest.

"Well, I have a research stipend for one year. It's for a study on atherosclerosis. I can't promise you a position after that, but we can see how things go over the year."

A moment passed before I realized he was offering me a job.

"Oh?" I said, "No, that would be fine."

We stood and shook hands.

∽

A few weeks before moving to New York, I pieced together my medical school application. I reviewed letters from Jeff Gotro and Paul Karmin who supported my candidacy.

Jeff wrote:

Pre-hospital critical care usually occurs in conditions that are less than optimum, and the controlled environment of the hospital is absent. This requires that the pre-hospital care provider be able to handle complex situations, usually with inadequate assistance, and perform in strange environments under tremendous pressure. John appears to be able to handle these types of situations with confidence. He has the ability to think quickly and make sound decisions under pressure. John is an excellent candidate for medical school.

Paul was no less generous in his appraisal of me:

Also worth detailing is the multifaceted nature of John's interests and personality. For example, John is a published author, with an article in the 10/87 issue of Emergency. He is the founder and a (recent) brother of Sigma Nu Fraternity. He was the founder and chairman of the Binghamton College Republicans, plus a Broome County Republican Committee man. His confréres included Senator Richard Lugar during a recent speaking engagement. He has always held a part-time job and knows the value of a dollar. Last, his communication skills are excellent.

It is thus my strong opinion that John is one of the best candidates for a career in medicine that I have ever met. He brings in a vibrancy and degree of self-motivation, tempered with compassion, that will serve him well. I believe he is headed toward a distinguished career in medical research, and may well pick up a Ph.D. along the way. John has my fullest endorsement, and I am sure he will abundantly succeed, God willing. If I can be of further assistance, please phone or write.

The application was comprehensive. I listed my parents' places of birth and occupations. I recorded all my jobs and extracurricular activities since Scouts. Painfully, I typed out my entire academic record.

Finally, I needed to compose a personal statement. I had multiple starts, trying to argue my case for acceptance. I questioned how much I should write about my paramedic experience and wondered how to broach my dismal GPA.

One day after a call, I pulled out a yellow legal pad, filled with thoughts and crude first drafts, intending to tackle the personal statement. I couldn't concentrate; there was too much on my mind. I turned to a blank page and wrote:

Thoughts of a Paramedic
John P. Pryor, July 1988

I had a well thought-out personal statement that I was going to present to you, but instead I want to write about what happened today.

I am a prehospital critical care technician with a volunteer ambulance squad. Six years ago, I joined mainly because of the excitement it offered. Over the years, I have completed hundreds of hours of training and have cared for countless patients.

Volunteer ambulance work is odd. The people who do it are in a way obsessed. We remain glued to our radios regardless of what activity we or our family are engaged in. Our mothers, friends and spouses curse "That Damn Ambulance" for taking so much time away from them. Today I am on call away from my family and friends; it is July 4th.

I was awakened at 7:00 a.m. by a call for a possible "Code 2," someone possibly dead. The tones were put out twice in a row because of a lack of volunteers. It's a holiday, and there would not be a guaranteed response. I got dressed and called for information. A woman had found her husband on the floor not breathing. Over the radio, another crew member called en route. I was relieved; at least there would be two of us.

The address was familiar, and I thought our captain, Dan, lived nearby. Shortly after we rolled the ambulance, the dispatcher notified us that our captain was at the scene. The patient was in cardiac arrest.

Tim drove as I assembled all the gear we would use in the back of the rig. The ride was rough, and rightfully so. We were responding to the gravest medical emergency possible, and literally seconds count. We would need all the advanced life support equipment. I threw it all on the stretcher. I assembled the bag mask, checked the monitor, and got the suction ready.

It is hard to describe what goes through my head when I'm en route to a call. Mostly, I run through a checklist of sorts: Check rhythm, watch pulses, keep a good airway, epinephrine, lidocaine, bretylium, bicarb. The latter is the sequence for medications. After six years, one has a solid picture of what is going to happen. I am ready to meet the patient and family in their own home.

As we neared the scene, Tim mentioned that the address may be Dan's uncle's house. I remember him saying it, but I was too busy to respond. We arrived and grabbed the stretcher full of equipment. As we approached the house, a man met us at the door, pointing down the hall. "In there." The man was Dan's father, the patient's brother.

As I took my first step into the house, I looked past a kitchen with two ladies, and saw two feet in the bedroom doorway. I turned the corner and entered the room where Dan had started CPR. Tim took over ventilations as I grabbed the defibrillator.

"Well, this is my uncle," Dan stated without missing a compression.

"How long has he been down?" I asked.

"Don't know."

Dan was quiet and reserved. I remember once arriving at a call for "child with leg laceration." Dan had arrived first and bandaged the wound. I asked him to describe the wound so I could relay the information to the Doc. He said it was about five inches, not too deep. On arrival at the ER, we unwrapped the bandages, and half this kid's leg unfurled on the table. Only Dan could under-emphasize an 18-inch gash to the bone with massive muscle and tendon damage as a five-inch cut. It was his nature to be very calm and relaxed.

Dan asked for suction. Tim had it ready in his hand when we

came in. Tim was a longtime veteran of the ambulance and instinctively anticipated our needs. Tim was a good EMT, one that made calls run smoothly because he always knew what needed to be done.

Just as I was checking the rhythm, Mike, a paramedic, came in.

"Hi, Mike," I said casually. I had been away and hadn't seen him in a while.

"Trouble?" he asked, walking into the room.

"Unknown downtime; looks like fine V-fib, agonal," I said, referring to the monitor.

It was then that I first noticed the patient's face. There is a lot in that moment, most of which I can't describe. It's an unpleasant sight: the skin is dark blue, vomit covers his cheek, and his eyelids are half open. At first glance, I always see the same picture: It is my father or grandfather or mother or brother. For a second or two, it is hard to disassociate these images, but then I recover quickly. For Dan, the image is real; I notice Dan staring at his uncle's half-opened eyes. Mike intubated as I charged the paddles to defibrillate. Tim was busy setting up the IV line, and Dan continued CPR. Mike got the endotracheal tube in on the first attempt. Then he turned to me and said, "Zap 'em."

The countershock changed the rhythm to flatline—no electrical activity at all. This is the point where the pace changes. We are all experienced providers who know when someone has a chance and when the door has closed. The third defib shut the door. I knew it Mike knew it; and, certainly, Dan knew it.

Dan's family (the patient's family), likewise, was acutely aware of what was happening. They had listened to Dan describe calls like this one countless times. Somewhat like families of a physician, families of paramedics pick up a lot about the practice; their understanding of exactly what was going on made me uneasy. Phrases like "Doing all we can" didn't fool them.

Mike began to radio the hospital while I stepped into the kitchen to ask the family some questions. I asked the basic ones, which always begin with the same question. "When was the last time you saw your husband?" I hate asking that question because it inevitably demands that the wife remember the last moment with her husband alive. With these types of calls, the answer is usually "last night." We call them "wake-up calls" because the scenario usually follows this pattern: went to bed feeling fine, died in his sleep, found dead in the morning. These patients typically have a poor prognosis because of the great amount of time between death and discovery.

As I was interviewing the wife, a few other people came in, frantic. They raced right past me and into the bedroom. One young girl leaned over a policeman to see what was happening. She came back into the kitchen and asked if he (the patient) was talking to us. Before I could answer, the patient's brother said, "No" and, turning to me, added, "and he ain't gonna talk, is he?" There was absolutely no way I could have stopped from saying, "Probably not."

The resuscitation continued with a host of medications given both down the lung tube and intravenously. We "packaged" the patient onto a board and began to move toward the ambulance. By this time, it was around 8:00 a.m., and it was a bright sunny day. There was a cool breeze. I thought what a great day for a 4th of July picnic. I went to prepare the rig for transport.

We loaded the patient and radioed "En route" to Ellis Hospital. On the way, the mood was flippant. Even with Dan in the rig, that eerie medical humor surfaced. Many people outside the medical profession find it hard to comprehend medical humor.

Health professionals are constantly joking and even making fun of patients and situations. Some say it is a defense mechanism; others think it is just a consequence of becoming very relaxed in a critical situation. Whatever the reason, today was no different from the many other times that calls like these were handled with a slice of humor.

Although we joked a little, we continued an all-out effort of resuscitation. If there was one thing my ambulance squad took seriously, it was the high level of patient care. Ignoring the poor, now even hopeless, prognosis, we continued to perform flawless CPR, administered medication, and kept in constant contact with the physician. We arrived at Ellis hospital around 9:00 a.m.

We unloaded the patient from the ambulance and entered the emergency room. It was a slow morning in the emergency room, probably fewer than five patients and some family members. We moved slowly because the person doing chest compression had to continue while walking beside the stretcher. The slow procession into the ward always hits me as symbolic. We walk in past a group of people in the waiting room with saddened faces. Once in a while, a woman will put her hand over her mouth with a tear in her eye and under her breath mutter, "Oh my God." It is especially uneasy for these people to view such a spectacle because chances are they have friends or family that are being treated in the ward. This scene is a vivid illumination of their greatest fear. It is, in a sense, a funeral procession; and just as funerals jolt us into a realization of our own mortality, so do scenes like these capture the minds of onlookers. We are past them in about twenty seconds.

Past the waiting room, we parade by the nursing station. In contrast to the waiting room, we rarely receive a glance from the nurses and physicians except, perhaps, from a triage nurse. "Room 10, thank you." It's no surprise, it's nothing new. We pull into room 10, where a team of professionals has assembled. We transfer the patient to the hospital bed and begin to summarize treatment given so far. For this type of medical problem, virtually every type of treatment possible has already been administered in the field. The physician re-administered a few medications, and waited.

After approximately ten minutes of futile efforts, the physician turned to the roomful of people and said, "Thank you all." That was a common way for physicians to end such resuscitating. I was amazed the first time I had witnessed it. There I was among twenty doctors, nurses, respiratory therapists and EMS personnel, all frantically pushing drugs, putting in tubes, drawing blood. With those subtle words "Thank you, folks," everyone stopped, packed up and left. Never had I been so in touch with the finality of death. It is an instant of time that I feel honored to share with the patient.

I didn't quite know what to say to Dan, so I said nothing. It was notably a mistake on my part, but I tried and couldn't start the conversation. I went out to begin the paperwork with Mike. I looked at the blank run report, filled in the date and looked at the blank space labeled "name." I didn't know the name, the person, or the family. However, I was summoned to enter their lives during their greatest life crisis and was asked to save the life of their father, brother or friend. I found the patient's name from the hospital chart; it was Fred.

Hello, Fred, I said to myself. *I'm very pleased to meet you.*

I didn't use this essay, but it felt good to write about my experience.

I completed the general application for medical school a.k.a. American Medical College Admission Service (AMCAS). This organization pulls together information from various sources, including college transcripts, composite letters and MCAT scores, and sends the material to individual medical schools. The schools send a "supplemental" application, mostly an excuse to charge another fee.

I indicated "early decision" for Upstate Medical Center in Syracuse. If Syracuse accepted me, I would drop my applications elsewhere and commit to attending that school. If rejected, the normal application process would continue.

I wasn't sure about how many schools to apply to. I heard crazy stories of students applying only to one or two. The average was ten to fifteen. I applied to twenty.

I remember dropping the application into the slot at the post office. *Alea iacta est,* I thought, *the die is cast.*

&

In July, I moved into a closet on West 58th Street. The windowless room was just large enough for a single bed and my brother's rolltop desk. My flatmate, a graduate student who needed help paying the rent, mostly kept to himself. It was an easy walk to the 1 train at Columbus Circle for the ride up to 168th.

Feeling like an impostor that first day, I swallowed my fears and forced myself throughout the entrance to Columbia Presbyterian. Past security, I stumbled into the bustling lobby. Prominent researchers, physicians and medical students strode purposefully to their stations while I tried not to get lost.

In the lab, I met my co-workers. A half-dozen grad students, researchers and Ph.D. students welcomed me. I was approached by one of them.

"What school do you come from?" asked Bernard. He was an M.D. from Belgium performing research before starting residency in the United States.

"SUNY Binghamton," I said.

"Binghamton?" Bernard's face soured. "What is this? This is a nothing school. I can't believe the crap Dekalbaum hires."

He withdrew in a snit, leaving me speechless.

"Don't worry about him," Narmer said as he grabbed my arm. "We think Bernard has a personality disorder."

Narmer Galeano was a pediatrician doing research before starting a fellowship in pediatric gastroenterology. His kind words saved me from a breakdown my first day.

Dr. Dekelbaum was great. His teaching style was reminiscent of McEvoy and Gotro back on the ambulance. Had I chosen to pursue research, Dekalbaum would have made an excellent mentor. As I gained greater confidence and ability, I saw less of him and worked mostly with the other lab rats. Despite our decreased contact, I always had his support, and I did my best not to disappoint him.

ᴇᴏ

Living in New York was amazing.

Stepping out on 8th Avenue was like waking from a deep sleep. Thrust into the bustling throngs, there is suddenly movement, action, life. Walking the sidewalk, my cadence is like a pulse. Honking cabs and woop-woop sirens punctuate the dissonant city noise. Venting steam from a manhole cover feels like a warm exhalation. The smell of roasted nuts from a corner vendor wafts as I wait for a walk signal. A subway rumbles underneath like the growling stomach of a sleeping dragon. Corner vendors hawk pretzels under a Sabrett's umbrella. The metropolis is synergistic, rising above the sum of its inhabitants, possessing a sentience that affects me, changes me.

It's a city of world leaders, famous actors, real estate moguls and Wall Street robber barons. The possibilities here are limitless, and I can't help but feel my esteem rise like a hot-air balloon. If you can make it here, you can make it anywhere; but more than that, walking these sidewalks, I felt like I could make it here.

I worked at Columbia Presbyterian, an Ivy League school with world-renowned researchers. I'm a part, granted a small part, but still, part of this team, able to contribute in some way. The door to this prestigious world had opened a crack, allowing me a glimpse. I'm shown great possibilities.

Wandering the hallowed, Ivy League halls, I spy physicians in long white coats, like cassocks of a priestly order, adorned with stethoscopes draped like medals. They roam in small congregations, each member representing a stage of doctor metamorphosis. A fresh-faced medical student, starched white coat cut short at the waist, hangs on every word, starving for crumbs of knowledge. The intern, haggard and unshaven, with half-open eyes from a sleepless night, fails to follow the conversation; his wrinkled long coat, soiled and coffee stained, holds pockets bulging with reference books and patient sheets. Speaking is the senior resident—clean, confident, well-rested. The hallway is his classroom. He shares his knowledge—teaching, yet still learning. All is presided under the tutelage of the attending physician, years of experience evidenced in his graying hair. The starched white coat has come full circle; his stethoscope is tucked neatly into a coat pocket. He nods as the resident speaks, occasionally interjecting a comment or correction.

I've worked alongside doctors in the ER and rode with Paul Karmin on the ambulance, but this was different. Here, the inner sanctum of medicine was exposed. My desire to join them blazed; for a moment, all doubt and uncertainty vanished.

If them, I thought, *why not me?*

Mesmerized, I failed to break my gaze and couldn't help but perceive my future laid out before me.

℘

I returned home one weekend in early November. A letter waited for me on the kitchen table. Syracuse had sent a response to my early admission request. I let out a breath as I tore open the envelope ...

Dear Mr. Pryor,

The admission committee has completed our evaluation of your application. We regret to inform you that you have not been selected for entry...

My first rejection. It felt like a kick in the balls, and I struggled to maintain my composure. Logic attempted a rescue: It's only the first response—It means nothing—I was to expect rejections—My GPA was going to make this a fight—There are plenty of other applications still out there. But my heart sank, flooded with depression and doubt.

I closed the door to my room and cried.

℃℧

Narmer and I became good friends. We frequently talked about world politics, social issues and u.s. medical education, comparing it to that of other countries. After a long day in the lab, I was ready to turn out the lights when Narmer found me.

"You still here?" he asked.

"Yeah, just about done," I replied.

"Wanna grab a coffee or something?" he asked.

It was a quick decision. My flatmate was usually out, and I hadn't made any friends outside of work. Nothing but an empty apartment waited for me at home.

We walked along 165th and headed south on Broadway. A few blocks later, we entered a cafe and ordered a couple of drinks. We sat near the front window to watch the passing New Yorkers.

"I was lecturing some of the second year medical students today," Narmer said. "I can't help but think there is a problem with the way we train doctors in the u.s."

"How do you mean?" I emptied a couple of sugar packets into my steaming mug.

"It seems like young doctors are more focused on the disease, the diagnosis and the treatment," he said; "they leave out the person—the human being."

I thought about my own experience on the ambulance.

"It may be too much science and technology," I said. "I think about the patients I've treated. Paramedics are limited in our medical care. Sometimes the only thing we can offer is compassion, like a shoulder to cry on. I think medicine used to be more like this. Years ago, doctors didn't have a lot of resources so the best they could do was empathize and give morphine."

"You've got a point," Narmer said. "Now with so many new drugs, CAT scans and specialists, the focus is on testing and treating, not listening and comforting."

"But what can we do about it?" I asked. "The system is set up with a priority on diagnosis and treatment, not empathy and understanding."

"Well," he said, "whenever I think of a great historical figure, I think that there was first a mentor who provided guidance and inspiration."

"That makes sense," I said.

"The mentor is there to pass on knowledge but also sets the bar for the student to reach, and exceed." He thought for a moment. "There's more to it than knowledge."

I thought about the people who inspired me. Mike McEvoy came first to mind. Why? What made Mike a mentor? He taught facts, but not more than my college professors. Yet, I didn't regard them as mentors.

"A mentor is an example of the kind of person we want to be," I said. "You only get that by working closely with him. I'm not sure you get that in medicine."

"Yeah," he said, "Ph.D. students work closely with an advisor, but medical students are taught by a series of lecturers. Then they rush around from one rotation to the next in the third and fourth years. How much time does that allow to really get to know a senior physician? I mean, how is it even possible to find a mentor in medical school?"

"I don't know." I took a sip of coffee.

"And without a mentor focusing on compassion treating the patient as a person, how do students learn these qualities?" asked Narmer.

"There needs to be a new approach in medical education," I suggested. "Maybe instead of focusing on the disease, students should spend time getting to know their patients. You know, meet them, talk to them, learn about their life, what they do or did, their fears, their hopes. This might teach them the value of compassion."

"It's a good thought, but I don't know how much you can teach compassion," Narmer said.

I gave him a confused look.

"Really?" I said. "You don't think so?"

"The way the world works today," Narmer continued, "it's mostly about competition and capitalism. Compassion and humanism are actually virtues and, by definition, rare. If everyone had them, then they wouldn't be virtues."

"So how do you teach compassion?" I asked.

"I think it has to do with one's personality and how he is raised.

It has more to do with environment. Have a child take care of a pet, and he will learn compassion."

"So you think it's too late by the time they're in medical school?" I asked.

"Maybe. I don't know. I think a lot of your personality is formed by then. But there is always room to grow. I think that is where the mentor comes in. A student trying to emulate his mentor might also become more compassionate."

"A mentor would teach by example, molding the student to his personality," I suggested.

"But the student must really want to emulate his mentor," he said; "otherwise it wouldn't work."

We all have visions of the person we want to be, but where do these ideas come from? I was still cultivating ideals that would become my adult personality, and this conversation made an impression on me. I wanted to be like my mentors, but I also thought about what it meant to be the example. I came to the conclusion that the only way to teach compassion and humanism is by example.

⌘

I'm standing on a road that curves in both directions around a steep mountain. The barren landscape, devoid of vegetation, is littered with volcanic rocks of various sizes. The dirt has the reddish hue reminiscent of a Martian landscape. A deep blue sky extends to the horizon. Out past the road, a sea of clouds floats below, stretching in all directions. I realize how high I am.

I close my eyes against the radiant sun and feel a cool breeze sweep across my body …

A ringing phone woke me, and I shook the image from my head. The dream was new but oddly familiar. Falling out of bed, I grabbed the phone.

"Hello?" I said, clearing my throat.

"John!" My dad shouted, excited. "John! You got an interview with Albany!"

"What? Really?"

You opened my mail? I thought.

"December 18, 8 a.m.," he said.

Holy shit! I thought.

I couldn't believe it. I got an interview! In my jubilant state, my brain went delusional. I started speculating on how many more interviews I would get, how many offers would follow. I even felt contempt for my college health advisor for suggesting it would be an uphill battle.

What did he know? I thought.

Boosted by a new sense of optimism, I headed for the Columbia Medical School bookstore. After a brief search along the walls of books, I found what I was after. A sales clerk rang up my selection.

"That'll be two hundred and ten dollars," he said.

Two hundred dollars!? I thought, *For ONE friggin' book?*

I swallowed hard and handed over my credit card. Harrison's Principles of Internal Medicine turned out to be worth every dime. Thicker than a phonebook with translucently thin pages, it covered every detail of Internal Medicine, making my paramedic text look like *Goodnight Moon*. It took hours to get through a few pages, and I quickly acquired a medical dictionary to help decipher the text.

My next visit to the library, I pulled a copy of the New England Journal of Medicine (NEJM) from the shelf. In the middle, I tore out the subscription card and filled it out. Fifty-two weeks of the journal was $160. I mailed it the same day.

A few weeks later, the first Journal arrived. The cover displayed its contents, and I scanned the original articles: "Zidovudine (AZT) in HIV Children," "Red Cell Calcium Pump Dysfunction in Hypercalciuria," "Intravenous Immunoglobulin in Chronic Lymphocytic Leukemia," "Echocardiogram Findings in Polycystic Kidney Disease."

Other content included letters, editorials, book reviews and essays. Review articles were a bit more introductory and helped explain certain diseases. But the best part about the Journal was the "Case Records of Massachusetts General Hospital."

The case records were amazing. They begin with a patient's chief complaint and proceed through the entire process including history, exam, laboratory values, radiology imaging, surgical photos, pathology, histology slides, differential diagnoses, discussion and final diagnosis.

The Journal assumes the reader has at least two years of medical education, so it was a struggle for me to understand a lot of the details. But with frequent references to Harrison's and the dictionary, I found I could get through it.

Each week I learned a new disease, how it presented and what it looked like. Amyloid thought to be Sjogren's, Leiomyoma of the stomach, Celiac Sprue, Sarcoidosis, Progressive Multifocal Leukoencephalopathy, Adrenal Myelolipoma, Nephropathic Cystinosis, Cholangiosarcoma, Pulmonary Histoplasmosis, Hypoparathyroidism in DiGeorge Syndrome, Cardiac Failure in Multiple Myeloma—each week there was another exciting new case to discover.

It was awesome.

Armed with Harrison's and the New England Journal, I didn't wait for medical school to begin my education.

ക

In December, I returned home for the Albany Medical College interview. On the train back to NYC, I pulled out my journal and wrote about the experience:

December 18, 1988

Today is Sunday. I'm riding on a train back to NYC, so excuse the messy handwriting. Friday was my interview with Albany Med. Much is said about such interviews, and I've heard some crazy stories about them, but mine went much like a few normal conversations. I recall being very calm throughout both interviews, a feeling that I thought was odd. I guess I felt so overwhelmingly that I truly belong there, that I didn't seem out of place or out of character. I felt like a medical student and acted like one.

The first interview (I had two) was with a fourth-year student named Lenny. I was very comfortable with him; we seemed to relate well. His first words were, "Interesting candidate. I look at all these things you've done, and I think 'wow, what a guy.' Then I look at your GPA, and it SUCKS. What happened?"

It is not by chance that I have been thinking about this type of question for the past year. I have thought about the answer a thousand times, and when he asked it, I was ready. I gave him my story, and he seemed to buy it. Again, my calmness amazed me, and I really enjoyed it. He told me that although I had outstanding credentials, the grades might bring me down and that he would do all he could for me. Lenny is going into orthopedic surgery. I wish him luck.

The second interview was with Gordon Kaye, an anatomy and pathology professor. We walked to his office and began to talk about Columbia (he worked there for some 15 years before Albany). I mentioned a pathologist, Daniel Knowles, who runs the path part of the CPC's at Columbia. It turns out that Gordon trained Dr. Knowles! I had made a connection (for good or bad). Anyhow, the conversation created a good feeling and even induced some excitement.

We arrived in a much cluttered office in which there were two red chairs. We sat in them to talk. He began with, "Why medicine?" I spilled another long story synthesized over the past year. His next question was "Account for the discrepancy between your GPA and your MCAT score," which I took only as a compliment. As I see it, I am not defending my intelligence. The MCAT and the host of accomplishments outside the classroom are evidence of that. I am defending my time-management skills, which I addressed in the answer. I got a lot of nods, and that was the end of the talk concerning grades.

Gordon began a long case history as an example of an ethical problem he presented for at least five minutes. The case ended with an 82-year-old female with coma intubated, decreased EEG and a son that said, "No extraordinary measures." I responded by listing the options DNR, no DNR, slow code and went on from there. We looked at around five cases. In all of them, I tried to relate patients I had in the past to our discussion. I felt as if I was having fun talking about medicine. On the walk back to the admissions office, we talked about old cars. A nice man. I wish him luck.

So now I am in limbo. Acceptance letters go out around next Friday. If I do not receive one, I will know if I'm in the hold category in one month. So the way I look at it, a letter before January 5 is an acceptance.

Closing the journal, I gazed out on the Hudson as the train pitched along the tracks. A heron swooped down and alighted upon the water. The interview went well; but more than that, I really felt like I belonged in medical school.

⁋

In January, Buffalo and Rochester rejected me without an interview. February followed with Columbia, NYU, Cornell, NY Med, and Stony Brook. Each letter chipped away my confidence.

The initial excitement and novelty of the lab, replaced with familiarity and routine, had finally degraded to boredom. Bench work wasn't difficult; it was tedious. Each day nearly identical to the last, I performed banal tasks with zombie-like enthusiasm. Reading the New England Journal between cholesterol determinations only reminded me of the life I could be leading, like pouring salt in the wound.

Doldrums set in, and I began to languish, praying for the end of the day, the end of the week. On my daily planner, I crossed off the days—one slash right before lunch and another before leaving—like some convict counting days in his cell. Between the rejections and doldrums, I fell deep into despair.

It was the lowest point of my life.

A letter finally arrived from Albany. Flipping it over in my hands, I could feel my heart pounding. I thought of Schrödenger's cat, all possibilities simultaneously existing in a spiritual void, both accepted and rejected, until, with a slice of my knife, all waveforms collapse, revealing one indisputable reality.

With little fanfare, I tore it open and read.

"Wait-listed," I said.

That cat was on a ventilator.

The purgatory of college admission, the wait list is pure torture. Good enough to be considered, but flawed enough to be ignored, I was now placed in limbo with the odds stacked high against me. Flashback to high school: I was accepted off the wait list for Binghamton. I didn't know if the memory provided reassurance or false hope.

❧

In March, I arrived at work to find the hallway filled with spacemen. Workers dressed in white contamination suits and respirators moved equipment out of our lab.

"What's going on?" I asked.

Narmer was filling a cardboard box with supplies.

"They found asbestos in the lab," he said; "they think it's from the pipes in the ceiling."

"Great," I said. "How long have we been sucking asbestos?"

"How long have you worked here?" Narmer smiled. "Don't worry; it's good for you."

Dr. Dekalbaum made arrangements for us to share a lab one flight down. We spent an hour moving the equipment we needed.

Bernard showed up as the spacemen unfolded large plastic sheets.

"What is this bullshit?" he asked. "I have no time for this; I have work to do."

"Bernard," I said, "this isn't fun for any of us; we all have work to do ..."

"You do not understand ..." he fumed.

I started to pick up the spectrometer when Narmer stopped me.

"No!" he said, "don't move the spec. It'll screw up the calibration."

"What?" Bernard asked; "I need the spec today. Can't you calibrate it?"

"No, it has to be done by the Beckman rep," he said. "Just leave it."

I replaced the cover on the spec.

"This is complete bullshit," Bernard muttered, storming out of the lab.

"That guy has problems," I said to Narmer.

We set up the lab downstairs and worked through the morning. When Narmer and I returned from lunch, we found our spectrometer downstairs. We looked at each other for a second.

Narmer powered up the spec. It took a minute to warm up before the display flashed "Error." Narmer called the Beckman rep; it would be a week before someone could come.

A typical move for Bernard and another example of what we had to put up with. Demeaning, abrasive and insulting, Bernard acted without regard for the rest of us. When he snuck back to the lab, I snapped.

"You moved the spec!" I shouted.

"I told you I needed ..." he began.

"And we told you not to move it!" I didn't hold back, letting my anger vent. "Now nobody can use it for a week! You have a mental abnormality, Bernard. I've never met someone who holds the world in such contempt. I have news for you: The world and this lab are not here to serve you."

It wasn't the spec that was bothering me.

My future was so uncertain. Medical school rejections forced me to cling to the idea of research as a career. The necessity of work put me in denial about the lab. I was miserable but still tried to convince myself that I could make it work or that it would get better.

The spec incident caused a sudden rush, a release of disillusion-ment. I stopped kidding myself that I wanted to be a biochemist. The truth snapped into focus, and I knew my future was in medicine. As much as I wanted to think biochemistry could be a career option, it really wasn't.

I hated the lab. I missed the ambulance. I missed the excitement, satisfaction and pride I felt treating patients. The lab provided none of this. From then on, my future was in medicine.

Psychologically, I closed the door on research as a career.

❦

In May, Rich traveled from Boston to visit. He was working at Mass General while trying to get a job as a paramedic. After dinner, we hailed a cab and headed to the East Village.

"Where we going?" Rich asked.

"McSorley's," I said.

"What's that?"

"McSorley's? It's the coolest bar ever," I said. "It's the oldest pub in the country. They didn't let women in until 1970. They brew their own beer served in small pint glasses that cost a dollar each. It's real easy to get shitfaced."

The cab pulled up as dusk settled in the East Village. A sign over the door read, "McSorley's Old Ale House, Est. 1854." Inside the atmosphere was dark and somber. Sawdust covered ancient hardwood floors. Every square inch of wall held old photographs, dusty mementos and antique signs. Any surface or shelf that could possibly hold something, held something; and whatever it was, it was old. A wooden icebox behind the bar was carved with the phrase, "Be good or be gone." In the corner sat a large cast iron coal-burning stove. The ceiling and rafters held hundreds of items precipitously suspended above our heads. A thick layer of dust covered everything.

McSorley's set the standard by which other bars were compared. Over the years, Rich and I would frequent many more establishments, all varying degrees of disappointment compared to this NYC landmark.

We parked our coats at a table toward the front windows with a good view of the street. I went to the bar and returned with ten mini pints. I had to go back for the other ten. The little table was covered with little pints of dark and light.

"Drink up," I said, picking up a dark.

Rich picked up a light. "Cheers!" We touched glasses and took a deep draught.

"So how's it going at the lab?"

"You know, Rich, I'm really glad I took this job."

"So it's going well?"

"No, it sucks beyond anything I ever imagined. I'm glad I took this job because now I realize this before I wasted my life going to grad school."

"So what's the plan? The job ends in a couple of months, right?"

"Yeah. Well, I applied to med school, but things don't look so good."

"You really applied? I thought you were just thinking about it."

I hadn't discussed my aspirations with him. Secretly, I feared I would be a failure if I didn't get in.

"I'll have you know I've been rejected by some of the most prestigious medical schools in the country."

"Impressive."

"Actually, at this point you have a better chance of getting into medical school." Rich had no college to speak of. He could start fresh, something I wished I could do.

He let out a genuine chuckle. "Uhhh, no," he said, "I don't think I'm doctor material. I just need to get a job as a paramedic, and I'll be happy."

"How's that going?"

"Well, it's a long story, but let me say the state of, oh, excuse me, the *commonwealth* of Massachusetts doesn't want me. I try not to take it personally."

One by one, the pints were drained. Soon we were down to our last light and dark. "We gotta keep drinking," I said, gathering some of the empties.

"No, thanks," Rich said; "I think I've had enough."

"No, I mean we literally have to keep drinking," I said. "It's a small place, and there's a line to get in. If we stop drinking, they'll kick us out for paying customers."

"Okay. One more tabletop. But then I'm done. Where's the bathroom?"

We worked our way through another twenty beers, talking about everything—religion, politics, girls, ambulance calls, music, college. The subject of church came up because our parents switched from St. Joseph's to Corpus Christi.

"Corpus Christi," Rich said, "sounds like a breakfast cereal, doesn't it?"

I let out a laugh.

"Try new Corpus Christies!" he continued, "little sugar-coated Jesus' that walk on milk!"

My head flew back and let out a guffaw. Sometimes he really cracked me up.

We stayed until closing. The crowds thinned as McSorley's staff gathered the empties. One of the bartenders invited himself to our table and struck up a conversation.

"How you young chaps doing tonight?" he asked.

"Couldn't be better!" Rich's voice slurred as he struggled to keep his head from teetering.

"Name's Bailey," he said with a warm smile. We shook hands. "Do you think beer exists for us to drink, or do we exist for beer to have a purpose?"

"Oh, you're a philosopher!" My liver was in better shape than Rich's, and I could engage in a more coherent conversation. Bailey proved to be quite a character.

"So what do you do, John?" he asked.

"I work in a lab at Columbia," I said.

"What kind of research?" he persisted.

"Lipoproteins and atherosclerosis," I responded, thinking this would end the subject.

"Ahh, yes. The wonderful world of lipod-apolipid interactions. It all starts with the dreaded mevalonic acid, eh? I always thought they should call it malevolent acid. A few pyrophosphates turn lanosterol into cholesterol, harden your arteries; next thing you know, you're having a heart attack. Sinister, ain't it?"

Bailey took a sip of beer.

I was dumbstruck.

"How does a bartender know so much about biochemistry?" I asked.

"I have a Ph.D. in biochem from NYU," he said with a smile.

"You have a Ph.D. in biochem and you're working at a bar?"

"Yeah."

"Why?"

"Cause I hated it," he said.

I let out a laugh.

"I kinda know what you mean," I said.

❧

As winter gave way to spring I received responses from the remaining schools: all rejections. In May, Albany Med achieved a full complement of students without me. As a final tease, they placed me on an "alternate list." If an accepted student failed to show up, names were called from the alternate list to fill the vacancy.

I tried not to wish ill on others, but I couldn't stop speculating about the odds.

Without a likely acceptance, I made plans to apply again. This time, I would broaden my scope to many more schools.

In June my time at Columbia was over. It didn't take long for my dad and me to empty the contents of my room into the rental van. Standing in the vacant space, I paused to reflect on my year in New York.

I arrived a child, fresh out of college, knowing no one and clueless at work. Very quickly I learned to adapt and survive. Gone was the fraternity brother engaging in juvenile antics and sleeping through class.

The lab taught me how to perform research and put the scientific method into practice. More importantly, it helped me realize I was not a researcher. I could have wasted many years in grad school deluding myself that I wanted to be a Ph.D. Sometimes life shows you the way if you are willing to open your eyes.

My future remained murky, but time was on my side. Surviving on my own in New York had given me the esteem and confidence to pursue future endeavors.

If I could make it here, I thought, *I can make it anywhere.*

Albany

The door to my office burst open. A squeaky janitorial cart pushed through the threshold and approached my desk, turbid water splashing from the pail. It stopped abruptly. A confused face appeared from behind the mop, scanning the nearly empty room before settling on my defeated countenance.

"So sorry," he said in broken English, giving me an apologetic smile.

"That's okay," I said, "it's been happening a lot lately."

The man meekly nodded, backed the cart out and closed the door. I buried my head in my hands.

What am I doing here? I wondered.

At 10 a.m., I gathered a stack of papers and headed for my first meeting. Stepping out of the recently refurbished janitorial closet, I headed to the critical care unit (CCU) conference room. Barbara Spath, RN, the nurse manager who hired me sat at the table surrounded by cardiologists, critical care nurses, hospital administrators and biomedical engineers. And the hospital CEO.

Barbara did most of the talking. She explained her plans for a central EKG-monitoring station while I tried to remain invisible. The new station, she explained, will monitor cardiac patients in the CCU,

M-4, C-8 and the ER. Also, patients being transported to the cath lab or nuclear medicine would be continually watched at the central station.

"How is it done now?" asked the CEO.

"Now, each floor monitors its own patients," Carol said. "This takes a nurse away from patient care. If a floor has no monitors, then patients are transferred to the unit—a waste of resources. With a central station, all floors and CCU patients will be monitored remotely by dedicated technicians."

The CEO glanced over the proposal.

"Makes sense," he said; "who's going to be in charge?"

"I'd like to introduce John Pryor," Barbara said, extending an open palm in my direction. "He will manage this project."

I gave a half-smile to the overly serious faces around the table.

One of the doctors spoke up.

"Welcome, John," he said. "I'm just a bit curious. What type of experience do you have organizing a program like this?"

Caught off guard, I was suddenly put on the spot.

"Well, ah…" I looked to Barbara for help. She offered none, so I continued, "no specific management but…"

"What experience do you have?" the CEO asked.

"I'm a paramedic," I said, "and I recently completed research at Columbia."

"Are you a nurse?" asked another administrator.

"No, but I'm confident I can set up the station like you want."

In fact, nothing was further from the truth. But this was no time for doubts. I can't remember what else I said, but I convinced the group to have faith in me. One thing college did teach me was how to bullshit persuasively.

"Okay, well, we'll see how it goes," the CEO said, looking squarely at Barbara. It was the closest to a vote of confidence I was going to get.

A big job lay ahead. I had to research and purchase monitors; interview, hire and train technicians; construct and furnish the room; and create a work schedule. I needed to transition the floors to the new system. Through it all, I would negotiate with physicians and department heads, my only clout being "some guy" they hired to do this.

The potential to screw up was enormous.

Albany

❧

After Columbia, I moved back home in the summer of 1989. I don't remember where I heard about the Albany Med job, but it made sense to work in a hospital. The position didn't involve clinical medicine, but I was on the floors, alongside doctors and so close to patients I could smell them.

Acceptance off the alternate list was as likely as being struck by a meteorite, so another AMCAS application headed for the typewriter. This time, I would list forty schools.

My dismal medical school prospects forced me to consider alternate career possibilities. Being a physician assistant (PA) was considered "the next best thing," so I applied to programs at Duke, Emory and Yale.

Rich now worked as a paramedic in New York City, and he loved it. I still considered working as a medic, but first I had to advance to the paramedic level. Frustrated that there was no other option, I enrolled in a year-long paramedic class.

Three nights a week, I parked in the commuter lot at Hudson Valley Community College and joined a small group of eager EMS providers. Until recently, our classroom had been a cadaver lab. On warm days, we could smell formaldehyde sweating from the tile walls.

Rich Beebe, a hefty round-faced man with an ebullient personality, taught the class. Clifton Park Ambulance Medical Director Dr. George Innes gave lectures and taught at the procedure lab. The students consisted of an eclectic mix of personalities: Ken Dott was a firefighter in Albany; "Diamond" Don Burkett turned out to be a Russian translator for the CIA during the cold war; Spencer Schoen looked like a surfer dude; and Jeff Rabrich went on to be an ER doc.

Spencer, Jeff and I competed for the highest grade. I usually won, but it wasn't fair, since most of the material was review for me. For the first time, I was head of my class and students started coming to me with questions. Right after an exam, I would be surrounded in the hallway, the de facto answer key, inciting consternation or jubilation with each query response.

It was a good feeling.

Alright, Let's Call It A Draw

✑

On August 16, 1989, I failed to keep myself occupied. Reading the Journal only made it worse. I wanted to escape the house but couldn't—I might miss a call.

Time inched by. Hopeless yet desperate, my mind raced with possibilities: Maybe someone got sick. Maybe there was a clerical error. Maybe someone revolted against familial pressure to enter medicine and ran away to become a dancer instead.

The phone remained mute. The kitchen clock ticked in silence, slowly reaching five o'clock. The first day of class at Albany Med was over; I had not been called as an alternate.

My final breath of hope was extinguished. In a way, I was glad the wait was over.

I now focused on the next round of applications.

✑

In November, Rich and I stand at the eighth mile along Lafayette Avenue in Brooklyn. A leaden sky spits icy drizzle as a chilly November wind blows through the crowds. Runners stream through the gloom. Bright reds, fluorescent yellows and electric blues brighten the street like a macaw strolling through a flock of pigeons. Continuous clapping and shouts are punctuated by an uproar of cheers as a neighbor runs by. Despite their toil, runners beam with enthusiasm, waving to the crowd. Small children reach into the torrent of runners for a slap from a passing marathoner.

My dad is running a marathon, I thought, *I can't freakin' believe it!*

Although he was a runner in high school, my dad's athleticism ended with an honorable discharge from the Marines. Weekly infusions of crullers while reading the Sunday paper and a languid lifestyle produced a large belly on his 6-foot, 4-inch frame. At one point, he tipped the scales at three hundred pounds.

But he kept a secret. He dreamed of running a marathon before turning fifty. A few years previously, he had realized time was running out, so he enrolled in a running program at work. During his lunch hour, he started walking, then jog / walking, then jogging.

Persistence paid off, and his transformation was startling. Fat melted away, especially around his face. He *looked thin*. Each week he extended long runs, until one Sunday he finished twenty miles—he was ready for the marathon.

"This is awesome!" Rich said.

Wave after wave of runners passed by; an endless river of marathoners.

"Yeah," I agreed. It was an amazing spectacle.

"Doesn't it make you want to run one?" he asked.

Hah! I had no interest in running twenty-six miles.

"I'll tell you what," I said, "whenever you decide to run a marathon, I'll be there to cheer you on."

"Deal," he said. I didn't think he was serious.

Eventually, we spied a fluorescent yellow headband atop an exceptionally tall marathoner. It was Dad.

"Dad, Dad," I yelled.

"Pryor!" Rich shouted.

He jogged over, un-shouldered a sweatshirt and took a swig of water.

"You're looking great!" I said, "How ya feeling?"

"Good," he said, "I'm averaging a nine-mile pace, feel good."

Rich took his picture before he ran off to complete his quest.

Near the finish, we saw him again. We screamed to get his attention, but pain and exhaustion made him oblivious to our clamoring. He crossed the finish line in 4:41:09.

I'd never been more proud of him.

❧

Work progressed well. I amazed myself at what could be done with a little assertiveness. I learned a little secret: Most administrators don't know what they're doing, but it doesn't stop them from doing it.

The monitor station was nearly ready. I assembled the chairs and desks myself. The monitors were ordered, and I interviewed prospective technicians. The caliber of applicant proved to be subpar; some hadn't completed high school. I wondered how many could learn to read EKGs.

In the CCU, I worked closely with staff and one cardiologist in particular, Dr. Drew Macina.

Thinning hair, glasses and a nasal voice, Drew was an affable colleague who always treated me with respect. One time, he walked in when I was taking a break.

"What are you reading?" he asked.

"Oh, just some light reading," I said.

"The New England Journal is definitely not light reading," he said. "Are you doing research for a paper?"

"Actually, I'm trying to get into medical school," I said.

"And reading the Journal will help you get in?" he asked.

"No," I said. "It'll make me a better doctor when I do get in."

I think I impressed him. Drew taught residents and medical students who rarely read the Journal for the hell of it. After this, he seemed to take me under his wing.

Walking through the CCU one day, I noticed Drew at the light box surrounded by a group of white coats.

"Hey, John," he poked out from the crowd, "come look at this."

Apprehensive, I timidly joined the clan of residents and students. My spine tingled as I rubbed shoulders with the white coats.

Drew regarded the chest x-ray—shades of gray-white outlined bone, tissue, heart and ribs. I discerned more subtle structures: trachea, bronchi, aorta.

"This is a seventy-year-old-male with a history of multiple heart attacks and hypertension. Now his pressure's in the toilet with an EF of 15%. You can see his heart is huge," Drew outlined the enormous silhouette, "and all these streaky lines in his lungs indicate pulmonary edema."

As a medic, I treated congestive heart failure (CHF), knew what it sounded like, watched patients struggling to breathe with it. It was fascinating to actually see what it looked like.

"Can't we start an inotrope?" a resident asked.

An inotrope increases the heart's contractility. My chest fluttered as I followed the conversation.

"Unfortunately, that's like rearranging deck chairs on the Titanic," Drew said.

We let out a laugh.

"I think if we pushed this guy's heart any more, it'll just give out."

"So what can we do for him?" a medical student asked.

"Keep him comfortable, speak to the family about hospice," Drew said.

I returned to work thinking about this patient. Something didn't sit well with me. Up until then, I was on the front lines initiating care as a paramedic and delivering patients to the hospital. I never gave much thought to what happened in the hospital. I always assumed they got better and went home. Some patients, I now realized, never make it out of the hospital alive.

Like rearranging deck chairs on the Titanic, I thought, unable to restrain a chuckle.

☙

On Friday mornings I would arrive at Albany Med an hour early to attend trauma conference. Each week surgeons, ER physicians, residents and medical students gathered in Huyck Auditorium to review recent trauma cases.

The scene was similar each week.

The audience falls silent; an intimidated resident cautiously approaches the podium like a lamb before the wolves. He begins in familiar territory—the mechanism of trauma, EMS response and paramedic treatment—but quickly enters deep waters of medicine and surgery. From the trauma bay to operating room to hospital admission and discharge, each step in the patient's care is precisely reviewed.

Comfortably seated in front, Dr. Fortune scrutinizes each decision, every lab value, and every action of the team. His queries bring out the Why. It is the basis of medicine: Why is the patient this way? Why did you give that medicine? Why didn't it work? Why did you choose the next course of action?

"Why didn't you transfuse the patient?" Fortune asks. His polite demeanor fails to mask a more ominous undertone.

Stuttering, forehead sweat glistening in the podium lights, the resident squirms, defending the indefensible. More questions assail him, and he struggles to explain the chosen course of action.

The point of this exercise is to learn, to share lessons and improve patient care. It was effective; I learned more from the questions than from the presentation, but at the moment it was more like an inquisition.

That I might be behind that podium someday gave me serious pause, but I couldn't help feeling it inevitable.

☙

As soon as my applications went out, the rejections started to roll in. In August, the University of Vermont, University of Maryland and the University of South Carolina all gave me the boot.

Things looked bleak until I received back-to-back responses from Eastern Virginia and Ohio; both put my application on "hold."

Then I was struck down.

Last year's interview and wait list at Albany buoyed my spirits and kept my dream alive. So close to admission, I fully expected another interview this year. I received a letter in early September:

Dear Mr. Pryor,

The admission committee has completed our evaluation of your application. We regret to inform you that you have not been selected for interview ….

Motherfucker! I thought, *Those god damn assholes! They interviewed me! They had me on the alternate list! And now they won't even consider me?*

"God damn it!" I shouted, crumpling the letter and throwing it hard. I pounded the table, I swore with each blow, "Fucking, goddamn, motherfucking, asshole, shit!"

Collapsing into the chair, I buried my face in my throbbing hand. *I fucking work there!* I thought.

Of all the rejections, this was the worst, draining my confidence. For the first time, I doubted I could be a doctor.

Maybe I'm meant to be a PA, I thought.

☙

It's sweltering and my sweat-soaked fatigues cling like a wet towel. The jungle is thick, and it takes effort to move even a few feet.

Exhausted, I stop to lean against a tree, closing my eyes for a few seconds. My patrol, barely visible in the darkness, slowly advances into the abyss of vegetation and swarming insects.

I hit the deck at the first cracking of AKs. We return fire at the muzzle flashes.

The firefight quickly escalates. Grenades exchange volleys with RPGs. Explosions ring in my ears, drowning out the shouts of our lieutenant.

I raise my rifle into the darkness, and I squeeze the trigger in rapid succession. The rifle dances in my arm, and I smell the shells leaping into the darkness.

I need to move. Firing a volley, I get to my feet and struggle through the thick underbrush.

Out of the corner of my eye, I see the RPG. I can't move. I can't fall. I'm frozen in place. The rocket comes at me in slow motion. I can feel my heart stop...

℃

My job was solitary but much more social than a sequestered lab rat. Constantly interacting with various departments and staff, I rarely sat in my office for long. One day in the CCU, I noticed a nurse reading a book on Judaism. I couldn't resist making a comment.

"Looking for the answer to life?" I asked.

She glanced back at the book, "I haven't come up with the right question yet."

"*God in Search of Man: A Philosophy of Judaism.* I tilted my head. "Looks interesting, are you Jewish?"

"No," she said, "just thought I'd explore all my options."

"I know, it's so hard to find the right god these days," I said. "It makes me want to come up with my own."

"Now, that's an option I haven't considered yet," she said.

"What, starting your own religion?"

"Yeah."

"Why not? It worked for the Mormons."

She let out a chuckle. "I guess you're right about that."

Our friendly banter turned into a conversation.

"I'm John, by the way," I said.

"Gemma," she said. "Nice talking to you."

I returned to my office with her phone number and plans for dinner.

e/s

In December, I sat before a small committee considering my application. The interviewers took turns grilling me about my paramedic experience and research at Columbia. My response stirred much enthusiasm.

All in all, I was an excellent physician's assistant candidate.

"Why do you want to be a PA?" one interviewer asked.

I forced a smile and recited some rehearsed bullshit about extending my role as a paramedic. It was met with nods all around.

Then came the dreaded question: "Have you ever considered medical school?"

Mentally, I writhed.

PA programs didn't want failing medical school aspirants. They wanted candidates committed to becoming a PA and, more important, staying a PA. The same question appeared on the written application, and it was difficult to tick the right box. In person, it was infinitely worse. I had to suck it up.

"No," I lied. "I don't think medical school is right for me. I wouldn't want all the responsibility of a physician."

More nods. My treachery was convincing.

I was a pathetic sellout.

e/s

Christmas, 1989. Smoke from the crackling hearth mixes with pine from a fresh balsam fir, and warms our living room against the chilly December air. The tree sags with ornaments, a living chronology of Christmas past. Extra tables in the dining room are laden with pies, cookies and cakes. Half-devoured shrimp cocktail lay on the coffee table, and candy dishes filled with nuts, M&M's and chocolates dot the house. Mom presides over dinner preparations—turkey, lasagna, stuffing and trimmings. Rich and I are seated, guitars in position, strumming Christmas carols as Bing Crosby croons "I'm Dreaming of a White Christmas." The scene is shattered by the shrill beep of my ambulance pager.

We froze, waiting for dispatch information. A squelch followed by the dispatcher's voice, "Ems dispatch to Clifton Park Halfmoon, a 9-4, cardiac arrest, at 24 Juniper Lane…"

Rich and I shot a glance. It took a heartbeat to decide. We jumped for our coats.

"Juniper's over in Aspenwood," Rich said. It was about a mile from the house.

"Ma, we gotta go!" I shouted, slipping on my sneakers.

"Where are you going?" Mom yelled from the kitchen. "We have people coming!"

"It's an arrest," I yelled back. "We have to go!"

"Is Richie going?"

"Yeah, I'm going too!" Rich shouted.

"Try to …" the door slammed behind us.

Our breath puffed in the cold as we ran to the Stanza. I floored it as Rich plugged in the green light.

The pager crackled with more information, "…1974, 24 Juniper Lane, 68-year-old female, cardiac arrest, possible drowning…"

Drowning?

We exchanged a look but said nothing. We both knew dispatch information could be wildly inaccurate.

A minute later, we pulled behind the sheriff's cruiser. Rich grabbed our ems bag and followed me to the door.

A panicked, wide-eyed man waited for us.

"Upstairs to the right!" he shouted.

I bounded up the stairs with Rich at my heels, turned into the bedroom and paused. Quickly scanning the room, I tried to make sense of it. To the left, a doorway led to the bathroom with a Jacuzzi filled with cranberry-red water. The trail of blood meandered across the carpet, in front of the bed, and encircled the patient like an expanding ink stain.

DEATH knelt beside the body. His hood turned purposely at me as he laid a hand squarely on her chest.

Okay, I thought, *I get it.*

DEATH vanished revealing an obese woman, completely naked, her extremities mottled and blue. A county sheriff pumped the woman's chest, making her fat jostle like grape Jell-O. More disturbing, however, was the blood erupting from her mouth. With each compression, air forced from her lungs expelled blood from her lips, spewing into the air and settling back like spray paint.

What the fuck? I thought.

I grabbed the bag and told Rich to get a towel.

Kneeling next to the patient's head, I pulled out the BVM. A family member stood near the door, a middle-aged woman, probably her daughter.

"What happened?" I asked, trying to get some clues as I put together the BVM.

"She was in the Jacuzzi," she said between sobs, "I came to check on her, but she wouldn't answer. When I opened the door, she was face down in the water. We took her out and called 911."

I tried to think of where the blood was coming from: Lung? Stomach? Esophageal varices?

"Is she a drinker?" I asked. "Does she have cirrhosis?"

"What, what …?" the daughter stammered.

Didn't matter. Now wasn't the time to ponder a diagnosis.

Rich returned holding a towel. I wiped away the blood as best I could.

"Hold CPR," I said, feeling the carotid. Rich relieved the sheriff.

"No pulse," I said.

"No! really?" Rich whispered facetiously.

"Wiseass," I said.

Rich resumed compressions as I fitted the mask over the patient's face and tilted her head back. Blood continued to seep from her mouth. I squeezed the bag, forcing air into her mouth, hoping for ventilation. Instead, air escaped from around the mask with a harsh farting noise that spewed blood everywhere.

"Well *that* was helpful," Rich muttered, wiping blood from his brow.

"Fuck you," I whispered back.

We tried again. This time, Rich paused as I squeezed air into her lungs. It seemed to work, but I wondered how much blood I was pumping into her lungs.

Lost in concentration, we didn't notice the crew arrive.

"What's going on, fellas?" Dwight appeared; a welcome relief.

"No idea," I said. "She was found facedown in the Jacuzzi bleeding from her mouth. Sheriff arrived and started CPR."

"Trauma?" asked Dwight.

"No," I said, "probably esophageal varices."

I learned from the Journal about alcoholics with cirrhosis. Veins around the stomach and esophagus become dilated and weak. At some point, they burst and bleed like stink.

She was dead, but we worked her anyway. Dwight sucked enough blood to find the trachea. I started an IV. The monitor remained flatline. We gave a few rounds of epinephrine to no avail.

The crew packaged her on the Reeves and made their way out. Loaded with gear, I followed slowly, pausing at the top of the stairs. I observed the family in the living room.

Sparkling Christmas lights cast the scene in a soft glow. Unwrapped presents littered the floor: open boxes of shirts, a Cabbage Patch doll, a fire truck and a remote-controlled car, all lay around the base of the tree. The woman's head was buried in her husband's chest; her shoulders shuddered as she sobbed. Children, two boys and a girl, were sitting on the couch, paralyzed with fear. The look of horror on their faces was indescribable. The patient must be their grandmother.

My heart ached for this family.

What a nightmare, I thought, *what a horrible fucking nightmare. Why? Why did she have to die on Christmas?*

The image burned an indelible memory in my brain.

ɕɞ

A few days later, Rich and I went out for a beer. We met up with our friend Jennifer Lanthier and her sister. Jen was currently using her marketing degree as a restaurant manager in Syracuse. Done playing maître d', she now searched for a serious career.

"I think I want to be a job coach," Jen said.

Rich and I exchanged a glance.

"What's a job coach?" asked Rich.

"A job coach helps other people get a job. They review and correct the client's resume. They help them prepare and get to the interviews. Then they help the client during the first weeks on the job, help with any training, that kind of thing. I think it's perfect for me. I would use my marketing background to help promote the client. I like to help people, and I like to teach. I think it would be a perfect match with my personality and college training."

Rich looked at me. I shrugged.

"Sounds good," I said, and took a swig.

"Either that," she added, "or I'd like to train dolphins."

I choked on my beer. Suds came out of Rich's nose.

"What?" we said in unison.

"I always thought it would be the coolest job—training dolphins."

An uncomfortable silence fell as we tried to get the joke.

She's serious, I thought.

"Uhh, yeah," said Rich, "but first you'd have to get in line behind the unemployed marine biologists."

"Really?" she asked.

❧

Rejections arrived daily in January: East Carolina, Uniformed Services Medical College, University of Connecticut, Stony Brook, Medical College of Pennsylvania. Not one interview. It was worse than the previous year.

In the midst of rejection and despair, I received a letter from the Emory PA program. Exasperated, I sat at the kitchen table and sliced the envelope.

My parents watched as I unfolded the letter.

"Great," I said in a defeated sigh, "I got in."

My parents tried to be excited for me. Dad reminded me it was a chance to practice medicine. In many fields, PAs functioned just like doctors. It was a better option than working as a paramedic. I even had a cousin on my father's side who, failing to get into medical school, became a PA. After working for a few years, he reapplied to medical school and was accepted. With no other prospects, everyone encouraged me to accept the offer. I agreed it was the only sane thing to do.

I mulled it over for two days before calling the number.

"Hi, this is John Pryor," I said on the phone.

"John, glad to hear from you," the director said. "We're looking forward to seeing you in the fall."

"Yeah, about that," I said, "I decided to decline your offer."

A bit of silence. "Oh, well we're sorry to hear that. Is there a reason?"

"No," I confessed. "I just don't want to be a PA."

It was cathartic to say out loud.

I don't want to be a PA, I thought. *I want to be a doctor.*

I'm going to be a doctor. I'm being rejected by every medical school in the country, and I have no idea of how I'm going to do it, but I'm going to be a doctor.

Either that, I thought, *or train dolphins.*

❧

"That's too fucking bad!" I shouted into the receiver. "I've been up for twenty-four hours covering assholes who don't come to work, and I'm not coming back in! If nobody's there to relieve you, then it's your fucking problem!"

I slammed the phone in the cradle, snapped the pager off my waist, and hurled it with all my might. It exploded against the wall, showering the floor with bits of plastic and a spinning battery. I jumped on the largest piece of circuit board.

That felt really good. I thought. *It doesn't solve any problems, but, man, did that feel good!*

Work was like running a daycare center. The administrative stuff I could handle, but personnel was a new experience in pain.

Granted, it was a tough sell. What person with an iota of intelligence would take a job staring at EKG monitors for eight hours? Some of my staff hadn't completed high school. But intelligence wasn't the problem; for the most part, everyone could do their job.

If they showed up.

Some employees thought coming to work was optional. If no one showed up, I had to stay and watch the monitors.

I worked the previous day, stayed overnight for a no-show, and then remained at work without sleep. I drove home shaking off head nods, struggling to stay awake. Exhausted, aching for sleep, I was now informed of another overnight no-show.

For a few moments I sat in silence, trying to calm down. Six o'clock. I could almost get four hours sleep before going back. I could take the next day off.

I called back and told the staff that I would be in later.

My days were numbered with this gig. I was proud to accomplish my goal, to get the monitor station up and running, but I couldn't go on covering for a bunch of dropouts every night.

Every medical school had rejected me. I declined acceptance to a PA program, and now I was ready to quit my job. I was starting to lose confidence about my future.

❧

On a bright spring morning in April, Gemma and I decided not to waste the day going to work. Three hours later, we strolled through lower Manhattan, deciding on a restaurant in Greenwich Village. After lunch, we returned to an empty space, noticing the "no parking sign" for the first time.

Recovering the car turned out to be an all-day affair. As evening approached, we decided to crash at a hotel and drive home the next day. I called my brother for an impromptu visit.

We met at the White Horse Tavern. Tilting back a few beers, I shared our adventure with the New York Police Department impound lot. When I was done, Rich had a story for us.

"I work for St. Vincent's, and we usually answer 911 calls for the city, but the hospital has a contract with the World Trade Center. We provide an ambulance for the buildings ..."

"What, all day?" Gemma asked.

"Yeah, we park in the basement garage and have a call room next to the jail."

"They have a jail?" I asked.

"Yeah," Rich said, "a little one. The buildings are like a small city. They even have their own zip codes. Anyway, occasionally I pull a shift in the towers. Last week, I was working with Danny Blum. We parked the ambulance and walked up to the concourse for breakfast. We ate and watched the river of people disgorge from the PATH escalators."

"PATH?" asked Gemma.

"The commuter train from New Jersey. It's fascinating, fifty thousand office workers flowing into the concourse. It's like the NYC marathon every day."

"I never realized there were so many people in those buildings," Gemma said.

"Yeah, so I'm watching this and I'm thinking about it, all these people, thousands of them, and if anything happens there are only two of us to take care of things. So I say to Danny, 'Wouldn't it be funny if there was a bomb or something? The place blows up. There are fifty thousand people to treat and just the two of us?' He agrees that it would be quite a scene."

"Talk about your MCI," I said.

"MCI?" Gemma asked.

"Mass casualty incident," I explained, "when there are a lot of patients and only a few paramedics."

"I didn't think anything more of it, and we went back to our cave in the basement to watch a movie. What I didn't know, and this will be important in a second, is that our little room was part of the police station, and it was supplied with emergency power. So we're watching a movie, but we hear all this chatter on the police radio. Finally, we can't ignore it, so we come out of our room, and it's dark!"

"What's dark?" asked Gemma.

"Everything. The power is out. We go up to the concourse, and everything is dead. Even the bank and its security system are out."

"What happened?" I asked.

"A transformer caught fire in lower Manhattan; power went out for half of downtown including the twin towers."

"So, no bomb?" I said.

"Luckily, no bomb. At first, I didn't think it was a big deal. But you have to remember, these buildings are more than a hundred stories tall, and the elevators were out. So people had to start walking down hundreds of flights of stairs."

"So?" said Gemma.

"That's what I thought. But a couple of things happened. First, everyone started to panic. That meant every asthmatic couldn't breathe, everyone with a heart history felt chest pain, and every pregnant woman started contractions. Normally, we get three or four calls a day, but now they came in every few minutes."

"And it's still just the two of you?" Gemma asked.

"You got it," Rich said.

"What'd you do?" I asked.

"We divided the equipment and split up. We each took a tower. Luckily, a freight elevator in each building ran on emergency power. We ran around checking people out and calming them down. Any real patients were brought down to the lobby.

"The other thing, it was hot last week. When the air-conditioning turned off, those buildings warmed up quickly. Thousands of unfit office workers were descending stairs in a stifling environment. We soon had calls for people passing out."

"Oh shit," Gemma said, "weren't there any other ambulances to help?"

"The first few hours EMS had their own problems. Eventually, we got some help and set up a command center in the lobby. We had dozens of people lying down with IVs hanging."

"That's wild," Gemma said.

"Yeah, just turning off the power in those buildings caused an MCI," Rich said. "I'd hate to think what would happen if a real bomb ever went off."

☙

Whenever I felt the need to procrastinate, I sought out Dr. Macina to engage in a discussion about ejection fractions or TIMI trials. Between the Journal and Harrison's I learned enough to ask intelligent questions and, more important, have a grasp of what he explained.

Our discussions were bittersweet. My gaining knowledge and

confidence in medicine made frustrations associated with med school rejections all the more acute.

"How's it going with the med school applications?" Drew asked one day. "Any interviews?"

Embarrassed about my rejections, I didn't like talking about it.

"Actually," I confessed, "it's not looking good this year. I think I'll to have to go back to grad school or something."

"Have you considered a foreign medical school?" he asked.

What's a foreign medical school? I thought.

"I never thought of it," I said. "I don't suppose it's a viable option."

Drew let out a little laugh.

"Well, it worked for me," he said. "I went to school in Italy."

I furrowed my brow, confused and speechless. What he said didn't make sense.

"You went to a foreign medical school?" I said at last.

"University of Bologna."

Another long pause followed as I again failed to comprehend. I'd been following Dr. Macina all year, hanging on his every word, gathering every scrap of knowledge he would share. He was my first physician colleague, and I considered him a mentor. Surely, he had no problem getting into medical school.

"You went to a foreign medical school?" I repeated.

He laughed again.

I assailed him with a thousand questions. Did he know Italian? Was it expensive? Did he get a loan for a foreign school? Was he allowed to sit for u.s. exams? How did he get back in the country? Was it difficult getting a residency?

Drew answered my questions. As he spoke, a light bulb went off in my head—something I'd seen while scanning the bulletin board near the bookstore. When our conversation was over, I hurried down to the bookstore.

My heart raced as I searched past ads for used books and requests for flat mates. I found the poster and tore off a coupon:

St. George's School of Medicine
Informational Seminar

Saturday, May 13
Sheridan Hotel, New York, NY

It felt like a lottery ticket.

&

In May, the paramedic program ended. I scored 96 on the written test.

The practical included IV insertion, intubation, medication administration and "mega-code," the paramedic equivalent of the EMT trauma station. The examiner presents various life-threatening cardiac problems and the examinee has to employ the right combination of medications or defibrillation to save the patient.

I passed without difficulty.

Three weeks later, I opened an envelope from the Department of Health.

John P. Pryor, AEMT-P
No. 078092
Expires 5/31/93

Finally, I was a full-fledged paramedic. I hoped I wouldn't have to use it.

&

A diverse ethnic population, dotted with turbans, filled the Sheridan conference room. Candidates from India, China along with American minorities crowded the rows. A pattern of small groups emerged: a prospective young student flanked by his or her parents. My parents and I made our way to some empty seats.

A half-dozen foreign languages fell silent as a man approached the podium.

"Hello, and welcome to the St. George's School of Medicine informational luncheon. We hope you come away with a better understanding about St. George's, what we are and what we are not."

He shared a little history about the country of Grenada.

Columbus discovered the island in 1498, but it wasn't settled until the French arrived in the 17th century. The British took over in 1762, cultivating sugar, cacao and nutmeg. In 1974, Grenada obtained independence, making it one of the smallest countries in the world. The medical school, founded in 1978, graduates physicians who practice throughout the world.

"If you are considering St. George's, you need to know what you can expect. The island is tropical. The weather can be very hot. It is a Third World country, which means it lacks many of the amenities and comforts that you take for granted in America.

"Most of you are either from the United States, or you will want to practice in the United States. If this is your goal, I must emphasize, any U.S. medical school is preferable to Grenada. Our school offers an excellent education. Our graduates go on to be successful physicians in many countries, but graduates from St. George's are foreign medical grads.

"What does that mean? It means it's much harder to get a residency in the United States—how hard will depend on the specialty and the institution. If you have your heart set on training at Harvard in neurosurgery, it's not going to happen. If you're looking for internal medicine, then you will definitely find a residency somewhere.

"Many of you can't get into American medical schools. There is probably a good reason for this. I must inform you, St. George's is no easier than the American schools. If students cannot perform satisfactorily, they will be dismissed. We follow the same curriculum, and our students sit for the same exam.

"We encourage our students to transfer to an American school after their second year. It's the best move for your career, and we are not offended. Unfortunately, only a few spots are available for transfer, so the selection is very competitive."

Listening to the speaker, I became convinced Grenada was my opportunity. This was it—this was my way in. I would transfer to an American school or, at the very worst, graduate a foreign medical grad. Either way, it wouldn't matter.

I was going to be a doctor.

ᴇↄ

In June, I filled out the application for St. George's. When writing the personal essay, I was relieved I didn't have to rationalize my flaws. This was Grenada—everyone would have similar imperfections. My essay was simple and straightforward:

PART VII PERSONAL EVALUATION ESSAY
St. George's School of Medicine

I was pleased to have the opportunity attend your open house meeting at the New York Sheridan. Many of the questions I had about foreign medical education were answered, and I gained the remaining information I needed to make a decision about your school. I was most impressed by the commitment of your faculty to teaching and the sense of "family" that I perceived between the faculty and student population.

I have completed two rounds of U.S. medical school applications, been on several interviews, and placed on two waiting lists. Most of the faculty I have interviewed with gave me the impression that although I had a solid background, strong recommendations and high MCAT scores, my cumulative GPA was not competitive enough. In response to this, I have completed 16 credits of coursework, with a combined GPA of 3.5, in an attempt to demonstrate my academic ability.

Although faced with the continuing disappointment of failing to obtain U.S. medical school admission, I am still deeply committed to becoming a physician. Since graduation, I have tried to use my time productively, gaining experience in research at Columbia and health care management at Albany Medical Center. In addition, I have continued my patient care involvement as a volunteer paramedic in my community.

I have taken the time to speak with several physicians who were educated in the Caribbean, both at St. George's and at American University. I understand the unique challenges that I will face at your school; I feel that it will be an exciting opportunity for me, and I look forward to the possibility of studying at St. George's University.

Enclosed is some additional support material for the committee to review. I apologize for making the decision to apply so late in the season, but there were a variety of variables that I had to consider before submitting this application. If I can supply any additional information, please feel free to contact me. Thank you for your time in consideration of my application.

John Pryor
June 6, 1990

⚭

In July, I gave my notice at Albany Med. The monitor station was up and running; it would be easy for someone to keep it going. I was proud of my accomplishment but was looking forward to turning in that infuriating pager.

With my resignation, I was equally free and rudderless. If I didn't get into Grenada, I didn't know what I was going to do.

⚭

Coney Island Hospital in Brooklyn, N.Y. began life as a boardwalk first-aid station in 1875. Now a 371-bed teaching hospital, it served as the main clinical location for students from St. George's. It was also where they conducted interviews for prospective students.

Dressed in a dark blue suit, I found my way to the office of Ellen Ferrone, admissions counselor, and sat with a few other candidates. Waiting my turn, I fought the idea that this was my last hope.

Presently, a woman appeared and introduced herself. We returned to Ms. Ferrone's office and spoke about my background and work experience. I discussed my accomplishments at the hospital and my volunteer work as a paramedic. Then she got down to the serious questions.

"How do you know you want to be a doctor?" she asked.

"I've spent a lot of time in my life trying to figure out what to do. I thought about being a biochemist, but after working in the lab, I knew it wasn't for me. I thought about being a paramedic, but it's not enough. I was accepted to several PA programs, but I know I'm capable of more. When I came up with the idea of being in medicine, when I settled on the idea that I needed to be a physician, I knew there was no other option."

"Why should we consider you?"

"I know you probably get this all the time, but I know I can succeed academically. If I am given a chance, I know I can do it. My grades are not a reflection of my ability. I really haven't given 100% effort in anything before. All I need is somebody to give me that avenue, to give me a try."

"What are your plans if you don't get in?"

"You know, I'm at the absolute end of my rope. I have got to get into your school. I see my future, like, to July of this year. I try to think beyond that, and it's all white and empty. I see no future in my life until the end of medical school. It's not like I'm depressed or anything; it's just that there is no other option."

Ms. Ferrone closed the manila folder, folded her hands and looked at me. It was exactly what she wanted to hear.

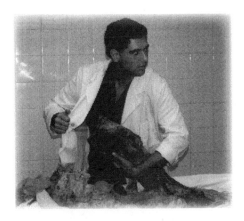

Grenada

August 1990, West Indies. Stepping from the plane, I squint in the bright equatorial sun. A wave of thick, humid heat consumes me—like entering a blast furnace. Beads of sweat dot my burning forehead as I descend to the tarmac. Struggling to move heavy air into my lungs, I fail to appreciate the sweet mix of ocean salinity and tropical flora.

Damn, it's hot, I thought.

I walk across the runway to Point Salines International Airport, a small terminal building bearing a sign welcoming me to Grenada. Inside the terminal, I pass through a rigorous customs procedure: A uniformed man eyes me suspiciously and, failing to cause me to crack under pressure, stamps my passport.

Out front, a small group of students huddle next to a rusted-out reggae bus. The driver holds a sign that reads, "Medical School."

I wonder if they mean St. George's? I joke to myself.

After introducing myself, the school representative checks my name on a clipboard. When our full complement arrives, we climb in the rickety vehicle. There are no seat belts.

"Ok, mon," the driver says, "welcome to Grenada!"

The bus lurches forward. We accelerate, and I wonder if there's a speed limit on the island. The driver brakes, speeds and swerves worse than any ambulance I'd ever ridden. Searching for a handhold, I settle on gripping the seat in front of me.

Outside, the passing landscape reveals houses—shacks mostly—in various stages of construction or degradation. Grenadians, clad in shoddy clothes, walk the roadside. Some are children dressed in school uniforms. Feral dogs roam the streets. Overall, the penury is striking.

The bus skids to a halt. I tense my grip, bracing against inertia's throw. The culprit of our sudden stop saunters by.

Is that a goat? I thought.

The goat leisured past. Jolted back in my seat, we resume our excursion.

The road sheds asphalt like a snakeskin; we acquire a dust tail. Emaciated cows and sickly chickens graze the sparse fields. At the top of a small hill, the bus abruptly stops. Dust billows past, obscuring the view.

"We're here, mon," the driver announces, "dis is da True Blue."

The dust clears, revealing an abandoned motel. I look out the other windows; there is nothing.

We're here? I think. *Where? Where are we?*

I jump out, searching for signs of civilization. A distinctive smell of burning garbage, like burning corn, assaults my nose. An ox, chewing the cud in an empty field, pauses his mastication to welcome us.

There's no "Here" here, I think. *There's gotta be a "Here" somewhere; let's go there!*

But this was it. We were here, my home for the next two years: True Blue.

℥

The abandoned hotel was my dorm. Ends of the long hallway lacked walls, a feature common in this winterless climate. On the second floor, my room reminded me of the college dorms, just big enough for matching twin beds and desks. Unlike college, we had our own bathroom with shower, minuscule as it was.

The balcony overlooked a rain forest; a tattered screen door proved little deterrence against crawling insects and salamanders.

Steve Foster, my new roommate, had arrived on an earlier flight.

Steve was from Rockland County; his father was a doctor. He offered me a beer but I declined. I couldn't resume old college habits even if class hadn't started yet.

Drenched in sweat, I unpacked a towel and headed to the bathroom, desperate to splash cool water on my face. Only a few drops dribbled from the faucet.

"Steve," I yelled, "was the water working when you got here?"

"They said no water today," he answered.

No water today? I thought. *What does that mean?*

Steve and I headed out to find dinner. Leery of indigenous cuisine, I suggested we get some pizza. After a good deal of searching and confused looks, we realized there wasn't any pizza on the island. None.

Nobody said there wouldn't be pizza, I thought.

Official orientation began the next day. Steve joined other students headed for a bar. I returned to the dorm eager to get some sleep.

The sun set, but the heat would not relent. Darkness fell, yet the sultry humidity refused to surrender. Less than a day in Grenada, and I had lost my entire body weight in sweat.

Lying sleepless on top of the sheets, naked except for my briefs, I continued to perspire.

Who can live in a place like this? I thought. *How can anyone go to school here?*

In the stifling darkness, I reflected on my recent actions. It all happened so fast: In May, I heard about Grenada, applied in June, interviewed in July and boarded a plane in August. Now I lay sweltering in a Third World country, surrounded by creeping fauna, lacking running water and starved for a slice of pizza.

I was in hell.

I made the biggest mistake of my life, I thought.

&

I couldn't believe it could get any hotter, but the next day proved me wrong. Fresh shorts and T-shirt were immediately dampened with sweat. Joining my classmates, I embarked on our first day orientation.

The school had two campuses: True Blue and Grand Anse. Besides my dorm, True Blue included the main lecture hall, labs, a library and a communal kitchen. One of the most spectacular beaches in the Caribbean, Grand Anse, was also home to air-conditioned dorms, an anatomy lab and an activity center. A shuttle bus provided transport between the two.

Large electric fans circulated air within the lecture hall. The indoor breeze made the heat marginally tolerable as we filled out papers and listened to instructions for the coming semester.

When we broke for lunch, I wandered from the group and found the library. I went in to take a look.

A sudden caress of cool air arrested my senses. Paralyzed, I closed my eyes, feeling the piloerection on my arms; the chill atmosphere lifted the smothering heat from my chest. The coolness was intoxicating. For the first time since stepping off the plane, I could breathe. I opened my eyes and walked forward.

Study carrels and tables filled most of the space not taken up by short stacks of medical books. It smelled like any other library. Around the perimeter, periodical-lined shelves covered the walls.

British Medical Journal, Chest, Dermatology, Endocrinology... I strolled along until I came upon my old friend, *The New England Journal.* Cradling the periodical in my hand, I flipped through pages, smelling the familiar ink.

This is the reason I'm here, I reminded myself. *I'm here to become a physician.*

I surveyed the quiet space, my new sanctuary. Outside remained the stifling heat, feral goats, sporadic plumbing and burning garbage. In here just me and the great expanse of medical knowledge.

Yes, I thought, *this'll do.*

❧

All medical schools follow the same basic curriculum; Grenada is no exception. The first year emphasized normal anatomy and physiology down to the molecular level. First-semester classes included biochemistry, embryology, genetics and anatomy.

My academic record at Binghamton proved I knew how to fail. Now, I needed to prove I could succeed. The difference was fear and motivation—fear I would fail out and motivation to transfer to an American school.

Employment cured my sleeping-in problem, and each morning I fought for a front-row seat in the lecture hall. During class, I took diligent notes. I allowed myself a break until after dinner before settling in the library from 6 p.m. until 1 a.m., every night. Saturday nights I went out, but Sunday was spent in the library.

Biochemistry, my major in college, was a gimme. I needed to re-memorize metabolic pathways like the Krebs cycle, glycolysis, hexose monophosphate pathway, etc., but for the most part it was all review.

Embryology detailed the journey from single cell to complete human. The process of growth, morphing and differentiation is complex and demanded all of my attention to understand.

Then there was anatomy, at once the simplest and the most difficult subject I've taken. Simple because there was little thinking involved. Observe: the facial artery. Period. Difficult because there were thousands of things to remember: This is the facial artery, and this is the cervical branch with the ascending palatine artery, the tonsilar artery, the submental artery and glandular arteries, the facial branch with inferior labial artery, superior labial artery, lateral nasal branch, ad infinitum.

I rewrote my class notes, filled countless 3 × 5 cards, read, reread, and re-reread the text until my face collapsed into the open page. I allowed no distractions during the week, ignoring intramural sports, social gatherings and the beach. For the first time, I was completely focused on the task at hand. For the past two years, I bitched that I could succeed if given the chance.

Grenada was my chance, and I wasn't going to blow it.

ભ

Over the coming weeks, I acclimated to my new environment. The heat wave broke. I was glad to hear it was hot even for the locals. I made friends with classmates, and together we commiserated about the conditions of the island.

The culture shock was not only of another country, but of a Third World country. Amenities taken for granted were now luxuries. On the island, police were ineffective, meals contained little meat, medical care was scant and the culture was nearly apathetic.

One night, I got up to take a piss. As I was doing my business, I casually looked up and jumped back, *"Jesus fucking Christ!"*

The largest cockroach I'd ever seen rested, motionless, on the wall. Five inches long, shiny brown, spindly legs, only the roving antennae showed signs of life. Arming myself with a shoe I returned to exterminate the monster, but he was too fast; he scurried into the closet.

Every night, he would be on the same part of the wall. Every night. I tried to kill him a few more times, but he was too fast.

So then I decided, look, I don't give a shit. I named him Henry and figured he'd lived here first and would probably survive long after I was gone.

Henry helped me realize Grenada was not the United States. No amount of complaining or wishful thinking would restore the electricity, produce a pizza restaurant or clear my room of cockroaches. Trying to force my expectations and culture onto this country was unfair and pointless. Once I resolved to this fact, I began to adjust.

So when I got up at 3 a.m. to go to the bathroom. I flicked the light on, and there was Henry on the wall in the same spot every night. Now I'd say, "Howya doin?"

One night, I heard Steve get up and go to the bathroom.

"Steve," I yelled from my bed, "turn on the light and look on the wall to your left."

He screamed.

"Yeah, that's Henry," I said. "He's there every night."

❧

True induction to Medicine occurs in a drab room smelling of newly opened vinyl shower curtains and filled with dead people.

The smell is formaldehyde. The dead people are cadavers.

Human dissection has a long and sordid history. Over the centuries, science and religion clashed, with most cultures and religions prohibiting human dissection. Early anatomists, forced to obtain bodies by unscrupulous methods, worked in clandestine laboratories.

Sacrilege. A perverse deed violating the sanctity of the human body and eternal spirit; medicine lay stagnant for centuries because of these beliefs. Physicians remained ignorant, their impotent healing tactics little better than witchcraft.

Before formaldehyde, anatomists worked in a race against time. The rotting stench of decomposing bodies tested the scientist's resolve. Within days, muscle began to putrefy, gas-filled bowel would distend and rupture. Pools of liquefied, fetid tissue would drip from the table.

Truly gruesome, but the reward was enlightenment and understanding. Early anatomists transcended the ageless mystery of who we are, what we are made of and how we work.

Now it was my turn.

After seeing my dorm and other facilities, I had low expectations for the anatomy lab. I wasn't disappointed.

Air-conditioners, cut into the pale green tile walls, remained as quiet and as lifeless as the cadavers. Dressed in green scrubs and a long white lab coat, I began to sweat in the windowless space. A single fan blew air from an open door like circulating heat in a convection oven. Overwhelmed by the smell, I tried breathing through my mouth; it didn't help. A dozen metal tables spanned the room; each held a shrouded form. Fluorescent lights cast the bodies in an eerie glow.

Tradition dictates many things in medicine; anatomy is no exception. It's a little thing, largely unknown to the outside world, but it has been done for years in anatomy labs the world over—naming the cadaver.

My dissection group circled the table as we discussed the small but meaningful detail.

"How about Cecil?" said Nadeem.

"That's good, what else?" I said.

"Igor?" said Kanel.

"Too cliché," said Steve.

"What about Edgar?" I asked.

There was a pause.

"Edgar is good," said Steve.

"Demetri?" offered Nadeem.

"Ehh.."

Put to a vote, Edgar won 4 to 2.

Hello Edgar, I thought, *I hope you don't mind our taking you apart this semester.*

Lab began with a lecture describing the day's dissection. We started on the back so we wouldn't have to attempt a cadaver flip when most of the chest and abdomen would be open.

Creating a human is an enormously complicated task, taking millions of years of evolution. Most of the process remains a mystery. Taking one apart, however, isn't nearly as difficult. All one needs, for the most part, is a scalpel, forceps and a few blunt dissection tools.

And lots of patience.

Steve and I struggled to flip Edgar onto his face. Formaldehyde made his heavy form slippery and difficult to negotiate. We managed to prevent him from sliding off the table.

Edgar's back glistened with formaldehyde-soaked skin. My bare hands—gloves were not an option—palpated his slimy spine. The scalpel made a long incision. Using forceps, I dissected a large flap of skin from underlying fat.

After only a few minutes, the scalpel became greasy with formaldehyde. Gripping the handle was a challenge, and I worried about slicing my own skin with the flesh and chemical-soaked blade.

Consulting *Netter,* the sine qua non of anatomy texts, my slimy fingers flipped to the appropriate illustration. There, Netter had a beautiful layout of the nerves and superficial back muscles.

It looked nothing like what I had done.

I went back to work, meticulously teasing out nerves from tissue, slowly separating muscles from fascia. Some structures were easy to identify; others took serious probing and a bit of imagination. With the body devoid of blood, many structures like arteries, veins, and nerves all looked the same to a novice.

When I was satisfied, nearly four hours had passed. I veiled Edgar in formaldehyde-soaked towels, draped him in plastic and hung my lab coat. Scrubbing my hands made them only marginally less greasy.

For the rest of the day and well into the next, I discovered a secret bonus of cadaver lab. One may leave the lab, but the lab doesn't leave you. Formaldehyde permeated my fingers and saturated my hair. I swore I could smell it in my sweat. Just when the smell began to abate, just when I could enjoy a meal without tasting Edgar, it was time to return to the lab.

Despite the heat and smell, I fell in love with anatomy. Each dissection, I delved deeper into the mysteries of the human form. I found a connection with manipulating tissues, an unfettered joy with identifying organs and an uncommon ability to find the most obscure structures.

It was awesome.

എ

A few weeks into the semester, I sat for my first exams. I had studied more in a few weeks than in my entire tenure at Binghamton, and I was eager to redeem myself.

The questions were K-type, much trickier than simple multiple choice:

Which planets have more than one moon?
1. Saturn
2. Neptune
3. Jupiter
4. Mars

A. 1,2,3 are correct
B. 1,3 are correct
C. 2,4 are correct
D. 4 only
E. All are correct

Despite the difficult format, I answered them easily. Page after page, I penciled in little circles. When finished, I reviewed my answers before turning in the exam. I was one of the first to be done.

Two days later, the lecture hall bulletin board produced our results. Grades were listed from highest to lowest and identified by social security number. I waited behind the crowd until it thinned enough for me to approach.

I placed my finger at the top of the social security list and slowly brought it down.

One, two… three. Holy shit!

Anatomy 99%!

The other lists were nearly the same. Biochem 97%, Genetics 96%, Embryology 98%.

Other students noticed where I stopped my finger and made comments about my grades. I didn't want to compete; from then on, I purposely slid my finger farther down so others wouldn't know how well I was doing.

The feeling of redemption was profound. For years, I tried to convince admissions committees I was capable of succeeding in medical school. Now, here was the first proof of my ability.

I was just getting started.

ɛↄ

By mid-semester, I began to really enjoy my island. Sure, some days we had no electricity, and various possessions would mysteriously disappear from my dorm, but where else could you take a study break by jumping in the ocean? While most of the United States entered the cold, darkness of winter, I was working on my tan.

We shopped at the Food Fair. Basic groceries lined the sparse shelves of this simple market. The store was not lacking compared to American stores, but absent was an entire aisle dedicated to sugary drinks or a hundred varieties of breakfast cereal. Instead, simple offerings like Coke or Pepsi, Cheerios or corn flakes made for easy-decision shopping. When I found pizza in the frozen food section, I couldn't have been happier.

On campus, we lunched and congregated at The Sugar Shack, a cafe just off the beach. The shack was home to one of the few televisions, usually tuned to CNN. My first experience of culture shock occurred here when I ordered a "meat pie." A pot pie arrived, and I picked through the crust and vegetables.

"Excuse me," I said to the waiter, "I think there's been a mistake, there's no meat in this."

He answered with a hearty laugh, "There's no *meat* in a meat pie!"

Of course!

Despite the island's dearth of red meat, food was sufficient; despite what my mother would tell you, I never starved. I found myself eating healthy meals, more fish and fresh fruits and even a vegetable now and again.

Restless from sitting on my ass all day, I started running. Each day, I finished three miles after class—one of only two times in my life I ran for exercise. My beer gut, started in college and cultivated in Albany, began to recede. Physically, I was in the best shape since high school.

The most conspicuously absent luxury was television. Withdrawal lasted a few weeks until I acclimated to the void. Liberation from television, however, allowed more time for studying, playing guitar, sending audio tapes back to Mom and Dad, going to the beach, playing volleyball or basketball and spending time with friends. CNN in the Sugar Shack was a novelty, otherwise I didn't miss it.

I became part of a community. On weekends, we gathered for movies at the lecture hall. The movie didn't matter, I enjoyed the sense of camaraderie and closeness with my peers. It reminded me of scout camp.

Except for Mom, Dad and Rich, I didn't miss the United States. I began to understand how people could live here happily. Life was harder on the island, but in many ways it was better.

⁂

My first image of her will always remain frozen in my mind, like a Polaroid snapshot. Fairly early, the first week of anatomy lab, I looked up from Edgar to see this scrawny little girl with curly black hair and a lab coat way down, too long for her. She was just kinda standing there looking totally disinterested.

Wow, I thought, *she's pretty cute.*

"Hey, Steve," I said.

"Yeah," he said.

"You know that girl," I pointed over with my eyes, "with the curly black hair?"

Steve looked up.

"Yeah," he said, "that's Carmela Calvo; she's friends with Tori."

I returned to Edgar and didn't give her any more thought.

A month later, I was in class when the instructor fell silent mid-sentence. I looked back to see a Grenadian walking into the lecture hall. Two hundred heads followed this guy down to the podium. He spoke to the instructor for a minute and then announced into the microphone, "Carmela Calvo? Carmela Calvo?"

Carmela raised her hand in the back. The Grenadian walked back up and gave her a box of flowers. Someone sent her flowers, delivered in the middle of class!

What the fuck? I thought. *Who the hell does she think she is?*

After that, she was shit in my books. After that day, I thought she and Tori could fall off the face of the earth for all I cared.

Of course, that wasn't the end of it.

Living on my own, I prepared meals in the common kitchen at True Blue. One evening while warming canned stew, I was joined by Carmela and Tori. Gabbing and gossiping, Carmela produced a parade of ingredients for a full-course meal. I tried to ignore them but finally broke down and joined the conversation.

I found it increasingly difficult to dislike Carmela. Our dialogue settled into a warm, comforting conversation, like two old friends reunited after years apart. And then there was that damn eye thing. I hadn't experienced it since I dated Cindy. When we spoke, our eyes embraced, words dissolved, and we fell, lost in each other's gaze. The world faded, and I lost all sense of time.

Maybe she wasn't shit in my books after all.

‹›

In December, I turned in my final exam, packed my bags and headed home for Christmas break. A few hours of flight returned me to modern civilization—indoor plumbing, television and fresh meat. My island life of the past few months became like a dream.

Sitting with Puppy, I told him my experience in Grenada. He sat forward in his leather recliner, puffing unfiltered Camels, hanging on every word.

"Well, well," he said, "it certainly sounds like you're going to be a fine doctor."

I was so happy that he was proud of me.

"It's because of you that I can go to medical school," I told him.

He gave a chuckle. "I don't think I had much to do with it," he said.

"That's not true," I said. "You raised Dad and sent him to college. He was able to send me to college. If I succeed in life, it's only because I was given the opportunity that you provided."

I meant every word, and I was glad to tell him how I felt.

Rich and I went out to Saratoga for our obligatory pint and deep conversation.

"So how's it going down there?" Rich asked.

"Man," I said, "the first few weeks were a nightmare. Hot as hell, freakin Third World, no pizza. But then a funny thing happened."

"What's that?"

"I began to like it."

"That's fine," Rich said, "just as long as you don't organize the 'Grenada Republicans.'"

"No worries there." I took a sip of beer. "So what are your plans?"

"You know, I love being a paramedic. Working at St. Vincent's is the best job I ever had, and I absolutely love it."

"But..." I said.

"But there's no future in it. You don't see fifty-year-old paramedics. There's only so much my back can endure, and I don't know how long I want to be called an ambulance driver."

He took a swig of beer.

"So?" I asked.

"So I'm going back to school. I figure two years at Hudson Valley then transfer into a PA program. I'll come out with a bachelor's and PA in one shot."

"That's a great plan," I said, "and if you change your mind, you could go to medical school."

He smiled. "Thanks, but I'd like to be realistic. I'm twenty-four this year, and time is running out to get my life in order."

I was glad Rich was making plans. He would be a great PA, but I didn't see why he couldn't be a great physician too.

❧

Returning to the warm sun, sandy beach and tropical flora was a welcome departure from the bleak Northeast winter. The final grades of the first semester were in: I had a 4.0 average. Certain I could maintain these grades, I was sure to transfer to an American school. But on January 17, I came close to quitting.

Crowded in the Sugar Shack, my colleagues and I sat, transfixed, watching reports of America's bombardment in Iraq. Night vision cameras showed grainy green images of downtown Baghdad lit up with tracers and explosions.

We were at war.

My family had a long tradition of enlisting during wartime although none had seen battle. Puppy was in his forties when he enlisted during World War II, contributing his skills as a CPA to the Army. Puppy's brother left Fordham to join the Navy during World War I, only to die of influenza at the Great Lakes Naval Station. The war ended months later. My dad was discharged from the Marines before Vietnam. I always felt an obligation to serve; recurrent dreams of battle only provoked my sense of duty and patriotism.

For weeks, I argued the pros and cons of leaving Grenada to serve. Steve called me crazy for even considering it. I continued my studies but secretly thought about finishing the semester and enlisting. I could always come back to school.

In February, however, as abruptly as it began, the Gulf War was over.

I had missed my chance.

❧

Whereas the first semester focused on anatomy and structure, the second delved into physiology and mechanics of how organs worked. *Guyton*, the book of physiology, revealed the mysteries of our innards: Actin and myosin of muscles, loop of Henle in the kidneys, bile-forming liver lobule, thyroxine-synthesizing thyroid, trypsinogen secreting pancreas, etc., etc.

Histology, anatomy on a microscopic level, introduced me to cellular structure. Cases in *The New England Journal* always include a histologic slide, but I never understood what I was looking at. Now I memorized slide after slide, hundreds of them, discerning liver cells, bladder cells, adrenal cells, and so on.

Struggling with this avalanche of information, I began studying on Saturday nights. One weekend, I finally needed a break and agreed to go out with Steve.

"Where we headed?" I asked.

"The Red Parrot," said Steve; "a bunch of people are headed down there."

"You know if Carmela's going?"

"I don't know. Why?"

"No reason, just wondering."

A shack of a cabana, the Red Parrot hosted most of our weekend parties. A dark wood roof, fringed with palm fronds, covered the enclosure. Simple lattice ironwork, extending to the ceiling from half-walls around the perimeter, admitted the occasional ocean breeze. The gusts were welcomed relief on the crowded dance floor.

Sparsely filled shelves behind the bar held bottles of rum, vodka and a few wine glasses. Carib beer and Coca Cola were served warm. Wire patio furniture, not seen since the 1950's, provided tacky, yet functional, decor.

Like a homely girl, the Parrot improved with darkness and alcohol.

When our group achieved quorum, I suggested we play Mexicali.

"What's that?" asked Dave.

"What, you didn't play this in college?" I asked.

"No," he said, "we just drank."

I explained the game: A cup held dice. You shake the cup then slam it upside down on the table and peek underneath. If your roll doesn't beat the previous roll, then you have to drink, but you can bluff. The person you are trying to beat can call your bluff, but if he's wrong then he has to drink.

"There's more, but we'll explain it as we go along," I said.

We drank and got rowdy. In between eruptions of cheers and laughter, I noticed Carmela enter with her friends. My heart pounded, and my mouth went dry.

The place got crowded. Dance music shook the walls. I stayed off to the side with my drinking buddies and watched, trying not to stare at Carmela.

Tori broke off from Carmela's group and wandered over to us.

"Hey, Steve," she said. "Hey, John."

"Hey, Tori," I said.

"Whacha drinking?" It was a running joke since there was only one beer available on the island.

"Carib. What you drinking?"

"Carib." We all let out a chuckle.

"Never gets old, does it?"

Tori and Steve talked about class for a bit, then she turned to me.

"Hey," she said, "what do you think about Carmela?"

I nearly choked on my beer.

"She's nice…" I tried to sound disinterested.

"Why don't you ask her to dance?" she said.

"I don't know" I demurred. "I don't really dance…"

"Go ask her to dance," Tori egged, "she won't say 'no'."

This sounded promising, and my spirits were lifted.

"Alright," I said, but I didn't have the nerve. Tori returned to her female congregate.

In due time, with sufficient alcohol, the right dance song and enough comrades covering my flank, I eased onto the dance floor. Periodically, through the mass of bouncing, twisting bodies, I caught a glimpse of that curly-haired girl with her bright smile. She looked over. For an instant, our eyes met and time seemed to stop.

A few songs later, the music ended, and the DJ cut in.

"We're gonna slow things down a little," he said. "This one's for you couples out there…"

I started walking off when I felt someone grab my arm. I turned to see her smiling at me.

"Let's dance," Carmela said.

I followed her. We embraced and danced slowly to the music. Four rounds of Mexicali did nothing to dull my shivering as I held Carmela and gazed into those beautiful eyes. I felt I should say something.

"Carmela…" Nervous, drunk and scared, I didn't want to blow it.

Keep it simple, I thought.

"Carmela... I think you're really nice."

And that, it turns out, was all I needed to say.

"I think you're nice too," she began. "You know I liked you last semester."

"Really?"

"Yeah, I was hoping you would ask me out..."

Carmela confessed how much she liked me, how she turned down other guys last semester because of me, and how she was waiting for me to ask her out.

Her soliloquy left me stunned. I had no idea.

Later, our groups merged, and we sat next to each other holding hands. It was Tori's turn to rant.

"Finally!" she said, "you wouldn't believe what we went through last semester."

"What do you mean?" asked Steve.

"We tried to get these two together all semester, finding out when John would be in the library and telling Carmela so she would be there too, where John went to lunch so she would be near to say 'Hi.' Really John, I can't believe you didn't notice..."

I couldn't keep from blushing.

"I guess I was too busy studying to put it all together," I tried to defend myself.

"It doesn't matter now; it was all fun," Tori concluded. "You guys make a really cute couple."

From then on, we were never apart.

❧

Mid-semester, while riding a reggae bus into town, an accident shattered any sense of security I had about Grenada. While chatting about class and the upcoming Sandblast, something shot toward us out of the corner of my eye. BANG! The van shook and swerved, throwing me to the floor. Tires skidded as the driver slammed the brakes. I heard more tires screech as other cars came to a stop.

"What the fuck!?" someone said.

"He came out of nowhere, mon!" the driver said, jumping out of the van.

A motorcyclist had rounded a curve too fast. He crossed the line and collided head-on with our bus. A crowd instantly formed around the prostrate body. Further down, a tangled mass of metal and wheels leaked onto the pavement. Initially reluctant about getting involved, it became obvious I was the most qualified practitioner there.

Probably the most qualified practitioner on the island, I thought.

I stopped the bystanders from moving the victim.

"Wait! Wait! We gotta hold his head!" I quickly surveyed the man's back while holding his head. So far, it didn't seem so bad.

"Okay, slowly!" I held cervical spine stabilization while the crowd rolled the flaccid man to his back.

Oh Jesus! I thought.

The man was FUBAR (Fucked Up Beyond All Recognition). Blood oozed from every orifice, his nose was flattened and his front teeth were missing. A slight moan was his only sign of life.

Airway, breathing—instinctively I became a paramedic; years of training and experience reflexively took over—*circulation*. I felt the carotid pulse, very fast and weak.

Compensated shock, I thought.

I looked lower. His chest moved with paradoxical motion. Bad. His right forearm bent at a disturbing angle around an expanding hematoma. Also bad. His hips were asymmetrical, one leg six inches shorter than the other, with pelvis bone jutting through his shorts.

Extremely bad.

In Clifton Park, I would get busy: Cervical collar, backboard, sandbag for the flail chest, saline-soaked trauma pad to the protruding bone, two large bore IVs and burn rubber to the trauma center.

But here, I had nothing.

A long time elapsed before the police arrived. One officer took charge, directing traffic; the other came over to us.

"Where's the ambulance?" I asked.

"No ambulance today," he declared. No other suggestion was forthcoming.

I'd been on the island long enough not to be surprised. The words "Third World" are meaningless until you come and experience it firsthand—a world where utilities are sporadic and municipal services unreliable. No water today, no electricity today, no ambulance today. One had to truly turn it on its head to make the best of it. Well, at least there is electricity some days.

I looked at the police car.

"No, mon, he can't go in the police vehicle." He looked down at the bleeding body, and shook his head.

Just then, another reggae driver staggered over.

"'E can come in my bus." The man swayed. "Come, we take him to the hospital."

Is he drunk? I thought.

The man was drunk.

The crowd carefully lifted the patient into the reggae van and laid him on the floor. Steve and I jumped in. The drunken man got behind the wheel.

"Hold on; we go really fast now!"

I did my best to keep the man's airway open while the van sped and swerved along the narrow hilltop streets. I stole a glance out the front window as the driver weaved through oncoming traffic.

I knew the motorcyclist was going to die. Now, I wondered about the rest of us.

Grenada Hospital, a modest two-story building, contained no emergency room, per se. There was a *room*. It had a door to the outside. But that's where any similarities ended.

We were in luck; it was open.

We laid the patient on the hospital gurney as the doctor arrived. I marveled at the antique medical equipment. The EKG machine had suction cups. In the corner, a pair of rubber gloves lay soaking in soapy water—those were *the* gloves. A microscope, at the windowsill, used the sun as a light source. Any corner drugstore in America would be the envy of the sparsely filled shelves.

DEATH appeared in the room.

The doctor performed a perfunctory exam, lifted his stethoscope from the man's chest and turned to me.

"This patient is stable," he announced.

DEATH took a step forward.

"*What?*" I couldn't stifle the outburst.

This man is about to become dead stable, I thought.

Unsettling as it was, the experience proved enlightening. We take good health for granted in the United States. Most of us are unaware of the huge safety net that lies just beneath our feet. One may complain about waiting times in the ER or expense or lack of health insurance. But in the end, the system is there. Ambulances respond. Hospitals are staffed with qualified doctors. Specialists are available even for the poor and indigent.

But in Grenada, no such safety net existed. There was no system, and the paucity of resources were available only sporadically. And you know what made Grenada different from other Third World countries? It was *better* than most.

My vulnerability registered like waking up naked in class. Suddenly the island wasn't so quaint. If I were struck by a van, my fate would be no different from this man's.

"You need a ride back to campus?" asked the inebriated driver.

Steve and I exchanged glances.

"No, we're good," I said; "thanks for all your help."

The next day, I wasn't surprised to hear the patient had died. I felt guilty. It didn't matter that I had no resources available. I shared responsibility for the man's death.

෮

The second semester came to an end, and I again finished with straight A's. I was ranked number three in the class, a remarkable accomplishment considering my collegiate history.

Summer, I worked as a girl's day camp counselor, a welcome break from studying medicine. Teaching at the camp, I had fun with the kids while imagining the kind of father I might be someday.

Rich was home, enrolled in summer classes during the week. We spent weekends together, going out to bars or visiting his friend's Adirondack cabin.

One time, I found Rich in his room typing at the computer. I picked up a brochure from Amnesty International.

"What're you doing?" I asked.

"Writing a dictator in Africa," he said, "informing him we know what he's doing to his people."

"Oh Jesus," I said, "my own brother, a bleeding heart liberal."

"What's a liberal?" he asked.

"It's what you are; next thing, you'll be voting for Ralph Nader."

"Who?" he said.

"How can you be so naïve? What, you think a few letters are gonna make a difference?"

"I don't know," he said. "It can't hurt. Maybe if we shed light on their atrocities, they might change their behavior. Would you steal something if you knew someone was watching?"

"No," I said, "but I care; these dictators don't care what anybody thinks."

"Well, at least it's something," he said. "What are you doing to help?"

"You're not helping," I replied. "You're wasting ink."

I didn't have time to join a crew on the ambulance, but Rich and I jumped second calls together. One night, a rollover on the Northway proved particularly gruesome. A teenage girl, ejected from the driver's seat, lay trapped with the car resting on her legs. I tried to intubate her while the fire department lifted the car, but all I could see was blood.

"Let me try," Rich said.

I shrugged and handed him the laryngoscope. A minute later, I was amazed to hear breath sounds as he bagged her.

"How'd you find the trachea?" I asked.

"Easy," he said. "Just aim for the bubbles."

⁊

August, 1991. The start of my second year in the Caribbean. I considered moving off campus with friends but changed my mind at the last minute, settling for an air-conditioned room at Grand Anse. After learning normal structure and function, it was time for the real meat of medicine: pathology.

Robbins, the bible of pathology, made me question every rash, lump and fever I experienced. Just a lymph node, or was it cancer?

Diarrhea, or did I have Crohn's? And that twinge of abdominal pain could be a dozen different diseases.

Parasitology, more germane considering my location, proved useful for an itchy, snake-like rash that appeared on my foot. I was the proud host of a hookworm, known as *Cutaneous Larval Migrans.* Considering all the tapeworms, liver flukes, intestinal nematodes and vector borne diseases, I considered myself fortunate.

Nutrition killed me. I have a philosophy that everything in medicine is important, that I will eventually use everything I am learning, but nutrition tested bounds of rationality. Really, how often would I encounter Vitamin A toxicity from overzealous polar bear liver consumption?

I promised myself I wouldn't get involved in extracurricular activities, but I allowed a single exception in my second year: I became a tutor for anatomy.

"Doctor" originates from Docere, to teach. Committed to becoming a doctor in every sense of the word, teaching would help me retain my anatomy skills while helping others learn.

Returning to the land of formaldehyde, I roved from cadaver to cadaver, identifying structures, liberating muscles and explaining connections. Knowing a subject well enough to teach is exhilarating. The combination of anatomy and teaching was synergistic. If forced to choose an alternate career, teaching anatomy would be an attractive option.

&

My social landscape shifted in my second year. I spent most of my free time with Carmela and saw less of my old roommate Steve, who was not doing well.

Medical school is grueling. Medical school in the Third World, isolated from friends and family is exponentially worse. In addition to challenges facing all of us, Steve battled additional psychosocial stressors: His girlfriend broke up with him, and his father, a physician with resources, refused to support him either financially or emotionally.

Then, there was his drinking.

He started to spiral: Depressed, he drank, missed class, performed badly, fell deeper into depression and drank more. One day, we found him shitfaced at two o'clock in the afternoon.

I worried about Steve committing suicide. Asked if he was depressed, he faced me and said, "I'm a bad person." Nothing I said could convince him otherwise. We called his father with our concerns, but he didn't feel it warranted interruption of his schedule. This made Steve feel even worse.

We intervened, convincing him to talk to a school counselor. Finally, his mother arrived and took Steve home for a "break." I didn't know if he would be coming back. It was very upsetting because I knew how smart and capable Steve was. He had the potential to be a truly great physician. I hoped that he would make it.

Meanwhile, my relationship with Carmela was frightening. For the first time, I felt everything was perfect: She was smart, beautiful, and came from a great Italian family. We had the best time together. Every day, I alternated between euphoria and panic, grateful to have her but paranoid that something would go wrong.

When upset, she would pout, and I made fun of her until she smiled. One time, she was fed up with studying.

"What are you pouting about now?" I asked.

"I'm not pouting," she said.

"Sure, you are. What's Italian for 'pouting'?"

"Fungia," she said.

"Fungus?"

"Not Fungus," she said laughing. "*Fungia.*"

Too late. The nickname stuck; for many years, I called her "My little fungus."

One evening, we walked along the ocean watching the sunset. I surprised her with a bottle of wine and cheese, hidden for the occasion. We drank and talked as the sun slipped below the horizon, lighting the sky with a brilliant burst of orange and fiery red.

We embraced on the beach. Drowsy from the wine, soft waves lulled me into a light sleep.

I am standing on a road that curves in both directions around a steep mountain. The land is strange because there is no vegetation, only scat-

tered volcanic rocks of various sizes. The dirt has a reddish hue, and I'm reminded of a Martian landscape. The deep blue sky extends to the horizon. I look out past the road. A sea of clouds floats below, stretching in all directions. I realize how high I am.

I close my eyes against the radiant sun and feel a cool breeze sweep across my body.

Suddenly, a car appears from around the bend and accelerates toward me. I am terrified, paralyzed as the car approaches. It speeds up, and I'm unable to move. Just as I prepare for impact, the car abruptly veers off. I watch as it crashes through the barrier and plummets over the cliff.

Startled, I awakened, distracted from my romantic evening by the recurrent dream.

What did it mean?

ↄ৴

When I received the news I booked a flight home the next day. My instructors, sympathetic and understanding, postponed my exams. The airline had been very helpful after I explained it was a family emergency.

Puppy had died.

My plane descended into the bleak, barren winter landscape that reflected my somber mood. Rich picked me up from the airport, and we drove in silence for a bit.

"So, what happened?" I asked.

"Well," he began, "Geraldine had come for a visit."

Geraldine was a family friend Puppy hadn't seen for years.

"They had a great time talking all morning. Smiling and laughing, they reminisced about life in Yonkers."

"The good old days," I said.

"Yeah, he always wanted to go back and visit, but it's better to remember it as it was. Anyway, I went out for a run. When I came back, Geraldine had left. I went down in the basement to stretch out.

"A few minutes later, Mom came down the stairs holding a lunch tray. She says, 'Richie, something's wrong with Puppy.' So I come up to see.

"I find him slumped over in his chair; of course, he's blue.

"So, I lower him to the floor and tell Mom to call 911. I shouted to Dad to get my EMS duffle—it was up in my room. While he's getting my kit, I'm checking, he's not breathing, and there's no pulse.

"Dad comes down with the kit. I take out the BVM. Dad starts compressions, and I bag him a bit and then I intubate him."

"You had a tube?" I asked.

"Yeah, a disposable blade and some tubes. So I intubated him. I was pretty sure I was in. I saw cords, but when I bagged him, it sounded awful."

"Did he aspirate?" I asked.

"No, I didn't see any vomit or anything. I'm thinking CHF or pneumonia."

"Or COPD." I didn't have to remind Rich of the unfiltered Camels Puppy smoked for eighty years.

"Yeah, probably a mix of everything."

"Then, what?" I asked.

"Bill Campbell, one of the first responders, showed up and took over compressions. Then the ambulance arrived. They didn't have paramedics, so there was no resuscitation. We loaded him on a backboard and put him in the rig. I jumped in the back, and we did CPR to Saratoga Hospital."

The irony was painful. My brother responded to thousands of calls as a paramedic, performing hundreds of resuscitations. But now, with his grandfather in need, there was nothing he could do. It must have been torture.

There was silence.

"He was a good man," I said.

"Yeah," Rich sighed. His eyes welled up.

"I'm sorry I wasn't there with you," I said.

Puppy's death wasn't the first family death, but this time was different. Puppy lived with us. Over the years, he became less a grandfather and more a friend to me and my brother. It was a strange relationship because we took care of him. We enjoyed him. I think I enjoyed him more as the years went on. When he died, it was one of the toughest times in my life. I still can't discuss it. It's strange because I always wanted to talk to Dad about it, but I couldn't. It was painful because I know how attached Dad was to Puppy. To see Dad hurt that bad was pretty rough. That was the toughest part, watching my father grieve.

∽

In March, 1992, I completed one final medical school application. This time, it was to transfer. I was on track to become a physician either way, but graduating from an American school was important. I didn't want to be a foreign medical grad.

I applied to the following schools:

- Albany Medical College
- Upstate Medical Center in Syracuse
- SUNY Buffalo
- Mt. Sinai
- Columbia
- Boston University
- Georgetown

∽

Every spring, right after midterms, St. George's hosts a raucous three-day blowout known as Sandblast. So when my brother asked when he could visit, there was only one weekend to consider.

A few minutes after his flight landed, I met him exiting the terminal with a large deflated duffle. He approached me and thrust the luggage into my chest.

"Here," he said by way of greeting, "this is from Mom."

"What is it?" I asked, leading him to the rental car.

"Meat," he said jumping into the topless Jeep.

"Meat?" I threw it in the back and got behind the wheel.

"Mom's worried you're too thin," he said; "my visit is part rescue mission."

I laughed.

"Thanks," I said. "I feel saved. Let me show you my island."

I took my brother on a tour of the island and headed to True Blue campus. Our first stop was a helicopter blade.

"What is it?" Rich asked.

In the middle of a little courtyard, flowers surrounded a small cement circle. In the center stood a black, six-foot-high rectangle. Inscribed signatures rose along the face.

"It's a memorial for the troops lost during the invasion," I said. "In October 1983, there was a coup, and the president was killed. Reagan worried that the country would fall under the control of Cuba, so he sent in the troops."

"I thought we were rescuing the medical students," Rich said.

"Yeah, that too," I said. "This is a rotor from one of the downed helicopters. It has the names of the casualties inscribed."

"Very nice," Rich said, taking a close look.

"Reagan was here for the dedication," I added.

"Ooo, Reagan? Really?" he joked. "Right here?" He got down and touched the grass gently.

"Cut it out," I said.

"Wait, I can feel his presence..."

I picked him up laughing and pushed him toward the Jeep. We headed for town.

"What do they do here?" Rich asked. Wind blew in our faces as we bounced along the unkempt roads.

"Well, I'll have you know Grenada is the world's leading exporter of nutmeg."

"Gotta have nutmeg for the eggnog," he said.

"Yeah, but get this: They're not selling it."

"What? Why?"

"I think they're waiting for a nutmeg shortage so they can cash in at a higher price."

"Sure," Rich said, "like the great nutmeg drought of '74?"

I laughed.

We drove to the city of St. George's, a quaint seaside village lining a small ocean inlet. Red-roofed houses layered the hillside. Shops and cafés adorned Young Street, adjacent to the harbor. Along the water, old-fashioned lampposts punctuate the walkway. A couple of red, English style phone booths mark the center of town.

At a café, we lunched while Rich explained his own academic

comeback. It would appear the Pryors could excel academically if we weren't screwing around.

After lunch, I drove him to campus.

"This is it?" he asked.

"I know," I said. "I thought the same thing. But the place grows on you. C'mon, take a look at this." I pointed to the seaside wall of my dorm.

"Are those *bullet holes?*" he asked.

"Yeah," I said. "They left them as a memento of the invasion."

"Nice."

We put his bag in my room, and I found a refrigerator for the meat. Then I showed him the lecture hall, library and anatomy lab.

"You really are desperate to become a doctor," he said.

"It's not so bad," I insisted. "The place really grows on you."

Around campus, I introduced Rich as my Liberal Ass Brother.

"Geez," Rich said, "write a couple of letters for Amnesty International and you're labeled for life."

We met up with Carmela, her sister, Nella, and their mother, Pauletta. Over the weekend, the five of us lounged on the beach sipping margaritas, dipping into the ocean and enjoying a rare treat on Grenada: barbecued meat. We toured the town, flew in a parasail and drove through the rain forest up Mount Saint Catherine, Grenada's inactive volcano.

After weeks of tireless studying, the weekend was like a breath of fresh air, and I was so happy Rich had come. Grenada had a large influence on my life, and of all my friends and family, the only one to visit was Rich. It meant a lot to me.

ভ

After Sandblast weekend, I was back to the library for the final push. As the end of second year approached, it became increasingly difficult to concentrate.

But I did it.

I continued my study schedule and hours in the library. When finals rolled around, it all paid off.

I finished two years of medical school with a 4.0 average.

In May, I flew home to find a few surprises waiting for me. George-town, Columbia, SUNY Buffalo and Boston University wanted to inter-view me. When not traveling, I returned to my room to study. True, classes were over, but one final task remained.

After completing two years of medical school, it was time to sit for The Boards. Step 1 of the United States Medical Licensing Examina-tion (USMLE) covers basic science, everything we learned in the first two years. All medical schools follow the same curriculum, and all medical students took the test at the same time.

I took Step 1 in ME-500, a lecture hall at Albany Medical Col-lege. As I sat waiting to begin, I briefly imagined how this might have been my classroom and the students who surrounded me might have been my peers.

Test packets were distributed, and I started to freak out. Once again, the course of my life hinged on a single event. The outcome of this exam would decide my fate as a foreign medical grad. It took a full minute for me to calm down enough to read the first question.

1.   A 25-year-old woman has a 3-day history of vomiting and diarrhea. She has postural hypotension and poor tissue turgor. Her serum sodium concentration is 130 mEq/L. Which of the following findings is most likely?

    (A)   Decreased serum aldosterone concentration
    (B)   Increased serum atrial natriuretic peptide concentration
    (C)   Increased effective circulating volume
    (D)   Increased serum ADH (vasopressin) concentration
    (E)   Urine osmolality less than serum osmolality

I wasn't sure of the answer and had to guess. I moved to the next question.

2.   A 50-year-old man with a history of alcoholism has difficulty with short-term memory. He is unable to recall the date and cannot remember what he ate for breakfast this morning. He thinks the examiner is a long-lost friend and carries on a conversation with the examiner as if they have known each other for years. His long-term memory appears intact.

The patient dies shortly thereafter of a myocardial infarct. Pathologic examination of his brain is most likely to disclose an abnormality involving which of the following?

(A)   Amygdala
(B)   Caudate nucleus
(C)   Hippocampus
(D)   Locus caeruleus
(E)   Mammillary bodies

Another hard one. Another guess. It continued like this, page after page. I've never studied so hard to feel so stupid.

At noon, we took a break for lunch. Feeling as if I'd just given birth, my pain was far from over. An afternoon session was about to begin.

And that was just the first day.

At the end of day two, I circled my 500th answer bubble and handed in my answer sheet, exhausted and emotionally spent. For two years, I studied continuously for this exam. I left feeling it wasn't enough.

I had certainly failed.

℅

With applications out and interviews done, the final contingency to transfer was my board scores. Several times a day, I checked the mailbox. Once again, my future hinged on the presence of an envelope in the post. Considering all the rejection letters I pulled out of the mailbox, I didn't have high expectations.

If accepted to an American school, I would have one month to find an apartment, move in and begin my clinical rotations. Not much time for such a life-changing event.

At least, I wasn't going through it alone. Carmela applied to American schools as well. We spoke each night, sharing news and commiserating about our plight.

An official-looking manila envelope finally arrived. I tore it open but didn't understand the results. I reread the printout and checked to see if it was the right name.

I scored in the 95th percentile.

This meant that I had performed better than 95% of all medical students around the country. Only 4% had done better than me. I not only passed; I kicked serious ass!

Carmela also passed, and we were relieved to have Step 1 behind us.

In only a few days, we received responses from the schools. Rejected by Boston, I was accepted by Georgetown and SUNY Buffalo. Columbia accepted me with the caveat that I repeat the second year. Carmela was accepted to New York Medical College.

I briefly fantasized about a triumphant return to Columbia, joining the white coats who inspired me years ago. Then I woke up.

Repeat an entire year? I thought. *Are they crazy?*

I tore the letter from Columbia.

That left Georgetown and SUNY Buffalo.

Georgetown was prestigious, but Buffalo was inexpensive. While mulling over the choice, it hit me: *I'm choosing which medical school to reject!*

Buffalo School of Medicine

Stand here," the nurse admonished, "and don't *touch* anything." Obediently, I became a statue, hands clasped against my chest, a stranger thrust into this unfamiliar role without any preparation or pre-thought. Legends tell of medical students screwing up in the operating room. I heard of one, a helpful third-year who replaced a dropped hemostat, gingerly contaminating an entire mayo stand. The surgeon was livid and kicked him out of the OR.

I wanted no such reputation, especially on my first day.

I stood silently, like a wallflower, observing various pre-op activities: the anesthetized patient lay bathed in halogen, a resident painted betadine on her belly, nurses counted instruments while anesthesia labeled drugs and monitored vital signs.

At least on the ambulance I could hold something, I thought.

I arrived in Buffalo, N.Y. on August 10, 1992. My new home was a small studio apartment on Linwood Avenue, close to the hospitals. Moving in consisted of sheeting a twin bed and unpacking a suitcase. A few shelves held my books from Grenada and a solitary aluminum pot—the one that sustained me in the Caribbean—sat on the stove.

A two-day orientation preceded the start of clinical rotations. Like

St. George's, each medical school class becomes a close-knit family. Now I was a stranger, joining a class that had bonded for the past two years. Though not entirely unwelcome, I felt like an outsider crashing the party.

My first clinical rotation was six weeks of obstetrics and gynecology. After a sleepless night and half a bottle of antacids, I entered at The Children's Hospital of Buffalo, strangled by a tie and stiff Oxford shirt. My virgin-white lab coat still showed starched packaging folds.

Security directed me to the correct floor. Almost an hour early, I sat near the nurses' station and cracked open my OB/GYN handbook. Eventually, other short white coats appeared, awkwardly loitering out of place. A senior resident corralled us into a conference room.

Three-inch binders, distributed around the table, contained our rotation syllabus. The first pages listed who would start Obstetrics or Gynecology and our call schedule. I would begin with GYN and spend my second three weeks trying to catch babies. The call roster had my name at the top.

Nothing like starting with a bang, I thought.

After the meeting, we dispersed to assigned floors, clinics or offices. I found my resident who, finished with rounds, was headed for the OR.

"Meet us in room 6," he said. "Case starts in thirty minutes."

"Got it," I said.

I didn't ask where I could find the operating room; the location of the lockers; how I could get scrubs; where they kept caps, masks and booties; how to scrub; what size gloves I wore, or even what the case was. None of these questions came to mind until I was hopelessly lost in the hallways of an unknown hospital. First lesson as a third-year: You have got to figure it out. You are expected to know things, and it is up to you to learn them. Whether it's how to treat myasthenia gravis or find the operating room, nobody's going to hold your hand and gently lead you along the path to becoming a doctor. If I didn't know something, I had to suck it up and figure it out.

It was an hourly occurrence.

My quest led me past common passageways of the hospital to the hallowed entrance to the operating theaters. I hesitated before passing into restricted space, resolute more than confident. Grim-faced nurses, barely concealing their disdain, guarded the reception area. My feeble student ID contained enough enchantment to allow passage to the inner sanctum.

I managed to stow my clothes and change into scrubs. I found a surgical cap, mask and booties. Last time I was dressed like this, I was making Sea-Monkeys in Binghamton. Thankfully, OR 6 lay straddled between ORS 5 and 7.

"Who are you, and what size gloves?" the circulation nurse greeted me.

"Uhh, John Pryor, third-year medical student," I paused to look at my hand, "Uhh..."

"Eight," the nurse said. "Go scrub."

Hands trembling, I nervously scrubbed each finger, palms, backs, arms up to elbows. Returning to the OR, I slipped into a gown and plunged my hands into sterile gloves. While waiting for my next command, I observed the activity around me.

A magical place, this world admits only a select few, where the hands of man transgress into realms God never intended. A distinctive smell, unique to the OR, is hard to describe. It's a clean, antiseptic aroma augmented by the surgical mask. The room is kept cool; I would be cold if not for my gown. The lighting is bright even without the surgical lamp. Anesthesia provides the soundtrack, a continuous beeping of the pulse oximeter with occasional bee-bee boop from the machine.

The gynecologist and resident entered, immediately attended to by the scrub nurse. They flanked the patient and prepared for the operation: Mayo stand wheeled close, Bovie plugged in and tested, lights focused, sponges dabbled pools of betadine. As an afterthought, the resident looked over his shoulder.

"You gonna join us?" he sneered.

I stepped up to the field, an expanse of blue surgical drapes surrounding the brown pool of exposed belly. My hands remained in prayer position, petrified of contamination. The resident forced them onto the drapes.

"Keep 'em where we can see 'em," he said.

"Yes sir," I said reflexively.

"This is Marjorie Davidson," the resident informed me. "She came to the ER last night with abdominal pain. An ultrasound showed an eight centimeter ovarian cyst…"

"Torsed?" I asked.

His brow furrowed. "You think we'd wait all night to go to the OR for a torsion!"

"Well… no," I conceded.

He rolled his eyes and turned back to the belly.

"Knife," the resident said, holding out his hand. A scalpel slapped into his palm. The incision was smooth and deliberate. Skin parted like the wake of an ocean liner. Little vessels oozed within the open flesh. The sound of the Bovie buzzed like a game of Operation! as a puff of acrid smoke rose from congealed flesh.

Dissecting into the peritoneum, a retractor was inserted, and the handle turned to me.

"Hold this," the resident ordered.

This is good, I thought. *I know how to hold.*

The attending and resident worked in perfect synchrony, each anticipating or complementing the other's actions. A ten-fingered dance, forceps pirouetted, sutures fluttered, organs dipped and bowed.

Poetic.

I identified the anatomy: bladder, uterus, fallopian tubes, bowel. The contrast with Edgar couldn't be more profound, like black and white to color. Glistening structures moved and flowed, tissue blushed with color, arteries pulsated against azure veins. Awestruck, I tried to take it all in.

I survived the operation. The patient did okay, too. Four others followed with a short break for lunch. With each case I became more adroit with the basics: scrubbing, gown and glove, and proper place-ment of my hands. Exposed bowel became routine, if not familiar. If I learned nothing else, I would have considered the day a success.

But the day was far from over.

After the final case, we headed to the floors. I followed my resident like a lost puppy, writing post-op notes on the recently incised, checking labs, dictating discharge summaries and changing wound dressings. Then we joined the rest of the team for afternoon attending rounds.

In the evening, the rest of the team signed out to my resident and me. Twelve hours, but my day was just beginning with admission notes to be written, ER consults and the periodic pages from the floor nurses. At two o'clock in the morning, the activity slowed enough for us to find the call rooms.

"GYN call is a lot better than OB," the resident said.

"Really?" I asked.

"Yeah, we sometimes get three or four hours sleep if there are no consults and the nurses are nice."

I wasn't worried about sleep. Years on the ambulance and my stint as a hospital supervisor had prepared me for the twenty-four hour days.

"What do they get on OB?" I asked.

"Usually none," he said.

We got a solid two hours. The ER woke us for a pregnant female with abdominal pain. Ultrasound showed a ruptured ectopic, a life-threatening condition. She needed to go to the OR immediately.

In the middle of the night, the mood of the OR reminded me of four a.m. ambulance calls. Somnolent staff, roused from call rooms or comfortable nurses' stations, moved like silent automatons. Incision made, bleeding ligated and fetal tissue removed; a life saved with little fanfare.

Emerging from the OR, I joined my short-coated colleagues on morning rounds. They asked me about my night on call, and I told them how much fun I had. After one more ER consult, we attended a conference, where I fought to stay awake. At noon, I handed off the call pager and returned to the OR, happy my clothes hadn't been stolen.

At home, I collapsed onto my bed fully dressed. I'd been up for thirty-two hours.

My first clinical day was over. As it would turn out, I had 5,973 to go.

⁊

It's hard to imagine a more demanding experience than that of a third-year medical student. Like some medieval tribulation, the process must have been deliberately designed to torment the student, a thinly veiled test; only those able to maintain sanity after two years would be allowed to graduate.

Every few weeks, my uprooted existence began a new hospital, a different specialty, and a new call schedule. Each week, I was forced to regain the trust of suspicious nurses, defend myself from abusive residents and prove my ability to cantankerous attendings. Just as I became familiar with a new environment, it was time to move on.

Despite these challenges, I not only survived; I excelled. I stood apart from my peers. I believe several factors contributed to my ability.

First, my paramedic experience provided a degree of clinical comfort and skill, especially in a crisis. I had run more codes than any of the residents; routine medicine was child's play in comparison.

Second, my fund of knowledge, for whatever reason, was greater than my peers. It's not intelligence, since I'm no more intelligent than the next guy. But between studying on a remote island for two years and reading the Journal each week, I managed to consistently pull the right answer from my ass.

Finally, I was still motivated. Much of the struggle and competitiveness are extinguished upon acceptance to medical school. By third year, interest is reduced to clerkships of possible career choice. Coming from a foreign medical school, I strove to prove I was worthy to be in an American school.

I sincerely believed everything was important. No matter what specialty I chose, someday even the most arcane aspect of medicine would come to bear on my patients. Giving a hundred percent, even in the specialties that didn't interest me, would make me the best physician possible.

❧

Pediatrics followed OB/GYN in the same hospital, so at least I began in familiar surroundings.

My first day, I joined the team for morning rounds. Our cluster of white coats shuffled along the hallway before settling near the doorway of our first patient. Dr. Sadowitz, a gruff pediatrician in his sixties, was all business. He reviewed the case of this four-year-old who presented to the ER with general edema. The child started with a cold, but his condition worsened; he had headaches and wasn't acting right. Dr. Sadowitz listed some of the labs.

"Nephrotic syndrome," I interrupted. The team looked in my direction.

"Very good, Mr. Pryor," he said. "What could give this little boy such a problem?"

"Strep, HUS, IgA nephropathy, HSP," I listed, "but the most common are from NSAIDS. Did the mother give him a lot of Motrin?"

There was a pause as Dr. Sadowitz sized me up with a scowl.

"You read the chart?" he asked.

"Uh, no." My eyes darted around the group. I had no intention of being a braggart. I was just answering the question.

"Hmmph," he muttered. Attendings didn't like to have their thunder stolen. We followed him into the room.

"Is this little Billy?" Mr. Rogers magically replaced Dr. Sadowitz in a striking transformation of personality. He beamed a great smile and tickled the patient.

"What? You like my tie?" he asked. "Are those duckies on my tie? Yes, they are! Those are duckies!"

My mouth hung open.

The lesson wasn't lost on me. We are each a composite of different roles. Sometimes it can be difficult to make the change between them. Dr. Sadowitz, in his years of experience, mastered the art of switching roles. Outside the door, he was a senior physician pimping me on renal failure. An instant later, he became a clown, gaining the trust of both child and parent. I, too, would adopt multiple roles in the course of my career, and knowing when to turn them on or off is an important skill.

Autumn arrived, turning the verdant foliage into a palette of bright oranges, blazing reds and brilliant yellows. After three years of perpetual summer in the Caribbean, I welcomed the colorful change of season. My student colleagues, however, were less enthusiastic. Geographically, Buffalo sat at the receiving end of a waterfall of precipitation from Lake Erie. In November, I completed pediatrics just as the first snow arrived like an avalanche.

Pediatrics

JOHN PRYOR's performance in Pediatrics was commendable to outstanding in all respects. He demonstrated a very strong knowledge base and was able to effectively apply this to the clinical setting. He was eager to expand his knowledge by reading about his patients' illnesses. His written work showed consistent improvement over the course of this rotation. He was most skillful in drawing blood and starting IVs and most willing to assist others with these duties.

John's clinical evaluators were impressed with his interest in learning and desire to work hard. He is a bright, articulate student who developed a good command of pediatric medicine during the course of this rotation. He consistently approached the patients he was assigned with empathy and professionalism.

His score on the written final examination was 77% (mean score 75%; passing score 65%).

John's final grade in Pediatrics is High Satisfactory.

☙

Christmas 1992. Medical school is such a kick in the balls; you need to focus on getting through each day to succeed. The enormity of it all can be overwhelming, so you look forward to certain milestones. Christmas break gave me a much needed breather, allowing reflection on my accomplishments while focusing on the challenges ahead.

Rich and I headed up to Saratoga to catch up. He finished two years of community college, but instead of transferring into a PA program he decided to complete his bachelor's and apply to medical school.

I knew he'd change his mind.

Carmela came to the house for a visit. I missed her so much; no amount of phone calls or letters could replace her warm embrace. I showed her my town and we drove past Shenendehowa. Then we picked up Rich and went out for dinner. In the coming years, most of my social life outside medicine consisted of the three of us, a triumvirate lasting until the birth of my daughter.

☙

In February, I began Medicine. My previous rotations were interesting but not what I considered career-worthy. Since opening my first New England Journal, I imagined myself as a consulting physician, straining my knowledge and ability to diagnose some mysterious disease tormenting the patient. No such opportunity had presented so far; but now, on the medicine service, I expected a challenge.

I adopted an active role, certain the best way to learn medicine was by practicing, not watching or following. I'd digested four years of the NEJM, aced the boards and gained confidence through previous rotations. It was time to assume a higher role.

I arrived two hours early my first day to read patient charts and familiarize myself with their problems. I learned who needed consults, who was going home, who was going to die and who needed x-rays. I recorded labs, interpreted test results and spoke to the nurses. In short, I assumed control of the medicine service.

When the team gathered, we divvied up the patients, but I closely followed them all. The more patients with whom I became involved, the more I would learn.

My four patients included

- A 72-year-old Black man with a history of adenocarcinoma s/p right hemicolectomy, who presented with shortness of breath, right-sided chest pain, cough with white sputum and itching over his entire body.
- A 38-year-old male with history of diabetes, seizures, alcoholism and hepatitis, who was admitted for seizure and hypoglycemia.
- A 34-year-old alcoholic, hypertensive male with a family history of coronary disease, admitted for chest pain.
- An 80-year-old female with history of COPD, on home oxygen, admitted for productive cough and difficulty breathing.

The rest of the team had similar patients: Diabetes, COPD, chest pain, kidney infections, hyponatremia. The most exciting diagnosis was lupus. So far, no mystery diagnosis, no multiple consults, no esoteric tests sent to Boston.

The routine on Medicine was similar to Pediatrics. During early morning pre-rounds, medical students and interns performed scut work, gathering data, reviewing overnight events and examining patients.

Resident rounds were slow and painful. With glacial speed, we progressed down the hallway, pausing at each doorway as a medical student or intern presented their patient's latest developments. Filing into the patient's room, we watched the resident interview and examine the patient. Back out in the hallway there would be more discussion about the plan before we inched along to the next room.

After resident rounds, we sat for hours, like cloistered monks, scribbling progress notes. Page after page, detailed symptoms, vital signs, lab data, physical findings, consults, and prognosis. Orders were written, and charts were flagged. A steady stream of pages interrupted our work, nurses asking questions, clarifying orders or reporting the slightest abnormalities.

Radiology rounds and noontime conferences provided welcome distractions from the mundane tasks. Rarely, a pharmaceutical lunch provided free pizza or sandwiches.

In the afternoon, the process was repeated. This time, rounds included the attending. Outside each patient room, the attending supervised academic discussions about current research and treatment. These "teaching rounds" are the crux of learning in the third year.

On teaching rounds, we formed a hallway thrombus, huddled around the attending, listening as a fellow third-year presented her first patient.

"This is Mrs. Lee," she began, "51-year-old female with history of CHF and known to be poorly compliant with her medications. She presented with shortness of breath. X-ray showed…"

"Whoa, whoa." The attending held up his hands. "You went from chief complaint right to imaging. This is no way to present a patient.

"Chief complaint, history of present illness, past medical history, past surgical history, medications, allergies, family history, social history. If applicable, travel, work, immunizations. Then differential diagnosis, labs and imaging, assessment and plan."

It was all academic for this particular patient. There was no mystery here. She failed to take her meds, filled up with fluid and wound up in the hospital. Still, each patient will teach you something; you just need to be receptive to the possibility.

"What are the causes of congestive heart failure?" the attending asked.

"Myocardial infarction, atrial fibrillation ..." She drifted. "... not taking her meds ..."

"Not taking medications causes CHF?" he derided.

Humiliated, she fell silent. Moments passed. I restrained myself from speaking out of turn.

"Doctor?" The attending faced the intern.

"Uhh, hypertension, valvular stenosis ...." He gazed at the ceiling. "Thyrotoxicosis ..."

Silence resumed as the intern exhausted his differential list.

"Anyone else?" asked the attending. Students took sudden notice of their shoes.

"Idiopathic cardiomyopathy," I offered, "renal failure, sepsis, myocarditis, chaga's, lupus, transplant rejection, Wegener's, sarcoid, amyloid, Gaucher's ..." I started to run out of ideas. "And beri beri."

The attending gave me a look I was growing accustomed to: eyes squinted, head turned a little to the side, speechless, perplexed. He appeared to be a man robbed of the basis for his argument.

"Hmmph," he managed.

As we followed him into the patient's room, I overheard another student whisper, "I would've never thought of beri beri."

෴

Two weeks into the rotation, Mrs. Lagrone, an admission from the overnight resident, appeared on my list.

"78-year-old female," the overnight resident yawned, "weak, dizzy, losing weight. Would've sent her home, but her blood pressure was in the toilet—probably dry. I would tank her up and decide whether to do a tumor hunt or send her home."

"Any history of previous cancer?" I asked.

"No, just hypothyroid and type II diabetes," he said.

At the computer, I copied lab results on my crib sheet. Mrs.

Lagrone won the prize for most abnormal labs. Her chart contained little information, so I decided to go see her.

The hospital is an impossible place to get any sleep, and I always felt a pang of guilt waking ill, sleep-deprived patients in the pre-dawn darkness.

"Mrs. Lagrone?" I laid a gentle hand on her shoulder. She woke easily and magically rose on the mechanized bed.

"Mrs. Lagrone, I'm John Pryor, one of the medical students. I heard you weren't feeling well …"

"I haven't been feeling well for a year," she said, "but my doctor thinks I'm crazy. Finally, it got so bad I went to the ER."

"What are you feeling?" I asked.

She described her symptoms of fatigue and weakness. Her doctor diagnosed hypothyroidism, but taking synthroid didn't help. Her condition slowly worsened over the months, and she began to lose weight. Over the past few weeks, she began having nausea, vomiting and abdominal pain.

"Did you ever smoke?" I asked. So far, her symptoms could be from cancer.

"No," she said, "never smoked."

"Any family history of cancer?" I persisted.

"I think my grandmother had skin cancer," she said.

"How old was she when she died?"

"In her nineties."

Hmm. No strong family history either. I reviewed her medical history, medications, allergies, family and social history. Nothing helped in making a diagnosis. I moved on to the physical exam.

"Mind if I turn on the light?" I asked.

"No, go ahead."

I pulled the light switch and turned back to the patient. In a flash, I had my diagnosis. My heart raced, and I couldn't hide my smile. I had been waiting for a case worthy of the NEJM.

The wait was over.

"Mrs. Lagrone," I said, softly grasping her arm, "tell me about your skin."

I decided to surreptitiously confirm the diagnosis before attending rounds. Presenting Mrs. Lagrone to the resident, I insinuated her symptoms stemmed from hypothyroidism, a plausible explanation. Thyroid studies had been ordered, I told him.

During the day, I conducted a diagnostic test. While waiting for results, I escaped to the library for a bit of research and photocopying. I wanted to be prepared for attending rounds.

"Next is Mrs. Lagrone," I said, as we stopped in front of her room. "She has Addison's disease."

The attending consulted his notes as the resident glared at me.

"You didn't tell me she had Addison's," the attending said to the resident.

"I diagnosed it this afternoon," I said.

"What makes you think she has Addison's?"

"I'm glad you asked." I distributed my hand-outs to the team. Starting from the top, I presented a complete history of Mrs. Lagrone. Then, my discovery on examination: a deep, golden tan.

"Who has a suntan in Buffalo during the winter?" I asked.

The resident mentally slapped his forehead. Primary adrenal insufficiency stimulates production of ACTH. A by-product of this process is MSH, melanocyte stimulating hormone, causing the skin to tan.

I lectured about Addison's disease—a slow, progressive destruction of the adrenal glands. Decreased production of glucocorticoid and mineralocorticoid steroids manifest with fatigue, weakness, hypotension, weight loss, and GI symptoms.

"Diagnosis is made with the cortico-stim test," I explained; "baseline cortisol level is drawn, then twenty-five units of cosyntropin are given. Repeat cortisol levels are drawn at thirty and sixty minutes. Minimal response should be greater than 200 nmol/L above baseline. She didn't break a hundred.

"I started her on 20 mg Hydrocortisone and .05 mg Fludrocortisone. We need to monitor her electrolytes for a few days and adjust the dose accordingly."

The attending flipped through the chart and reviewed the labs, trying to find a flaw in my diagnosis.

"Hmmph," he muttered.

Finally, he looked up.

"Who co-signed your orders?" he asked.

"Uhhh … What?" I said.

"Students aren't allowed to write orders independently," he said. "Next time, you discuss it with the resident first."

"Yes, sir," I said.

Mrs. Lagrone taught me two things. First, the importance of the physical exam. I perform a complete exam on each of my patients, from head to toe, including a rectal, every time. The resident missed Mrs. Lagrone's diagnosis because he examined her in the dark and didn't identify the skin changes.

Second, I knew what I was doing. For some reason, my knowledge, experience and confidence placed me on a par with the residents. I had *ability*, and I refused to capitulate to the attending simply because I was a student.

My evaluation for medicine arrived in the mail:

Medicine Evaluation

Buffalo General

Mr. Pryor is a very good student who performed well during his four weeks of medicine at Buffalo General Hospital. He was rated at the high satisfactory level by the ward attending, who noted that although Mr. Pryor was clearly above average that he was at times overconfident in some areas, including being overly concise in his initial patient write-ups. He was rated at the honors level by all of the house staff, who felt that he was one of the best third-year students with whom they have worked. His fund of knowledge was extremely advanced for a third-year student, and he was an exceptionally hard worker. He willingly and eagerly participated in code situations utilizing his prior paramedic training appropriately. He was also noted to be well-organized and to show very good clinical judgment.

Overall, it was felt that with further experience he has the potential to become an excellent house officer and is very strongly encouraged to pursue a career in internal medicine.

John Pryor received a grade of Honors.

Erie County Medical Center

John is a very mature, self-directed individual with an exceptional fund of knowledge and an equally exceptional ability to apply his knowledge to the clinical setting.

John functioned as an intern on his service (which was extremely busy). He displayed enthusiasm for medicine and was instrumental in the care of his patients.

John is a well-organized individual. His histories and physicals, as well as his daily progress notes, reflected his organizational skills. His oral presentations were also outstanding. John presented not only the patient in chief of service but also the discussion (Addison's disease).

John is extremely talented and would be a great asset to Internal Medicine.

I laughed at the overconfident accusation. The comment that I functioned as an intern even though I was a third-year student was high praise and boosted my confidence. I was very happy to read that I should pursue a career in internal medicine.

It's always nice to feel wanted.

છ

I completed medicine as Buffalo's tenacious winter finally relented. Lengthening daylight, receding snowbanks and apple blossoms heralded the coming Spring. As I started my surgical rotation, I couldn't help but think it a good omen.

Suspecting my future lay down the surgical path, I approached the rotation with excited trepidation. I elected two of the most demanding specialties, cardiothoracic and pediatric surgery. I would learn everything General surgery had to offer plus gain exposure to two of the most demanding surgical specialties. A strong showing over the next few weeks could determine my future.

Contrasting starkly with medicine, surgery rounds started at 5 a.m. and progressed at lightning speed. Progress notes, reduced to a few lines, got right to the point: Avss, Chest–CLEAR, Heart–RRR, Abd–SOFT NT/ND, Incision C/D/I, Plan–OOB, ADVANCE DIET.

Next.

Surgeons can't afford to spend all day documenting minutia. We have shit to do.

My OR experience in OB/GYN served to prep me for surgery. Returning to the OR was like coming home. Here was a place where things got done. Patients wheel in with a problem and wheel out with the problem solved. Something about the immediacy and definitiveness of surgery appealed to me.

I'll never forget the first time we opened a chest. The skin was incised and retracted exposing bone. Using a sternal saw we sliced open the sternum like a Zip Lock bag. Inserting the retractor, I cranked it open, raising the curtain on our pulsating soloist.

"Ever feel a beating human heart?" the surgeon asked me.

"No," I said.

He gently placed my hand on the heart. Muscular contractions bounced against my palm. The feeling was almost deviant, an aberrant violation of natural law. My hand was *inside the patient's chest!* I have never experienced anything like it since.

After three weeks of cardiothoracic, I returned to the Children's Hospital of Buffalo to begin pediatric surgery. Here, I met Dr. Rob Kelly.

Dr. Kelly impressed me with his incredible diversity as a clinician, a trait seldom seen in medicine these days. Most doctors provide limited care to their patients, deferring to others when a problems lies outside their specialty. Some surgeons consult medicine even for the most mundane blood pressure issues, and social problems are quickly handed off to the social worker.

Dr. Kelly showed me it didn't have to be this way. Yes, he was an outstanding surgeon. But beyond that, he was an outstanding pediatrician, he could practice medicine, and he functioned as a social worker.

He was the complete package.

I worked with Dr. Kelly for only four weeks, but it was enough to change me. When I thought about it, I wanted to be like Dr. Kelly, a surgeon who has utility beyond the operating room.

For seven weeks, I worked my ass off. I was first to arrive and last to leave. Like medicine, I assumed the role of resident and raised my own expectations. Residents and attendings, recognizing my ability, trusted me with increasing responsibilities and autonomy.

When it was over, I looked forward to my surgery evaluation:

Surgical Evaluation
WRITTEN EXAMINATION: 86
ORAL EXAMINATION: Honors
RECOMMENDED GRADE: Honors

The student's recommended grade of Honors is strongly supported by an honors performance in all clinical areas of the course and on the oral examination. This student's clinical experience included rotations at the Buffalo General Hospital and the Children's Hospital of Buffalo.

He demonstrated an outstanding clinical and basic science knowledge base. He was far advanced in his case presentations and assessments of patients. He has an excellent knowledge of patients' clinical problems and contributes on rounds and all patient care issues. He communicates well with the staff and often stimulated conversation and asked probing questions. He was enthusiastic and went above and beyond his responsibility in reading about problems present on this service. These same skills were noted at the Children's Hospital also. He consistently presented patients at an "intern level or better." He knew his patients and had an outstanding ability to grasp the difference between major and minor problems. He is helpful and will be an outstanding role model.

Obviously, this student has no clinical problems. He is at home in the surgical services and functions extremely well. The Department is pleased to recommend a grade of Honors for this outstanding student. We recommend he continue his present level of development and would be happy to support his candidacy for postgraduate training in any clinical area. We certainly suggest he seek a career in Surgery in view of his outstanding ability demonstrated in this course.

I felt honored. Seven weeks. Such a short time on the scale of life, but what a significant change in my life! I could be a surgeon if I chose. One particular line made me swell with pride: "I would be an outstanding role model." I couldn't help but think back to my discussion with Narmer at Columbia. It was too early to consider myself a mentor, but now I could see it happening.

The end of surgery marked the completion of third year. I came home for a few weeks and helped Rich fill out his medical school applications. Excited for him, I couldn't help but think my success influenced his decision.

"You suck," I told him, looking over his transcript.

"What?" he asked.

"You're totally gonna get in," I said. "I had to suffer in Grenada."

"I saw Grenada," he said; "it didn't look like suffering to me."

"Yeah, well you didn't have to go to class in hundred-degree weather without showering because there was no water."

"You don't shower even if there is water," he said.

"That's not the point."

❧

I missed my little fungus. During summer break, I was able to see her, but it wasn't enough. The past year had been difficult, separated by hundreds of miles and preoccupied with the demands of our clinical rotations. Through it all, my feelings for Carmela never dimmed, and I fully expected our relationship to continue during residency.

"I think we should couples match," I said to her.

Couples-matching is a process where two people intertwine their fate to obtain residencies in the same location.

"Don't you think we should have more of a *commitment* first?"

"What do you mean?" I asked, knowing exactly what she meant.

"I'm not going to follow you in a couples match as boyfriend-girlfriend?"

"Why?" I asked. "Why not?"

"Because what if we break up?" she asked.

I knew she wanted to get married. Emotionally, I felt the same, but I was a male, and my Y chromosome disabled the speech center of the brain from articulating the word "Marriage."

Really, it's true! I learned about it in neuroscience.

This issue came to a head when a distant relative died and Carmela asked me to attend the funeral. I could see if it were her mother or some close family member, but this was her cousin's-father-in-law-once-removed. I didn't see the point.

"I'm not going," I said. "You don't need me there."

"Then, I'm not couples matching with you," she said; "if you can't be here for me, then I don't see how I can make a commitment with you."

I realized there was no way out of this. The only way to keep her as my girlfriend was to ask her to marry me.

Carmela comes from a traditional Italian family, and I had to approach things in similar tradition. The next break between rotations, I drove to Brooklyn. While Carmela was at school, I knocked on her parent's door.

Inside, I sat trembling with Franco and Pauletta at the kitchen table. After coffee and small talk, I settled on the purpose of my visit.

"Mr. Calvo," I said, clearing my throat, "I came here to ask for your daughter's hand in marriage."

He beamed with delight.

❧

Only a few months into my fourth year, I was forced to make the most important decision of my life: Who I was going to be.

One does not become a doctor in medical school. Doctors are made in residency. Residency is an apprenticeship of gradually increasing responsibility. At the end, one is prepared to function as an independent physician or surgeon. The time had come for me to choose which residency, or specialty, to pursue.

I narrowed the decision between internal medicine and surgery.

Looking back, I can't remember if I was honestly conflicted or lacked confidence and wanted to cover all my bases.

In medicine I liked the diagnostics, creating a differential list and thinking about the diagnosis. The fun was in the detective work. A lot of this came from reading the NEJM. But the cases in the NEJM are *The Cases of The New England Journal*. These cases are, by definition, difficult and fascinating. Day-to-day medicine, however, is much more mundane—mostly diabetes, CHF and COPD. The most interesting case was Mrs. Lagrone's Addison's disease. I realized my career would never be like the NEJM.

Alright, Let's Call It A Draw

Sitting at the computer, I began a personal statement for medicine:

Medicine Personal Statement

I wanted to expand on some aspects of my experiences that convinced me to choose Medicine as a career. The first is my involvement in prehospital care as a paramedic. I spent a lot of time and energy as a volunteer paramedic, both for my home and college community. Being a part of emergency services for nine years has been much more than an activity; it has been a way of life. What I enjoyed most about being a medic was having the confidence to act calmly and effectively in horribly chaotic situations. Perhaps the most unpleasant aspect was seeing untimely death, usually young, healthy victims of trauma.

I stopped at the word "trauma."

Memories of my trauma patients surfaced. Chaos at the scene, the smell of blood, desperately searching for a vein, tossing around in the back of a wailing ambulance, mayhem in the trauma bay and Dr. Fortune calmly in control of the resuscitation.

Rotating in the emergency room, I learned the next steps: chest tubes, DPL, x-rays, resuscitation. Then what? Then the patient is whisked away to the OR, where the real magic happened. If I pursued medicine, I would never know that final step, the complete care of the trauma patient.

On introspection, I recognized the signs: The epiphany in Binghamton—*These are the Hands of a Surgeon*; my enthusiasm teaching anatomy in Grenada, and the excitement I felt treating trauma patients as a paramedic. I enjoyed fast paced critical patients, fixing things, and getting tasks done. This is a surgeon's personality.

This was my personality.

The clincher was envisioning my mentors, the people I wanted to emulate. As a new EMT, I looked up to Mike, Dwight and Kevin and thought, I want to be like them some day. Now, I thought of the type of doctor I wanted to be. Dr. Fortune, Dr. Kelly and Dr. Hassett came to mind.

All were surgeons.

I opened a new document and began again.

Surgery Personal Statement

The decision to pursue a career in Surgery was a difficult one for me because there are many aspects of both Medicine and Surgery that I enjoy. In the final analysis, however, I believe that my interests and talents are best suited for a career in Surgery. I am looking for a solid program that has a real commitment to house staff education. In my conversations with several surgeons over the past few months, the program here in Buffalo has consistently been highly regarded.

My experience in health care began in high school when I joined a local volunteer ambulance corps and became an Emergency Medical Technician. During my college years at Binghamton, I continued riding with a volunteer squad and trained at night to become a Paramedic. I spent many hours every week on the ambulance, often neglecting the enormous workload of a biochemistry major. It was in my senior year that I knew I wanted to become a physician and combine the science I was learning in school with the patient care I was providing in the community.

Unfortunately, I finished college with less than a competitive grade point average and was not accepted to medical school. My friends and family, knowing my dedication to becoming a doctor, were not surprised when I told them of my plans to attend St. George's University in Grenada, West Indies. Living outside the country, especially in a Third World nation, is an experience that I will never regret. I was a very serious student for those first two years and was pleased to score in the 95th percentile on Part I of the USMLE. I was even more pleased to accept a third-year transfer position at the State University of New York at Buffalo.

In the two years between college and medical school, I was able to spend time in research and administration. I spent a year as a full-time research assistant at the Columbia University College of Physicians and Surgeons as a member of the atherosclerosis research team. Although I would have liked to stay longer, I was offered a very exciting position at the Albany Medical Center Hospital. As Director of the Remote Central Monitoring Station, I was responsible for the development and supervision of a unit that continually monitored EKG telemetry from more than sixty beds throughout the hospital I continued volunteering as a paramedic and had the opportunity to develop several teaching conferences including "Topics in Pediatric Advanced Life Support" with Martin Eichelberger, M.D. of the Children's National Medical Center.

Objectively, I would consider myself mature and self-directed. I enjoy solving complex problems and making difficult decisions. There are times in medicine to be warm and compassionate and times to be assertive and strong. I feel comfortable with both aspects. Those close to me say that I can be stubborn and strict at times, flippant and childish at others. I am extremely dedicated in the hospital, but I also believe that there is much more to life than a career.

The future for John Pryor looks exciting. I want to remain academic, teach and do some research. As of now, I am interested in General Surgery with an emphasis on trauma and critical care. I have a special interest in information management and would like to be on the leading edge of integrating computers into the daily lives of physicians. My free time will be spent with my very special fiancée Carmela, a gifted future pediatrician and my partner in the couples match. I look forward to meeting with the faculty on a formal basis this winter. Thank you for taking time to review these comments.

Still uncommitted, I applied to both Medicine and Surgical programs. Keeping them separate was logistically very difficult. Over the next few weeks, I interviewed at many programs. Dusting off my suit, I wandered the halls of unfamiliar hospitals, listening to residents detail their program's strengths.

In January, Carmela and I traveled to Boston for interviews. Rich forged through a blizzard to meet us at Boston University School of Medicine. Afterward, he brought us to "Joe's" on Newbury Street for dinner.

"How's school going?" I asked, cradling my beer.

"It sucks," he said. "Each day I bounce between two negative poles. I can't stand being at home, so I drive to school. At SUNY, I spend the entire day without speaking to another soul. Finally, I get sick of being there and drive home."

It was hard to see him depressed.

"You're still going out with Karen?" Carmela asked.

"Yeah …" he sighed, "Karen's great; she's my best friend; but, I don't know, I just can't commit to her 100 percent. Know what I mean?"

"Any word from medical schools?"

"I got interviews for Albany Med, NY Med and Mt. Sinai," he said, "still waiting from four others."

"Look, it's gonna be okay," I said. "Just keep your head down and get the work done. In a few months, you'll be in medical school and it'll be a whole new world."

"Yeah, I guess," he said. "I don't have a lot of hope that I'll get in."

"You can't go in with that attitude," I told him. "You've got to remain positive."

"I know," he said. "I'll try."

❧

January 1994. Albany Medical Center had changed little in the few years I'd been away, but walking past the pillars I entered an unfamiliar hospital. No longer a paramedic or an administrator, I was now part of the patient care team, the doctor team, an exclusive club that wielded power yet bore ultimate responsibility.

I wore my new role like a costume; nurses and staff I had worked with failed to recognize me.

I chose a visiting surgical clerkship to broaden my experience and spend time at home for a month. That and a slew of psychiatrists would suggest I wanted to validate my ability at the school that rejected me twice.

I found my surgical team on morning rounds. My chest started to flutter when Dr. Fortune joined us. It was like meeting a rock star.

"I'm... I'm John Pryor," I stammered, "I used to deliver trauma patients to you from Clifton Park."

"Really?" he said.

"Yeah, I also attended trauma conference when I worked here."

He tried to place me, but I was a nameless face in the crowd.

"Well," he said, "it's good to have you aboard."

I assumed responsibility for more than my share of patients plus the overnight admission. During the day, I managed the floors and consults while the team went to the OR. Near the end of the day, I was called to the ER for a consult. I walked down and searched the nurses' station for the patient's chart.

"Hi, John," one of the nurses said. I looked up trying in vain to recognize her. A moment later, I realized she was speaking to the resident who appeared by my side; his name was John, too.

"This is Mr. Carpenter," I told the resident. "Fifty-three-year-old male who presented to the ER with fever and right upper abdominal pain. Ultrasound shows a hot gallbladder."

I followed the resident into the room. He reviewed his history and confirmed my exam.

"He needs a scar," he said. "Can you get him set up for the OR? I'll tell Fortune we have an add-on."

I took care of the scut work: calling the OR, signing consents, ordering pre-op labs and x-rays. I rolled him to pre-op holding for anesthesia evaluation. When the room opened up, we wheeled him in.

Anesthesia put him down, and I prepped the abdomen—soapy sponges followed by three coats of betadine.

"What size gloves?" the scrub nurse asked.

"Eight," I said and walked out to scrub.

I returned to the OR, donned my gown and gloves, and, lacking an attending or a resident, enlisted the scrub nurse to help me unfold the sterile drapes.

A few minutes later, Dr. Fortune backed into the OR, hands dripping.

"Oh, John, you're here," he said. "Are we ready?"

"Yeah," I said, omitting the obvious lack of a resident.

Dr. Fortune tied off his gown, approached the opposite side of the patient and adjusted the light.

"Ok," he said. "Knife to John."

The scrub nurse exchanged a confused glance with the circulating nurse, who shrugged her shoulders. The scalpel was offered to me.

I need to stop here and explain something.

Medical students don't operate.

Maybe in fiction or on television or in the movies they do, but not in real life. Medical students are at the bottom of a hierarchical totem that starts with the attending, descends to senior residents, then junior residents and finally the intern. Medical students are underground somewhere. Students are permitted to observe and hold retractors. If they're lucky, they're allowed to trim sutures or suck some blood. The absolute best-case scenario for a student is to suture skin closure under the watchful eye of the resident.

As the moment stretched, many thoughts quickly bubbled through my brain. Perhaps Dr. Fortune considered me special because of my paramedic experience. Maybe it was a test. Maybe this is how they do things in Albany. Maybe he was simply allowing me the first incision.

None seemed plausible.

I didn't stop to ask. I didn't consider the consequences if I screwed up. Mostly, I thought that I was ready.

Cold steel cooled my palm, I pulled skin taught and I sliced into the abdomen. Skin opened like a large mouth bass, and Dr. Fortune cauterized the bleeders. We dissected down to peritoneum.

"Metzenbaum," I said holding out my hand. The scissors slapped into my hand. I cut through the peritoneum.

"Umm, hmm," Dr. Fortune said.

"Rigby," I said. Inserting the retractor, I adjusted light into the field. Liver and bowel were retracted, revealing a swollen, gangrenous gallbladder. It looked like a grenade about to go off.

Dr. Fortune gently lifted the gallbladder cephalad above the liver.

I identified Calot's triangle containing the hepatic artery and hepatic duct—two structures not to be fucked with. Identifying the cystic duct, I bluntly dissected it free from surrounding tissue.

"Umm, hmm," Dr. Fortune again indicated his approval.

With the cystic duct free, I tied two ligatures, one proximal and one distal. Holding up the duct, Dr. Fortune cut between the ligatures. I then identified the cystic artery ...

The door banged open. I looked up to see the resident backing into the OR.

"Sorry I'm late ..." his voice trailed off as he turned to see the operation in progress.

A moment of awkward silence descended as Dr. Fortune looked between me and the resident.

"John?" he asked the resident.

"Yeah," he said.

Dr. Fortune turned to me.

"Then who the hell are you?" he asked.

"I'm John *Pryor*," I explained, "the fourth-year student,"

He blinked as the situation sank in.

"Well," he finally said, "you certainly fooled me!"

∞

In January, Carmela and I submitted our rank order list—the list of residency programs we desired to attend, ranked in order of preference. In March, a computer would compare our list to the list submitted by residency programs and "match" students to programs all over the country.

Complicating the process, Carmela and I participated in couples matching. The computer examined four sets of variables instead of two. If either of us didn't match in the same location, then the computer would move on to the next choice.

My list reflected my indecision about specialties:

1. Surgery – Boston University
2. Surgery – Buffalo
3. Surgery – Emory
4. Medicine – Columbia

5. Medicine – New York University
6. Medicine – UMass Medical Center
7. Surgery – Rochester

I didn't think we would fall below our third choice; if I did, the match would not only choose my location, but my specialty as well.

ℰℛ

In February, I spent a month on the nephrology service at Buffalo General. I was lucky to have another case worthy of the NEJM, although it was too little to make me think of changing my rank order list.

Mr. Denier was a sixty-four-year-old homeless alcoholic admitted for renal failure. This was his third admission for renal failure, but no one could figure out why. A large part of the problem was that nobody cared why a homeless drunk had renal failure. He was admitted, his labs normalized and he was discharged.

End of story.

But he kept coming back. There was something more going on, and I figured it out, not because I was super smart, but because I asked the most important question:

Why?

Turns out Mr. Denier had hepatitis C. This was well known. However, patients with hepatitis C can form abnormal proteins, known as cryoglobulins, which coagulate in cold temperatures. Once formed, cryoglobulins can clog the kidney, resulting in renal failure. When the body rewarms, the proteins liquefy, the clogs resolve and the kidney function is restored. Each time Mr. Denier was sent back to the wintery Buffalo streets, his proteins would coagulate and cause his kidneys to fail. In the hospital, he warmed up and got better.

"Who," the attending asked, "ordered cryoglobulins?" He looked at the chief resident.

"That would be Pryor," the resident admitted.

"Who the hell is Pryor?" he asked. "An off-service resident?"

"No," the resident pointed to me. "He's the medical student."

The attending found my face in the group.

"You mean a *medical student* figured this out?"

"Well," the resident explained, "not just any medical student …"
I couldn't help but smile.

&

In the Spring of 1994, my life began to coalesce.

I sat for Step 2 of the boards, emerging from the test with doubt about the proverb *Two Years for Step 1, Two Months for Step 2 and Bring a No. 2 Pencil for Step 3*. The test was difficult, but when the results came in, I landed in the 87th percentile. Later that week, I was inducted into Alpha Omega Alpha, the Phi Beta Kappa of medical schools.

Then, on March 17, I assembled with fellow students, faculty and staff for the most significant day of my life. Across the country, fourth-year medical students at similar gatherings waited anxiously. At precisely 1 p.m., EST, envelopes containing match results were distributed. I held my envelope for a few moments, turning it over in my hand. Another Schrödenger's cat: I am a surgeon in Boston, an internist in Columbia, a surgeon in Atlanta, an internist at UMass.

Around me, students tore their envelopes; delighted girls screamed excitedly and hugged; the guys shouted or pumped the air. I took a deep breath and tore mine open, collapsing all waveforms into one single reality:

Congratulations! You have matched.

- John Pryor   Categorical   Surgery   SUNY Buffalo
- Carmela Calvo   Categorical   Pediatrics   SUNY Buffalo

It figured.

I felt a little deflated for not getting into Boston, but Buffalo was a solid program. They would train me to become a great surgeon.

Years later, I learned the match isn't as objective as I thought. Programs are run by physicians who usually know each other. A few phone calls among directors, and selection is reduced to the process like children divvied up for a game of kickball. I think Buffalo didn't want to give me up.

&

In April, I stopped home before heading to New York City to meet Carmela. I showed Rich the ring.

"Oh, man," he said, "you're really going to do it?"

"Yeah, she's been hounding me," I said. "I figure this will buy me some more time."

He threw back his head and laughed.

"Yeah," he said, "asking her to marry you will get her off your back alright."

A funny thing occurs to me as I think back. I never explicitly asked Rich to be my best man. I think we both naturally assumed it.

I met Carmela at her house in Brooklyn. After a visit with her family, we rode the subway into Manhattan. After lunch, we walked to Central Park.

Enticing sunshine from a cloudless sky breathed life into the park. Rollerbladers and joggers competed with pedestrians along Terrace Drive.

Holding hands, we strolled the paths, finding our way to Bethesda Fountain. An angelic statue appeared to float against a sapphire sky as cardinals and mourning doves fluttered in the breeze. The angel stood poised, blessing the water, giving it healing powers, before it cascaded down to the reflecting pool. Warm sun on our faces, the fragrance of spring, cascading water trickling in the background, laughter of children splashing the water, sparrows and warblers bathing in the fountain—what a perfect day.

"Isn't this romantic?" she asked.

"Very," I agreed.

"This would be a great place to get engaged," she said.

I kept my mouth shut but couldn't suppress a smile. My fingers felt the small box deep inside my pocket.

"Let's go sit by the water," I suggested.

We walked over to the lake's edge. I palmed the box before sitting. For some reason, I wasn't nervous. I couldn't help but feel we were meant for each other, our fate inexorably entwined.

"Carmela?" I said turning to face her; my tone became serious.

"What?" she looked at me nervously.

I held up the little velvet box. She raised trembling hands to her mouth.

"Carmela," I opened the box; the ring sparkled in the sunlight. "Will you marry me?"

Throwing her arms around me, I felt her shaking. She pulled back smiling, wiping her eyes.

"Yes," she said through a sniffle. She took the ring. "Yes, of course, I'll marry you."

She placed the ring on her finger and looked at it. Then she kissed me, and we embraced again.

"I love you," I whispered in her ear.

"I love you, too."

∽

Graduation weekend, May 20, 1994.

Rich, Carmela and my parents came out for the festivities: a lavish banquet Friday night with an awards ceremony and graduation the next day.

At the apartment, my parents presented me with their graduation gift. Thanking them, I pulled out a Lladro ceramic sculpture of a bearded physician in deep contemplation.

"Thanks," I said again.

"Here," Rich said, handing me a gift-wrapped box, "I got you something you might actually use."

Ripping off the wrapping, I was surprised he got me something so expensive.

"What? A cell phone?"

"Wave of the future," he said. "Soon everyone will have one."

At the time, I didn't think I would use it much. After a few weeks as an intern, however, I couldn't imagine life without it. From then on, the cell phone bound me to the hospital like no previous generation of physician could imagine.

Friday was also the day my new car was delivered. After lunch, my parents drove me to the dealership where staff welcomed me to the Saturn family. A Polaroid was taken and added to the wall of satisfied Saturn customers. I drove off the showroom floor to the cheerful applause of Saturn employees.

Thirteen miles later, the vehicle sputtered, coughed and died. I silently rolled it to the shoulder as my parents parked behind me. What followed next prompted a letter to the president of Saturn Corporation:

June 26, 1994

Richard G. LeFauve
President, Saturn Corporation
P.O. Box 7008
Troy, Michigan 48007 -7008

Dear Mr. LeFauve:

I am writing to express my deep dissatisfaction with a purchase of one of your automobiles.

Having recently graduated from medical school, I was looking forward to making my first car purchase.

I was attracted to your company because of what I felt was a sincere commitment to service and because it provided a reliable product. On May 20, the day before graduation and the night of the graduation gala, I drove off the Saturn dealership lot with a brand new SLI. It was four o'clock.

I drove exactly thirteen miles when, at a stop light, the car bucked and stopped. The car rolled, unresponsive to the accelerator, and it was soon obvious that it was not functional. Ironically, the incident occurred directly in front of the banquet hall where the graduation Gala was to be held at six-thirty that evening. My parents were following behind, en route to their hotel room to change for the dinner. It was now four-thirty.

I decided to stay with the vehicle while my father went to call for assistance. Having left the dealership less than a half-hour earlier, he decided to call the sales associate who had just sold us the car. He explained the situation to the associate, who being inexperienced with such situations consulted the sales manager. The sales associate came back to the phone and said, "call the 800 service number." There was no initial effort to send a car for us, help us contact the 800 number, or help us get roadside assistance. The reaction of the sales team infuriated my father—I think rightfully so. It was now five-thirty.

We contacted the 800 number, which dispatched a tow service with an estimated arrival time of one hour. We waited outside the hotel room for an hour with no sign of assistance. My father recontacted the dealership and got no answer, not even an answering machine. If we were once part of the Saturn family, we were now orphans. As we made calls on the pay phone from inside the banquet hall, dressed in blue jeans and T-shirts, the guests began to arrive around us for the dinner. It was now six-thirty.

We recontacted the 800 number operator, who thought of the idea to leave the car keys at the banquet hall so that we could leave to get dressed and still make the dinner that we paid $250.00 to attend. We were grateful for that assistance. The car was eventually picked up as we prepared for dinner. We arrived at eight o'clock at the affair, tired and incredibly irritated.

Mr. Lefauve, it was not a good night for one of your dealership people to make such mistakes. The dinner that night had more than six hundred professionals, doctors, lawyers, and businessmen in attendance. Because dinner was held up for us, the news quickly spread about our day with the Saturn "people," and I don't believe that there was a person in that hall by the end of the night who didn't hear about the disaster that took place that day. It was midnight, and we went home.

The next business day, I meet with the dealership people, who were extremely apologetic. They stated that they had sent a car to us eventually, but that it never found us. I returned the car promptly. The dealership made honest efforts to replace the vehicle at my convenience. It even offered to drive a new one out to Albany, where I was going to be for the next few weeks. However, it was all too little too late.

Had the story ended there, I never would have bothered writing to you. However, to my amazement, the saga continued. Shortly after returning the car, I received a package of cookies from the dealership. I thought, "Oh, isn't this nice, a little gift to say sorry that things didn't work out with the car." Instead, the note inside is thanking me for buying a Saturn. Then I received information of the Saturn homecoming: "Hope you can make it!" More than three weeks later, I received a letter from Jeff Stacey, again thanking me for buying the car, etc. Not once have I received a letter from anyone either explaining what happened to the car, why we were treated so poorly on the 8th, or even, "Sorry that things didn't work out." At first, I thought perhaps your records were somehow incorrect and that I was still listed as an owner. But today, I have a letter again from Mr. Stacey asking me to "... Please return the Saturn Ownership Key." It was the final insult that prompted me to write this involved letter, one that I am convinced will never even cross your desk, Mr. LeFauve.

A poor effort and a poor result. Thank you for your time,

John P. Pryor, MD
SUNY at Buffalo Graduate Medical and Dental Consortium

On Saturday, we attended the awards ceremony, where I was presented with the John R. Paine Award for Excellence in Surgery. Graduation was held in the Center for the Arts, on the North Campus. Zipping up a flowing gown and donning the floppy hat, I sat among the graduation class, listening to speeches of increasingly important people.

Graduation from medical school is a bit of a mixed bag. From the outside, one would assume it is a tremendous accomplishment. I struggled for years to achieve this goal, and it was about to become a reality.

I should be ecstatic.

But, enmeshed in the medical culture as a student, I realized I stood at the beginning of a continuum of learning that stretches through residency, possibly fellowship, and long into one's career. Awarding of the medical degree is barely the first step in the process.

The speeches concluded, and we began to line up.

"Dr. John Pryor," the speaker announced.

I climbed the stage and accepted my diploma to enthusiastic applause.

There was no epiphany that I was now a doctor. Through third and fourth year, I assumed the role of physician and tried to act accordingly. The diploma felt like a technicality. I was proud and felt a sense of accomplishment, but as far as feeling like a physician, I was already there.

The best feeling was reflected in the smiles of my parents. I was happy to make them so proud. In their eyes, I had made it; I was now a doctor.

I knew better. This was not an end but the beginning. I now stood at the base of a huge mountain called residency. It would take five years to climb. At this point, I couldn't imagine the summit.

But I knew it was there.

Surgical Residency

M r. Ward?" I gently shook the old man's bony shoulder. Snooz-
ing, head arched back, his gaping 'O' shaped mouth revealed a
dry, toothless cavity. Sometimes they slept so soundly I wondered if
it were a code. I glanced at the medical student before trying again.

"Mr. Ward?" I shook a bit more vigorously.

"Uh?" he grunted, slowly opening his eyes and smacking cracked
lips

"Mr. Ward, it's Dr. Pryor," I said, "I looked at the angiogram; it
looks like we need to amputate your leg."

"Okay doc," he coughed, "whatever you think."

Captain James Ward, World War II veteran, survivor of the Normandy Invasion, closed his eyes, and returned to a dream world infinitely more pleasant than the dark, gloomy reality surrounding him.

I stood over him in a bit in an awkward silence until I realized
there was nothing else to say. The student followed me into the hallway.

"Well," she said, "that went pretty well."

"That's how it is at the VA (Veterans Administration)," I explained,
"no questions, no arguments, no 'what else can we try?' Just 'okay,
Doc.' It's kinda amazing."

"Wonder why that is," she said.

"These guys are all military, so they know how to take orders," I said, as we walked the hallway. "They come from an era when doctors weren't questioned, and, let's face it, most are at the end; their friends are gone. It's pretty much 'game over', so they're not so concerned about what happens to them anymore."

"I guess … still seems odd though," she said. "Tell someone you're taking their leg, and they just shrug and say, 'Ok.'" She shook her head.

"Reminds me of a joke," I said with a smile. "What do you call a patient at the VA with two legs?"

"What?" she asked, cringing.

"Pre-op!"

She tried not to laugh.

"Thanks for going over the angio," she said. "I couldn't get a hold of my resident."

"No problem," I said. "Order all the pre-op stuff, EKG, CXR, and book him for the OR tomorrow. I've got to get back to the unit."

"By the way," she said, "I should let you know, students started circulating your pager number. I was told, 'When all else fails, call Pryor, even if he's off-service at another hospital; he'll call you back and tell you what to do.'"

"That's funny," I said with a smile. "It explains why I get so many pages."

The Buffalo VA had changed little since the Kennedy administration, and the ICU showed its age—fading paint peeling from the walls, worn paths in the tile, a nurses' station with rotary phones and a tattered patchwork of reference numbers under glass blotters.

Individual patient rooms surrounded the nurses' station. Each bed bore a moribund veteran buried under a multitude of tubes and wires. DEATH meandered impatiently; his efforts constantly thwarted by a ventilator, IV medications and me.

The ICU doors opened, and a new patient was wheeled in. Staff moved him into the last empty room. A medical student squeezed the BVM while a nurse maneuvered two IV poles. A small flurry ensued as IVs were secured, vent was set up and the monitor was attached. I approached the bedside next to the senior resident.

"Eighty-two-year-old male, three-vessel bypass," the senior resident yawned. His eyes were at half mast as he handed over the chart.

"Don't let his pressure get too high; don't let his pressure get too low. I got another case." He turned and walked away.

Great sign out, I thought facetiously.

I reviewed the chart at bedside as the staff finished settling him in. He had good lung sounds. Just a hint of pink blushed beneath the sternotomy pads. Heart sounds clear. JP drains were half full. Abdomen was soft. Foley was draining with good urine output. Toes were pink. The monitor plugged along at eighty. The BP cuff cycled and displayed: 140/90.

I scribbled my findings in a post-op note and moved on to the next room.

Working in the ICU is like playing 'whack a mole.' Your time is spent bouncing from patient to patient, juggling various problems in attempts to keep everyone alive until morning. Just as one problem is solved, another arises; if you're not fast enough, problems become overwhelming.

Then you're screwed.

It was an hour before I returned to the post-op patient.

"How's he doing?" I asked the nurse while scanning the bedside flow sheet.

"No problems," she replied. "Heart rate is up a bit, but probably from pain. I just medicated him."

True, the heart rate was up, but the blood pressure was down to 120/70. I expected the pressure to be higher if the increased heart rate was from pain.

Huh, I thought, *still within normal limits, though.*

I moved on to a patient with a clotted central line. Changing out the line took twenty minutes. Just as I finished, the nurse came in.

"Could you come look at the post-op heart?" she said.

"What?" I asked.

"He's not doing so well," she said.

Shit! I sutured the line in place and covered it with tegaderm. Leaving the mess, I walked directly to the post-op patient.

Pulse 120, pressure down to 90, urine output dropped off. Vent pressures still normal. I examined the patient: lung sounds clear, heart sounds muffled, JP drains empty, and toes now blue.

"What're his sats?" I asked, looking up at the monitor.

"Ninety, but not a good waveform," replied the nurse. "Maybe you should call the resident."

"Yeah, let's increase the FiO_2 on the vent and hang dopamine; start it at ten micrograms." I wrote the orders and headed for the nurses' station.

I paged my senior.

"I'm up to my elbows in a chest," he said while a nurse held the phone to his ear. "What's his pressure?"

"Ninety," I said. "I'm hanging dopamine, but that's not the problem."

An exasperated sigh said it all: The patient's crapping out in front of a clueless intern.

"Listen," he said, "I'll be there as soon as I can, DON'T DO ANYTHING, okay? Up the dopamine but ..."

"He's got a tamponade," I interrupted. "The drains are empty, and his heart sounds ..."

"I know," he said. "I'll be there as soon as I can. Don't go near that incision. Understand?"

Most interns would welcome this command. An elderly man, fresh from open heart surgery, losing his blood pressure and turning blue—not something an intern is ready to handle. When told to wait and do nothing, most interns would obey without question.

"Right." I hung up and met the gaze of the ICU charge nurse. "The attending wouldn't be in the hospital, would he?"

"Attending?" she asked? "What's that?"

"That's what I thought," I said. "Get me the thoracotomy tray."

She didn't budge. "What'd the fellow say?" She folded her arms.

"He said if the pressure continues to drop," I lied, "that I should open the chest."

"Interns don't do that here," she said.

"We'll just get things set up, then," I said.

Satisfied with this approach, she retrieved the thoracotomy tray.

I returned to the bedside. DEATH's undivided attention was focused on the patient. Heart rate now 180, blood pressure 60; ashen blue fingers made sats unmeasurable.

I removed the dressing, exposed the incision site, and swabbed it with betadine. Donning a gown and sterile gloves, I opened the thoracotomy tray. While selecting forceps and scissors, the nurse confronted me.

"What are you doing?" she asked.

I paused.

"Look at him," I said, "you wanna watch him die waiting for the resident, or do you want to help me?"

The nurse bit her lip at the monitor and weighed her options.

"They clip the bottom wire for a pericardial window ..." she advised.

Cutting subcutaneous sutures, I opened the skin. Flesh parted without bleeding. A row of metal wires ran down the sternum, twisty tie ends folded flat against the bone.

"Wire cutters," I said.

The nurse donned sterile gloves and handed me the wire cutters. "You've done this before?" she asked hopefully.

"Uhh, I've *seen* it done ..." I clipped the lower sternal wire, allowing an opening. A small amount of blood evacuated, but not what I expected.

We all looked up at the monitor. There was no change.

"It's probably all clot ..." I said.

I need to open him up, I thought.

I snipped each wire as the nurse shifted her weight uneasily.

"I need the retractor," I said. The nurse handed it over, and I parted the chest like an open book.

Such a scene is expected in the operating room, but in the ICU, it seemed wholly unnatural: Chest split wide, a beating heart visible to any passerby.

I scooped out a large clot that was strangling the ventricles. Like throwing a switch, his blood pressure and pulse jumped to normal. Within seconds, the extremities turned pink and his sats returned to normal. DEATH wandered away, foiled but not defeated.

"Stop the dopamine," I told the nurse, "and I need some better light."

With the clot removed, I went after the culprit: Somewhere a bleeding vessel was causing trouble. A portable light was wheeled over, shining into the field so I could see.

"You got 3-0 silk and a driver?"

Handed the instrument and suture, I isolated the bleeder and tied it off. A few pats with a surgical sponge showed no reaccumulation of blood. Satisfied, I removed the retractor and approximated the sternum. I placed a sterile sheet and taped fresh dressing in place. The patient would need to go back the OR for a proper closure.

The resident arrived about five minutes later, slightly panicked and a little out of breath. He observed normal vital signs on the monitor. The patient looked fine.

"False alarm?" he asked.

I looked at him with surprise. "Not quite," I said, glancing at the open thoracotomy tray.

"What the fuck did you do?" he asked.

I just saved his life, I hoped.

ℰℐ

After graduation Carmela joined me in Buffalo and rented a one-bedroom flat in the same apartment complex. Franco, Carmela's father, sent a clear message when he purchased Carmela's child-sized bed. It didn't matter that we were engaged or that we were doctors, we weren't to sleep together until after the wedding. I solved that problem by lugging my queen-sized mattress over to her apartment. It was removed when her parents came to visit.

On July 1, 1994, I began my surgical residency. Walking into Buffalo General that first day was like sitting in a roller coaster, poised at its zenith, just as it's loosed into free fall. My gut actually tickled with nervous excitement.

I worried about fitting in. I have a fear of meeting people and being embarrassed. I'm very self-conscious about what people think about me and what people say about me. It's part of what drives me to be good, gracious and friendly. But it's also insecurity that goes back to when I was a kid and not being accepted on the playground. I wanted to be a great doctor, but I also wanted to be liked. I wanted my peers and co-workers to respect me, but if I had to choose, I'd rather be liked than respected.

I hoped to accomplish both.

I also worried about first impressions. In medical school, I picked up the folkways of medical culture. Residents gossiped in whispers, and I realized how easy it was to pick up a reputation, either good or bad. I remember one intern placed an NG tube into the trachea by mistake. The nurse delivered 50 milliliters of Ensure into the lungs before it was discovered. The intern wasn't a bad guy; he just fucked up. But from then on, he was the idiot who drowned a man with tube feeds.

It's hard to recoup from such a stigma.

My program organized into three teams, one team taking call each night. Being on call every third day left only one day in three that I wasn't either on call or post call. After a few weeks, I learned what this *meant*.

Each step in becoming a doctor is more difficult than the last by several orders of magnitude. First-year classes made getting in seem easy. Basic sciences were difficult until I hit the floors. Now residency makes medical school seem like a vacation.

Describing residency is like writing about sex: I can tell you about it, but you won't really understand unless you've done it. Residency is an apprenticeship consisting of rounds, operating, lectures, and conferences. But the bane of residency is *call*.

An admixture of sleep deprivation, uncertainty, and boredom punctuated by moments of sheer terror, surgery call is epitomized by the dictum, "Eat when you can, sleep when you can, and don't fuck with the pancreas."

It hurts.

It's painful.

Forced, it would be considered torture.

But the process toughens you, forcing you to mature, to change. There is no alternative. The pounding is necessary, else the sword cannot be forged. If you ever wonder about the difference between a nurse and surgeon or a PA and a surgeon, the answer is simple: Five years of being on call.

After twelve hours in the hospital, you begin call around 6 p.m.

with sign out from the other two teams. Almost immediately, your pager beeps; nurses pepper you with queries on patients you've never met.

Armed with metaphorical helmet and extinguisher, you embark on hospital rounds, putting out fires and checking off items on your scut list. Operating, rounds and admissions cluttered daylight hours, but at night there is time to change dressings, place a central line or pull a chest tube.

Finally, you can get shit done.

Every night on call is different. Some nights are slower than others, but generally scut keeps you busy well past midnight. Er consults and emergency cases interrupt any well-laid plans. Some nights, medical students keep you company; but mostly, banter with the nursing staff makes the time enjoyable.

Downtime might be spent in the call room, but there is little sleep. If you manage a solid two hours, consider yourself golden. A successful night on call is when housekeeping finds a pristine bed in the morning.

When hypoglycemia sets in, you realize you haven't eaten since lunch. The cafeteria is closed, so you're forced to scavenge the kitchenettes for peanut butter and jelly, graham crackers, ginger ale or, if you're lucky, ice cream cups. In desperation, you suck down a few cans of Ensure.

Soon the night begins to ache. Fatigue becomes a disagreeable intoxication. You're slower to respond to pages. Wandering the halls, you need to stop and actively remember where you're headed. You read the chart but have to blink and begin again because nothing made sense.

The Sandman comes even though you're awake. Rubbing the crusts from your eyes, you feel a day's growth of stubble on your cheeks. You acquire cotton mouth and notice a film on your teeth. You suddenly want to brush, but the call room is too far away, and you never get around to it.

3-5 a.m. separates men from the boys. At this point, fatigue weighs anchor, clouding your brain with toxic fumes. The exhaustion is cumulative. It's not that you've been up for 20 hours; it's that you've been up for 20 hours after never recouping from being up 30 hours two days ago and 34 hours three days before that. Cat naps and daytime slumber fail to restore enough REM sleep. The deficiency accumulates, dragging you down, pulling you to sit, to lie, to close your eyes. Your brain pleads, just for a moment. Your eyes sink, your head nods. You shake it off and move ahead.

Keep moving—keep moving, you think, *like a shark.*

Stop moving, and you'll crash.

A patient is dying. Any other resident would wake their senior, but you see that as weakness, failure. Instead, you place a central line, transfer him to the ICU and call the attending directly. You'd rather be admonished than follow protocol.

"Morning" is designated by rounds. First, you might get a chance to splash cold water on your face or to gargle some Scope. A normal person would shower and shave, but usually there's no time. During rounds, you feel slight vertigo; you swear you feel the earth rotate beneath your feet.

Your diurnal cycle kicks in, and your body assumes the new day. Involved in daytime activities, you catch a second wind. For a while, a full day's beard is the only evidence of your night on call.

It all catches up with you on the drive home. Head nods begin, and you pray for a red light so you can close your eyes for a minute. You collapse onto the couch, still in scrubs, next to your wife. It's early evening or, if you're lucky, late afternoon, and you want to use the free time, get the oil changed, play guitar or take your wife to a movie. But your strength is sapped. The cushions cradle you, your lids sink, and the next thing you know she's waking you up for dinner or bed.

You have one normal day before it begins again.

For five years.

Despite the brutal demands, I loved it. On call, in the dead of night, I *owned* the hospital. While my senior slept, I was in charge, first to know about new patients or complications. I couldn't believe I even considered Internal Medicine.

"You know the worst part about being on call every third night?" I asked my dad once.

"What?" he asked.

"Missing out on two-thirds of the cases!"

He laughed, but I meant it.

My intern year I rotated through GYN, Neurosurgery, Urology, Vascular, ICU, Anesthesia and General Surgery. I bounced between Buffalo General, Millard Fillmore, Erie County Medical Center and the VA. By the end of the year, I had a dozen ID badges and security cards.

In April 1995, I had a month vacation. While my colleagues used their time to travel, visit home or go on vacation, I headed to Brooklyn, N.Y.

Matrimony beckoned.

⁊

Like most men, I knew few details about my own wedding. I knew it was in Brooklyn, and I knew the girl. Beyond that, I had two uncompromising demands:

No wicker chairs.

No stupid chicken dance.

On the morning of April 8, I peeked out the window of the Golden Gate Motel. The sun failed to pierce an overcast sky, and rain looked likely. My dad was up, but my mom and brother slept in. I searched for coffee in the sparse hotel room, but there was none. Luckily, the door burst open and a parade of my parents' friends entered, bearing coffee and donuts.

We took turns in the bathroom as the cluster of family and friends exchanged pre-wedding banter.

"I can't believe Johnny's getting married …"

"Baby John, are you ready for this?"

"Rich is going to save me," I said, and the group let out a laugh. "You know, like in the movies when they're about to hang a guy and, at the last minute, a horse comes riding in." More laughs. "Rich is going to do something like that. I know it."

The breakfast party broke up, and we changed into formal attire. Half-dressed in my unbuttoned tuxedo shirt, my dad started quizzing me.

"So, what are your lines?" he asked.

I counted each finger. "You look beautiful. I do …" I squinted at the ceiling trying to remember the third thing. "Uhh, I love you." I smiled. "I got it."

"Good," he said, "they don't even have to be in that order."

The Guardian Angel Catholic Church, an iconic stone structure on Ocean Parkway, served parishioners of Brooklyn since 1880. As Rich and I entered the vestibule, we were accosted by a video crew.

"Okay, I want you here." Rich was positioned. "John, you stand here. Don't look at the camera, and you don't need to say anything. This will be overdubbed with music."

He directed us to shake hands and told Rich to adjust my flower.

We couldn't stop laughing.

"Okay, I want you two to shake hands, and maybe your brother could look at his watch," the cameraman started to hover.

We smiled at each other and shook hands. When Rich looked at his watch, I tried to escape toward the exit. Rich grabbed my shoulders and forced me toward the aisle. I started to shake my head, pretending to cry. Rich pretended to slap me and pointed sternly toward the altar. I begrudgingly started to nod. Rich dusted off my shoulders and straightened my tie.

So much for Rich's escape plan.

At the altar, I waited with Rich beside me. Nella, dressed in turquoise and holding a bouquet, stood across the aisle. The priest nodded, and the organist began the opening notes to *Here Comes the Bride*. The congregation stood and turned as Carmela made her entrance.

A flower girl scattered rose pedals on the runner. Franco escorted his daughter down the aisle. She radiated a smile as friends and relatives blotted their eyes. Joining me at the altar, I was speechless, my mouth slightly open. She was angelic. Rich nudged me from behind. I blinked and swallowed.

"You look beautiful," I said.

One out of three, I thought.

The priest proceeded with the ceremony. I needed no prompting for 'I do' or 'I love you' after we kissed. I couldn't stop smiling as we walked down the aisle together, waving to my family and my new family.

Just outside the doors, Rich and Nella joined us as guests threw birdseed and cameras flashed. An antique limousine pulled up, waiting to deliver us to the photo session and on to the reception.

We arrived at the banquet hall and waited in the foyer with our parents. Behind closed doors, guests took their seats as the DJ prepared to announce our entrance. My dad cracked the door, peeking quickly before closing it.

"John," he said, "I need to tell you something."

"What?" I asked. "What is it?"

The DJ announced the wedding party, beginning with Carmela's parents. A burst of applause erupted as they strolled through the door.

"Marriage is all about compromise," my dad said; "you can't get upset about the small stuff."

I didn't know what he was talking about. Before I could ask, the DJ called his name, and my parents disappeared through the door.

We were next. I heard them announce Dr. and Mrs. Pryor. The doors opened, and we made our entrance. I kept smiling, but instantly understood what my dad was saying. At the head table were two of the largest fan-backed wicker chairs I'd ever seen.

Figures, I thought.

Brooklyn-Italian culture, worlds away from my upbringing, was on full display at the reception. White marble, glass and mirrors filled the inner decor. Fluent Italian was spoken among Carmela's side of the hall. Waves of hors d'oeuvres flowed from the kitchen, and not a glass was allowed to fall half-empty. When the dancing started, it wasn't long before they played the chicken dance.

So much for my demands!

Before dinner was served, the music fell silent, and my brother walked onto the dance floor. It was time for his speech.

"What I wanted to do today," Rich said, "was to tell you about how John and Carmela met. I wasn't in Grenada at the time; but, fortunately, I have a first-person account of what transpired."

What's he getting at? I wondered.

Rich signaled the DJ, and a tape began to play. It was my voice.

"Carmela. Okay, where do I start with Carmela?"

Rich was playing a tape I had sent home to my parents. I blushed as the congregation focused on me. Rich gave a satisfied smile.

"I'm gonna kill you," I mouthed, drawing my hand across my neck. He laughed.

"All last semester," my voice continued, "I would say hi to this girl, and I would just say hi, but we had that same kind of thing where you say hi to that person but you look straight at the person, you look straight into her eyes. It's something I can't really explain, but I knew it was there all last semester."

My voice filled the hall, detailing our story, the flowers in class, meeting in the kitchen and finally getting together at the Red Parrot. Deeply personal thoughts, never intended beyond my parents' ears, were now broadcast among complete strangers.

"But anyway, so we started hanging out and talking more. And it all just ... it just all came together. It's just really weird. So, anyway, I like this girl a lot."

The tape ended to a standing ovation. Older women were dabbing their eyes. I kept shaking my head, looking at my brother.

He got me good, I thought.

"My brother and I have lived two versions of the same life," he said. "We were Boy Scouts together, played guitar together and rode on the ambulance together. Until now. I've been lucky that I've had him all to myself. But now he's getting married and, in a way, I have to give him up.

"Carmela, I give you my brother knowing he'll be safe in your capable hands. May you both live, love and prosper."

Another round of applause. Rich came over, hugged me and kissed Carmela. It was the best wedding speech ever.

Officially wedded, Carmela and I moved in together. A large three-bedroom apartment became available in our complex, and Rich came out to help us move. Kitchen, dining room, living room with fireplace—there was even a small servants' quarters with mini bathroom. At 1,500 square feet, I could fit every previous apartment and dorm I had lived in with space left over. But the apartment was more than a larger living space.

With Carmela, it was home.

❧

Our residencies continued into our second year, PGY-2. Carmela's program was lighter, but juggling two call schedules made it challenging to see each other without falling asleep. Complicating matters was my desire to stay at work until my tasks were done. The problem being, tasks were never done.

One time, Carmela and I planned dinner and movie. Toward the end of my shift, a patient came in with a dead foot. He needed to go to the OR to restore blood flow.

"I can't come home," I told her on the phone. "I got a guy with a dead foot."

"What?" Carmela said. "We have plans!"

"I know, but this came up," I said. "I have to take care of it."

I pulled my head away from the screaming earpiece.

"Here," I handed the phone to my senior, "it's for you."

By the time the case was done, it was too late to go out. Sure, I missed the movie, but the upshot was that I saved someone's foot.

⁊

Rich matriculated at Albany Med in the fall of 1995. When he came to visit, there was no time for going out or kicking back beers. Instead, he joined me at work and followed me on call.

"Hey, everybody," I introduced him, "this is my liberal ass brother, Rich."

"He looks just like you, John," they said, "but thinner."

"Yeah, I'm John-light," Rich quipped, "just as much fun with half the fat."

Everyone laughed.

Always a wiseass, I thought.

Even though he was a medical student, Rich wasn't allowed to do much. We had fun anyway as he shadowed me, following me on rounds and observing me in the OR. In the afternoon, we wrote post-op notes, completed scut and put out fires.

Slowly, the hospital would empty. Around five, all the administrators headed home. By seven, most of the medical students were gone. At midnight, the evening shift had signed out and the hallways darkened. Only a skeleton crew remained overnight.

"I love the night," I told him. "It's the only time I can get anything done."

We moved from patient to patient, packing wounds, ordering antibiotics, checking x-rays. My pager constantly interrupted us.

Between patients, we talked about life.

"School going okay?" I asked.

"Yeah," Rich said. "I'm doing well. I still can't believe I made it into medical school."

"What's going on with Karen?" I asked.

"Karen and I broke up," Rich said. "I've been talking to Deidre."

Deidre was a girl Rich met at SUNY. He'd talked about her on and off for years, but I didn't know how serious it was.

"Yeah?"

"Yeah, I figure if I can get her to break up with her boyfriend, I've got a shot," he said.

"Maybe you should find a girl without a boyfriend," I suggested.

"That's another option," he said. "We'll see."

"Wanna take out some staples?" I asked.

"Sure."

Switching on the light, we disturbed an elderly man from sleep.

"It's Dr. Pryor," I said. "We need to look at your incision."

Handing Rich a staple remover, I took down the dressing and examined the wound. Satisfied with the healing, I nodded to Rich, and he started to remove the staples.

"Good," I said with each liberated staple. When they were out I handed him Steri-Strips. He placed the first strip. When he started the second one, I stopped him.

"No," I said and took the strip from his fingers.

"Your first one started on the left, and you pulled skin tension over to the right, see?"

"Yeah," he said.

"Then the next one should start over here on the right and pull skin tension over to the left. See?"

"Okay," he said.

"This way, the skin tension is equally left and right," I explained, "otherwise all the tension is one direction and the wound can pucker. The scar would be worse."

I paused for a second then delivered the real lesson:

"There is something to be learned in everything you do in medicine," I said, "even the simplest procedure has a lesson to be learned. Everything you do, everything you say, every medication you give, there is a deeper meaning. There is a reason. Sometimes that meaning is lost or forgotten, and it is your job to stop and ask why? Why is it done this way? Why do we do the things we do? Anyone can simply mimic certain actions—monkey see monkey do. The greatest quality you can have as a physician is being inquisitive and understanding the Why."

ᴄ⁓

As a second-year. I spent my life in the OR. Rotating through cardiac, ortho, thoracic, trauma and general surgery, I performed case after case after case. Scrub, gown, glove, cut; scrub, gown, glove, cut; scrub, gown, glove, cut. Gallbladders, appendectomies, hernias, bowel resections, vascular bypass, cardiac valves, thyroidectomies, breast masses, ovarian tumor resections, tracheotomies, lung resections, pannectomies, fistulas, portacaths, amputations, Whipples, splenectomies, transplants, organ harvesting, on and on and on. I had my finger on every organ and vessel from the chin down.

The most demanding and emotionally draining time was spent in the Burn Unit. Burn care is intense and complicated; patients face months of painful debridement with countless trips to the OR for grafts. The course is plagued by complications—pneumonia, fungemia, sepsis, ARDS, malnutrition. Mortality remained high despite my efforts. For some, those with extensive burns who were tortured daily, I almost felt relief to see an end to the pain.

I learned to hate burns.

Third-year (PGY-3) started with four months of pediatric surgery at the Children's Hospital of Buffalo. For a while, Carmela and I were in the same place and, on occasion, we had time for lunch. Now in her final year of residency, Carmela decided to apply for a fellowship in Pediatric Emergency Medicine. But on June 12, 1997, a little pink line changed our plans.

Carmela was pregnant.

Surgical Residency

⁂

The emergency room at Buffalo General was unusually still on Friday night. Other adjectives include peaceful, tranquil, calm or inactive.

But it wasn't quiet.

You never use the word quiet in the ER. A universal superstition pervades emergency departments around the world, causing panic in otherwise educated and clearly thinking individuals. Black cat cross your path? So what? Break a mirror, and you're in for bad luck. Ridiculous!

But don't ever say "quiet" in the ER. It's not done. Anyone using the "Q" word puts himself at grave risk. Otherwise polite and sensible nurses have been known to become violent.

"I can't believe how *quiet* it is tonight," I announced as loud as I could without shouting.

I drew the attention of the nurses.

"Shut up!" said one.

"What are you doing?" added another.

"Hey, I'm just pointing out that it's really *quiet* tonight." I goaded with a big smile. "I don't think it's ever been this *quiet* on a Friday."

A nurse marched over and started punching my shoulder. "Stop— saying—that—word!"

I flinched defensively, laughing, "Okay, okay! Stop!"

"It's not funny," she said.

Lisa Reyes, a third-year medical student starting her surgical clerkship, sat silently and observed the banter. She seemed amazed at my behavior.

"Alright, alright," I continued as the blows stopped, "I guess if there are no patients to treat, we can do some teaching instead."

As a fourth-year resident, I began to expand my role as teacher and mentor. During downtime, I tutored the residents and students.

"Sal, you were thinking of going into GI, right?" I asked one of the students.

"Yeah," he said.

"Okay, let's think of something good for you. I squinted and tapped my cheek. "Alright, how much bile does the gallbladder produce in a twenty-four hour period?"

Sal glanced at Lisa. He thought it was a stupid question.

"I'd say about a hundred to two hundred mls?" he guessed.

"Wrong!" I said with a smile, a little too enthusiastically.

"Lisa?" I asked.

Lisa thought for a moment but then gave up: "I have no idea."

I glanced at the interns, who also didn't know but didn't want to admit it in front of the medical students. The second-year shook his head and rolled his eyes.

"None!" I announced. "It's a trick question. The *liver* produces bile; the gallbladder *stores* it!"

Groans all around. Lisa cracked a smile.

"No really, I think there is a lesson in here somewhere," I continued. "It goes back to understanding the physiology. Without understanding the physiology, you can't understand the pathophysiology. It's like when McKinley was shot. Do you know that story?"

The interns and medical students shook their heads no.

"So, in 1901 Buffalo hosted the Pan-American Expo. It was like a world's fair with different venues showcasing new technology.

"While McKinley was giving a speech, some guy pulled out a revolver and shot him twice. One bullet grazed his shoulder; the other went into his belly. He went down but remained conscious.

"Instead of taking him to Buffalo General, they moved him to a temporary hospital created for the expo. This gives you an idea of the trauma care they had back then.

"The staff surgeon was called away before the shooting." My listeners gave me astonished looks. "Right, the President is in town, and the only surgeon leaves town. It was a long time ago.

"Anyway, the only other "surgeon" available was Dr. Mann. What kind of surgeon was Dr. Mann?"

The rhetorical question drew some shoulder shrugs.

"That's right. He was a gynecologist." The group let out a laugh. A few nurses had joined my ad hoc lecture.

"Now, because this was an expo for new and amazing technology, there was a medical device being demonstrated. They called it an x-ray machine, but it was so new and unproven that the doctors were afraid to use it on the President.

"Dr. Mann decided to operate. Electric lights were on display outside, but in the operating room they're forced to use mirrors, capturing light from the setting sun.

"He finds damage to the stomach, pancreas and kidney. They patch him up and, surprisingly, he lives. He rallied for a few days but then began to decline. The physicians noticed that he was tachycardic. And here is the point of the story: They observed his heart rate was high and he was getting sicker. A healthy person has a low heart rate. On a very superficial level, one could infer a correlation between these two observations. Low pulse healthy, high pulse sick. So what did they do?"

There were no guesses.

"They gave him digitalis. Why? Because dig will lower the heart rate." The group was astonished. Even the medical student knew the last thing you'd give a trauma patient is digitalis.

"It's crazy, right? But on some very simple level, it makes sense—but only because they had such poor understanding of physiology and pathophysiology. They observed the heart rate was high but didn't understand why. It's your job in medicine to understand the why. Why is your patient hypotensive? Why are the O_2 sats low? Why is there a fever? You can treat the symptoms, but don't ever think you're done. There is always the Why you need to answer."

A brief silence ensued as the young doctors pondered my words.

"So what happened to him?" asked Lisa.

"Who, McKinley?" I said. "He got septic and died like a dog."

I looked at my watch; it was nearly eleven o'clock, and still nothing was coming in.

"Okay, this is ridiculous," I announced. "If nothing happens soon, I'm gonna have to do the trauma dance."

The entire nursing staff jumped up and yelled out in unison, "NO!"

"Yeah, I think we need the trauma dance," I repeated.

"What?" asked Lisa. "What's he talking about?"

The second-year let out a sigh of exasperation. "It's like an Indian rain dance, but instead of rain, he is trying to summon a trauma patient."

"You're kidding, right?" she said.

"Oh, you want to see it?" I asked. "I need a chest tube."

Defying the protests, I grabbed a chest tube and trauma shears. I started to shuffle and chant like an Indian around a campfire.

"HEH YA YA YA, HEY YA YA YA," I sang, dropping my head low, then raising it to the ceiling. I danced in a broad circle around the trauma bay.

"Dr. Pryor!" one of the nurses tried to shout over my chants.

One of the interns turned over a plastic bedpan and started pounding on it like an Indian drum.

BOOM boom boom boom BOOM boom boom boom ...

"Guys! Really!" the nurses protested.

The interns and medical students joined in behind me. Lisa couldn't control her giggling. The others were adding to the chorus of HEY YA YA's.

"Oh, TuBeers! God of trauma!" I prayed. "Send us a victim of trauma so that we may heal him and he may be saved!"

"TuBeers?" someone asked

"Two Beers," the resident explained. The most dangerous thing one can do in Buffalo is have two beers and mind your own business. Whenever a beaten and bloody assault victim wheeled into the trauma bay, the same questions would be asked:

"What happened?"

"I was minding my own business."

"How much have you had to drink?"

"Two beers."

Crackling from the EMS radio interrupted our dance. The conga line froze and fell silent.

"Buffalo General, Rural-Metro Ambulance."

Everyone held their breath as the nurse answered. "This is Buffalo General. Go ahead Rural Metro."

"Buff General, we are en route to your location with a 22-year-old male. Patient is victim of an assault ..."

The rest of the report was drowned out as the groups let out a mixture of laughter, whoo-hoos or god dammits, depending on the staff.

ᕮᕮ

Carmela had one scare with some spotting, but otherwise our

gestation progressed well. As physicians, we knew the complications of pregnancy and childbirth, but we did our best to act like a normal expectant couple.

At twenty weeks, I met Carmela at the Children's Hospital for our first ultrasound. Despite being post-call and officially off duty, I received pages about my patients. I walked into the ultrasound suite on the phone, discussing a case. I hung up as Carmela lay on the table, exposing her gravid belly.

While the technician entered information into the ultrasound, my pager went off again.

"Pryor," I answered, walking away from my wife, "I'm not in the hospital right now. Get a portable chest x-ray and call the junior." I hung up and returned to the show.

The ultrasound probe spread glistening gel around her abdomen. A grainy image formed on the monitor. My pager went off again.

"Look," I said into the phone, "I need a few minutes. If there's a problem, Dr. Boulenger's on call now, okay?" I returned again to my wife and baby.

Finally, we saw him on the screen. I squeezed Carmela's hand as the tech measured crown, rump length, and femur length. She moved the probe, revealing an intact spine and normal heart. My pager went off again.

"God damn it!" I said.

I dialed the number. "What do you want? What do you want?" I yelled at the unlucky nurse who disturbed me, "I'm trying to look at my son on the ultrasound!"

The tech looked up at Carmela and me.

"Uhhh," she said, "I don't think it's a *he*."

She pointed out the triple stripe sign. My mouth hung open as the phone fell away from my ear.

We were going to have a girl.

☙

In December 1997, the *New York Times* infuriated me with an article, "Exhaustion is Still the Rule for Medical Residents." The report criticized resident work schedules, stating many hospitals ignore legal restrictions on resident work hours.

"These people have no fucking idea of what they're talking about," I said to Carmela.

"What, is that about the Bell Commission?" she asked, looking over the article.

"Yeah, they think we can do this job in eighty hours a week," I fumed; "it's complete bullshit."

"They're not doctors," she said. "They're bureaucrats passing laws about things they know nothing about. What do you expect?"

"Look at this," I said, quoting the article: 'The senior doctors are often just not here, and there's a real taboo about calling them at home when there's a problem in the middle of the night. It's scary. I'm smart. I'm a good doctor. But I just don't have enough experience to be making these calls myself.' I dropped the paper. "That's not true, or this person doesn't have the balls to call his senior. You either handle it yourself, or you call your senior. How fucking hard is that?"

Incensed, I went straight to my computer and opened up a new document:

December 14, 1997

New York Times
229 West 43rd Street
New York, NY 10036-3959

Dear Mr. Raines,

I was annoyed by your December 14, 1997 article "Exhaustion is Still the Rule for Medical Residents." I read it through weary eyes, having just finished a thirty-six hour shift as a surgical resident in an upstate New York hospital. I work on average 100 to 120 hours a week and frequently deal with 'fatigue.' It is not justified to blame bad medical decisions and poor outcomes on the physician being fatigued. Most medical decisions during the course of a long shift are routine, and complicated decisions are rarely made quickly and without input from several physicians. If anything, it is more dangerous to make major decisions when the physician does not know the patient's case well, when intricacies of the management are not clear. These mistakes are often made by physicians who are covering overnight and on weekends for physicians who are taking time off because of the Bell Commission rules. As a resident surgeon, I believe that continuity of care by the same physician is the best way to take care of patients, especially acutely ill or injured patients. I don't make mistakes when I am tired. I make them when I have had a day off and don't know the recent events in my patient's care.

As for supervision, I rarely have trouble getting help from more experienced physicians when needed. In addition to the more senior residents who are usually in the hospital, the attending physician is always just a phone call away. Last night, I had to call the Chairman of the Department of Surgery at 2:00 a.m. because he was on call to cover an emergency case. He was in the hospital in thirty minutes without any disagreement and without any "pervasive hospital atmosphere that discourages [me] from turning to the attending physician for guidance."

The Libby Zion trial was a case of an angry father who was financially and politically capable to sublimate his anger at the death of his daughter into a trial of American medical education. The fact remains that the graduate medical system in this country is the epitome of the world, and medical residents are the pillars of this system.

John P. Pryor, MD

Senior Resident in General Surgery
State University of New York at Buffalo

I dropped it in a mailbox, feeling righteous, and forgot all about it.

A few days later, Scott Boulenger approached me during morning rounds.

"Nice job, Pryor," he said.

"What?" I asked.

"Your letter in the Times," he said. "Way to go."

"They *printed* that?" I asked.

Scott retrieved the paper from the nurses' station and folded it over. On the Op-Ed page under "Letters" was an edited version of my letter. I read it through with fresh eyes and immediately spotted a problem.

"You might have left out the part about working a hundred twenty hours a week," Scott said. "You know, publicly decrying our hospital is violating the law; it's bad form."

Just then my pager went off. Dr. Hassett's office number blinked at me. When I called back, I got his secretary.

"Dr. Pryor?" she asked.

"Yeah," I swallowed.

"Dr. Hassett wants to see you right away," she said.

Oh shit, I thought.

When I came home that night, Carmela noticed my subdued demeanor.

"You get fired?" she asked holding up the Times.

"No," I said, "but I came close."

I learned that expressing my opinions in a public venue could have consequences. It would become important as e-mail became more ubiquitous. Whenever I was hot and bothered about a topic, I always remembered my letter to the Times before sending a reply.

☙

Carmela was due in February 1998. I fully realized this when she found a copy of my resident schedule.

"You took *January* off?" she said.

Oh shit, I thought, *what'd I do now?*

"Yeah...," I cringed, "isn't that when you're due?"

"February!" she shouted. "The baby's coming in *February!*"

You know, I'll never understand women. I was only off by a month, and still she was pissed.

"Well," I said hopefully, "maybe she'll come early."

"You're impossible!" she huffed.

The week before Carmela was due, I received a phone call from my brother.

"My schedule changed," he said. "How about I come out for one last weekend together before your life is over?"

"Thanks," I said. "I'll have you know becoming a father is the most wonderful ..."

"Yeah, yeah," he said. "I can come Thursday if that's okay; it'll give us a long weekend."

"Yeah, come out," I said. "I only have morning rounds on Saturday and Sunday."

As Carmela approached her due date, I became increasingly anxious about the whole baby thing. I was relieved Rich was coming to visit.

On Thursday evening, I was on the computer when Carm appeared in the doorway.

"What?" I asked.

"My water broke," she said.

"Really?" I smiled. "Now?"

"We should call the ob," Carm said.

"What, now?"

"Yes now, what did you think?"

"I thought we had until tomorrow."

"What are you? Stupid?"

She was right. We packed a bag and waited for my brother. Finally, there was a knock at the door.

"Thank God, you're here!" I said, tossing his bag into the foyer.

"What?" Rich stood motionless as Carmela appeared in the doorway.

"We're going to the hospital," I said.

"What, *now?*"

At the Children's Hospital of Buffalo, we checked in. Carm was poked, prodded, and plugged in. She finally settled in her bed, and I dug out the video camera.

"What are you doing?" Carmela asked.

"Don't worry, you'll thank me later," I said, pointing the camera at her.

"Hello and welcome," Rich said, "to another edition of *We're Having A Baby...*"

It dawned on Carmela that she was alone with two rambunctious Pryor brothers armed with a video camera. She was not amused.

"Ooo, looky, what we have here!" I narrated as the camera focused on the tocometer. "Forty! Wow, that looks painful. Carmela, can you confirm pain?"

"John ... really ..." she protested.

I ignored her. "And the baby will go from here," I aimed at Carmela's abdomen, "over to here ..." I panned over to the baby warmer.

Rich was back in frame holding a plastic visual aid showing progressively larger circles from a closed cervix up to ten centimeters of dilation.

"This is our cervical road map," said Rich, laughing.

I was laughing so hard that I couldn't hold the camera still. "Where are we now?" I asked.

"We're here at two," Rich pointed to a relatively closed circle.

"And where do we have to get to?" I asked.

"We need to get all the way to ten!" Rich pointed to the largest circle.

"Oooo, looks painful!" I said.

Carmela's look of disgust was mixed with disbelief.

I gotta go through labor with these bozos? she was thinking.

I turned the camera off. A resident came in to check Carm's cervix; Rich excused himself. A few minutes later, I joined him in the hallway.

"C'mon," I said, handing Rich his coat. "Let's go get some coffee."

"She kicked us out?"

"Yup."

"Where's she at?"

"Three, not even four," I said. "We've got plenty of time."

We walked downstairs and outside into the frigid Buffalo winter. Less than a block away, there was a twenty-four hour convenience store. Inside, we stocked up on supplies for the night.

Nothing prepares one for parenthood like medical school. We'd been through obstetrics clerkships and knew better than anyone what to expect. For some, childbirth is an arduous, sleep-depriving experience. For us, it was just another night on call.

Carmela labored throughout the night. Our antics died down as her contractions took center stage. I tried to remain upbeat and encouraging despite the increasing pain intensity. It was hard to see her suffer.

At long last, Carmela was fully dilated and effaced; it was time to push. I supported one leg, and Rich held the other. Carmela gritted her teeth and bore down.

"Push push push push push push push, okay, deep breath and relax," the obstetrician directed the process.

"You're doing so great, honey," I said as I rubbed her leg. "Almost there, we could see the head that time …"

"Push push push push push!"

Then, her head was out.

"Okay, hold it!" the obstetrician grabbed a bulb syringe and suctioned out her nose and mouth.

"She's there!" I said, "one more time, and she's out!"

Her shoulder was delivered and gently lifted. When the posterior shoulder was clear, Danielle came shooting out into the doctor's arms. He suctioned her mouth a few more times and then gingerly placed her on Carmela's abdomen.

Carmela gave a shuddered laugh, and I wiped a tear from my eye. I bent down and kissed her.

"You did it," I said. "She's here."

Danielle lay swaddled with a cap placed on her head while the doctor cut the cord.

We looked down at our daughter. The thought of raising a child was daunting. The best thing was to not think about it. But now, with those little eyes staring up at you, the enormity of it hits home. Like most new parents, we had no idea of what to expect. But that's life—not knowing what to do, but doing it anyway.

⚘

I began feeling like a real attending during my fourth year. Most cases I worked with a junior resident, the attending poking in occasionally to see if I needed anything.

I felt even more autonomous rotating in private community hospitals around Buffalo. As the only surgeon in house, I took care of everything while the attending slept at home.

One time, I was working with Dr. LaScola, a short overweight Italian who was into fine wine and gourmet food. It seemed his interest in being a surgeon had waned over the years. A patient came in with an acute abdomen and needed to go right away to the OR.

"Nah," said Dr. LaScola over the phone, "we'll take him in the morning."

"You can go back to sleep," I told him. "I'm taking the patient to the OR."

So I did.

Halfway through the operation, Dr. LaScola backed in, hands dripping.

"Jonny," he said with a thick accent, "why didn't you wait for me?"

"Dr. LaScola," I said, "with all due respect, I wouldn't let you operate on my dog."

I was tired and pissed, and it just came out. But it showed you where I was in my training. I was on par, if not better than, some of the attendings.

Only one case caused me real trouble.

Two in the morning, Buffalo General paramedics wheeled in a bloody, multiple gunshot victim.

"Twenty-three-year-old male, multiple shots at the scene, we got holes in the chest and abdomen; pulse 180; pressure 60; intubated without sedation; he's got two 16s in each AC, unknown medical history."

On "three," a limp body flopped onto our stretcher, and the trauma dance began: Intubation, chest tubes, trauma line, blood, x-rays. We ran him to the OR, and I opened him stem to stern. In the chest, I repaired a hole in his atria; in the belly, multiple bowel and vascular repairs were needed.

Meanwhile the attending, called in from home, was stranded in a blizzard. I finished closing the patient just as he arrived.

"Who was in on the case with you?" the attending asked me.

"Nobody," I said. "It was me and the junior."

"Then who's going to sign off on the case?"

"You were on call," I said.

"But I wasn't here," he explained. "I'm not going to accept responsibility if I don't know what you did."

What a fucking dick, I thought.

"What? I was supposed to wait for you?"

"I'm sorry," he said, "but I'm not going to accept liability for surgery I wasn't present for."

The patient spent his entire hospital stay with no official attending on record. Not that he needed one, because I was taking care of him, but legally it was a problem. The discussion continued for weeks, but the attending remained obstinate. Eventually, my chairman signed off on the case.

∽

Unbelievably, the end of residency was fast approaching. With each case, each sleepless night, each lecture, I conquered Mt. Residency. Now, above the tree line with summit in sight, I needed to decide my next move.

I wanted to practice Critical Care and Trauma pretty much since starting residency. Bill Flynn, a Trauma and Critical Care surgeon at ECMC, was my role model. That's what I wanted to do: General Surgery with Trauma and Critical Care.

I decided to do a fellowship because I wanted to be the best at what I do. I also wanted to run a trauma center; to do that, you need critical care; you need to be formally trained. It's a pain in the ass because I'm giving up two years of salary. I'd been poor my whole life and would continue to be poor for two more years.

Meanwhile, every service wanted me: Urology, Vascular, Colorectal, even Neurosurgery offered me a spot to switch residency. Flattering, but my decision was made.

"You hear what Pryor wants to do?" I overheard in the locker room one day, "Trauma. Fucking waste of talent."

It made me smile.

In a way, they were right. Far from prestigious, trauma is the bastard child of surgery. Blunt trauma receives little attention or research dollars, and penetrating trauma was a problem for poor inner-city males nobody cared about. Nobody ever got rich or famous being a trauma surgeon.

I didn't care what they thought. I loved it. Besides, there's no better surgeon than a good trauma surgeon. A bullet can land in any part of the body—and at 3 a.m.; there's no time to call a cardiac surgeon or a vascular surgeon or a colorectal surgeon. I needed to be as good as all of them.

Applications to fellowships in trauma / critical care went out to programs all along the East Coast. Eventually, it came down to three, with pros and cons for each.

- **Louisville**
  They have several well-know surgeons. The program is very laid back without formal rotations. Fellows direct themselves. Dr. Harmon Polk is very interesting. J.D. Richards is highly respected. The city is small, and the people seem inbred. Could be boring. Lots of good research.

- **University of Pennsylvania**
  This is a very academic program and very well funded. They have eight fellows and fourteen attendings. They get about the same penetrating trauma as Buffalo. Less demand on operating, but lots of detail-oriented care. I would learn how to research and present well. Dr. Schwab is very connected. I don't like that the program doesn't interact much with general surgery. I suspect lots of "Ego."

- **Emory**
  A very clinical program with lots of operating. Dr. Feliciano is the hot shot. I suspect not a lot of time for research. Dr. Rosezky would be great to work for. Most people seem happy there. Er is great. I would need to be assured that I would have protected time. Atlanta is the biggest draw. It's a clean and upcoming city with 120 bars!

Which would it be?

My gut said Emory.

☙

I learned as a medic and continued to learn as a surgeon how patients can change you. Most patients are forgettable; they arrive, are treated and are discharged. Some are more memorable, an interesting diagnosis or a complication that teaches you something. Then there are the few who change you, patients who affect you in profound and lasting ways.

Cody was eighteen when his car went off the road. It took an hour to extricate him from the wreckage. He wheeled into my trauma bay, awake but writhing in pain.

DEATH appeared moments later.

"My chest! My chest!" he yelled. No amount of morphine could dull his pain. The chest x-ray was snapped up on the viewer, and my sphincter puckered. A large blush obscured his mediastinum.

"Type and cross for ten units," I told the junior. "Let's run him to the scanner but then right to the OR. Who's on for cardiothoracic?"

Cody had an aortic dissection, bleeding into his mediastinum. I needed the CT to confirm the diagnosis, but I had little doubt. His odds for survival were slim.

"Dr. Pryor?" the nurse said, "his parents are here."

I didn't have much time to talk. I told them it was very serious and we needed to go to the OR right away. They were good people, pleasant, understanding. It's easy to say they didn't deserve this nightmare, but then again, nobody deserved this nightmare.

In the scanner, I looked over the technician's shoulder as he scrolled through the slices. Images of the chest flashed by, revealing a torn aorta. I grabbed the stretcher and helped wheel Cody to the OR.

DEATH kept pace with us.

"Doc! Doc!" Cody's eyes were wild. "Don't let me die!"

He looked between me and DEATH.

"Please!" he glanced at DEATH then back to me. "Don't let him take me!"

It was my turn to freak out.

You can see him? I thought.

In all my years, I never met someone who saw DEATH the way I could.

"Don't worry, Cody," I said. "I won't let him take you."

I ran through a quick scrub and kicked into the OR. I told Dr. Grosner about the CT findings as we zipped open Cody's chest. Blood welled up into the field like an overflowing sink. I plunged my hand, feeling for the aorta.

"Clamp!" I barked.

I cross-clamped the descending aorta and started to feel for the hole.

"Pressure's dropping," anesthesia announced.

"Then hang more blood!" I shouted. "Where's the fucking hole?"

My fingers slid along the slippery pulsating snake until my index finger fell in. I plugged the tear, but blood continued to pump out. DEATH inched closer as bags of blood drained into Cody's arms.

"God damn it!" I sent in a needle driver and used my finger to guide it. The needle bit my finger over and over as I felt for it. I managed to tie a few sutures.

The bleeding started to slow. I hoped it was from my efforts, but his heart began to race.

"Pressure's 60," said anesthesia.

"Fuck! FUCK!" I looked up to see empty rapid infusers. "We need more blood!"

DEATH stepped closer.

"It's coming," someone said.

"WE NEED IT NOW!" I yelled.

DEATH was shoulder to shoulder. Cody's heart started to fibrillate.

"V-fib," anesthesia said flatly.

"Where are the paddles?" My hands shook. "Give me the fucking paddles..."

"John ..." said Dr. Grosner.

"Is the blood here yet? Charge the paddles ..."

"John ..."

The bleeding ceased; a Yankauer sucked the field dry. I shocked Cody into asystole. DEATH vanished, his mission accomplished.

"GOD DAMN IT!" I threw the paddles. "GOD DAMN IT!" I strode away from the table and punched the door, leaving a bloody fist print. I walked back to the table and threw my hands in the air.

"WHAT THE FUCK!" my voice cracked as tears welled in my eyes.

"I told him …." I choked up. Snapping off my gloves, I buried my face in my hands.

Oh God, I told him he'd be okay. I promised he wouldn't die. I failed him.

I felt a hand on my shoulder.

"I'm okay," I said, wiping the snot on my sleeve. "I just need a minute."

Then I had to tell Cody's parents I killed their son.

ಲ

When the time came for a final decision on fellowship, I chose Emory. But then I got a call from Grace Rosezky, who said they took someone else. I suspected there was more going on behind the scene, but what could I do? I called Penn and accepted their offer.

Why Philly? I looked at different programs throughout the whole country, but it was obvious that Carmela wanted to stay on the East Coast. So that eliminated a lot of programs. Really strong programs on the East Coast include Penn, Memphis with Tim Fabian, Atlanta with Dave Feliciano and Gary Rusziki. We didn't want to go to Miami. We looked at Chapel Hill which had some good people, but Chapel Hill would be ten times worse than Buffalo. New Haven and Hartford were possibilities, but they didn't have the recognition.

Basically, it came down to Penn or Emory at Grady Memorial. I liked Grady a lot. I thought I'd fit in well down there. It's a very clinical program. It's a very poor hospital; the program is poor. Dave Feliciano one of the world leaders in trauma, has an ugly, run-down office. I would've worked my butt off clinically and would have been a better clinical surgeon. But I wouldn't have protected time and financial support, and I wouldn't have the mentorship. I believe in a firm foundation in the clinical ability, so Emory was my first choice. I made it clear to them, but they picked someone else.

I think, in the long run, going to Penn was a better choice. First of all, everybody advised me to go to Penn, and nobody thought I should go to Emory. Penn's got a shitload of money, and they have ten faculty members. When you have ten faculty members, ten people all interested in the same thing as you, that's an amazing amount of intellectual asset. They are a very protective group run by a guy named Bill Schwab, who really knows what he's doing. He's best friends with Jim Hassett, and that deal was done. I don't think I had much to do with it. In fact, it could very well be that they just decided that I was going there and the powers that be said I'm going to Penn, and that was the end of that.

Quite frankly, that's fine with me. I learned that you have to trust your mentors. If Jim Hassett, a national leader in trauma, tells me to go work with Schwab, another national leader in trauma, the answer will be, "Yes, Sir."

❧

Spring of 1999 was a busy time for everyone. While I finished my residency and prepared to move to Philadelphia, Rich graduated medical school and would soon begin his residency in Emergency Medicine.

But first, he would marry Deidre.

I suffered his rants about Deidre for the previous four years. She finally came around during medical school, and now they were getting married.

The Inn at Stone Ridge, an 18th century Dutch colonial mansion, hosted their ceremony and reception. Like my wedding, there were only four in the party—Rich, me, Deidre and her sister. The reception was held outside under a white party tent. Not a single wicker chair in sight.

Danielle, a year and a half by then, tore up the dance floor in a white lace dress. She was so cute.

I heard someone say, "Dr. Pryor." I instinctively looked up. I was surprised to see my brother being addressed. It made me smile. I was so proud of him.

Doctor, married to Deidre, I thought. *He's really got his act together.*

❧

In June 1999, I completed my general surgery residency in Buffalo. It was five years. In those five years, I learned how to be a surgeon and how to be a physician. It's been the best time of my life after Grenada and high school.

There's a lot to be said about training for surgery. It's different from becoming any other type of physician. It's not only intellectual but also emotional, physical and spiritual. You become a different person. I think I developed my own style, how to take care of people and how to interact with other professionals.

I throw myself 100 percent into my patients. That's not easy, because it takes up time: It takes time away from your family; it takes time away from sleep. There's emotional cost and spiritual sacrifice. When you take care of your patients 100 percent, you dedicate yourself for two or three days to get through a critical period. If you lose a patient, you lose a chunk of yourself.

I lost a lot of chunks.

I think, if anything, that's probably what sets me apart from most of the other people who work here. The patients I take care of—now, this is not all of the patients, because emotionally I can't do it, but there are patients I chose to put forth 100 percent effort—they need a physician, not just a shift doctor, but a doctor who can be there twenty-four hours a day for four or five days in a row. Not just physically but also emotionally. This means I go home and I think about the patient. I call from home. I'm there in the morning. I'm there in the afternoon. I'm always worried about the person as if he were my own family. You commit a big part of your psyche to that patient.

And these patients had better do well. If they don't, it hurts. And it takes a big chunk.

Over the five years, I've had a lot of chunks taken out. And it changes you. It makes you tired. In the last year, especially after fourth year, which was a big push year, I've felt emotionally tired. It goes back to high school. I've been doing this since I was a paramedic, and there are cases from when I was a paramedic that still weigh on my mind. I gave out chunks as a paramedic. I gave a chunk to the young kid who died from asthma, the eight-month-old who drowned in the sink, all the arrests that I couldn't get back, the grandmother who died on Christmas—they all take chunks. In residency, it's even worse; patients taken a lot out of you.

The other thing that I decided is that in my life, in my career, in my career as trauma and critical care is that DEATH is the enemy. If my patient dies, it is a direct failure of me not as a surgeon but as a person because I didn't give to that patient as much effort as he/she deserved. If I had given that patient 110 percent, the patient should live; if the patient doesn't live, then I have failed.

You can't be the physician that makes excuses, saying "Oh, the patient is diseased." "The circumstances." "This failed." "That failed." "This regimen didn't work." When it comes down to it, it's a battle between you and the disease and you and the patient, and you have to win. There is no second place. When I lost, I took it personally. It was a personal loss to me. The people who have been lost have been personal losses. Not all the patients, because some I decided that I'm not going to be responsible for. The patients I *have* been responsible for, who have died, I consider a clean "kill." It's no different from a war. In *Saving Private Ryan,* Captain Miller says people who died under his command were people he killed. Basically, it's the same thing: If I fail, then I killed that person just as much as the trauma killed the patient.

Thinking like that makes me a better surgeon and a better physician. I feel that if one of my family members were sick, I would want somebody who cares about the patient as much as I do and who would put in as much effort as if it were his own brother. That's the test, every time you're tired and you want to go home and you don't want to check another lab value or you don't want to check another x-ray, say to yourself, "If that were my brother, would I check the x-ray? Would I put the Swan in? Would I transfuse tonight?"

When you use that test, you're there all the time.

Fellowship

It's a warm Saturday night in July. If you know anything about West Philly, you know there's gonna be trouble.

At 2 a.m., the Purple Lounge is hopping. Jared lowers his beer to see his girlfriend talking to some stranger on the dance floor.

What the shit?

"Who the fuck are you?"

"Get the fuck away from my bitch."

The guy was quick. One-two, and Jared hits the dance floor. Next thing he knows, he's getting tossed out into the street. So is the other motherfucker.

In the street, it starts up again.

Jared lands a few and knocks the stranger back.

"I've had enough of you, nigger." He pulls out the Glock.

Pop, pop, pop—all at close range. Bystanders duck for cover. The stranger conceals the gun and sprints away.

Jared hits the street. There's a scream. A crowd forms. Someone rolls him over. Blood pours onto the asphalt.

"Oh, shit, he's fucked up."

"He still alive?"

"Someone call an *am-blance.*"

While Jared bled out in the ambulance, I was trying to get my bearings in a new environment. It was my first night on call as a Fellow with nurses who didn't know me, a whole service of new patients and an unfamiliar paging system. I felt like a clueless medical student.

I teamed up with the junior resident, who showed me the ropes. After a while, I could navigate my way through the hallways and find the bathroom on my own. When two problems came up, I was confident enough to head out on my own.

"Divide and conquer," I said to the resident. "You want to do the ER consult or see the guy in PACU."

"I'll do the consult," he said.

The trauma alert pager pierced my ear.

"Or," I said, "we could do the trauma instead." We walked briskly to the ER.

In the trauma bay, staff appeared unnervingly animated for this time of night. I knew what this kind of flurry meant.

"Something wicked this way comes," I said. The resident gave me a smile.

"What'd we got?" I asked no one in particular.

"Eighteen-year-old, gunshot wound to the chest and abdomen, obtunded, agonal, ETA five minutes ..."

Beeping from the ambulance backup alarm rattled my nerves.

"ETA, zero minutes," I said, putting on lead and gown.

"Okay, who's here?" I surveyed the scene trying to remember who were interns and who were senior residents.

"Who's got airway?" I stood at the foot of the stretcher mentally preparing for the resuscitation. "Okay, Steve, survey and right chest tube; Stacey, get a trauma line ready." Then to the resident, "You get the left chest tube if we need it."

Paramedics wheeled in the patient, flanked by a police escort.

"Eighteen-year-old male, three shots at the scene, we have two holes in the chest and one in the abdomen, pulse 160, pressure was 80 palp, couldn't get an airway, he's got two 16's in each AC, unknown medical history or allergies."

On "three," Jared's limp body flopped onto the stretcher, and the trauma dance began: Intubation, chest tubes, trauma line, blood, x-rays.

I like to think Jared helped me that night as much as I helped him. When he rolled in, my fear and anxiety vanished. I became a surgeon treating my patient. Nothing else mattered. Do right by the patient; do everything you can to heal him; put in 110 percent, and the rest will follow. The hospital may be new. I might not know the nurses or the computer system, but trauma is the same. Bleeding is the same. I fell back on five years of surgical training.

The resident's hands trembled as he tried to place the chest tube. I broke from my role as team leader to help. Amid this tempest of chaos and confusion, my voice was calm and my hand steady.

"You're deep enough. Now push with the hemostat and pop through the intercostals, push... harder. C'mon push like his life depends on it. Oh that's right; his life *does* depend on it." I smiled then added, "No pressure."

The resident let out a nervous laugh. He put his weight behind the hemostat, popping through muscle.

"Good, now spread." I divided my attention between the chest tube tutorial and getting the patient to the OR. "Can we call the OR and let them know we're coming? Good, now insert the tube. Yes, hang the other blood ..."

In the OR, Pat Riley, head of the trauma program, helped me repair holes in Jared's heart, great vessels and gut. We moved him to PACU, and I went to find his family.

Jared's parents sat among a dozen family members and friends. Jared's father, a laborer, wore paint-splattered overalls and thick calluses on his hands. His mother was fat, missing a canine and wore a dirty Michael Jackson T-shirt. The remainder were a mixture of obese, unhygienic, beggarly people—the face of poverty, unfortunate victims of urban blight.

The American Dream had abandoned these people.

"Jared is alive," I said. Tears of relief erupted all around, "But, he's in very critical condition."

I explained the extent of his injuries.

"Oh, lord," I heard in the crowd, "oh, Lord Jesus."

"When can I see him?" his mother asked. "When can I see my baby?"

"He's in the PACU right now," I explained. "You can see him we he's transferred to the ICU."

When can I see my baby?

The words struck me as a parent. It's so easy to stereotype the poor: lazy, stupid, dangerous. We distance ourselves from them; we dehumanize them. It's done out of fear, ignorance. We do it to protect ourselves emotionally.

What I learned in Buffalo held true in Philadelphia: Being poor doesn't make you any less human. Jared's mother loved him as much as I loved Danielle. Her grief was no less than my grief for Danielle would be if she were hurt.

I made Jared my responsibility. In the first few days, he required twenty-four hour attention. Then complications sprouted like dandelions: an obstruction, seizures, sepsis. All the while, Jared's mother maintained her bedside vigil.

One morning, I led the team into Jared's room and discovered a problem.

"Oh, Dr. Pryor," Jared's mother accosted me, "thank God you're here. They wouldn't restart his feeds last night."

I looked up to see an empty bag of Ensure.

"What?" I said. "Why not?"

"I asked the nurse, Dr. Pryor, but she wouldn't listen to me."

Infuriating.

You see? This is why I can't take time off—because shit gets missed and someone drops the ball. This time, it was tube feeds, but it could have been something serious.

"I'll take care of it," I said. Then I ripped out a blank progress note, wrote some numbers and handed it to her.

"Listen," I said, "this is my personal cell phone, okay? If you call this number you won't get a page operator or an office. You'll get me. If something like this happens again, you call me, day or night; it doesn't matter. Okay?"

Her look of relief and appreciation made me choke up. My unorthodox move drew concern from my colleagues.

"You gave her your cell phone number?" Mark asked incredulously.

"Yeah, why?"

"Are you nuts?" he asked. "Do you realize what kind of neighborhood they come from?"

"What's that got to do with it?"

"You just don't do that, JP," he said. "Who knows where that number will turn up?"

"I don't see it that way," I said. "I see a mother concerned about her kid who's on the brink of death. If she needs me, I want to be there."

&

The end of my general surgical residency marked a stressful transition point. I had lived in Buffalo for seven years, became master of my environment, and gained the trust and respect of my colleagues at work. Now I embarked into the unknown—a new location, a new hospital, a new life. I was starting over from scratch

At Penn, an Ivy League institution, I would be working alongside some of the best surgeons in the country.

As my start date approached, I began having panic attacks.

Plagued by self-doubt, I chewed Tums like candy and struggled with insomnia. The anxiety finally manifested somatically while we were visiting Carmela's parents in Brooklyn. At 5 a.m. Danielle woke us with a fever. I went to the bathroom while Carmela dosed her with Tylenol. I came out, feeling my pulse racing at over 150 beats per minute. I looked at Carmela.

"I'm in A-fib," I said. "Call an ambulance."

While waiting for the ambulance, I laid a bag of ice on my face and tried to use the valsalva maneuver to return to a normal rhythm. It didn't work. NYC EMS arrived, started an IV and confirmed the arrhythmia on their lifepak. During the ride to Maimonmides, I allowed a brief reminiscence of my ambulance days.

"You guys hiring?" I asked the medic.

In the ER a cardiology fellow started me on procainamide. If I didn't convert in 24 hours, they'd have to shock me. Considering the move, my new job at Penn and Danielle being sick, I didn't have time for this shit.

Luckily, I converted overnight. I started Toprol before discharge the following day. After a few weeks, I weaned myself off. I never had another episode of the arrhythmia, and I'm sure it was from all the stress.

Philadelphia is quite a distance from Buffalo, so we worked with a realtor to find our apartment. She recommended a place in Chestnut Hill, a suburb just north of Philly. This was before the Internet, so we signed the lease pretty much sight unseen.

Compared to our apartment in Buffalo, it sucked. The 1,500 square footage on paper belied the actual layout. The space was divided into three levels: upstairs, downstairs and basement.

A metal balustrade separated the step-down living room from the anterior dining room. Our furniture barely squeezed into the space. Dining room chairs couldn't clear the table, and only a small gap remained between ottoman and facing couches.

It was difficult moving backward from such a comfortable apartment in Buffalo, but it was only temporary, and I would be spending most of my time at work.

Ben Franklin founded the University of Pennsylvania in 1740, making it the fourth oldest Ivy. The hospital was constructed in 1874 to train physicians and surgeons for the school of medicine. Now a 700-bed teaching hospital, the Hospital of the University of Pennsylvania (HUP) had become a regional trauma and tertiary referral center.

The Fellowship in Trauma and Critical Care took place over two years, integrating the disciplines of Trauma Surgery, Emergency General Surgery, and Surgical Critical Care.

During my first year, rotations in surgical critical care training were interspersed with rotations on a trauma service. There was heavy academic emphasis, and I was quickly brought up to speed writing papers and giving presentations.

Penn's style was meticulous and precise, from the arrangement of providers around the trauma stretcher to the background color and layout of the Power Point slides. Some would find it constraining, but I appreciated the discipline. By the end of my first year, my name appeared on several publications, and I had given three lectures.

During the second year, the balance of the Surgical Critical Care

Fellowship occurred. After passing my boards, I served as a Fellow in Exception (FIE) in General Surgery. FIEs are able to practice surgery and traumatology independently at HUP and St. Luke's Hospital, located 60 miles north of Philadelphia. St. Luke's Hospital provided a community-based environment with more blunt trauma and pediatric injuries.

Like every new place I've been, I worried about fitting in. This was the real deal, a prestigious teaching hospital with residents from Princeton, Harvard, Stanford, Columbia—the list went on. Arriving from Buffalo caused some confusion.

"Buffalo?" They would frown. "You mean, like, Cornell?"

"Yeah," I would bullshit. "Cornell had an outreach program at Buffalo."

"Oh."

It was hard for people to get their head around. And forget about Grenada, I couldn't even *mention* Grenada.

Despite my convoluted past, what mattered now were my actions going forward. That meant continuing the same effort and enthusiasm for surgery that allowed me to succeed in residency.

In short, I continued to be myself.

Clinically, I spent my time divided among three places: the trauma bay, the operating room and Rhoads 5 surgical intensive care unit (SICU).

HUP's 1,400-square-foot trauma resuscitation bay could handle three patients simultaneously. Large, clean and state of the art, the bay saw constant use with daily gunshot victims, blunt trauma and facility transfers. Video cameras mounted on the ceiling recorded each resuscitation for later critique. I assumed responsibilities for maintaining the videos.

I liked Penn's approach to trauma. Each resuscitation proceeded "by the book," following Advanced Trauma Life Support (ATLS) protocols. Staff donned lead aprons, blue gowns, gloves and masks. Each nurse, resident and attending, positioned around the stretcher, assumed a specific role. The airway person remained at the head, a primary assessor stood to the patient's right, a trauma nurse and procedure resident stood to the patient's left, the team leader observed from the foot, and a recorder documenting the resuscitation stood to his side.

After evaluation and stabilization, our next step frequently led to the OR. A transitional time for me, I mastered new surgical techniques while teaching basics to the residents. I found Penn residents to be super smart, widely published and nearly incompetent in the OR. One of my fears coming to Penn was an emphasis on publishing without a firm basis in clinical skills. That's why I preferred Emory. Observing the residents made me appreciate my training at Buffalo.

Rhoads 5, a 56-bed surgical intensive care unit, became my second home. Sign-out occurred at 7 a.m. in the conference room, where new admissions and problems were discussed. Morning rounds commenced at 8. We moved from patient to patient assessing treatment and formulating a plan. Radiology rounds were held at 11 a.m., followed by conferences. Afternoon rounds began at 3:30, and evening sign-out started at 7 p.m.

The trauma service organized into two teams, each with four residents and a fellow. My call schedule put me on every fourth night.

Luxury.

Post-call, I could leave after morning rounds. I always left when I was supposed to and never violated the resident work hour restrictions. I wouldn't want to violate the work hour regulations, right?

In the SICU, I earned the nickname "Super-Intern." I found it impossible to remain in my call room at night, as I was equally worried about my patients and eager to participate in new cases. During orientation, residents were given a list of "Fellow Call Triggers," actions that required the Fellow to be called: intubation, resuscitation greater than two liters, vasopressors, etc. Someone added "Dr. Pryor on call." Frequently, I placed a line or checked labs while the intern slept. I remember telling Rich about it.

"John, you're the Fellow now," he said. "Remember when you were a resident and you took care of shit while your senior slept?"

"Yeah, but..."

"Well, it's your turn to take it easy; you've earned it. You can't keep doing everything all the time. You'll burn out."

I knew what he was saying, but he didn't understand.

The learning curve was steep, especially when you work so many hours. After only a few weeks, I became comfortable in my new role.

Fellowship

Of course, we couldn't keep things simple. In October, just as we began to settle in our new environment, Carmela discovered she was pregnant again. Our second child would arrive while I was still in my first year of fellowship.

⁊

The gunfire finally peters out like the last few popcorn kernels. The smoke starts to clear, and I see silhouettes roving the hill. They approach a foxhole, pop off a few rounds, and yell, "Clear!"

I grab my bag and shoulder my rifle. Starting toward the line, I hear shouts, "Medic! Medic!" My heart pounds as I run toward the shouts. Wisps of smoke dissolve, and the scene becomes visible. Two men hunch over the wounded man. His exposed chest weeping blood from the bullet holes.

Dropping my bag, I realize how helpless I am. No IVs, no chest tube, no scalpel, no operating room. I look around the desolate battlefield. No ambulance—no place to go if there was one.

I pull out trauma pads and press them tight against his chest and belly. They blush bright red and begin to ooze blood. His face drains, ashen. He starts to gasp.

"Shit!"

I could save him. If I had him in the operating room, I could save him. I look up to see DEATH *looming over me. I fall into his hood, and the silent blackness envelopes me. I'm stunned by the empty nothingness of death.*

Carmela shook me awake.
"Danielle's crying," she mumbled, half asleep. "Can you go get her?"

⁊

My schedule kept me at work most of the time, but Carmela didn't have it any easier. In addition to keeping the house, preparing meals, doing laundry and taking care of Danielle, she worked part time in a pediatric emergency department.

Her gestation made it that much more miserable.

Luckily, the pregnancy progressed without complications. At the ultrasound, we learned it was a boy and began to discuss names.

"I like Christopher," I said. "It was my father's middle name."

"What's wrong with Frank?" Carmela wanted to name the baby after her father, Franco. "He can be Francis Xavier like your grandfather."

Puppy's name was Francis Xavier. It was a good idea. We could honor both families in one fell swoop. But, Francis?

"Okay," I conceded, "as long as we use Hatshepsut for a middle name if the next one is a girl."

"Hat shit what?"

"Hatshepsut," I said. "She was the Queen Pharaoh of Egypt."

"You're crazy. You know that?"

"I'll take that as a yes."

ℰ℘

Carmela's due date was June 4, and I have to tell you, I came really close to getting it right this time.

Really close.

I had off May 21-27. Frankie came on the 29th. She'll tell you I screwed up again, but I could only take a week this time—and, really, who can predict when a baby's going to arrive?

Sunday the 28th, I rounded in the morning and came home. That night, contractions started, and she labored all night. I was supposed to take call at 5 a.m. in the SICU but found someone to cover me. Contractions got bad at 3 a.m., and we pulled into Chestnut Hill Hospital at 4:30.

As far as deliveries go, it was pretty horrible. Anesthesia placed an epidural, but it didn't take. She felt everything; it was basically natural childbirth. At 9 a.m., he came out: Francis Xavier Pryor.

I stayed as long as I could, but at 11 a.m. I had to get back to work.

"You good?" I asked her.

"What?" she asked. "You're really going to leave?"

"I'm on call," I said, as if that explained everything. "Besides, there's nothing for me to do anyway. I don't have breasts."

I never realized how close I came to getting divorced that day.

Too wrapped up in work to appreciate my family, I showed up during radiology rounds in the SICU.

"John?" Katie was surprised to see me. "What are you doing here?"

"Didn't your wife just give birth?" asked Mark, one of my cofellows.

"She's fine," I told them.

At midnight, I jotted down the events of the day:

5/29/00

What a great day! Francis Xavier Pryor was born today at 08:46. Seven pounds, ten ounces, 20 inches and sooo cute. Mom started serious contractions at about 3:00 a.m.—went to the hospital at 4:30. There was a lot of pain involved, an epidural was placed, but it wasn't working and the contractions were brutal. Carmela did great, however, and after several hours of pushing, a little black-haired munchkin poked his head out. The first view I got was his cheek, then his face—big lips, small nose—not like Danielle, big nose and squished face. He cried just a little bit and went right to sleep. Pauletta was in town to help watch Danielle. I was to bring them to the hospital around noon. Danielle was very excited to see "The Baby." She played with him, held him and kissed him. She watched Mom breast feed and didn't even get jealous.

I have so many hopes and apprehensions for Francis. The 90s are very prosperous times. Economy is great, crime is down—world is mostly at peace. I know how the times cycle, and I am afraid Francis will face adversity much more than my generation. I am especially afraid that his generation will fight a war. We are due for a conflict. I want Danielle and Francis to be happy. Carmela and I work so hard for that. I am tired. I work so much, I am getting older, and it is getting so hard to work these 36-hour shifts. Right now, it is 11 p.m. on Monday. I really haven't slept since Sunday. I still have 12 hours to go. I am in the SICU at Hosp Univ of Penn—several real sick patients tonight. I spend my time just trying to keep everyone alive until the morning. I love my work, but it is getting tougher each day. I can't imagine doing anything else. Maybe someday Francis or Danielle will fall in love with medicine the way I have.

I need sleep.

I didn't sleep that night. When I returned to Carmela, it was 1 p.m. the next day. Fifty-six hours. Awake for fifty-six hours, a new personal record. I remember holding Frankie in my arms in the Barcalounger before passing out. Pauletta rescued him as my arms went slack.

❦

There are some points in your life that are so miserable that you wonder how you ever survived. For me, it was summer 2000.

Philly experienced a heat wave, and our air-conditioner died. The stifling heat reminded me of Grenada. The apartment was a mess; baby toys littered the floor, and the diaper genie pumped out toxic fumes. Sitting at the dining table, I tried to work on my paper while one child or the other constantly interrupted me.

I had a name for it: Baby Hell.

When Carmela worked, I struggled to stay awake watching the kids. One would start crying, then the other would join the cry fest. At meals, I fought to get Danielle to eat. Bedtime meant more crying.

Desperate for a break, I needed to get away for a while—a holiday from the hospital, an escape from that claustrophobic apartment, and relief from the heat. And sleep. I felt I could sleep for a week straight. But I had no time off, and we didn't have any money even if I did.

The stress caught up with me. I finally snapped.

Trying to sleep post-call, the crying woke me. Incensed, I picked up a hammer and smashed picture frames as I walked down the stairs.

"I. Can't. Fucking. Stand. This. Place!" Glass shattered around me and tumbled down the stairs. The babies started to wail. Carmela just stared at me in disbelief.

And then disgust.

I got to the bottom of the stairs and dropped the hammer.

"I quit," I announced. "I can't fucking take it anymore. I quit."

I stood, palms on my forehead, while Carmela calmed the children. Finally, I looked at the stairs and back at Carmela. I sighed heavily. "Where's the broom?"

ↄ

Fellowship prepared me for four types of clinical scenarios. Beyond the obvious acute trauma and surgical critical care, two other patient populations kept me busy: emergency surgery and critical transfers.

Emergency surgery, an emerging category, constitutes those cases that can't wait for the next day's OR schedule. Traditionally, an acute appy or hot gallbladder would be taken by the general surgeon on call. Most of these surgeons took call from home and returned in the middle of the night to operate. But as the trauma surgeon, I was in house all the time, available to go right to the OR if necessary. This was less of an issue at major teaching hospitals that had residents, but at local community hospitals it made sense. The patient received better care, and the case would be transferred to the general surgery service the next day.

Critical transfers added an extra burden to a service beyond capacity. Most followed a similar scenario: Grandma develops severe abdominal pain. Concerned family takes Grandma to Rinky-Dink Hospital in Boondocks, PA, where a myopic, nearly retired, surgeon operates. After botching the case, he keeps Grandma at Rinky-Dink until nearly dead. As a last ditch effort, the surgeon packages Grandma in a helicopter and flies her to me. Problem solved.

For him.

For me, it's an instant train wreck. Sickest of the sickest, these patients arrive harboring multiple complications and infections. They require intensive care and multiple operations to repair failed or botched procedures. Most of my trauma patients got better or died, but the transfers lingered for months, draining resources and incurring astronomical expense. Despite my efforts, mortality remained high. Transfer patients tested my clinical ability, mental resolve and emotional capacity.

In a way, both emergency surgeries and transfers are patient dumps, cases where other surgeons didn't have the interest or ability to do their jobs. I viewed it differently; these patients, either at 3 a.m. or after multiple failed surgeries, had no other option. I was their only hope, the wall that stood between them and DEATH. It was an extension of my attitude as a volunteer medic, that I was the "someone else" in "let someone else take care of it."

Fellowship allowed me to expand my role beyond the bedside. In Buffalo, I performed administrative duties, but the priority was clinical skills and ability. Now, especially in my second year, I became involved in administrative duties. I was given an office and shared an assistant. I participated in committees, taught ATLS and learned how to run a trauma center.

Above all, however, I honed my skills as a team leader.

Medicine, and trauma especially, is a team effort. Surgeons are notorious for their egos, and that can cause friction when trying to get everyone to work together. The surgeon is important, but he cannot function in a vacuum, just as a quarterback cannot execute a pass without the linemen protecting him. The surgery team includes nurses, residents, fellows, respiratory therapists, dietitians, PharmDs and students. If you think any member is expendable, try replacing one for a day.

One episode in the trauma bay highlighted my approach. The patient was critical, so everyone was high strung. There was a new nurse on the team, and she was just overwhelmed. She couldn't get a vein to draw blood, couldn't get the Foley in and made a medication error. As the patient wheeled to CT, I noticed she was shaken and tears were welling up.

"Listen," I pulled her to the side, "we all have bad days. You can't let it bother you too much." I told her a story of when I was a paramedic. "I had a patient in cardiac arrest, couldn't get the tube, couldn't get an IV. I was completely fucking useless. By the grace of God, the guy survived, no thanks to me. It happens, but you have to shake it off and do better the next time."

She wiped her eyes, gave me a nod, and walked out of the hospital, never to be seen again.

No, I'm just kidding. She got through it, just as we all get through it because we're a team.

It's my job to keep the team together.

❧

While I tried to control my hectic time in Philly, Rich was preoccupied as an ER resident in Syracuse. Unable to visit together, we were lucky to find time for a phone call every few weeks.

I called him before the presidential election in 2000.

"Hey," I said, "just got back from Sweden."

"No shit!" Rich said. "How was that?"

"Pretty wild. They don't get much of penetrating trauma there."

"That's 'cause they don't have enough guns."

"Right. So they shoot live pigs with assault rifles and then rush them to the treatment area. Then the instructor says, 'Okay, now save the pig.'"

"Yeah," he laughed, "that'd go over real well in this country."

"Right, can you imagine?"

"Hey, I've got some news."

"Yeah, what?"

"Deidre's pregnant," he said.

"Really?! Holy crap, that's great!" I couldn't believe my little brother was going to be a daddy.

We talked shop for a while before turning to the election.

"So, you gonna vote for Gore?" I asked.

"Well, what's the alternative? Bush? You can't be serious."

"What's wrong with Bush?"

"Are you kidding? The guy's a moron. He's nothing like his father."

"It's okay," I said. "He'll be surrounded by good people; he's got Dick Cheney and Colin Powell ..."

"John, he's an idiot; it's got nothing to do with ideology. I would vote for McCain if he were the nominee. I like him. Bush isn't qualified ..."

"He's qualified ..."

"Yeah, because he's well connected—not because he possesses any intelligence or ability."

"Rich, it won't matter; if he wins, he's gonna have a lot of smart advisers, and he'll do what they tell him."

"Is that what Republicans call leadership?"

❧

In the spring of 2001, Schwab offered me a job. I considered my options: Buffalo was desperate to have me back, but we were done with Buffalo. I considered offers in Boston and New York and could easily get a job at Albany Med. But I was very happy with the people at HUP, and the hospital began to feel like home. Penn was fertile with academic opportunities; it fostered an environment where I could continue to grow and mature both as a surgeon and teacher.

Carmela and I began our search for better living conditions. We considered the Philly suburbs but decided to live across the river in New Jersey. From here it was only an hour on the Jersey Turnpike to Carmela's parents in Brooklyn.

Our real estate agent showed us several houses in Cherry Hill and Haddonfield. We settled on a nice two-story colonial on Europa Boulevard in Cherry Hill. It had a room for my office and a furnished basement for all the toys. Danielle ran from room to room, excited about all the space in her new house.

The house was a huge improvement from the cage in Chestnut Hill, but I had my sights on something better down the road.

"It's a nice starter house," I said to the agent.

"It's a nice house," she corrected me.

❧

In June, I was in and out of the garage, packing boxes for the move. Frankie toddled after me.

"I need to go out for a minute," Carmela said, "You have to watch him."

"He's fine," I said.

"Really," she said. "He's going to get hurt out here."

"You're being paranoid," I said.

When she returned home, I was holding pressure to his lip. At least, he'd stopped crying.

"What happened?" She was furious.

"He fell," I said.

"Let me see."

I removed the cloth. A stellate laceration crossed the vermillion border, where the skin meets the lip. If it wasn't lined up properly, it would scar badly.

"Fuck!" she said.

We loaded up the car and headed for the Children's Hospital of Philadelphia (CHOP). Once settled in a room, we instantly started to argue.

"It'll be one or two stitches," Carmela said. "We can just hold him still."

"No," I said. "If he moves, it won't line up right. He needs to be sedated."

"He just ate. We'll be here for hours."

"Carm, I'd rather get it done right."

We waited in a crowded, bustling, screaming-baby filled emergency room while Frankie digested his stomach contents. Danielle started to whine immediately. During this time, I learned which resident was on for plastic surgery.

"Oh, no," I said. "I know her. She ain't touching Frankie."

"Then, who?" Carmela asked.

As the most qualified person present, I briefly entertained the idea of doing it myself. But then I thought of the asthma kid and my vow never to treat my own family.

"Let's just have the ER attending do it," I conceded.

Four hours later, Frankie was given a shot of Ketamine and drifted into unconsciousness. While his eyes beat slow sideways nystagmus, the ER attending placed a single vicryl stitch.

"That looks good," he said and started packing up the instruments.

"What, one?!" I looked at his lip. It came together nicely.

Carmela shook her head at me, frustrated by the whole ordeal. "All that for one stitch?"

"Well, how was I to know it would only need one?"

We packed up our stuff and headed home.

Two days later, the stitch fell out.

✧

In July 2001, I completed my fellowship and began the transition to faculty attending. My salary increased. I was given a better office and a full-time assistant. The call schedule got much better. I made Sunday my protected time for home; usually, I rounded early but then spent the rest of the day with Danielle and Frankie.

We moved to Cherry Hill, and I leased a silver Jetta. Over the next few weeks I started to settle into my new role as attending. I had finally arrived: a beautiful wife, two great kids, a house, two cars and my dream job.

So why was I so miserable?

I suppose it was like post-partum depression. I had struggled for so long: fighting to get into medical school, proving myself at Buffalo, slaving as a resident and striving to fit in at Penn. Suddenly the fight was over. I had won.

I had no idea how to handle it.

"What's the matter with you?" Carmela confronted me.

"I don't know," I said. "It all seems so easy."

"Easy? *Easy!?*" she was aghast. "What was easy? You were never home, and when you were, you were dead to the world exhausted. We have no money, we never go anywhere, we never go out! What the hell was so easy?!"

She didn't understand. I had focused on a life purpose, a career goal. Now that it was accomplished, I didn't know what to do with my life.

I would have to think of something.

September 11th

The commute to Philly from Cherry Hill was a breeze at 5 a.m., and I remember looking forward to a light schedule over the next few days. While rounding on my critical patients, I paused after writing the date for my orders.

9-11, I thought, *they should make it national* EMS *day.*

At 8 a.m. we began morning report. A cloistered group of surgeons, fellows, and residents busily reviewed radiology studies and labs on our SICU players.

At 9:00 I excused myself from the group to answer a page. Before I could get to a phone I was approached by one of the nurses.

"Did you see that a plane hit the World Trade Center?" she asked.

I always feared a plane might accidentally crash into the Twin Towers, so the news wasn't particularly surprising. Word quickly got around, and we abandoned morning report to watch the live video on ABC.

Thick black smoke rose from the North Tower as we sat, stunned. I began to comment on my time in New York when the screen exploded with an enormous fireball.

"What was that?"

"Holy shit!"

The initial impact was disturbing, but nobody imagined it was deliberate. The second impact, however, caused serious confusion. Unable to accept the reality, I could not yet comprehend this was a terrorist attack.

The scale of the buildings made perspective difficult, but I knew the fires were enormous. I feared for the people above the impact, engulfed in smoke, but I assumed they would climb to the roof and be rescued. People below could probably evacuate safely.

When images of a smoking Pentagon filled the television, my knees went weak. Now it was clear—we were under attack. Philadelphia was located halfway between New York and Washington, and I feared we would be next.

I watched the coverage in the ICU for a while before joining Dr. Shapiro in the call room; he was glued to CNN.

"What was that?" he yelled.

The camera panned back revealing a column of smoke, like a ghost tower.

"It collapsed!" I said.

I couldn't reconcile what my eyes were seeing.

How could it collapse? I thought.

Up until then, the catastrophe was contained. But with the collapse, I imagined debris spread over several blocks. Casualties could be in the thousands.

A wave of emotion flooded over me. Images of the WTC surfaced from my subconscious. In second grade, I learned of the world's tallest building under construction. I came home and showed my father a picture of the half-completed structure. He laughed and said, "I know. That's where I go to work." My dad was always kidding me, and I giggled. But this time, he wasn't joking. He really did work there. In 1976, I remember having my nose pressed against the window of the 32nd floor, gazing out on the Hudson as an armada of tall ships, celebrating the country's bicentennial, slowly sailed past. In the summer of 1988, I pulled my girlfriend close against a chill wind atop the South Tower as we looked out on the city from 1,300 feet.

I recalled my brother's story when the towers lost power. A mass casualty incident with just the power going out—now, two planes and a tower collapse!

My heart began to race.

I became a sixteen-year-old EMT with an ambulance pager blaring in my head.

I have to go, I thought.

This was a disaster of unprecedented proportions; even the resources of New York City would be overwhelmed. They needed my help.

I have to go NOW!

I wasn't on call and had few clinical responsibilities that day and for the next few days. Still, absconding from work would make a lot of people angry. I decided to pray for forgiveness rather than ask for permission. Hopefully, I wouldn't get fired.

I found Dr. Dabrowski, who kept equipment prepared for disasters. He offered me his pack. It had two large compartments—one with basic equipment, the other with field amputation instruments. He removed the amputation equipment and suggested I fill both compartments with basic supplies.

It would be a fateful error.

I stopped by my office to get a few things. Lauren, my administrative assistant, noticed the duffle and quickly surmised my intentions.

"What are you doing?" she asked, following me to my desk.

"Listen," I said, "if Carmela calls, tell her you don't know where I am."

I stuffed a spare battery and charger into the duffle and headed out the door.

"You're going to New York?!" she said. "I can't lie to her about that!"

"The hell you can't," I said. "I'll see you when I get back."

I slung the duffel over my shoulder and headed for the parking garage. I had $100 in cash, a fully charged cell phone and half a cup of coffee.

I drove north on Route 76, heading for the New Jersey Turnpike. Attempts to call my wife were thwarted with the recording, "We're sorry, all our circuits are busy …" I tuned to 1010 WINS, New York's news channel. I learned they closed the NJ Turnpike northbound. This would be a real problem, and I thought I might not be able to get near the city. I envisioned thousands of people trying to evacuate

Manhattan with cars driving south in northbound lanes. However, I continued on, eager to see how bad it really was.

At a rest stop, I pulled off for gas. In the convenience store, I grabbed a flashlight, lighters, pens, work gloves, three gallons of bottled water, and some Cliff bars. The meager provisions hardly prepared me for what lay ahead.

Continuing north, 1010 WINS reported all routes into NYC were closed. They also reported the second tower had collapsed and lower Manhattan was being evacuated. Instructions were given to walk uptown and over the Brooklyn Bridge. I envisioned hordes of walking wounded evacuating lower Manhattan. Initially, my plan was to get to the NJ side of the Holland Tunnel, park, and set up an aid station to help with the wounded coming out of the tunnel from downtown.

Speeding north, a request went out for any available plastic and burn surgeons to report to St. Vincent's Hospital. This was my ticket in, and I decided to head for St. Vincent's. Near exit 11, traffic slowed to a crawl. Ahead, flashing cruisers directed traffic toward the off ramp. Slowly breaking rank, I approached the road block as a dozen troopers grabbed their holsters.

I spoke to the officer in charge and showed my ID.

"Be careful, son," he said, handing back my badge. His concern was unsettling and made me feel as if I were going off to war. He stepped back, waving me onto an empty highway.

I arrived at the Holland Tunnel amazed to find it quiet and empty. No hordes of exiting New Yorkers, only a barricade of police and national guardsmen. I spoke with several officers, telling them I needed to get to St. Vincent's. I figured I would hop an ambulance or cruiser to get to the hospital. To my surprise, they waived me through. Alone in the tunnel, I realized I was driving through a prime terrorist target. I floored the accelerator.

From Canal Street, I headed up Hudson to 8th Ave. Driving through the Village, I was struck at the sight: Pedestrians strolled the sidewalks; patrons dined in outdoor cafes. By all appearances, it was a normal late summer's day.

At 14th Street, I talked my way through a final road block and parked across from Vinnie's ER. A flurry of activity enveloped 7th Avenue: ambulance and police cars filled the street, hordes of news crews set up across the street in the Village Green, and the family practice center had hundreds of volunteers lined up to donate blood. Dozens of stretchers lined the sidewalk outside the ER; a virtual wall of supplies was stacked behind them. Doctors and staff, dressed in scrubs and lab coats, waited outside for patients to arrive.

I gathered my equipment: wallet, cell phone, two pens, pager, and trauma shears tucked into my belt. I wore a blue scrub shirt, blue pants and white sneakers. It was 10:30 a.m.

St. Vincent's had activated its disaster plan. Staff wore fluorescent bibs with labels like "Incident Commander" or "Communications." I approached "Medical," who had me sign in with my name and license number. She led me to the surgeon staging room and told me to wait until called. Surgeons of all specialties, including orthopedics, plastics, ENT, and general surgery, mingled and loitered. As I waited, another twenty surgeons filled the space to capacity.

Clearly, they had more than enough surgeons sitting idle. I decided to leave and search for a role in the field. On the way out, I ran into Neil Reich, an anesthesiologist I knew from residency. I asked about the wounded. He said there were a few burns and one DOA from a crush injury. The rest had only minor injuries.

Walking south on 7th Avenue, I waved down an ambulance and hitched a ride to a staging area at Chambers Street and West Side Drive near Stuyvesant High School. As we made our way to this area, I could see hundreds of firefighters and police lining West Side Drive. The ambulance slowly waded through the crowd. We parked on Chambers Street and I got out.

On the corner of Chambers and West Side Drive, fire and police set up a command center. A group of medical personnel surrounded the Mobile Emergency Response Vehicle (MERV). I introduced myself to the physician in charge. His name was Scott, a surgeon from Mt. Sinai. Around me, physicians, residents, medical students and nurses had come to help. I recognized Carlos Puyana, a trauma surgeon from Pittsburgh, who recently spoke in Philadelphia.

We organized into three teams, each headed by a surgeon. Inside the MERV, we cleaned dust from the collapse and organized the equipment. Initially, we planned for the critical patients to be brought into the MERV for stabilization. However, the space was cramped and could only accommodate a few patients at a time. Scott suggested we set up a field hospital in one of the nearby buildings.

I walked across the street to Stuyvesant High School. The lobby was large and spacious, perfect for our needs. Police cleared out the area and cordoned off a perimeter. EMS supervisors took over setting up equipment and treatment bays.

Rescuers continued to pour in, filling West Side Drive with ambulances and fire apparatus. Equipment from Jersey, Rockland County, Poughkeepsie, New Haven, Connecticut, and Long Island packed the road. An EMS lieutenant was frantically trying to untangle the gridlock.

Throughout the day, a steady stream of "walking wounded" exited the danger zone. They were mostly firefighters with eye complaints, asthma, burns or minor injuries. There were no critical patients.

At one point, a dazed fire captain came shuffling out of the danger zone. He carried the remnants of a white helmet. It looked as if it had been chewed and spat by a giant beast. He approached the fire command center calling for the chaplain. I saw tears streaked against his dust-caked face. The helmet belonged to the fire commissioner, killed in the collapse with hundreds of others. I choked up, fighting back my own tears.

As the afternoon progressed, we became better prepared for casualties. Still, there were none.

At five o'clock, the earth began to rumble, and WTC 7 vanished from view. A huge cloud of debris erupted from behind the building in front of us. The cloud burst upward and rushed toward us. A crowd of firefighters turned and ran uptown screaming for everyone to run. I jumped into the MERV, quickly followed by about 40 rescuers. There were shouts to close the doors, kneel on the floor and cover your heads. Through a small window, I saw the rolling cloud envelop the MERV. But the impact was feeble. After the dust settled, we went out to see if anyone was hurt. The dust was very fine, not a lot of heavy debris; the workers were okay. Luckily, the collapse happened after the vast majority of firefighters were out of the scene.

From this point on, there was a lot of waiting. Without an active rescue effort, there were no patients to care for. The EMS captain mentioned there might be a need for some doctors to go into the inner zone. Scott, Carlos and I decided if patients didn't start coming out, Scott and I would go in.

I returned to Stuyvesant and observed the progress. The police had secured the building, admitting only appropriate medical personnel. A triage desk recorded incoming patients. Bays were set up for specific complaints: eye irrigation stations, burn care, simple lacerations, asthma, etc. They even set up an area for critical patients including two "operating rooms." Any operation here would be standard of care for the Civil War. I decided anyone needing an OR would be sent to NYU downtown hospital, less than a mile away.

I asked a nurse who was in charge of the field hospital. She looked at me blankly and replied, "You are." I felt uneasy that a surgeon from Philadelphia could arrive at a disaster in New York and be in charge of anything. By ten o'clock, the field hospital was wall-to-wall medical personnel with nary a patient to be seen.

I was struck by the lack of EMS organization. Fire and Police had elaborate command centers, but no one seemed to be in charge of the medical response. EMS captains and lieutenants loitered, but no one took charge. A paramedic supervisor (a woman, don't remember her name) was doing an excellent job of organizing the field hospital in the high school, but no one outside was clearly in command. Scott had taken charge of the medical personnel, but he was not part of EMS. I assumed control only because everyone was coming to me as the only trauma surgeon. At one point, an emergency physician with a badge and a radio showed up. I introduced myself as a surgeon and told him what we were doing. He walked aimlessly; he was completely useless. None of this was relevant without patients to treat; but if casualties did start to mount, the system would have collapsed. I'm sure of it.

For hours I languished, anticipating some kind of activity. Passing the time, I chatted with other volunteers as a plume of smoke continued to rise from lower Manhattan. I met Mike, an EMT and photojournalist from Long Island. In his excitement to respond, he forgot his camera. However, he did bring some very useful halogen caving helmets. I also met Bob, a former Navy SEAL and paramedic with expertise in search and rescue. We were all getting restless.

Meanwhile, police formed a formal barrier along Chambers Street to control entry to the inner zone.

I tracked down an EMS lieutenant and asked what happened to Scott, whom I hadn't seen in some time. Scott had entered the danger zone an hour earlier. No one knew what was going on down there. I heard rumors about a staging area near Battery Park, south of the collapse site. I couldn't believe anyone could get to the other side of the scene without going right through it. If anyone could use my help, it would be in the inner zone, and possibly closer at ground zero.

Mike, Bob and I decided to enter the inner zone, but first we would need to get past the police barricade.

"I can get us past them," Bob said.

"Bob," I said to the ex-Navy SEAL, "we can't kill anyone. You know that, right?"

"Have it your way," he shrugged.

Our break came at one o'clock in the morning. The danger zone was deemed "safe," and waves of replacement firefighters were being sent in. Next, groups of EMS personnel were gathered to go. A call went out for volunteers, and we jumped at the chance. Bob and I joined a group of ten nurses and paramedics. There was one other physician, but I was the only surgeon. A paramedic who had been at ground zero led us through the barrier, and we headed south.

Almost immediately, the scene changed. Darkness enveloped us as we left the staging area. Only our flashlights and headlamps pierced the blackness. The dust was thicker, almost six inches deep in some places. It was like walking through snow. The most unnerving feature, though, was the silence. Even our footfalls were muffled by the dust. Pitch black and quiet, I entered a void between worlds. I couldn't believe this was Manhattan.

As I walked south, the air became heavy. The smell of smoke and dry cement was so thick I could taste it. I donned a mask that had been hanging around my neck all day. It was uncomfortable and suffocating. My eyes began to tear from the caustic smog.

We came upon firemen sitting on piles of rubble. They seemed to be in a daze, absently staring at the destroyed buildings. We stopped at each firefighter to check his condition. Most agreed to eye irrigation, but otherwise refused any care.

Ahead, there was a glow in the darkness. It cast a light against the black background like a giant campfire in the woods.

Ground Zero.

We stopped at the bridge that led to the financial center. Several pumpers and ladder trucks aimed hoses at the smoldering twisted remains of WTC 6. Runoff mixed with the heavy soot, creating a lake of mud. The team went around flushing eyes. I approached one of the firefighters.

"Do you know if they're extricating victims anywhere?" I asked.

"No way," he said absently. "There's nothing, nobody."

I shuddered.

Bob and I surveyed the scene as the medics irrigated eyes. Bob looked east, down Vesey street.

"Nobody's helping those guys down there," he pointed.

"Down there" was a narrow remnant of street now filled with treacherous mounds of sharp, twisted metal. Perched on either side, precipitous girders and debris loomed over the narrow passage. Occasionally a "bang" punctured the silence as debris fell to the street.

Oblivious to the hazards, Bob began gathering a few duffels of equipment.

"Ah …" I started to protest. I glanced down Vesey again before grabbing a duffle.

Right, I thought, *this is probably a bad idea.*

We started east down Vesey. Soon we were away from the lights and sounds of the pumper. The darkness returned, and I heard my ears ringing in the silence.

I shone my light at the walls of destruction. A shredded facade disappeared into the smoke-filled darkness. Beyond ten stories, nothing was visible. I worried what dangers lurked precariously above my head.

We were flanked by rows of cars that took the brunt of the collapse. Those still with a body were stripped of their paint. Some were reduced to little more than a drivetrain. Even the seats were stripped of their padding, leaving only steel frame and springs. It was like the set of a horror movie.

The dust was now a foot thick with more significant debris. Besides paper, I could identify fragments of office equipment, bits of tables, chairs and computers. Nothing larger than a few inches across.

"Ever see anything like this before?" I asked, my voiced muted by the dust.

"Yeah, sort of," replied Bob.

"You notice anything strange?" I asked, as if there was anything one could add to such a surreal scene. But there was. I sensed it but didn't want to say anything.

"No bodies," Bob answered flatly.

No bodies, I thought.

When I entered the danger zone, I prepared myself for the dead. I saw none. Now, only two blocks from ground zero, there were still no signs of the deceased.

"Looking at the condition of those cars," Bob added, "anyone standing on the street was probably incinerated. The rest are probably under the wreckage."

It was then, in the middle of the destruction of Vesey, among the thousands of ghosts circling the smoldering rubble that I had a sudden grip of fear. The rational part of my brain briefly penetrated my defenses and made an unwelcome appearance.

What the hell am I doing here? I thought.

I had foolishly run into this catastrophe. I put my life in jeopardy without even thinking. What if something happened to me? What would my wife and kids do without me? What if I never saw my children again? Now, as I made my way through this canyon of annihilation, I felt I had bitten off more than I could chew. It reminded me of being on the top of a roller coaster. I suddenly wanted to get off.

I became flushed. My heart started to race. The mask choked my sweaty face, and the feeling of suffocation intensified. I wanted to rip it off, but here the smoke had gotten thicker. It would be worse without it.

I'm panicking, I thought.

In all my years as a paramedic and surgeon, I had never panicked. I was always the one taking control of the chaos. Here the chaos was overwhelming and inescapable. I needed to calm down and regain control. I forced myself to breathe slowly. I stopped looking up and focused on the lights ahead. The hysteria abated, and I regained my composure.

Seriously, I thought, *what's the worst that could happen?*

A loud crash answered in the darkness behind me.

We arrived at the fire apparatus. Several fixed hoses were spraying another pile of rubble; somehow I identified it as WTC 7. We spoke with the firefighters; none needed medical attention. Most were sitting or standing like statues, despondently staring into the mangled pile. Their faces expressionless, they would answer direct questions but otherwise remained silent.

The whole scene ran counter to my experiences as a paramedic. I had been to many fires and countless car accidents. Usually, there is mayhem with movement, action and shouting of commands. Here, however, were silence and stillness. No rushing. No shouting. No efforts to dig for victims. No attempts to attack the flames. The mood seemed defeated and hopeless. With five city blocks covered with two 110-story buildings, where does one possibly start?

Now, separated from our group, we moved on hoping to find an active search and rescue operation. We followed another narrow street and came upon Church Street. As we moved south along Church, I was suddenly was presented with a view of ground zero.

Holy Jesus, I thought.

A huge metal crown rose amid a field of endless twisted steel and pulverized concrete. It was backlit by raised stadium lights on portable generators. The crown was made from remnants of the external vertical girders that rose for three stories. The steel beams were arranged in a semicircle with the top half fanning out from the ground. Construction crews wielded acetylene torches to slice beams leaning against the crown. I wondered why they were attacking those girders in particular.

Throughout the day, I had heard rumors of buried victims making cell phone calls from beneath the rubble. I thought it was doubtful, but if there were any chance of saving someone tonight, it would be here at ground zero.

I found a fire captain and asked who was in charge of medical.

He directed me toward One Liberty Plaza, referred to as "Liberty," across from the South Tower. The building was in shambles. The facade appeared bombed with debris hanging from the windows. The smoke was still heavy, and I couldn't see above ten or so floors. The damage seemed so severe that I questioned the integrity of the structure.

Around the corner, we found a few ambulances parked outside the main entrance of Liberty. A surgical resident from NYU had organized a field hospital just inside the lobby. Three cots were surrounded with a fair amount of equipment. There was excellent organization with a triage station outside and two teams inside to render care. Again, there was one problem: No patients.

It was now 3:30 a.m., and I hadn't sat down for a long time. I decided to take a rest and find something to eat. Amazingly, in this crater of desolate destruction, there was plenty of food. On Liberty Street, a station was set up to hand out sandwiches, fruit, water and juice. Even a Burger King being used as a police command station opened its kitchen and started distributing hamburgers.

After a sandwich and a short rest, I walked out to the front of Liberty. The building had an overhang which offered protection from falling debris. The terrace was elevated above street level, providing an excellent view of the heavy metal cutting.

I joined a small group watching the sparks spray into the dark like mini fireworks. A minister from New Orleans attending a conference in the city felt compelled to help. Along with a priest, he tried to identify victims from wallets and IDs found in the pile. He also created a temporary morgue for the bodies. So far, there were only six.

A group of firefighters quickly approached Liberty. They were running for the lobby, yelling "Take cover!"

I stood motionless asking, "Take cover from what?" Then I felt rumbling and bolted into the lobby.

I slammed into the side of an elevator shaft and knelt down, hands over my head. The walls shook, and I braced for the roof to cave in on me. A crash outside spawned a dust cloud that flowed into the lobby. Part of an adjacent building had lost its façade, but there was no major collapse.

I made a note not to question running firefighters in the future.

Back in the lobby, I chose an empty cot and lay down. I hoped to get a solid hour of sleep, but just as I closed my eyes, I heard someone in the lobby.

"Is that surgeon in here?" It was one of the EMS lieutenants.

I was up in a flash.

"What's going on?" I asked after introducing myself.

"They sent me here to get you and some oxygen," he said. "There's a rescue in the plaza."

I felt an adrenaline surge and eagerly followed the paramedic out of Liberty. We walked past the ironworkers and up Church Street to what was once a wide-open space between the towers. Now, a few steps led to a pile of twisted metal and concrete.

Hell couldn't be any more gruesome.

A baleful darkness permeated the site. Hundreds of crimson eyes burned from the windows of the remaining buildings. The glowing flames mixed with the thick smoke to produce a dark aura. My eyes stung from the toxic vapors.

The footing was murderous. Nothing I stepped on was stable. Sharp, twisted metal shot up from the debris like metal fangs. Black holes of unknown depth pitted the landscape, hungry for a careless step.

I thought of my paramedic training and the first rule of rescue: Don't become a victim.

One fall, one misstep, I thought, *and I become a victim.*

I made my way toward the center of the plaza. I passed many firefighters, all with the same despondent stare. Some stood near difficult areas to help people across the terrain. So many of their brethren were dead. I wondered how they could still function.

In the distance, flames danced in the windows of every building. Smoke vented from the rubble. There was a lot of shifting of debris, especially if someone walked too close to a pit. Rescuers coming in from the plaza kept along a line of firefighters, who formed a path. This marked the safest route in.

As I walked deeper into the plaza, the lights and noise faded until there was again absolute silence. Wind whistled through the building remains. A dull moaning vibrated beneath my feet, and I froze in my tracks. Metal creaked, like the shifting of a ship's hull at sea.

The pile is going to collapse, I thought. *I'm going to die.*

"Don't worry about that," offered the paramedic. "It's been creaking like that all night."

His reassurance was negligible. I pressed on.

We passed between the burned-out structures of WTC 4 and WTC 5. Fires continued to burn in both buildings, especially the top floors. I was amazed they remained standing. I paused to look at the building on my right. Part of the roof seemed to have an odd overhang. It took a minute to realize the structure was a huge piece of wall that had impaled the side of the building.

That doesn't look stable, I thought.

The wind shifted. For a moment, the smoke cleared revealing the tortured remains of the North Tower. I recognized the distinctive outer columns that once formed the base of the building. It was like observing a loved one in the casket. As silly as it sounds, this was the first time I accepted the fact that this was the WTC. It really happened.

DEATH surrounded me. Not the DEATH I was used to—a single DEATH come for a single patient. Here, DEATH was everywhere, walking the pile and swooping through the darkness like broomstick-riding witches.

I'm standing on thousands innocent souls, I thought.

My eyes welled up and began to tear. I fought it, shook my head and shined the flashlight in my eyes. The feeling passed. Usually in a tragedy, there are things to do, patients to treat. The activity protects the rescuer from the emotional devastation. The lack of patients was becoming a serious psychological burden.

Halfway through the pile, we met up with a battalion chief in radio communication with the rescue team. The victim was confined in a deep hole, buried up to his chest. A surgeon and ER doc were down in the hole with him.

"They were able to dig him out to his thighs," the chief informed me.

"Both legs?" I asked.

"Yeah," he said.

"Amputation isn't an option at this level," I explained. "If you try to cut his legs, he'll bleed to death before you could get him out."

"Are you sure?" he asked.

"Just because someone is going to die doesn't mean you have to kill him."

It was a phrase I used frequently with my residents, and it just slipped out. I regretted saying it, but the chief understood what I meant.

A second rescue effort started in a nearby hole, and I went to investigate. This victim was not seriously trapped, and rescuers were able to quickly extricate him. The man was uninjured and didn't require my care. A paramedic started an IV, and the patient was carried from the pile.

It was one small victory, but there was an immediate boost to morale. Rescuers awakened as if a spell had been lifted. Firefighters began to spread out and search holes and crevices with renewed vigor. I was called back to the battalion chief.

"What's up?" I asked.

"The guy is vomiting," he said. "They need a drug, comrasine or something."

"Compazine. I don't have any." I hadn't brought any medications with me. There was none at the aid station either.

"And they want blood, too," added the chief.

"We'll have to send someone to the hospital to get it," I said.

We sent a runner to NYU downtown hospital for the medications and blood.

There was more chatter on the radio and the chief turned to me: "The Doc says he needs some equipment down in the hole. He's not saying much because he doesn't want to upset the patient."

I imagined the surgeon was considering a field amputation but didn't want to say it over the radio. I thought of how I could confirm this. "Ask him if he needs the Gigli," I said. A Gigli is a flexible wire saw used by surgeons to cut bone. It would be needed for any amputation attempt.

I heard the crackling response over the radio, "That's affirmative on the Gigli."

Shit! I thought. Back in Philadelphia, in the office of Dr. Dabrowski, a Gigli saw and amputation equipment lay uselessly in the dark.

I double checked my equipment, but there was no saw.

"What do we do?" asked the chief.

"Send another runner to the hospital," I said. "The other guy is going to take a while before he gets back."

As we waited for the saw, I observed the activity of the firefighters. One hole was very deep, and they were calling for a 34-foot ladder. When the ladder finally arrived, the firefighters explored the hole, but no one was found.

With the increased activity, firefighters were finding body parts. A hand was found and brought to one of the doctors. He took it, and became frantic. He tried to remove the wedding band. "We might be able to identify her by the ring," he said. It was not the time or place for identification, and the doctor was spooking the firefighters. I had to walk over and relieve him of the hand.

Other parts were found, including a decapitated torso. It was close to twenty hours since the attack, and the remains had begun to smell. The fetid odor reminded me of my paramedic days when neighbors called 911 because of a bad odor coming from an adjacent apartment. Other parts smelled of charred flesh. I spoke with the battalion chief about the remains.

"There's no way we can put each piece in its own body bag," I said. "We should set up a temporary morgue to place all the remains. Then forensics can take over when they get here."

The chief agreed.

I sent a medical resident on a quest to find body bags. He dutifully returned with a package, but when we opened it, we found hazmat garments. We did our best, wrapping the remains with what we had. I ordered the torso to the morgue at Liberty. It was the closest thing to a body I saw all day.

The runners had returned with the compazine and Gigli, but the hospital had refused to release blood. In the end, neither was needed. The victim was extricated without the need for amputation and was transported to the hospital. Again, there was nothing for me to do.

I was cold for the first time in the twilight just before dawn. Police were handing out coats to other volunteers and rescuers. I noticed they were brand new coats that still had the price tag attached. I declined a coat and donned an OR gown instead.

The sun rose. Light was shining—not only a new day, but a new era. In the blink of an eye, the world I'd grown up in had ended. Like many Americans, I had believed the United States was impenetrable. In the light of day, the destruction was unbelievable. Bombed-out buildings and smoldering rubble were the realm of Third World countries on distant continents, not lower Manhattan.

Like Britain during the blitzkrieg, I thought.

The paucity of workers overnight conveyed a sense of intimacy and isolation, but soon there would be thousands working on the pile. I imagined an army of rescue workers would soon descend on lower Manhattan.

I heard a radio report that hundreds of health care workers were still standing ready at Chelsea Piers and each of the hospitals. I wondered what they were waiting for. I was one of ten doctors at ground zero; it turned out to be ten more than were needed.

At 10:00 a.m., I packed up my duffle and made my way north on Church Street. When I arrived at Chambers, I noticed a large crowd contained by a police barricade. I ducked under the yellow police tape and was instantly accosted by a swarm of reporters. There were people from the *New York Times, Daily News* and some European papers.

"What's your name?" someone asked.

"What were you doing there?" added another.

I kept walking and answered some basic questions without elaborating. I didn't want to be rude, but I was exhausted and emotionally drained.

Then I was approached by a reporter from 1010 WINS. I felt obligated to stop because I felt 1010 WINS helped me get here in the first place.

"What's the rescue effort like?" the reporter asked.

"There is no rescue effort," I replied solemnly.

"Well, if there were thousands of people in the buildings and there is no rescue effort, what does that mean?" he asked.

I returned a look of despair but wouldn't give him the sound bite he was looking for.

They're all dead, I thought.

℃℈

Looking back on that day, I remember the main emotion I felt while standing on the pile of rubble was not anger, but profound sadness—not only for those who died and the rescuers who were missing, but for all the deaths to come. I knew this was the start of a long war, with many more casualties in the future.

After leaving New York, it took days to come off the adrenaline rush. Then, I fell into a deep depression for several weeks. I still have trouble talking about that day or when seeing images of it on television.

However, what I do not have is regrets. I take solace in believing that, however useless, I did everything I possibly could to help that day. I risked my job, my career and, at times, my life to be there.

I have no regrets.

That was the most important lesson I learned. If I were told I had inoperable cancer or had suffered a massive heart attack, I would want to lie in my bed knowing I lived my life without regrets—that I was a faithful and loving husband; that I raised my children as best I could; that I loved my children as much as a human heart could; that I prepared our finances, insurances, trust funds so my family would be cared for in my absence; and that I had completed, to the best of my ability, my life "To do" list. Without regrets, I would be able to accept death and gently pass from this world.

That is what I learned from 9-11.

Casus Belli

September 12, 2001. Europa continued her Jovian dance with Io and Ganymede as the gas giant swirled in multicolored turbulence. Unabated, the sun fused hydrogen in a fiery furnace of plasma and radiation, just as it had for millions of years. Winds blew across the Martian terrain, shifting the rusty sands across the barren landscape.

On a grand scale, the universe moved on with little regard to the events of September 11.

But on the third planet, great changes were afoot. Few events in modern history produced such disruption, setting enormous geopolitical wheels in motion.

The attack produced fear; fear that would influence presidential power, Middle East politics, foreign policy and the lives of millions of people. Repercussions would ripple for decades, redefining habeas corpus, torture, legal surveillance and justification for war.

At the time, I couldn't imagine how it would affect me.

Within hours of the attack, the media had reached a verdict: Osama Bin Laden and his Al-Qaeda network were found guilty. Less than a month later, our military launched an offensive against Al-Qaeda in Afghanistan.

Feelings of patriotism and duty, dormant since the first Iraq war, began to resurface. Briefly, I thought this might be another chance to serve my country; but the sides were grossly mismatched in our favor. This conflict would certainly be over before I could complete the paperwork to enlist.

It wasn't a war; it was a manhunt.

I turned my attention back to my family and tried to settle into my new role as attending. Completing my fellowship marked an end to some lifelong struggles: medical school, residency, getting a job. But like all commencements, it marked the beginning—the beginning of my professional career.

I continued to publish, lecture and operate, but my proudest moments came when I watched young residents take the reins for the first time.

"Don't worry," I would tell them, "I can get you out of any trouble you get yourself into."

This statement helped them focus on operating without worrying about screwing up. When I could observe a case without scrubbing in, it meant my kids were ready to fly solo.

I still obsessed over some patients, but I became increasingly stretched thin, unable to function as "super intern" like I used to. Struggling to find balance, I remember one case that helped put things in perspective.

My pager awoke me from a sound sleep in the middle of the night. I wasn't on call, but the fellows knew "on call" was a relative term for me. "If there's anything cool happening," I told them, "I want to know about it." I called back Gary Lombardo, one of the fellows.

"Gary," I croaked, clearing my throat, "It's Pryor. What's up?"

"JP—Niels has a kid open on the table, and we want to run something by you."

A young man had been shot multiple times. Niels Martin had taken him to the OR, opening him stem to stern to repair almost every major organ. But then Niels had come across a very complex, life threatening injury and wasn't sure how to proceed. He called Gary for help. They discussed it and decided on a course of action, but their plan was risky and unorthodox.

"Let's call JP," they said.

So, Niels was elbow deep in this kid's belly, Gary was describing the injuries and his plan. I received a real-time narration of what was going on. What they wanted to do was very difficult, and there was a good chance it wouldn't work, but I couldn't think of an alternative.

"Go for it," I told them. "It's what I would do."

In the morning, I rushed in to see if the patient survived. I met Niels and Gary at the patient's bed in the SICU. We were all beaming at each other. The patient was alive and stable. I was so fucking proud of those guys.

"Good stuff!" I said.

It was then that I experienced an epiphany. The time for me to take care of everything was coming to an end. Between traveling to conferences, writing papers, teaching, and raising two kids at home, I could not physically be present like I used to.

I realized my role was to train young surgeons to work in my stead. I needed to instill the same enthusiasm and dedication into the next generation of surgeons. My job was not so much to take care of patients anymore but to create outstanding surgeons who could take care of patients. If I could guide young residents to excel, then they, in turn, would pass on these skills. It was exponential.

I still needed to be the best surgeon possible. But now I was the example, the role model, the mentor Narmer and I had discussed so many years ago.

℘

Our military quickly dominated the conflict in Afghanistan, but Osama Bin Laden eluded our grasp. Then, during the 2002 State of the Union speech, President George W. Bush introduced a new player in the geopolitical equation:

"Iraq continues to flaunt its hostility toward America and to support terror. The Iraqi regime has plotted to develop anthrax, and nerve gas, and nuclear weapons for over a decade. This is a regime that has already used poison gas to murder thousands of its own citizens— leaving the bodies of mothers huddled over their dead children. This is a regime that agreed to international inspections—then kicked out the inspectors. This is a regime that has something to hide from the civilized world.

States like these, and their terrorist allies, constitute an axis of evil, arming to threaten the peace of the world. By seeking weapons of mass destruction, these regimes pose a grave and growing danger. They could provide these arms to terrorists, giving them the means to match their hatred. They could attack our allies or attempt to black-mail the United States. In any of these cases, the price of indifference would be catastrophic."[1]

Over the next year, Bush began to beat the war drums louder and louder. In speech after speech, Bush and Vice President Dick Cheney alluded to the dangers Iraq posed, citing past atrocities, active chemical weapons programs and a desire to obtain nuclear material. Cheney warned of the marriage between state-sponsored weapons of mass destruction with Al-Qaeda or other terrorist networks. The threat, he said, posed an unacceptable risk to the United States.

Iraq propaganda appeared in nearly every public address Bush made. In a speech to the Troops in Alaska:

"... One of the most dangerous things that can happen to the future of our nation is that these kind of terrorist organizations hook up with nations that develop weapons of mass destruction. One of the worst things that could possibly happen to freedom-loving people, whether it be the United States or our friends or allies, is to allow nations that have got a dark history and an ugly past to develop weapons of mass destruction like nuclear weapons or chemical weapons, or biological weapons which could, for example, be delivered by long-range mis-sile, to become a part of the terrorist network. And there are such nations in the world.

Of course, we'd like for them to change their ways, and we'll con-tinue to pressure them to do so. We'd like for them to conform to normal ways of treating their own people, plus their neighborhood, plus the world. We expect there to be transparency. People who have got something to hide make us nervous, particularly those who have gassed their own citizens in the past, for example.

---

[1] http://georgewbush-whitehouse.archives.gov/news/releases/2002/01/20020129-11.html

And so we expect them—and so do other freedom-loving countries—to change their behavior. But if they do not, the United States will do what it takes to defend our freedom. Make no mistake about it."[2]

During a March 2002 press conference:

"… I am deeply concerned about Iraq. And so should the American people be concerned about Iraq. And so should people who love freedom be concerned about Iraq.

This is a nation run by a man who is willing to kill his own people by using chemical weapons; a man who won't let inspectors into the country; a man who's obviously got something to hide. And he is a problem, and we're going to deal with him. But the first stage is to consult with our allies and friends, and that's exactly what we're doing."[3]

In May, while speaking with French president Chirac:

"… Let me start with the Iraqi regime. The stated policy of my government is that we have a regime change. And as I told President Chirac, I have no war plans on my desk. And I will continue to consult closely with him. We do view Saddam Hussein as a serious, significant serious threat to stability and peace."[4]

In a commencement speech at West Point:

"… For much of the last century, America's defense relied on the Cold War doctrines of deterrence and containment. In some cases, those strategies still apply. But new threats also require new thinking. Deterrence—the promise of massive retaliation against nations—means nothing against shadowy terrorist networks with no nation or citizens to defend. Containment is not possible when unbalanced dictators with weapons of mass destruction can deliver those weapons on missiles or secretly provide them to terrorist allies.

We cannot defend America and our friends by hoping for the best. We cannot put our faith in the word of tyrants who solemnly sign non-proliferation treaties and then systemically break them. If we wait for threats to fully materialize, we will have waited too long."[5]

During a press conference in Crawford, TX:

2   http://georgewbush-whitehouse.archives.gov/news/releases/2002/02/20020216-1.html
3   http://georgewbush-whitehouse.archives.gov/news/releases/2002/03/20020313-8.html
4   http://georgewbush-whitehouse.archives.gov/news/releases/2002/05/20020526-2.html
5   http://georgewbush-whitehouse.archives.gov/news/releases/2002/06/20020601-3.html

"There should be no doubt in anybody's mind this man [Hussein] is thumbing his nose at the world, that he has gassed his own people, that he is trouble in his neighborhood, that he desires weapons of mass destruction. I will use all the latest intelligence to make informed decisions about how best to keep the world at peace, how best to defend freedom for the long run.

We'll continue to consult. Listen, it's a healthy debate for people to express their opinion. People should be allowed to express their opinion. But America needs to know, I'll be making up my mind based upon the latest intelligence and how best to protect our own country plus our friends and allies."[6]

In September, Bush appeared before the United Nations:

"My nation will work with the u.n. Security Council to meet our common challenge. If Iraq's regime defies us again, the world must move deliberately, decisively to hold Iraq to account. We will work with the u.n. Security Council for the necessary resolutions. But the purposes of the United States should not be doubted. The Security Council resolutions will be enforced—the just demands of peace and security will be met—or action will be unavoidable. And a regime that has lost its legitimacy will also lose its power."[7]

At a September press conference:

"At the United Nations Security Council, it is very important that the members understand that the credibility of the United Nations is at stake, that the Security Council must be firm in its resolve to deal with a truth threat to world peace, and that is Saddam Hussein. That the United Nations Security Council must work with the United States and Britain and other concerned parties to send a clear message that we expect Saddam to disarm. And if the United Nations Security Council won't deal with the problem, the United States and some of our friends will."[8]

With the fear of 9-11 fresh in the American psyche, the Bush Doctrine became easy to swallow—that a pre-emptive attack against foreign threats is a justifiable policy of defense. Although many countries

---

6 http://georgewbush-whitehouse.archives.gov/news/releases/2002/08/20020816-3.html
7 http://georgewbush-whitehouse.archives.gov/news/releases/2002/09/20020912-1.html
8 http://georgewbush-whitehouse.archives.gov/news/releases/2002/09/20020919-1.html

fell within this definition, including Iran and North Korea, Iraq was singled out as the country most in need of "regime change."

☙

In July 2002, Rich completed his residency and accepted a position at Albany Medical Center. He moved into his first house with Deidre and one-year-old daughter, Sophia.

I was so proud of him.

When I came home in August for a visit, Rich and I were able to escape to a pub. It seemed like years since we'd been out for a beer together.

"So how's life in baby hell?" I asked him.

"Well, you know, it was hard in the beginning with all the crying," he said, "but now it's a lot better."

"Yeah?"

"Yeah, now I can finally sleep through the crying."

"Wait until the next one comes. When is she due?"

"March. Should be interesting."

As usual, our conversation turned to politics and Bush's interest in Iraq.

"I don't get it," Rich said, "we were attacked by Al-Qaeda, and now Bush is saber rattling against Iraq. It just doesn't make any sense. What does Iraq have to do with anything?"

"Are you nuts?" I said. "Saddam is dangerous."

"Yeah, but he's always been dangerous, and we never cared ..."

"But ..."

"He was dangerous when he invaded Kuwait, but we didn't need to take him out of power then ..."

"Rich, we were attacked. 9-11 changed everything."

"But we weren't attacked by Iraq. Saddam has nothing to do with religious extremists. You know about Middle East stuff. You should know that."

"He's got chemical and biological weapons ..."

"John, half the country is a no-fly zone patrolled by our planes. How much of a threat can they possibly be?"

"Rich, he gassed his own people."

"In 1988! Why didn't we care back then? Where was Reagan when Hussein gassed his own people?"

"You're not getting it. He's continued to develop chemical and biological weapons. Can you imagine if he gets them into New York or Philadelphia?"

"I don't see how this is possible. I mean, if he could attack the U.S., then why hasn't he? And if a terrorist attack is linked to Saddam, we'd nuke Iraq back to the Stone Age. So why risk it? What would he accomplish?"

"There's gotta be something," I said. "There's information or intelligence that the president has that he can't tell us."

"You think the government has a reason to invade Iraq but they can't tell us?"

"They must," I said.

"Well," he said, "I don't believe it."

વ્ક

On October 2nd 2002, legislation was introduced to congress authorizing the president to use force against Iraq. Over the next few days Bush maintained his argument:

"On its present course, the Iraqi regime is a threat of unique urgency. We know the treacherous history of the regime. It has waged a war against its neighbors; it has sponsored and sheltered terrorists; it has developed weapons of mass death; it has used them against innocent men, women and children. We know the designs of the Iraqi regime. In defiance of pledges to the U.N., it has stockpiled biological and chemical weapons. It is rebuilding the facilities used to make those weapons.

U.N. inspectors believe that Iraq could have produce enough biological and chemical agent to kill millions of people. The regime has the scientists and facilities to build nuclear weapons, and is seeking the materials needed to do so.

We know the methods of this regime. They buy time with hollow promises. They move incriminating evidence to stay ahead of inspectors. They concede just enough to escape—to escape punishment, and then violate every pledge when the attention of the world is turned away.

We also know the nature of Iraq's dictator. On his orders, opponents have been decapitated and their heads displayed outside their homes. Women have been systematically raped as a method of intimidation. Political prisoners are made to watch their own children being tortured. The dictator is a student of Stalin, using murder as a tool of terror and control within his own cabinet, within his own army, even within his own family. We will not leave the future of peace and the security of America in the hands of this cruel and dangerous man.

None of us here today desire to see military conflict, because we know the awful nature of war. Our country values life, and never seeks war unless it is essential to security and to justice. America's leadership and willingness to use force, confirmed by the Congress, is the best way to ensure compliance and avoid conflict. Saddam must disarm, period. If, however, he chooses to do otherwise, if he persists in his defiance, the use of force may become unavoidable."[9]

While congress debated the issue, Rich and I continued our dispute over the subject.

"I still don't see a case for war," he said. "If Saddam does have biological or chemical weapons, what would stop him from using them in a conflict? If his back is against the wall, it could get ugly."

"So now you think he does have weapons?" I said.

"Whether he does or doesn't is not the point," he said. "North Korea has a nuke, but we're not going to war against them."

"That's different ..."

"And they keep shouting "regime change," but don't bother with specifics. Regime change to what? What's the plan? How come they never mention the plan?"

"What, you think they would invade Iraq without a plan?"

"Well what's the plan?"

"I don't know, but don't be ridiculous. Of course, they have a plan."

"John, you've always been gung-ho Republican. Politics never really interested me. But this Iraq shit is driving me insane. It makes no sense. For the first time in my life, I wrote my senators asking them to vote against this bullshit."

"Really? What were you hoping for?"

---

9   http://georgewbush-whitehouse.archives.gov/news/releases/2002/10/20021002-7.html

"I don't know, a bit of sanity maybe. Or democracy."

Rich's letters to Clinton and Schumer proved unconvincing. On October 10th, congress voted to authorize the use of force in Iraq; the measure passed in the house 297 to 133. Later that night the senate concurred, 77 to 23.

Bush's comments after the house vote revealed the inevitability of our gathering conflict with Iraq:

"The House of Representatives has spoken clearly to the world and to the United Nations Security Council: the gathering threat of Iraq must be confronted fully and finally. Today's vote also sends a clear message to the Iraqi regime: it must disarm and comply with all existing U.N. resolutions, or it will be forced to comply. There are no other options for the Iraqi regime. There can be no negotiations. The days of Iraq acting as an outlaw state are coming to an end."[10]

In November, the U.N. Security Council passed Resolution 1441, finding "Iraq has been and remains in material breach of its obligations under relevant [post-Gulf War resolutions], in particular through Iraq's failure to cooperate with United Nations inspectors and the IAEA."

The resolution granted weapons inspectors admission to the country and gave Iraq thirty days to "provide a currently accurate, full, and complete declaration of all aspects of its programmes to develop chemical, biological, and nuclear weapons, ballistic missiles, ... stocks of agents, and related material and equipment, the locations and work of its research, development and production facilities, as well as all other chemical, biological, and nuclear programmes including any which it claims are for purposes not related to weapon production or material."[11]

The resolution stopped short of threatening military action for noncompliance.

In January 2003, I watched the President deliver his State of the Union speech. Bush articulated his final indictment against Iraq:

---

10 http://georgewbush-whitehouse.archives.gov/news/releases/2002/10/20021010-5.html
11 http://daccess-dds-ny.un.org/doc/UNDOC/GEN/N02/682/26/PDF/N0268226.
pdf?OpenElement

Casus Belli

State of the Union Address
George W. Bush
January 2003

"… Today, the gravest danger in the war on terror, the gravest danger facing America and the world, is outlaw regimes that seek and possess nuclear, chemical, and biological weapons. These regimes could use such weapons for blackmail, terror, and mass murder. They could also give or sell those weapons to terrorist allies, who would use them without the least hesitation.

This threat is new; America's duty is familiar. Throughout the 20th century, small groups of men seized control of great nations, built armies and arsenals, and set out to dominate the weak and intimidate the world. In each case, their ambitions of cruelty and murder had no limit. In each case, the ambitions of Hitlerism, militarism, and communism were defeated by the will of free peoples, by the strength of great alliances, and by the might of the United States of America.

Now, in this century, the ideology of power and domination has appeared again, and seeks to gain the ultimate weapons of terror. Once again, this nation and all our friends are all that stand between a world at peace, and a world of chaos and constant alarm. Once again, we are called to defend the safety of our people, and the hopes of all mankind. And we accept this responsibility.

America is making a broad and determined effort to confront these dangers. We have called on the United Nations to fulfill its charter and stand by its demand that Iraq disarm …

In all these efforts, however, America's purpose is more than to follow a process — it is to achieve a result: the end of terrible threats to the civilized world. All free nations have a stake in preventing sudden and catastrophic attacks. And we're asking them to join us, and many are doing so. Yet the course of this nation does not depend on the decisions of others. Whatever action is required, whenever action is necessary, I will defend the freedom and security of the American people.

... Our nation and the world must learn the lessons of the Korean Peninsula and not allow an even greater threat to rise up in Iraq. A brutal dictator, with a history of reckless aggression, with ties to terrorism, with great potential wealth, will not be permitted to dominate a vital region and threaten the United States.

Twelve years ago, Saddam Hussein faced the prospect of being the last casualty in a war he had started and lost. To spare himself, he agreed to disarm of all weapons of mass destruction. For the next 12 years, he systematically violated that agreement. He pursued chemical, biological, and nuclear weapons, even while inspectors were in his country. Nothing to date has restrained him from his pursuit of these weapons — not economic sanctions, not isolation from the civilized world, not even cruise missile strikes on his military facilities.

Almost three months ago, the United Nations Security Council gave Saddam Hussein his final chance to disarm. He has shown instead utter contempt for the United Nations, and for the opinion of the world. The 108 U.N. inspectors were sent to conduct — were not sent to conduct a scavenger hunt for hidden materials across a country the size of California. The job of the inspectors is to verify that Iraq's regime is disarming. It is up to Iraq to show exactly where it is hiding its banned weapons, lay those weapons out for the world to see, and destroy them as directed. Nothing like this has happened.

The United Nations concluded in 1999 that Saddam Hussein had biological weapons sufficient to produce over 25,000 liters of anthrax — enough doses to kill several million people. He hasn't accounted for that material. He's given no evidence that he has destroyed it.

The United Nations concluded that Saddam Hussein had materials sufficient to produce more than 38,000 liters of botulinum toxin — enough to subject millions of people to death by respiratory failure. He hadn't accounted for that material. He's given no evidence that he has destroyed it.

Our intelligence officials estimate that Saddam Hussein had the materials to produce as much as 500 tons of sarin, mustard and vx nerve agent. In such quantities, these chemical agents could also kill untold thousands. He's not accounted for these materials. He has given no evidence that he has destroyed them.

U.S. intelligence indicates that Saddam Hussein had upwards of 30,000 munitions capable of delivering chemical agents. Inspectors recently turned up 16 of them — despite Iraq's recent declaration denying their existence. Saddam Hussein has not accounted for the remaining 29,984 of these prohibited munitions. He's given no evidence that he has destroyed them.

From three Iraqi defectors we know that Iraq, in the late 1990s, had several mobile biological weapons labs. These are designed to produce germ warfare agents, and can be moved from place to a place to evade inspectors. Saddam Hussein has not disclosed these facilities. He's given no evidence that he has destroyed them.

The International Atomic Energy Agency confirmed in the 1990s that Saddam Hussein had an advanced nuclear weapons development program, had a design for a nuclear weapon and was working on five different methods of enriching uranium for a bomb. The British government has learned that Saddam Hussein recently sought significant quantities of uranium from Africa. Our intelligence sources tell us that he has attempted to purchase high-strength aluminum tubes suitable for nuclear weapons production. Saddam Hussein has not credibly explained these activities. He clearly has much to hide.

The dictator of Iraq is not disarming. To the contrary; he is deceiving. From intelligence sources we know, for instance, that thousands of Iraqi security personnel are at work hiding documents and materials from the U.N. inspectors, sanitizing inspection sites and monitoring the inspectors themselves. Iraqi officials accompany the inspectors in order to intimidate witnesses.

Iraq is blocking U-2 surveillance flights requested by the United Nations. Iraqi intelligence officers are posing as the scientists inspectors are supposed to interview. Real scientists have been coached by Iraqi officials on what to say. Intelligence sources indicate that Saddam Hussein has ordered that scientists who cooperate with U.N. inspectors in disarming Iraq will be killed, along with their families.

Year after year, Saddam Hussein has gone to elaborate lengths, spent enormous sums, taken great risks to build and keep weapons of mass destruction. But why? The only possible explanation, the only possible use he could have for those weapons, is to dominate, intimidate, or attack.

With nuclear arms or a full arsenal of chemical and biological weapons, Saddam Hussein could resume his ambitions of conquest in the Middle East and create deadly havoc in that region. And this Congress and the America people must recognize another threat. Evidence from intelligence sources, secret communications, and statements by people now in custody reveal that Saddam Hussein aids and protects terrorists, including members of al Qaeda. Secretly, and without fingerprints, he could provide one of his hidden weapons to terrorists, or help them develop their own.

Casus Belli

Before September the 11th, many in the world believed that Saddam Hussein could be contained. But chemical agents, lethal viruses and shadowy terrorist networks are not easily contained. Imagine those 19 hijackers with other weapons and other plans — this time armed by Saddam Hussein. It would take one vial, one canister, one crate slipped into this country to bring a day of horror like none we have ever known. We will do everything in our power to make sure that that day never comes.

Some have said we must not act until the threat is imminent. Since when have terrorists and tyrants announced their intentions, politely putting us on notice before they strike? If this threat is permitted to fully and suddenly emerge, all actions, all words, and all recriminations would come too late. Trusting in the sanity and restraint of Saddam Hussein is not a strategy, and it is not an option.

The dictator who is assembling the world's most dangerous weapons has already used them on whole villages — leaving thousands of his own citizens dead, blind, or disfigured. Iraqi refugees tell us how forced confessions are obtained — by torturing children while their parents are made to watch. International human rights groups have catalogued other methods used in the torture chambers of Iraq: electric shock, burning with hot irons, dripping acid on the skin, mutilation with electric drills, cutting out tongues, and rape. If this is not evil, then evil has no meaning.

And tonight I have a message for the brave and oppressed people of Iraq: Your enemy is not surrounding your country — your enemy is ruling your country. And the day he and his regime are removed from power will be the day of your liberation.

The world has waited 12 years for Iraq to disarm. America will not accept a serious and mounting threat to our country, and our friends and our allies. The United States will ask the u.n. Security Council to convene on February the 5th to consider the facts of Iraq's ongoing defiance of the world. Secretary of State Powell will present information and intelligence about Iraqi's legal — Iraq's illegal weapons programs, its attempt to hide those weapons from inspectors, and its links to terrorist groups.

We will consult. But let there be no misunderstanding: If Saddam Hussein does not fully disarm, for the safety of our people and for the peace of the world, we will lead a coalition to disarm him.

Tonight I have a message for the men and women who will keep the peace, members of the American Armed Forces: Many of you are assembling in or near the Middle East, and some crucial hours may lay ahead. In those hours, the success of our cause will depend on you. Your training has prepared you. Your honor will guide you. You believe in America, and America believes in you.

Sending Americans into battle is the most profound decision a President can make. The technologies of war have changed; the risks and suffering of war have not. For the brave Americans who bear the risk, no victory is free from sorrow. This nation fights reluctantly, because we know the cost and we dread the days of mourning that always come.

We seek peace. We strive for peace. And sometimes peace must be defended. A future lived at the mercy of terrible threats is no peace at all. If war is forced upon us, we will fight in a just cause and by just means — sparing, in every way we can, the innocent. And if war is forced upon us, we will fight with the full force and might of the United States military — and we will prevail.

And as we and our coalition partners are doing in Afghanistan, we will bring to the Iraqi people food and medicines and supplies — and freedom.

… We Americans have faith in ourselves, but not in ourselves alone. We do not know — we do not claim to know all the ways of Providence, yet we can trust in them, placing our confidence in the loving God behind all of life, and all of history.

May He guide us now. And may God continue to bless the United States of America."[12]

On February 5, Secretary of State Colin Powell performed an impassioned speech before the u.n. Security Council, presenting indisputable evidence regarding Iraq's chemical and nuclear weapons programs. Powell produced transcripts, displayed mobile biological weapons labs and held up a vial of powder for emphasis.[13]

The speech was an attempt to persuade the Council to vote for military action against Iraq.

The Council, however, remained unconvinced as reported in the Los Angeles Times:

War Still Not the Answer, Say France, Russia, China

February 06, 2003 Maggie Farley Times Staff Writer
The three veto-holding Security Council members prefer stepped-up inspections. Paris says use of force must be 'final recourse.'

UNITED NATIONS — France, Russia and China, the key opponents to using military action to disarm Iraq, said Wednesday that Secretary of State Colin L. Powell's presentation to the U.N. Security Council failed to persuade them that war is yet necessary.

By summoning the Security Council to argue that Iraq is in "further material breach," the U.S. has technically fulfilled its requirements under Resolution 144—the November measure that led to weapons inspections—to convene and consult the council members before taking action. Washington, U.S. officials said, can now launch a military strike at any moment but will wait a little while

---

12 http://georgewbush-whitehouse.archives.gov/news/releases/2003/01/20030128-19.html
13 http://2001-2009.state.gov/secretary/former/powell/remarks/2003/17300.htm

longer for the council's benediction, if not a second resolution endorsing the use of force.

We wouldn't wait long.

✃

I'm standing on a road that curves in both directions around a steep mountain. The strange land is barren of vegetation, only scattered volcanic rocks of various sizes. The dirt has a reddish hue, and I'm reminded of a Martian landscape. The deep blue sky extends to the horizon. I look out past the road. A sea of clouds floats below, stretching in all directions. I realize how high I am.

I close my eyes against the radiant sun and feel a cool breeze sweep across my body.

Suddenly, a car appears from around the bend and accelerates towards me. I'm terrified, paralyzed as the car approaches. It gains speed, and I'm unable to move. Just as I prepare for impact, the car abruptly veers off. I watch as it crashes through the barrier and plummets over the cliff.

An image rises from beyond the cliff. At first it's like a bright cloud, but then it begins to take shape. It moves closer, becoming more solid and more defined. I realize it's a man dressed in tan camouflage fatigues.

I awoke in the call room, pager beeping. This recurring dream, it felt more like another reality. I couldn't make sense of it, but it made me feel so … emotional.

I dialed the ER.

"Pryor," I said, still half asleep.

"JP, it's Ed."

I need to pause and tell you about Ed Dickinson. Like me, Ed began his medical career in EMS before becoming a physician. However, Ed never stopped being a paramedic. Even as a doctor, he continued to ride the ambulance. The embroidery above his lab coat pocket said it all, "Ed Dickinson, MD, EMT-P."

Before HUP, Ed worked at Albany Med and Colonie EMS. We knew a lot of the same EMS people.

"Listen," he continued, "I got a 38-year-old guy with fever and right lower quadrant pain, probably an appy, but I wanted to ask if you could do a lecture for the national EMS conference this month; we had a speaker bail."

"Huh?" In the dead of the night, I struggled to understand what he was saying.

"Do you think you can do it?"

"Yeah," I said. "Yeah, sure."

I hung up the phone and closed my eyes for a second. A few minutes later, I woke myself up, struggling to remember whether I was going to the OR or preparing for a lecture.

In March 2003, Philadelphia hosted "EMS Today," the national conference for mmergency medical personnel. Vendors filled the Pennsylvania Convention Centre, displaying the latest defibrillators, airway devices, ambulance accessories and medical equipment. My head was flooded with memories of my days on the ambulance.

I meandered among many rural volunteers. These people were the salt of the earth. Many were overweight and poorly dressed, but they shared a rare trait in today's society: they sacrificed sleep, weekends, holidays and time with family to help strangers in need.

I met up with Ed, who introduced me to A.J. Heightman, the editor of JEMS (*Journal of Emergency Medical Services*).

"Hey, John," said A.J., "we'd love to have you on board at JEMS, whatever your schedule would allow."

"Sure," I said. JEMS was the magazine that published my first article back in college. Now, they wanted me to be a contributor.

I gave two lectures during the conference: "Severe Chest Trauma: a Problem-Based Approach" and "Multiple Gunshot Wounds: Care of the Street Warrior." The audience was huge, and I had a lot of people approach me afterward with comments and questions.

I then discovered an unforeseen complication with giving a lecture at the national EMS conference. Who attends the national EMS conference? Usually state EMS directors. When those directors need speakers for their state conference, whom do they think of?

Invitations to speak at state conferences began to roll in. Lauren, my administrative assistant, screened many requests. Otherwise, I would've been traveling to a different state every month. It was hard for me to say no.

The lectures were always fun, and I was glad to discover a way to give back to the EMS community. One time, I found myself in an ambulance bay speaking to a packed crowd of volunteers. I tried to imagine what it would be like to have Dr. Fortune speak at our ambulance station.

From clueless EMT to competent paramedic, now I returned as a national leader in trauma. I had come full circle in EMS.

❧

On March 19, 2003, my brother's wife delivered their second daughter, Olivia. We bombed Iraq the next day.

The "shock and awe" on CNN instigated another pang of guilt; the United States again at war without me there to help. Thoughts of enlisting again surfaced, but I imagined our involvement in Iraq would again be measured in weeks.

I followed the events in Iraq closely. As predicted, our troops decimated the Iraqis. Within a month, Baghdad fell to the cheering crowds of liberated Iraqis.

On May 1, President Bush landed in a jet fighter aboard the USS *Abraham Lincoln* anchored thirty miles off the California coast. Before a banner that read "Mission Accomplished," Bush declared an end to combat operations stating, "In the Battle of Iraq, the United States and our allies have prevailed."

From all outward appearances, this conflict mirrored the first Gulf War. Doom and gloom predicted by opponents failed to materialize. Two months, and the war was over.

I missed another opportunity to serve.

But it wasn't over. A rising insurgency and sectarian hostilities produced an environment most unlike Iraq I. Military activity and casualties began to climb. This conflict was far from "accomplished."

Several of my reservist colleagues were called up for active duty. It wasn't long before I heard the Army was struggling to find qualified surgeons.

Our hospital's chief medical officer, Dr. Bernie Johnson, a dermatologist, retold of his experience in Vietnam. I asked what a dermatologist did with trauma. His answer was, "Everything." In times of need, doctors in the military performed what was required, not what they were trained for. I tried to imagine a gynecologist caring for complex war trauma and shook my head in disbelief.

Dr. Schwab trained in the Navy and served nine years on active duty. An advocate for military service, Schwab explained how the military provided experience not available in the civilian world, especially trauma.

The pull to enlist intensified. Some residents, including a few women, were deployed. The insurgency worsened; casualties mounted. I heard more stories about inadequate or poorly trained surgeons on the front lines. It was hard, knowing I could do a better job. All of this combined with my innate desire to serve pushed me to join.

Only one thing stopped me: Carmela was pregnant again.

⁊

While the war raged and Carmela gestated, I continued my busy schedule at work. I joined hospital committees, taught ATLS, coordinated the trauma bay videos, lectured and continued to publish.

I was so busy I didn't know what I was doing next until Lauren told me. She handled my schedule, booked my flights and hotel rooms and took care of the bulk of my paperwork.

One time, I was headed out the door to give a lecture somewhere. Lauren forced the airline tickets in my hand and told me I was late. I rushed to the airport, quickly checked in and ran to the security gate.

"What's your destination?" the TSA agent asked me.

"What?" I said, "Isn't it on the ticket?"

I had no idea where I was going. It took a bit of explaining to the suspicious agents that I was more clueless than terrorist.

I frequently advised medical students interested in trauma or critical care. One time, I was speaking with a student about his career plans. He stopped before leaving my office and turned back.

"Hey, since I'm here, I have this idea," he said. "I think you might be the one to talk to about it."

"Sure," I said. "What's up?"

"I was thinking of starting a trauma club at Penn."

"Hey, that sounds cool."

I got up from my desk, and we filled a white board with ideas. We imagined a lecture series, clinical skills workshops, even research programs. The more we discussed it, the more I got excited about it.

"Hey," he said as we concluded our thoughts, "we'll need an advisor for the club. Would you consider being the advisor?"

Before I opened my mouth, we heard a shout from the outer office.

"NO!" Lauren yelled. "He's too damn busy. Try someone else!"

We froze like a pair of mischievous children caught in the act. I put my finger to my lips, glancing out the office door, then back to the student. I smiled, and nodded vigorously. He smiled, and we fist bumped.

"Send me an e-mail," I whispered.

ↀ

In December 2003, grainy, black-and-white images of our third child appeared on the ultrasound monitor. Having two children previously did nothing to dull our excitement.

"It's a boy," the tech said. I smiled at the thought of another son.

Later, we started to discuss names.

"I still like Christopher," I said, "or how about Luke?"

"You know," said Carmela, "I like John; can we name him after you?"

I had mixed feelings about this. I never thought to name a child after me.

"Okay," I said, "but not just for me."

Frankie was named after my paternal grandfather. I felt my mom's family had been left out. John was my maternal grandfather's name.

"What about a middle name?" Carmela asked.

"Joseph," I said. "It's my brother's middle name."

"John Joseph," Carmela smiled. "I like that."

In the coming months, we prepared for John John's arrival. We had a crib in our bedroom, but it saw little use. Frankie, almost three, would be usurped from sleeping with us, just as he had done to his sister. In April, I sent out a mass e-mail at work:

From: **Pryor,John**
Subject: My Son's Birth
Date: April 8, 2004 5:17:39 EST
To: <Staff>
CC:

Dear Colleagues and Staff,

My wife Carmela is pregnant with our third child and is due at the end of May. For our first two children, I was unable to get time off after the deliveries. This did not go over well with my wife.

Carmela has threatened to leave me if I screw up this time.

I am writing to notify you that when the baby comes, I will be unavailable for at least a week afterwards. I will speak with you individually about coverage, but I wanted everyone to be aware if I'm suddenly absent from the hospital.

Thank you for your cooperation and support.

John P. Pryor, MD, FACS

On May 31, Carmela came downstairs as I was heading to work. "I think the baby's coming," she said.

I called Lauren to let her know I wasn't coming in, then I gathered our stuff. An hour later, Carmela was being examined by the OB resident at the Pennsylvania Hospital.

"You're only about a centimeter," the resident said. "I think you can go home."

Carmela looked at him, aghast.

"This is my *third* baby," she said. "There's no way I'm going home."

At 11 a.m., anesthesia placed an epidural. This time, it worked. For the first time, Carmela was comfortable during labor. At noon, the nurses went to lunch.

While reading the paper, I noticed the resident enter the room. I glanced over to see him checking Carmela and returned my gaze to the *Times*.

"Okay, why don't you give a little push?" I heard behind the paper.

There was a little pause and then a panicked voice, "Oh shit!"

I dropped the paper and jumped up.

"What? What is it?" Carmela shouted.

The baby's head was out—not just crowning; his entire head was out!

"Baby's here!" I said.

No time for gloves, I held his head and turned gently. The resident ran for help as I suctioned John John's nose and mouth. Flashbacks to my obstetrics rotation in medical school guided my actions. In a few seconds, I tried to remember everything I learned twelve years earlier.

His anterior shoulder popped out. I slowly lifted. When the posterior shoulder cleared, he fell out into my arms.

I delivered my son! I thought.

"Is he coming?" Carmela asked. The room began to flood with staff.

"He's here! He's here!" I held him up a bit for her to see before handing him off to the delivery team.

"Oh my God," Carmela broke into tears. "I didn't feel anything."

Whatever ease John John allowed during the delivery, he made up in post-delivery complications. By 1 p.m., he was tachycardic and hypothermic. They moved him to the nursery, placed an orogastric tube and shot a chest x-ray.

The next day, he developed a fever of 100.4, prompting a mini-sepsis workup. They started a line, drew CBC, blood cultures and started empiric antibiotics. Luckily, the labs were normal, and cultures grew nothing. We came home two days later.

Danielle, Frankie and now John John. Three beautiful children. You never know how you're going to be as a parent, right? Now, as a father of three, I couldn't imagine life without them. They were my life, and they would define me more than anything I could accomplish as a surgeon.

United States Army

Iraq was becoming a clusterfuck. In March, Iraqi insurgents attacked a convoy of U.S. contractors. The Americans were killed, set on fire, and dragged through the streets. The charred remains were suspended on display on a bridge above the Euphrates. The military retaliation in April failed to take control of the city.

About the same time, the Abu Ghraib torture and prisoner abuse story broke. Images of tortured and humiliated prisoners appeared on television, prompting a public outcry.

The mounting insurgency, defeat in Fallujah and prisoner abuse scandal painted a bleak picture of our mission in Iraq.

I knew we weren't getting out of there anytime soon.

☙

In August 2004, I drove to the Army recruitment office in Cherry Hill. Pacing between a Starbuck's and a Florist, I tried to muster the nerve to enter.

This was the most difficult decision of my life. Carmela didn't understand my desire to serve, and whenever I brought it up, she went ballistic.

"Are you crazy?" she yelled. "We just had a baby! You have three kids at home! You think the Army *needs* you? What about your family? Don't we count for anything?"

I knew what she was saying. It's not like I didn't consider what my deployment would mean to her and the children. But I felt I had an equally valid point in joining.

"Those kids in the desert deserve to have someone like me out there treating them, not some gynecologist or small-town general surgeon," I told her. "Like it or not, I'm the most qualified person for combat surgery, and it tortures me to stand idle when I'm needed in Iraq."

"You're not idle, John; you're taking care of your family."

She didn't understand. She didn't understand my need to give back to my country or my commitment to military service. I would never get her blessing and had to decide whether to follow my gut or acquiesce.

I entered the recruiter's office.

Inside, a corporal in full military dress sat behind a desk. Posters covered the walls displaying proud soldiers jumping out of helicopters or providing aid to Third World countries. A rack filled with brochures boasted the benefits of a military career. A TV, tuned to CNN, hung from the ceiling. A few other potential recruits, young kids, milled about. One sat with a man, probably his father. Another stood by the rack examining a brochure.

I approached a desk and waited for the corporal to get off the phone.

"May I help you?" he asked.

"My name is John Pryor. I'm a surgeon and would like to speak to someone about enlisting in the reserve."

The corporal scanned his desk and selected a manila folder.

"Let's have you fill out some basic information, and I'll tell the sergeant you're here."

I took a seat and read through some of the forms.

A pudgy, pimple-faced kid sat with his back to the TV. A Gameboy demanded his full attention, thumbs flickering, tongue poised at the corner of his mouth. Behind him, black smoke billowed from a destroyed HUMVEE on CNN.

How ironically poignant, I thought.

Here's a kid, joining the Army, who didn't have a clue about what he was getting himself into. I imagined him struggling through basic training, deploying to the desert and facing enemy fire within a year. His future seemed to be playing out right behind him … if only he were aware enough to turn around.

"Dr. Pryor," the corporal said, "the sergeant will see you now."

The application introduced me to Army bureaucracy. Included in the stack of forms and questionnaires hid a mostly blank sheet of paper. A single question asked, roughly translated, "Why do you want to join the Army?"

I took time to articulate my thoughts before typing my response:

Statement of Professional Interest
John P. Pryor, MD

My mother and father are great parents, and although we were by no means wealthy, I never remember them saying no to anything that I needed. I never had to work to support myself during high school or college. I always had close friends and was lucky enough to meet and marry my wife, Carmela, during medical school. After completing surgical training, I became a faculty member of one of the most respected surgical programs in the country. We are financially secure with very little debt. I have been blessed with three wonderful children from ages six months to six years. I am settled in my career and have a beautiful wife and family, with plenty of free time to spend together. My life is, by all accounts, great.

But all during this time, from high school through surgical training, I have always felt as if I was taking much more from American society than I was giving back. I have strong convictions, which include a strong sense of citizenship and patriotism. I feel it is my duty to serve in some capacity, and to give back to a country that has allowed me to have such a great life. Recently with the War in Iraq and Afghanistan, these convictions have become stronger and better defined. However, at the same time, the sacrifices of deployment, especially for my wife and children, have been becoming more real. After many months of soul searching, my family and I are ready to interrupt our great life and to make a sacrifice for the country and to repay the debt that we owe so many soldiers that have sacrificed for us throughout the years.

My contribution is my experience and expertise in trauma surgery. For many years, I have been taking care of victims of the ongoing street violence in America. Our trauma center treats more than 2,500 patients a year, 500 of whom have penetrating injuries, mostly handgun wounds. In addition, my training in surgical critical care has given me the opportunity to care for the sickest patients from the trauma bay all the way through their definitive care stay.

When I see reports of young American soldiers getting hurt or killed, I feel a stab in the pit of my stomach. I take solace in knowing that they are being cared for by some of the greatest medics, nurses, and physicians in the world. But I also realize that the medical ranks are being stretched and that there is a real need for more surgeons with trauma experience to join in the fight. This is the time for me to serve. I have made all the necessary arrangements for my reserve responsibilities and my inevitable deployment. I realize that I have a lot to learn about being a soldier, and about war surgery. I assure you that I will work tirelessly to earn the right to wear the uniform as a United States Army Medical Corps Officer.

∾

John John was a good baby, but let me tell you, three is a whole new world. You'd think with a six- and four-year-old, we'd be used to this, but you forget about diapers and 3 a.m. feedings.

We were back in baby hell.

We took John John to a pediatric urologist concerning possible hypodspadias. His anatomy was a little off, but not what the urologist would call abnormal. While there, we scheduled a date for circumcision.

On the day of the procedure we got lost on the way to the hospital and arrived late for the appointment. The circumcision went well, and we were told there were no complications. Driving home we hit a traffic jam and J.J. wailed continuously as we crawled along in bumper-to-bumper traffic.

"Probably an accident," I fumed, losing my patience.

When we finally got home, Carmela noticed the baby's diaper was purple. She removed the diaper and blood squirted in her face.

"JOHN!" she screamed, holding pressure.

I ran over. She pulled her hand away, and blood pumped into the air.

"GOD DAMN IT! GOD DAMN IT! " I yelled. "I deal with fucking bleeding every fucking day. Why does it have to follow me home?"

We called the urologist. He told us to go to CHOP.

On the way there, I called the urology resident, who was to meet us in the ER.

"Uh huh, uh huh. Okay. Alright," I dropped the cell phone and started punching the steering wheel, swearing with each blow.

"Fuck! Fuck! Fuck! Fuck!" I couldn't deal with this shit happening to my own kids.

"What'd he say?" asked Carmela.

"He wants to place a Foley and wrap a pressure dressing."

By the time we met the urology resident, the bleeding had stopped. The resident decided against a Foley and sent us home. It's okay with me. I'd rather look like an idiot than have to put a Foley in J.J. In hindsight, the whole episode was no big deal, but it showed how poorly I handled medical problems with my own family.

℘

In October of 2004, I was alone in the house. Frankie was at Karate, and Carmela took Danielle and John John to the mall. An official envelope appeared in the mail. I tore it open and read the contents with a bit of trepidation. It was official: I was a soldier in the United Sates Army Reserve.

I dialed my brother and heard him pick up on the third ring.

"Hey, what's up?" I said.

"John, how are you?"

We spoke for a while before I turned to the purpose of my call.

"Listen, I've got some news I need to tell you." I glanced at the letter.

"What?"

"I've joined the Army Reserve."

There was a pause.

"You *have* joined the Army Reserve, or you're *going* to join the Army Reserve?"

"I enlisted. Signed. It's a done deal."

More silence.

"I don't think it's a good idea," Rich said.

"Rich, you don't understand. The military is stretched thin. They don't have enough surgeons to treat the wounded.

"I still don't think it's a good idea." Rich sounded exasperated.

"Why not?"

"Because this is not your battle to fight. Whatever this thing is in Iraq, it's not for you to get involved with."

"Why not? I've always felt a need to do something for my country, and now I have a way to contribute."

"You know, if Dick Cheney wants to have a war and most of the country believes the bullshit he puts out, I can't do anything about it. But it doesn't mean I have to like it or agree with it. And I certainly don't need to get involved in it. Doesn't that bother you? That we've invaded a country on a bunch of reasons that turned out to be false?"

"Right now, it doesn't matter how we got there. The fact is we *are* there, and American lives are being lost, and I can help."

"Spoken like a true Republican. 'It doesn't matter how we got there.' I think it does matter why we are there. If it were a just cause, if it were truly a matter of defending America, then I would be enlisting with you. But my gut feeling is Iraq was all based on a lie, and I can't see risking my life for a lie."

"So what are we supposed to do? Ignore the troops that are there?"

"This isn't about the troops."

"I think it is …"

"No, this is about you joining …"

"To help the troops …"

"You have no obligation there. The military has an obligation for the troops, and if they can't meet that obligation then ..."

"And they can't. That's why..."

"I can't feel bad for the United States Army, John. They have billions of dollars at their disposal. If they really want something, they usually get it. If they need surgeons, I'm sure they can get them somehow."

"Rich, you're not getting it ..."

"Really? There are private contractors in Iraq, right? And they need truck drivers, so if I'm a truck driver I can go over there and make—what—two, three times my salary. Is the military going to pay you twice your salary?"

"That's not the point."

"I think it is because you say that they are stretched thin and need surgeons, right? Well, don't you think, considering all the millions of dollars they are throwing around, that they would spend some of it making sure the troops receive appropriate medical care?"

"It's got nothing to do about money."

"Well, no, not for you. But I would think that if the military were so desperate, as you say, then they would at least be offering you a ton of money."

"My salary will be the same."

There was another pause.

"You realize they own you now, right?"

"No, it will be two tours ..."

"I'm sure that's what they told you; but after you sign, they can change their mind and ..."

"I know what you're talking about, but it's different now. That used to be the case; they would promise something and then make physicians deploy more or for longer tours. But then word got out, and they had a hard time recruiting. So now they don't do that because it hurts recruitment in the long term."

"I hope you're right."

"It'll be two tours."

"How long?"

"They call it ninety days 'boots on the ground,' which means it's ninety days in the theater of operation. It doesn't count the time it takes to get in and out."

"When will you have to go?"

"I don't know yet. The first step is officer training in January. I could go as early as late winter or early spring."

"Uh, huh. Did you tell Mom yet?"

There was a pause.

"Well ... no, not yet."

"Good luck with *that*."

"Could you tell her?" I joked.

Rich let out a laugh. "Yeah, right. Like I said, good luck with that."

I hung up the phone and sighed. I hoped for more support from Rich. I needed it to make my next call to Mom and Dad.

For several hours, I tried to dial my mother. It wasn't going to be pretty. Finally, I gave up and instead sat down at the computer. I opened a new Word document and began typing:

October 9, 2004
Dear Mom and Dad,

I am writing because I want to convey my thoughts on a very complex decision I have made. I decided to write instead of speaking to you face-to-face so that you and mom may try to understand why I have come to this decision, and to avoid a flaring emotional argument. It is important for you to realize that the decision is already made, the die has already been cast, and that discussing this with you is the toughest part of the entire process.

I have decided to become an officer in the United States Army Medical Corps Reserve. This is a reserve position, and I will keep my regular job. However, with the situation now in the world, it is clear that I will be deployed almost immediately. Thus, I am essentially enlisting for active duty. As it stands now, I will go through officer basic school in January for two weeks, and will be deployed for four months in the late winter/early spring.

Why? Okay, that is a tough question with a complex answer. The short answer is you know why. You raised me. You know me better than anyone. You both know I have a voice in my head that demands I contribute … that I go where I'm needed. I have been toying with the idea of military service for many years, and I have always suppressed the notions for you, Carmela, and the kids. But now is the time for me to serve. This is when I am needed. There are many, many fathers, MOTHERS, and brothers being killed and horrifically injured over there—6,000 injuries thus far, and it is not letting up. The medical resources are stretched beyond capabilities, and OB/GYN docs are staffing the combat support hospitals because there is such a lack of general surgeons, not even trauma surgeons, but plain general surgeons. I can't just sit by anymore when I know that I have a critical skill needed to care for these kids. It's my time to serve.

What about the kids and Carmela? The hardest thing I will ever do in my life is to leave them for four months. It will break my heart. It is devastating. Carmela will suffer the most caring for the kids alone for such a long period of time. It may even affect the kids long term. I realize all of this. But, why should our family be so special? Why do thousands of families of servicemen suffer, but not us? What makes us so immune? Not to mention the thousands of families that lost or will lose a family member in the war. Why do only they suffer? Because they are poor and have no other choice? That is not right. This will be the biggest sacrifice my family will ever make, but we will earn the right to say we did our part, and will earn the right to enjoy life in this country and this world. Attached is the personal statement I sent with the application. It says many of the same things.

Financially, we will be okay. I am working with the University to make sure that my salary is covered and that the benefits continue while I am away. All of my partners are concerned and supportive. I have made the necessary changes to the schedule to allow my time away.

Last, what about my safety. This is the toughest part to deal with—not for myself—I have lived a great life and have absolutely no regrets. But obviously, for the kids. I have thought about this endlessly—about the pain for the kids if I don't return home. The thought of hurting the kids makes me cry every time I deal with it. I love them so much, as I do Carmela and you two. But as much as I love them, I also think of the children of servicemen who are getting hurt and killed. The emotions are all so complicated. The easy and safe answer is to stay home and work in a homeless shelter to make myself feel needed. I know that, but my soul is telling me that this is important and that this is a necessary risk for me and my family to take. Having said that, every time I move two feet, I will think of the kids and do everything possible to keep myself out of harm's way. I am not going there to be a hero—just the opposite—I declare that I am a non-combatant chicken. My only dedication is to doing the job and getting home as soon as possible. That I promise you. Also, there is good evidence that I will be perfectly safe: The combat support hospitals (CSH) are very well fortified and defended, with no casualties to date of any medical personnel.

I can hear Mom now saying, "Don't do it, John; let someone else do it." Mom, you have tried that argument from my first day on the ambulance corps to the last day of my fellowship, and it never worked. I am "Someone else."

Will talk to you soon.

CPT John P. Pryor, MC, USA

My commission took place in a backyard ceremony at my house. My recruiter, SFC Nichols, reservist colleagues Dr. Dabrowski, Dr. Bilski and others served as witnesses. Carmela held John John on her hip, Danielle stood at attention in front of me and Frankie held the American flag. I raised my hand and repeated as Dr. Schwab recited the oath of office.

United States Army

I, John Pryor, do solemnly swear that I will support and defend the Constitution of the United States against all enemies, foreign and domestic; that I will bear true faith and allegiance to the same; that I take this obligation freely, without any mental reservation or purpose of evasion; and that I will well and faithfully discharge the duties of the office on which I am about to enter. So help me God.

Later, I set up the video camera on the back porch and rounded up Danielle and Frankie. I sat them both on my lap facing the camera.

"Come here," I said, pulling Frankie closer, "I want to tell you something. Today is October 9th two thousand and…" I prompted Danielle.

"Four," she said.

"2004," I repeated, "and today we're going to have a special party. Do you know what that party is for?"

Danielle looked sideways and smiled. "Umm, no," she said. I whispered into her ear.

"My dad is going to be a soldier doctor," she repeated.

"That's right, a soldier doctor. And the reason we're doing that is why, Danielle?"

"Cause we have to help the people who get hurt in the war."

"Right," I said, "and Frankie, I want you to know that daddy loves you very, very much and when daddy goes away, I'm going to miss you very much, but it's not going to be … forever; it's only going to be for a while."

"Excuse me," interrupted Frankie, "I have to go bathroom!"

"Okay, wait a second; listen; look at me." Frankie turned to me. "I love you very much and all I did was think of you guys, and it's a very difficult day for daddy because when you're a soldier doctor, sometimes you have to go away from your kids for a while.

"But not for a long time. We're going to have Christmas and your birthday, and then daddy has to go away for a little bit.

"But, the good news is, all those boys and girls that are getting hurt, daddy can go help them. Okay? How does that sound to you, Dan?"

"Good," Danielle said.

"And Frankie, come here. This is important. A hundred years from now, this is going to be important. Look at me. I love you more than anything in the whole world. You two are the most special, special kids in the whole world. I'll love you forever."

"What about baby John?"

"I'll love baby John forever, but he's too small to understand, alright? So listen, I just want you to remember that daddy will love you forever and ever. Do you understand what I'm saying?"

"Yeah," said Frankie.

"No you don't, but someday you will."

∾

In November, the U.S. launched a major "we'll teach you to fuck with us" assault on the city of Fallujah. The siege lasted forty-six days, claiming the lives of 95 Americans and 1,350 insurgents. I wondered how bad things would get before I deployed.

That same month, my brother came down to run the Philadelphia Marathon.

Inspired by Dad, Rich started running marathons in 1994. Since then, he usually completed one each year. I gradually got hooked as well—as a spectator. No, I still had no idea why anyone would want to run twenty-six miles, but on a nice day they were enjoyable events to watch.

Rich arrived with his family the day before the race. In the pre-dawn darkness, I drove him to the start before going to work.

"Must be nice to have so much time to go running," I teased.

"Yeah, well you know, ER docs work only a few hours a day," he said, "like twelve."

"Yeah, three or four days a week," I ribbed, "some people have to work, you know, *every* day."

I fought through traffic to get close to the start. Crowds of emaciated runners flowed in and out of large event tents. The Philadelphia Museum of Art reflected the first light of dawn.

"What's your goal?" I asked as he got out of the car.

"I need 3:15 to qualify for Boston," he said.

"You can do that no problem," I said.

"I've never been under 3:25."

"Until today," I said smiling.

After rounds, I left work early. I met Carmela, Deidre and the kids near the finish. Waves of runners in bright colors flowed by until we spotted Rich. Hearing our shouts, he waved just before crossing the finish in 3:08.

I'd be heading North in a few months to watch him run Boston.

 భా

In January 2005, I traveled to Ft. Sam Houston, San Antonio, Texas, for Army Medical Department (AMEDD) Basic Officer Leader Course (BOLC). This three-week training camp provided a smooth transition into Army life. During my time, I became familiar with military culture, increased my understanding of our missions and learned tactical medical doctrine and principles of leadership.

Induction into the Army is pretty much what you'd expect: uniforms, physicals, standing in line, lectures, mess hall, training, drills, etc.—similar to the Boy Scouts but with M-16's.

During one briefing, they dropped the facade and gave it to us straight.

"The reality is this—the Army is a dangerous place. Soldiers get hurt and die. They die in training exercises, they die in accidents and they die in combat. The best thing you can do for your family and loved ones is to prepare for the worst-case scenario, before deployment."

As a surgeon, my risk would be minimal. Unlike the grunts on patrol, drawing fire and triggering improvised explosive devices (IEDS), I would be sequestered behind barricades and fortifications. There were few medical casualties, and I felt my only risk was traveling in and out of the combat arena.

Still, the message was not lost on me. Anything could happen, even an accident, and I had to prepare as best I could for such a contingency.

When I returned home, I made arrangements with a lawyer and financial planner. My will was finalized, and we created trust funds for the kids.

I collected copies of vital documents and placed them in a large green three-ring binder. It contained information about the lawyer, financial information, life insurance policies and all my passwords.

I called it the "doomsday binder."

I then sat at the computer and opened a new word document entitled "Letter of Instruction." I thought for a minute, then began typing:

To be read only upon the death of John P. Pryor

This is a document to provide my final instructions upon my death. I have thought these things out for a long time, and I would like the instructions followed as best you can. This information can be shared freely with all those involved in making the appropriate arrangements

I. Supervision...

Over the next few days, I worked on this document, carefully detailing what I wanted done if I did not to return from Iraq. When finished, I opened another document entitled "Obituary." It took me another few days to finalize my thoughts on this document.

I printed these documents, placed them in the doomsday binder and stored it in our fireproof safe.

This left one final task to address.

Lankenau Funeral Home occupied a large Victorian house a few blocks off Main Street in Moorestown, NJ. Steve Lankenau, a quiet and well-mannered man, had run the family business since 1989. We sat in his office.

"What can I do for you, Dr. Pryor?" he asked.

"I'm here for a couple of reasons," I said. "I'm a trauma surgeon, and every day I see sudden catastrophic deaths. I realize that I'm not immune to such a fate and that it is never too early to prepare for some unforeseen accident.

"The other thing is that I recently enlisted in the Army Reserve, which means I'll be deployed sometime this year."

"I see," he said.

"I need to make arrangements as best I can for the worst-case scenario."

"I think that's a smart move," said Steve.

He took out a fresh information file and a pencil. "We've resisted the Computer Age and still do things a little old-fashionedly; let me have your full name."

For the next half hour, we discussed my education and training, my family and children. Steve was surprised that my youngest was less than a year old.

With the form completed, we toured the downstairs parlors. Sliding doors could divide the space into three separate rooms.

"This is very nice," I said. "I hope we never have to use it."

"Me, too," he said.

Reassured, I thanked Steve for his time. The arrangements were a bit overkill, but it's never a bad idea to be prepared.

☙

At the time of deployment, I needed to pass the Army Physical Fitness Test (APFT): sixty sit-ups, twenty push-ups and run two miles in less than 18 minutes. Doesn't sound like much, but I was in the worst shape of my life at the time. During residency, my addiction to Little Debbie's star crunches and pizza had piled on the pounds. Even if I wanted to exercise, my schedule did not allow it. Now forty pounds overweight and winded after a minute jog, I needed to get in shape.

The potential embarrassment of failure kept me motivated. I ate less, started to jog and began a routine of sit-ups and push-ups. Slowly, I noticed a difference, and my weight began to drop.

There was one final task before heading to Iraq.

I felt strongly about the larger purpose of our involvement in the Middle East. I wanted the Iraqi people to know Americans were there to help improve their country. For me, winning the hearts and minds of the people was more than just a catchphrase.

To that end, I decided to learn Arabic.

I had no illusions that I could learn a foreign language in a few months, but I could learn a lot. Even a few questions and phrases here and there would convey a bigger message: Americans were sincere in our effort to help.

I sent out an e-mail asking if anyone spoke Arabic. An Egyptian anesthesiologist had taught Arabic and agreed to meet me. We arrived in a conference room and discussed some hospital issues and people we knew in common.

Finally, he looked at me with all sincerity and said, "Why do you want to learn Arabic? This is very unusual for Americans."

"I'm going to Iraq soon," I told him, "I want to be able to communicate with my patients there."

He thought for a moment before slowly nodding his head. "سوف يعلمك اللغة العربية," he said. "I will teach you Arabic."

&

Throughout 2005, I waited for my deployment orders. In the meantime, I read up on combat surgery, increased my running endurance and practiced Arabic while commuting to work. I made arrangements for a satellite phone and loaded video chat software on my computer.

Iraq was going to be the most demanding adventure I've ever attempted. It would affect my entire family. I needed to be ready when the time came.

&

With three kids, our house shrank to half its size; we decided to find something larger. My friend Raj suggested we take a look at Moorestown. Carmela and I took a tour; we fell in love with the town.

In May of 2005, we moved into a new house only a few minutes from downtown Moorestown. Our development consisted of large 3,000-4,000 square-foot homes surrounding a golf course, which would be even better if I played golf. Obtaining the mortgage wasn't difficult, but our budget was stretched thin. The schools were great, and there was plenty of shopping close by. My predawn commute across the Ben Franklin Bridge took only a half hour.

The house was nice. Off the foyer to the left was the formal living room / dining room with access to the detached sun room. To the right, I had my own office separated by French doors. A large kitchen opened to the spacious living room with vaulted ceiling and gas fireplace.

Upstairs, we had four bedrooms. Danielle had her own bathroom;

the boys shared a Jack and Jill bathroom. The master bedroom was enormous with a huge walk-in closet and a Jacuzzi-equipped bathroom.

My bedroom was bigger than the apartment I had in New York.

The vast basement was divided into two playrooms, a guest bedroom and storage. I created a little music studio with my guitars, my brother's keyboard and a drum kit donated by Carmela's cousin.

After moving in, I felt my life had finally settled. This house would accommodate us for as long as I worked at Penn. No more moving, no more training. I had finally arrived, ready to grow some roots. A beautiful wife, three great kids, a job I loved and now a house better than I ever imagined.

In November, we invited Rich and his family to celebrate our first Thanksgiving in the our location.

Frankie and John John jumped on Rich, who was down on all fours and neighing like a horse. I sat back and reflected on our accomplishments. Rich and I had gotten through medical school. We had survived residency and baby hell. Now we both had nice houses, secure jobs and great families.

Life was turning out pretty good.

But watching our kids play, I realized we had advanced to the next generation. So much of my life had been focused on my career, my wife or my brother. But now, as five young children screamed and ran around the living room, the focus was on them.

On the Friday after Thanksgiving, my holiday mood was tempered when I received a letter from the military.

My orders had arrived.

I would be deployed in three months.

☙

I had seen my brother on a regular basis over the years, but we rarely had time alone. Between work and family, it was tough just getting out for an hour to have a beer. But with my deployment rapidly approaching, I wanted to spend a few days with him.

Our last weekend alone was during my last year of residency. We took a road trip to Cedar Point Amusement Park in Ohio. Making plans in late January, our options were limited.

"What ya wanna do?" I asked.

"Too cold for camping," he said.

"Not enough time for Las Vegas," I said.

"Spamalot is playing on Broadway," he said. "That's the Monty Python musical."

"You read my mind," I said.

We were both big fans of Monty Python, and I was excited to hear they turned "The Holy Grail" into a musical. I made hotel reservations, and Rich bought the tickets.

The Manhattan Westin is on 43rd Street in the Theater District. I met Rich in the lobby, and we checked in. After a rest, we headed out to find food.

While meandering through the crowded streets, we reminisced about our time in the city.

"Did I tell you about the time Bernard released radiation into the lab? They had to evacuate the building and decontaminate it?"

"Wasn't that how you lost your calculator?"

"Yeah, nice HP scientific calculator," I said, "rendered radioactive."

"I ever tell you about the homeless guy who could fake a seizure so well they hired him for the paramedic class?"

"Really?"

"Yeah. Or the EMS medic who got fired? He was so pissed off he gave his uniforms to the homeless drunks at the bus depot. So it looked like a bunch of city EMS paramedics were sleeping in front of the Port Authority."

"That's hysterical," I laughed.

We entered one of those chain restaurants with vintage heirlooms stuck to the wall and overly friendly wait staff covered in flair. McSorely's it was not, but they had beer.

Our conversation settled on work and kids. We gave politics a rest

When the check came, I interrupted Rich and blurted, "Hey, how would you like to come work at Penn?"

He blinked at the sudden change in conversation.

"Uhh, I don't think so …" he said.

"Well, at least we talked about it," I said, slapping my Penn credit card onto the table.

"Oh!" he said with a laugh. "I'd pick it up, but Albany Med doesn't give me an expense account. Guess I'm not that important."

On the way to Shubert Theater I answered a call from the hospital. After discussing a case with the resident, I hung up and turned to Rich.

"You know, sometimes I feel like the patients are all blindfolded, slowly walking toward a cliff and all I do all day is continually run around turning them around before they fall off the cliff."

"That's a good analogy," Rich said.

"And then, once in a while, I find a resident leading them straight for the edge."

Rich laughed. "It's not that bad; they're not *trying* to kill the patients. It only looks that way."

We had seats in the balcony and talked before the show started.

"What other shows have you seen?" Rich asked.

"Sunset Boulevard," "Les Mis," not a lot..."

"I saw 'Cats.' Did you see 'Cats?'"

"No."

"Absolutely sucked. I had no idea what it was about. There was no story I could figure out."

"Too bad."

"Yeah, ever see 'Blue Man Group?'"

"No."

"Me neither; always wanted to see them."

There was a pause before we started to recite our favorite Python lines.

"It's only a flesh wound!"

"WHAT is your favorite COLOR?"

"Someday, son, all this will be yours. What, the curtains?"

"It's not a question of where he grips it! It's a simple question of weight ratios!"

We chuckled at each line.

"I ever tell you the dream I had, that you died?" I said.

"Really?" Rich asked.

"Yeah, it was awful ..."

"Sorry ..."

"Yeah, your tombstone read, 'Alright, let's call it a draw.'"

"That's hysterical," Rich said. "That would make an awesome tombstone."

"I thought you'd like it."

"Wow, is that a premonition or a self-fulfilling prophecy?"

"Let's not find out."

The lights dimmed, and the show began. Over the next few hours, one of our favorite movies played out on stage with singing and dancing. It was a great show. At the conclusion, Rich stopped at the souvenir counter and purchased a T-shirt that read, "I'm not dead yet."

"You want one?" he asked.

"No thanks," I said. "I'm good."

Back at the Westin, we got ready for bed. Rich opened his suitcase and pulled out a book.

"You ever think about what happened on 9-11?"

"Why? What do you mean?"

"I mean there are a lot of questions about that day that remain unanswered."

"Like what?"

"Well, like why Bush just sat in a classroom for half an hour while the country was under attack?"

"Well, that's just Bush for you; he really didn't know what to do."

"Yeah, but other people, like the secret service, did know what to do, but ..."

"But what are you saying? Are you suggesting ..."

"Hold on, hold on. Why is it whenever someone asks questions about 9-11 there's always a jump to some conclusion?"

"Because you are implying ..."

"No, wait, I'm just asking a question, right? Like why did World Trade Center 7 collapse?"

"It was from fire ..."

"Have you seen it? It collapses straight down. I mean, it's perfectly straight, and you know what the 9-11 Commission said about its collapse?"

"No, what did they say?"

"Nothing. They never even mentioned it."

"So?"

"So? Isn't that a little strange? A forty-seven story building collapses because of fire, and they don't even mention it?"

"That doesn't mean anything."

"Would you do me a favor?"

"What?"

"Would you read this and then tell me what you think?" Rich handed me the book, *The New Pearl Harbor* by David Ray Griffin.

"What is this?" I leaned over on an elbow and flipped through the pages. "This is crap," I added, looking at the back cover. "Who published this? Who the hell is Interlink Books?"

"What, you won't read it because of *who published it?*"

"Look, I don't see what you're getting at. Are you saying the government was involved in 9/11?"

"I'm not saying anything. I just have a lot of questions, and I think the government does a poor job of answering them. I think, hmmm, that doesn't make sense ..."

"But where do ..."

"And since you are about to head off to Iraq, you might be interested in thinking critically about why we have an Army there and why you're going."

"We're there because Saddam is a baaaad man," I teased, and started to laugh. I tossed the book at him.

"You're such an ass," said Rich.

I was glad he dropped the subject. Sometimes Rich doesn't make any sense.

Sunday morning I enjoyed a rare treat: sleeping in. Mercifully, even my cell phone remained silent. Rich had been up and showered, but he let me sleep late.

"Man," I said with a yawn, "no rounds, no kids, no wife. Remember when life was this simple?"

"I remember you being home from Binghamton. I would come home at noon, and you'd still be in bed."

"Those were definitely the days."

"I'm so impressed with you. Not of your accomplishments, but at the fact that you found something that you love more than sleep."

"It's a tradeoff. I'll get to sleep when I die."

"C'mon, go take a shower. We need to check out soon."

I got out of bed and headed for the bathroom. I showered and shaved. Then, we packed up and stopped in the hotel restaurant for breakfast.

"What time's your train?" I asked him.

"Not 'till three," said Rich, "I'll walk over to Penn Station with you and then hang out at Grand Central—you know, get a cardboard sign and put out a coffee cup for donations."

"Could be your new career," I said.

"Sure, grow a beard, become an alcoholic, piss in my pants, I don't see a downside."

"Either that," I said, "or train dolphins."

We headed along 42nd Street, shivering among the crowds of New Yorkers. A few minutes later, we stopped in front of Penn Station.

We didn't talk about Iraq other than about when I was going and when I would be back. The fact that it was a war zone wasn't lost on us. We weren't in denial of the danger. We just didn't speak of it.

Pushed to the farthest reaches of our minds was the thought that this would be our last time together. I felt as if I was balancing delicately on a tightrope, that any mention of the danger would jinx me.

"Well …" said Rich, struggling for the right words, "have a good trip back."

I couldn't bring myself to say 'goodbye.' There was an uneasy permanence to it. Instead, I said, "Alright, I'll give you a call soon."

We parted ways. I headed for my train.

344th Combat Support Hospital

Iclinched my eyelids tight and grappled for the seat in front of me. I felt my testicles rise into my abdomen as the sensation of free-fall intensified. Like a roller-coaster uncoupled from its rails, we plunged toward earth in near free fall. As we plummet, time distorts, seconds feel like minutes. I struggle to keep down my breakfast.

Sure, I thought, *have that extra helping of eggs this morning.*

That was a mistake.

I swallowed the bitter regurge, refusing to vomit on the soldier in front of me.

A few hundred feet from the tarmac, the c-17 pulled out of its death plunge, three Gs drilled me into the seat before levelling off. We landed hard, rattling my kidneys. My helmet shook over my eyes and I fell forward into the harness as we decelerated. The plane came to a bumpy stop then slowly started to taxi. I started to breathe again and relaxed my white-knuckled grip.

"Welcome to Baghdad." The pilot's tone was emotionless.

ℰℐ

My journey to Iraq began with my premature departure on February 11, 2006. A nor'easter charging up the East Coast spawned flight delays and cancellations in its wake. I couldn't risk missing my arrival date at Fort Bliss, Texas, so I was forced to leave before the storm's arrival.

The change in plans cut my "goodbye" time by about twelve hours—a big blow. Before I was ready, as if I could ever be ready, Carmela and I huddled together with Danielle, Frankie and John John. Rational discussions, preparation and planning broke down into a horrid cluster of sobbing. Repressed anxiety and fear bubbled to the surface as we realized this was it—I was really leaving. I wouldn't be home to watch "American Idol" or laugh at Frankie's childish antics. I wouldn't be there to hear Danielle singing along to her karaoke machine or to run around the house with John John on my shoulders.

I pulled Danielle into my arms, smelling her hair. I gazed at my wife's face, trying to memorize each freckle, and squeezed the air out of the boys. I cried unlike I had ever done before. Then, with a knock at the door, the airport shuttle ended our time for goodbyes. With one last kiss from everyone, I walked out. The sound of Frankie's gut-wrenching cry faded behind me.

This scene must play out for the thousands of families with a loved one leaving for active duty. It has been the same for past wars, and when this conflict is over, there will be some future conflict, and it will be the next generation's turn to defend freedom. Much has been written and glorified about going off to war, but for me, it was a pain that ripped a hole in my heart.

It was the worst day of my life.

 C/3

Most soldiers headed to Iraq and Afghanistan are deployed as units. Some units are as large as a division, with thousands of men. Others are smaller, such as Special Forces (SF) and Forward Surgical Teams (FST) that have twenty or fewer. Units deployed for a year or more will need to rotate individual personnel in and out. Such is the case with physicians in the Army Reserve; we are mobilized for four-month blocks.

To prepare and mobilize individuals to join the fight, the military has processing centers called "CONUS" (Continental United States)

Replacement Centers (CRC). Independent Replacements (IRS) are processed and prepared at the CRC to join units already in theater. They say in times of war every soldier can rely on two things: their training and their buddies. IRS frequently have neither—CRC is an attempt to provide a little of both.

The training at the CRC was top notch. Of course, nobody can learn to be an infantry officer in five days, but we did get some basic skills in weapons, tactics, first aid, chemical/biological attack, law of war and cultural sensitivity training. Physicians are issued a sidearm, the Beretta 9-mm handgun. If a physician carrying a weapon sounds strange, I can tell you it is only one of the dozen of convoluted ethical and moral challenges of being a combat surgeon. It certainly feels out of place holding this thing, let alone firing it. However, the realities of war dictate that although physicians are by nature non-combatants, everyone within a war zone has the right to self-defense and thus needs to carry a weapon. During the firing exercises, I joked about physicians being "life-savers, life-takers," but the fact is I prayed to God that I never had to use the weapon.

Camaraderie is one of the most important parts of the combat team. Friendship in the military has several levels, and the depth of the commitment is related to the situation. We all have friends from similar occupations and work environments. Friendships tend to be stronger when you endure hardships together, such as those I recall from my days in high school football. Combat and preparing for combat is the ultimate experience that binds people together. It has been said many times by many veterans that strength and courage to accomplish difficult missions come not from patriotism, heroic thoughts, or dedication, but from the fear that you will let your buddy down. Of course, in five days, I had not made these kinds of connections. However, I met some outstanding individuals, many with whom I would work over the next few months.

When I called home, Carmela was still upset. Often, her anxiety manifested as anger, and she continued to express her disapproval of my decision to join. Earlier that day, I sat in a room for a need-to-know-only briefing on Improvised Explosive Devices (IEDS). We watched graphic videos of soldiers wounded and killed. Afterwards, the instructor asked how many have experienced an IED or knew someone who had been injured. Half in the room raised their hands. Later, the chaplain asked how many had recently been to a military funeral. Virtually every person, besides me, raised their hands. Many of these soldiers are on their second and third deployments, often for a year in heavy-combat conditions. I met one officer with fresh scars on his face from an IED. He was processing through for his second volunteer deployment.

After a day like this, I was in no mood to hear my wife complain about the inconveniences we were going through for a paltry four months. I knew how hard this was on my wife and my children, but the sacrifices our family and I were making were inconsequential compared to those of the men and women I sat with that day. I felt inadequate and humble. I went to sleep praying that if any of these soldiers ever needed my care that I would not fail them.

The night before I shipped out, I aimed my video camera at a mirror. I wanted to record my experiences during this tour.

"Dear video diary," I said, "today is the 16th of February. Tomorrow, we ship out to Kuwait. I have to pack tonight. The good news is that formation is not until 9:40 p.m., but then we start packing the plane at midnight and all through the night so whatever sleep I get tonight will be the last sleep for about three or four days. I'm excited."

The next day, I kept the camera rolling as I walked out to the tarmac. As we approached the DC-10, I joked with one of my buddies, "Hey if they call the plane coming home the 'Freedom Bird' what do you call this one—'The 'Incarceration Bird?'"

We flew first to Bangor, Maine, for our first layover. In the dead of night, a small cluster of people brought life to an otherwise empty terminal. A group of civilians and ex-military men had sacrificed sleep to come see us off. They waved little flags, shook our hands and wished us luck.

A swell of emotion rose in my throat.

We traversed the Atlantic and landed in Hahn, Germany, for

breakfast of bratwurst and sauerkraut. When our final flight landed in Kuwait, I pulled my Beretta from the seat-back pocket and slowly followed the line of soldiers down the aisle. With nervous excitement, I tried to anticipate the new world that awaited outside the plane.

It was pitch black. I hesitated for a moment at the top of the stairs, searching for a star or city lights, anything as a point of reference. There was nothing. I descended into the void, thinking that I knew what Neil Armstrong felt stepping from the Apollo lander. Sounds of the aircraft faded as I walked the tarmac and silence enveloped me. The quiet darkness would not be the last similarity to Ground Zero.

We drove into the night toward a cluster of lights on the horizon: Camp Virginia, Kuwait. Sand, piled into high mounds, flanked the road obstructing any view of the desert. As we approached the camp, floodlights lit up barricades and check points. Constantina wire lay everywhere, covering mounds of dirt and straddling the walls around the camp.

I spent three days at Camp Virginia; there were more briefings and weapons checks. The tents and enclosed toilets on the base would be a luxury compared to what was in store. As a final farewell, we received our ammunition.

Hours before sunrise, I boarded the c-17, a huge flying behemoth used to transport vehicles and tons of cargo. Rows of seats were clipped down the center, converting the plane into a flying movie theater. We packed in shoulder to shoulder, and I looked up at the high interior space. As if someone had ripped out the plane's walls and ceiling, wires, pipes and technical guts lay exposed.

"Ever fly a combat landing?" the guy next to me asked.

"No," I said.

"You're in for a wild ride," he said with a smile.

After our suicide landing, we disembarked and gathered our duffles. By this time, the group of docs and nurses I was with throughout this process whittled down to five others, all headed to the same combat hospital. Baghdad International Airport (BIAP) was a desolate, burnt-out shell of a place. With imagination, I could visualize what it was like in more civilized times.

I stood on the tarmac breathing in my new environment, trying to adjust my bearings. Baghdad, Iraq. Something seemed familiar but disconcerting. Then I saw him out of the corner of my eye. I turned my head, but he was gone. I realized it was like being at the pile at ground zero: DEATH was everywhere.

"Now what?" someone asked.

"Now we take the helicopter the rest of the way," I heard.

Obviously, Iraq was a dangerous place; I knew the risks I would take coming here. I tried to rationalize the risk by explaining how I would be safe and secure once inside the base. The only risk, I argued, is transporting in and out.

A thin, square-jawed sergeant major approached our small group. He stood facing us for a moment, gnawing on a cigar stump.

"You the docs?" he asked

"Yeah."

He pulled out the stogie and spit. "Well, c'mon. I got yer ride."

Ride? I thought.

I caught up to the sergeant major. "I thought we were going by helo."

"Can't. You guys picked the day they started a civil war. All the helos are out on combat missions.

"Then how do we get to the 344th?" I thought about the previous week of training and lectures. Images of IED destruction popped into my brain. The message was simple and clear: Don't convoy.

"It's only a twenty-minute convoy," replied the sergeant.

Shit!

Any convoy is, by definition, a combat mission. As such, it is prepared and equipped for battle. The team assembled. It included the sergeant major, a first sergeant, and fifteen soldiers to provide force protection.

I was struck by the youthful faces of these 18- or 19-year-old soldiers. At their age, I was getting drunk in college, thinking I was hot shit because I ran around on an ambulance.

Nobody was shooting at me on the ambulance, I thought.

A soldier helped me attach axillary and shoulder plates to my Individual Body Armor (IBA). I stood near my escorts: driver, gunner, and a female MP riding shotgun on the Comm. They recounted previous convoys that ended badly—IEDs, small arms fire and RPGs—there was always something. Convoys, it seemed, were large, moving bullseye.

With our armor in place, we huddled for convoy brief.

"Okay, listen up!" the sergeant shouted. "You've been through this before, so you know the routine. This is a convoy from BIAP to Abu Ghraib. Convoy consists of six vehicles ..."

He went on to map the route to be taken, list communication frequencies, and recommend spacing between vehicles. He reported the latest intelligence on insurgent activity and reviewed the current Rules of Engagement (ROE). Finally, he went over the plans for when they get hit.

"When?" I thought.

The huddle broke. My gunner locked and loaded his roof-mounted M2 'Ma Deuce' 50 caliber machine gun. I sat next to him as he stood in the turret. The Humvee fired up, and the hundred-pound armored doors were slammed shut. I never had a problem with claustrophobia.

Until now.

"Captain Pryor?" It was the female MP turned around in her seat. She was shouting over the noise of the engine.

"Yeah?" I said.

"When we get hit, it's your job to grab the gunner's legs. Usually, the vehicle rolls after an IED. Your job is to hold onto his legs so he's not crushed in the rollover."

"Got it!" I tried to sound confident.

What's with this fucking 'when' shit? I thought.

The vehicles moved out, and we passed the outer gate of the airport. As we turned onto the main road, my heart pounded into my throat.

Accelerating along the dark, empty highway, my thoughts returned to the day I spoke to my father about my decision to join. Dad had served in the Marines, but never during combat. Still, his experience provided valuable insight.

"You think it's a great idea to serve," he said; "you think of serving your country; you think of the adventure and excitement. But before you know it, you're huddled in a foxhole with artillery exploding around you. And then you wonder, "What the hell was I thinking?"

I thought I knew exactly what I was doing when I signed up.

Cognitively, I knew there would be danger. I knew one day I would be in a convoy just like this, and I mentally prepared for it. I thought I was ready for this.

We drove down a dark road. Headlights lit up potential threats for only a second before they flashed past. I held my breath past each box or piece of garbage. Small arms fire echoed, and I could see fires burning off in the distance—the whole scene was surreal.

We approached an overpass—God's gift to the insurgents. Not only could they launch RPGs from the road above, but a huge blind spot on the other side was perfect for concealing an ambush. I held my breath passing under the bridge. Just as we emerged on the other side, a blinding flash lit up the darkness. Our vehicle swerved, and I flinched, bracing for impact.

There was none. A second later, we heard a muffled blast. The explosion was in the distance, but in the darkness, the flash appeared to be right next to us.

I remained silent, but in my head I was screaming, *Faster, Faster, get me the hell off this road!*

Nothing can prepare you for this, I thought, wiping sweat from my palms. *What the fuck was I thinking?*

After what seemed like hours, the convoy safely reached the Forward Operating Base (FOB). Dismounting soldiers immediately grouped together with shouts of relief and slapping high-fives, as if my team had scored a touchdown.

"God damn!"

"Hoo Rah!"

"Nearly crapped my pants!"

The soldiers' ebullience relieved me. I wasn't the only one freaked out by the blast.

"I wasn't worried," a driver said. "When the real deal hits, you don't see the flash. You just feel the impact."

"Well, that was the closest I came so far," said one of the privates.

"I thought you said you'd been on dozens of convoys," I asked another soldier.

"Not *together*," he said. "This was our first convoy as a group."

It's hard to come up with an analogy for this experience. Imagine wearing a blindfold and walking across a busy highway. That's what it felt like out on the road. Glad to be done with my one convoy, I couldn't believe these kids would go out and do it again the next day. Raw courage. Truly astounding.

☙

The care of soldiers injured in combat is a highly developed and ever evolving discipline. Each conflict teaches us new lessons on how to care for combat injuries. The modern concept of field care has a hierarchy, also referred to as "echelons of care."

It begins at echelon I with self and buddy care. Here, all soldiers use their brief training in first aid skills to stop bleeding, recognize shock and stabilize fractures. Each soldier carries limited first aid equipment in his or her gear, such as a field dressing and a self-applying tourniquet. Immediate care during the fight is also rendered by "combat lifesavers"—soldiers with some additional training and skills.

The combat medic provides the first step into organized Army medical care. These special soldiers are highly skilled medical providers. They have excellent infantry skills with the ability to render complex medical care to very sick and injured patients. They render care under the worst possible conditions. Soldiers and medics bring patients off the battlefield to casualty collection points (CCP). From here, ambulance companies transport patients to battalion aid stations (BAS).

The BAS is considered echelon II care and is staffed by a physician, a physician assistant, medics and technicians, making up two treatment teams. The teams care for incoming wounded when needed and also provide essential continuing health care to the troops on a daily basis. The physician staff is usually comprised of family practitioners, internal medicine or emergency medicine doctors. Care at the BAS is also very basic, strictly stabilization, before being sent to echelon III.

Over the past fifteen years, since before the first Gulf War, a new concept in war surgery emerged called the "Forward Surgical Team" (FST). Taking lessons learned from civilian trauma centers, the methods of damage control were applied to war surgery. Damage-control techniques involve using multiple short surgeries instead of one long surgery to care for severe trauma. This concept allows more time for the body to catch up with blood loss and infection, and has proven a very important part of the increased survival of severely injured patients on the civilian side. The military responded to this by forming these small, highly mobile surgery units that could move with combat units and provide front-line surgical care. In keeping with damage control concept, the surgery done at FSTs is brief and not complex. Bleeding and ongoing contamination from leaking bowels are controlled, and the patient is quickly transferred to a higher level of care. Because of the dichotomy of being highly specialized, but in a very forward position, FSTs fall outside the usual echelon classification system.

The Combat Support Hospital (CSH) is the modern equivalent of the old MASH units and represents echelon III. The modern CSH is housed in a tent and container system called a "DEPMED." The hospital is a maze of tents, attached to rigid containers housing the CT scanner, OR, or Laboratory. The CSH is a dynamic asset that can be as compact as eight ICU beds with twenty ward beds and as large as 258 beds in its fully expanded form. The CSH provides a wide variety of services including surgery, surgical specialties, internal medicine, ophthalmology, psychiatry, and rehabilitation. It's the first level of care that can provide extended in-patient care for those unable to be evacuated.

The OR in our CSH was essentially a small metal container, approximately 100 square feet—the size of a small bedroom. In this box, two OR tables provide the ability to run two cases at once. Our staff consists of a general surgeon, an orthopedist, a CRNA, an anesthesiologist, and about seven OR nurses and technicians. The book says we can provide up to 36 hours of continuous operations. I can tell you from experience we could do that. Despite the cramped space, it had the look, feel and the efficacy of any OR I ever worked in. The nurses and technicians are highly skilled and motivated—some of the best I ever worked with.

After treatment at the CSH, patients were sent to one of three destinations depending on their status. U.S. soldiers are immediately evacuated to another CSH connected to a major airfield. There, they are stabilized for transport to Landstuhl, Germany, for what is considered echelon IV care. Eventually, they will make it back to a hospital in the United States, such as Walter Reed Army Medical Center, which represents the fifth and final echelon of treatment. Iraqi citizens are stabilized, cared for and transferred to an Iraqi civilian hospital. The remainder of the patients are detainees who have no place to go and make up most of the long-term patients at the CSH.

☙

The infamous Abu Ghraib prison complex was home to the 344th CSH. Since the scandal, the prison had been emptied out. Tents and containers of the CSH had been set up inside a large warehouse. The solid structure provided protection from sandstorms and enemy artillery.

I was shown to my barracks and stored my gear. After a brief rest, it was time to meet my new colleagues. Lieutenant Colonel (LTC) Leslie Rice was the nursing supervisor who kept the place running. She led me around the facility, introducing me to the others: Goodspeed, orthopod; Woletz, anesthesia; Costello and Rees, internal medicine; Wenstrup, podiatry; Cushing, radiology; and in the ER, Walsh, VanEvry and Smith.

The tour led along the back hallway of the CSH lined with cement floor and plywood walls. Passageways led to large tents set up within the building. One large tent just inside the entrance functioned as the Emergency Treatment Room (ETR); another served as pre-op; a third was the ICU.

In the ICU, neon lights dangled from the white fabric ceiling. Large plastic sheets secured with duct tape covered the floor. In between, a medley of ordered chaos prevailed. Patient beds, separated by blue curtains, crowded next to each other. Large oxygen cylinders flanked each bed while cardiac monitors hung on foot boards. Nurses and techs bustled along the narrow walkway cluttered with code carts, equipment bins and documentation stations.

I looked for the outgoing surgeon to receive report, a process in the military known as "right seat, left seat." She wasn't hard to find.

"Hold CPR," she said.

The monitor showed v-tach.

"Okay, let's shock him," she said.

"Hi, I'm John Pryor," I said as the defibrillator charged. "I'm your replacement."

"Sheri Johnson," she said, "very glad to see you."

She got right to the point. "This is a 22-year-old Iraqi who was caught in the crossfire of a patrol looking for bad guys. He's post op day four from a bowel resection."

"Clear!" yelled one of the techs. The patient convulsed from the charge. The monitor returned to a regular rhythm, and I quickly assessed the situation.

So much for an orientation, I thought.

"Is there a pulse?" I asked, assuming responsibility.

"We got a pulse," responded a tech.

The resuscitation slowed, allowing our conversation to continue.

"Sorry to leave you with a mess, but he just crashed this morning," said Major (MAJ) Johnson. "Otherwise, the unit is pretty stable. You got two intubated soldiers with head injuries, three Iraqi civilians and one insurgent."

She quickly rattled off the injuries and basic plan for each. "What you need to know is in the chart. What's not in the chart, the nurses know.

She handed me a portable radio. My new appendage would be clipped to my chest for the next 90 days and never be turned off. Ever. It accompanied me to meals, slept with me, took a shit with me and stayed within reaching distance when I showered. And it was never quiet for more than a few hours.

"I don't mean to leave in such a rush, but I've been here for two tours, back to back, and I've got a helo to catch."

"No problem," I said. "I'm sure I'll figure it out."

MAJ Johnson headed for the exit. I was officially "it."

My first day in Iraq was another in a series of stressful situations I had to overcome in my life. Not only a new environment with new staff, but this was the military, in a different country, a war zone. Half of my patients didn't speak English. Again, I relied on my surgical training to get me through. The saving grace was the patient. Hospitals may change, staff could go on strike, the entire earth may shift from beneath my feet, but patients are always the same. Bleeding doesn't change. Bowel perforations don't change. Pus doesn't change.

I reviewed the patient's chart then placed a hand on his belly. Such a simple act yet it takes years to appreciate the information gleaned by such a maneuver. I tallied up the information.

"What do you think?" one of the nurses asked.

"We have a scanner?" I asked.

"Yeah, but it's broken today," she said.

I raised my hand to my chin to think a minute. The scan would be standard of care in the u.s. to cinch the diagnosis. It didn't matter. I had a pretty good idea of the problem.

"So how do we get him to the or?" I asked.

"You tell me you want to take him to the or," said the nurse.

"I think we need to open his belly."

The operating room was proceeded by "pre-op," a series of tents with furled dividers and "rooms" formed by draping sheets of fabric. The or entrance lay beyond a set of double doors displaying a white placard labeled "or" flanked by two red crosses. Windowless white plastic walls and low-lying ceilings made the space feel confined.

An orderly moved the patient and began the prep. I found the scrub sink and backed my way into the box. Woletz prepared the anesthesia, and I adjusted the surgical lights. Before I could ask, a scalpel was placed in my hand. I was amazed at how fast this team moved.

Cutting into peritoneum released a good amount of pus.

I've seen worse, I thought.

I resected the worst of the infection and irrigated the belly with antibiotic lavage. As I closed, I felt relieved this was my first case, something simple to get me acclimated.

The next few days, I provided routine care to the existing patients. Some were very sick, and the icu care was similar to that in the u.s., the difference here was that once these patients were stable, most were transported out.

My real introduction to war surgery came on a beautiful sunny afternoon a few days later. While lounging with Goodspeed and Walsh outside the etr, our radios came alive with an alert tone followed by crackling voices.

"All personnel to etr. Incoming wounded. Repeat: all personnel ..."

Conversations stopped mid sentence, and soldiers hustled to the

ETR. I was slow on the uptake, but Goodspeed prompted me, and we jogged to the entrance.

"We're about to get busy," he said.

I hadn't experienced an adrenaline rush this intense since I was a medic. It's hard to describe such feelings of excitement and anxiety— not knowing what is about to happen, but knowing it's going to be bad. In a few moments, a life may be saved or lost depending on my actions. The anxiety arrested my thoughts, wiping my mind of all knowledge. Only when I start to act, when I start doing something, would the fear abate and my ability return.

The team gathered equipment and readied stretchers. Combat hardened nurses, and staff knew what was about to arrive. I felt so naïve.

They said wounded would come in groups. In Philly, shootings were sporadic, and it was unusual to get more than three patients at once. In Iraq, however, there could be five or more soldiers injured by an IED, more if there was a subsequent firefight. These are called mass casualty incidents or "Mascals" for short. Mascals are challenging even for experienced providers because decisions about whom to treat first and how to allocate resources become difficult. At HUP, I had dozens of fellows, residents and colleagues to lend a hand if there were multiple patients.

Here, I was the only general surgeon.

With staff preparing the ETR, I stepped into the bright sunlight outside the ETR doors. The choppy thunder of the approaching Chinook vibrated the air. I glanced at the front gate of the base. A pair of ambulances led a dust cloud, making a beeline for the ETR.

Here they come, I thought.

The officer in charge (OIC) and the clinical director of emergency medicine remained outside to initiate triage. I headed inside.

The first patient, an Iraqi soldier, wheeled in and was transferred to the hospital stretcher. I was taken aback a bit because I had been expecting Americans. A heavy smell of gasoline and charred flesh filled the air. A large metal fragment had ripped into his neck and upper chest; his face and arm were badly burned. Unconscious and ghostly pale, he was in shock from significant blood loss.

The team sprung into action. The Emergency Medicine (EM) doc cut deeper into his badly damaged neck to place an improvised tracheotomy. Corpsmen placed IVs, blood was hung and radiology moved in.

Obviously, this patient would be first to the operating room to control bleeding in the neck.

The second patient came a moment later. He had a chunk taken out of his right pelvis; exposed bone was peeking through mounds of blood-soaked trauma pads. His legs were a tangled mess. The soldier was also ghostly pale from blood loss. He, too, needed to go to the OR right away.

I was suddenly caught in the bane of triage: Who goes first?

As tasks were completed on the first patient, the staff moved quickly to the next. Then the next. Then the next. Within minutes, seven more patients filled the ETR. Fractures, burns, blast injuries. These others weren't critical, but they were badly wounded.

Amidst the chaos of rushing staff and screams of pain, DEATH strolled silently along the corridor. He appeared different here—larger, his robe, worn and tattered; his sickle blunt from overuse. He stopped at the head of the first patient and leaned heavily on his staff, like an old man in need of rest.

In times of need, military personnel must be able to multitask and function in multiple roles. The adaptability of the team was impressive. In most hospitals, radiologists remain sequestered in a back room gazing at x-rays. The hospital chaplain might visit patients but avoid any crisis. Lab technicians spend the day running blood samples. But in combat, everyone is involved, and everyone helps. Patients were tended to by nurses from all areas of the hospital, the radiologist, nurse anesthetists, the internal medicine doc, the chaplain, lab techs—everyone was present in the ETR.

In all, nine casualties arrived from this IED blast. The neck and the open pelvis were both taken to the OR. I worked on the neck as ortho started on the pelvis. It was the closest I had come to operating on two patients at once. Both were saved and remained stable until transfer the next day.

When the dust settled, I noticed one of the young Iraqi soldiers. In charred and blood-soaked fatigues, he retold his ordeal through glazed eyes, almost as if he weren't really there.

"There was a flash. One moment we're driving along, and the next was complete chaos. We all got out except Rahim. He was trapped. We tried to get him out, but the fire started to spread. We could hear him screaming ..."

Most soldiers know that it's only a matter of time before they are going to get hit with something like this. Today was their day. If they were fortunate in any way, it was that they were brought to this hospital with amazing and dedicated care-givers—all reservists, all volunteers, all here sacrificing time from family and a normal life to serve their fellow man selflessly. I was honored to be part of the team.

∽

I had the opportunity to meet and care for many Iraqi citizens. They come to the CSH under many different circumstances, but invariably they all are seeking the coveted care of an American medical system. Many of them have conditions that would be easily and routinely cared for in the states. But in Iraq, a routine problem could easily become life threatening.

Early Monday morning, a week after my arrival, Chief Medical Officer (CMO) Crawford walked to the gate; he was flanked by a few armed soldiers and an Iraqi interpreter. The sun broke over a sea of sand chasing away the early morning twilight. A group of Iraqi women had already gathered at the entrance. The women immediately approached and began their pleas for help. Two of the women held small children in their arms.

It was a daily ritual. The Iraqi medical system was never the envy of the Middle East. After the invasion, the medical facilities, like most public services, had been devastated. There were still private hospitals and if you had money, you could pay for relatively good care. But the poor were out of luck. I heard stories from Iraqis, in their own language, of patients literally being put out in the street for not being able to pay—quadriplegics left to die, medication and food stolen from patients and sold on the black market.

In a system like this, patients beg to be treated at our hospital. Of course, we can't treat everyone. Most of us will never know such torture—to have a loved one so sick whose survival rested on the decision of a foreign Army commander. But such was the reality; and the reality was a lot of people died.

The Army has strict guidelines as to who is allowed to be a patient at the CSH. Obviously U.S. and coalition troops are given priority—then American contractors and U.S. nationals, then Iraqi civilians who are victims of collateral damage or friendly fire. Finally came the injured enemy combatants and insurgents who are in U.S. custody. Regular Iraqi civilians weren't on the list.

The mother of Najeem pleaded for help through an interpreter; her voice was filled with anguish and desperation. Geography may change; cultures may be completely foreign, but some human traits are universal. One such trait is that a mother will do anything to save her son.

Najeem was burned in a kerosene fire in the town of Abu Ghraib. Police suspected he was working with insurgents and had him in custody but couldn't care for his burns. He was eleven years old.

"He is a good boy," the interpreter translated as his mother rambled: "He ... she says he's always been such a good boy. Then he, then the insurgents come, and she says they convince him to work for them. She says he was forced into it and that he didn't know what he was doing ..."

Crawford let out a heavy sigh and shook his head. Implementing Army protocol was one thing but standing in front of these desperate women listening to their heart-wrenching stories, knowing a denial was the same as a death sentence, was completely different.

"Where is he?" he asked the interpreter.

"The local police have him," said the interpreter, "but they're not providing any medical care."

"How bad are his injuries?"

The interpreter spoke to Najeem's mother then turned back to the commander. "Burns. He's burned from the waist down."

Burns? Crawford thought. *How hard can that be to take care of?*

Technically, there was no reason to take Najeem. He was in custody, but not American custody. He was not injured as a result of American actions. Crawford would be completely justified in turning Najeem's mother away.

"Ok," the CMO conceded, "tell her we'll take him."

Before the translator could finish his sentence, Najeem's mother collapsed to the ground in tears.

"She says, Thank you. Allah thanks you."

"Yeah, yeah, okay."

⁓

I stood at the foot of the bed and surveyed Najeem for the first time. I stared at him silently with my arms folded. Bony and malnourished, he appeared like a lightly veiled skeleton that breathed. Unconscious, mouth open, he occasionally gasped as if it were his last breath. Nurses unwrapped fetid dressing, revealing raw flesh, eschar and pus. It smelled like pseudomonas. His temp was 104.6, heart rate 140 and blood pressure 60 over nothing. Third-degree burns encircled both legs and ascended to his waist; his penis and testicles were barely recognizable, and burns extended into his anus. Every bowel movement would be a nightmare.

Goodspeed flanked me.

"This kid's a mess," I said without looking up.

"Yeah."

"He's already septic," I continued. "His legs are all third degree. If we can keep him alive, he'll need dozens of grafts, daily debridements, antibiotics. We're talking months and months of care."

"Yeah."

"Who the hell thought this was a good idea?"

"Crawford."

"Did he have any idea of what this kid will require?"

"I guess not."

"I don't think he's gonna make it." I weighed the odds, the care he required with the resources we could offer. "He's malnourished. He needs to be at a burn center."

"John …"

"Do they have morphine at the local hospitals? Maybe they should have just made him comfortable …"

"John…"

"Yeah?"

"Just do the best you can." He slapped my back.

I picked up the brown manila chart that contained two sheets of paper. One was a brief history of Najeem's injuries. The other was a blank ICU order sheet. I let out a sigh and glanced at the emaciated child in the bed.

DEATH hovered close, waiting my decision.

What if that were Frankie? I thought.

I began writing admission orders: antibiotics, dressing orders, IV fluids, tube feeds. When I looked up, DEATH had retreated a few feet but remained close, leaning on his sickle.

✂

Departing for Iraq, I knew I was headed into a war zone. I didn't know what that really *meant*. Nobody does until you hear the gunfire and feel the base rattle with each explosion. But not all explosions are the same, and it takes time to sort them out.

My first real explosion occurred when I was in the OR opening a neck abscess. A bunch of the other docs and staff observed me in the OR. As I draped the patient, the entire room rattled. I flinched, almost falling to the floor.

Everyone laughed.

"Ah, John," someone offered, "that was a controlled det."

A controlled detonation was a scheduled explosion usually to eliminate unexploded ordinance. It was a routine occurrence.

"Could someone please put the war on hold while I'm operating?" I joked.

A few days later, I was trying to sleep when the sounds of mortar fire caught my attention.

"Mortar attack!" I said into my video camera, recording the incident. I struggled into my battle rattle and headed for the bunker. But when I came out to the main corridor, I found it empty.

"JP," one of the staff, was up watching a movie. "What are you doing?"

"I heard mortars," I said.

"Those are *outgoing*."

A rookie mistake. Luckily, there was a steep learning curve. After a couple of weeks, I could distinguish a mortar from a rocket from an IED, incoming versus outgoing and how far away. It was life in a war zone.

∞

If you haven't already seen the HBO mini-series, *"Band of Brothers,"* I highly recommend it. It's a historically accurate account of a company of soldiers from the 101st Airborne Division as they fight from Normandy to Berlin in World War II.

One episode entitled *"Why We Fight"* tells of Easy Company discovering a concentration camp. Finding these camps and rescuing the prisoners gave the soldiers great strength of purpose. All the struggles they endured, all the friends they lost and all of the sacrifices made were justified. Clearly, World War II was a war against evil. The future of freedom throughout the world was at stake.

I think it is safe to say that many of the wars and conflicts since World War II have had less clear purpose. The lines between good and evil have been blurred. This is true in Iraq where much of the evil of Saddam's regime remained hidden from the American people.

On March 5th, I had the opportunity to understand the evil we were fighting in Iraq. I joined a tour of the Abu Ghraib prison.

We arrived at the desolate prison and entered a silent metal hallway. The cells, rooms and holding areas were devoid of furniture or equipment. Tan-colored paint peeled from barren walls. A dusting of sand lightly covered the floor. Heavy metal doors separated each large room. Wind whistled through the space like distant screams. Fenestrated outer walls permitted sunlight and sounds of chirping birds that belied the sense of captivity.

We followed our guide as he spoke of the horrors that occurred here. Presently, we came to a stop within a very long hallway covered by an inch of sand.

"Welcome to the 'Brown Mile'," he said. "The Iraqis won't come here; most of them are too afraid. This is where one of the worst atrocities happened, sometime in the '90s."

I wondered what could be worse than the stories I had already heard about torture and death.

"The prison had become overcrowded to a point where the prison officials needed to do something. You can probably imagine it wasn't fun to complain to Saddam about any problems, but the officials told him of the overcrowding of the prison.

"Saddam sent his son, Qusai, to take care of it. The prisoners were lined up along this hallway so they could 'meet' the arriving dignitaries. They were told it was like an inspection. They stood there, bound, while Qusai walked down the line executing every third prisoner. In the end, something like a thousand prisoners died that day. Afterwards, he was heard saying, 'No more overcrowding problem.'"

Hearing this story while standing in this spot was like hearing a ghost story around the campfire as a child. The difference was that this story was true. I could almost hear the gunshots echo down the hall and feel the terror of those who stood in line, not knowing if they would live or die. I imagined the prostrate bodies lying in pools of blood.

We continued our tour.

In one holding cell, walls were covered with murals: a woman's face, a scenic view with mountains and river, a steamship headed for a tropical island, a woman holding a dove, a bare-chested man waist-deep in the ocean embracing a woman and flanked by leaping dolphins, scenes of mountains, dreams of freedom.

The group moved on. We came to a small holding cell where prisoners were confined until called to the 'death house.' On the wall, scratched with fingernails or small stones was written graffiti of the condemned. Even with my limited Arabic, I could make out some words—names, pleas, 'mother,' 'children', 'goodbye.'

We walked outside into a bright courtyard surrounded by high walls and a circular guard tower in one corner. The death house was a square building about four feet taller than an adjacent single-story prison. The sound of a metal latch echoed in the courtyard; hinges screeched as a heavy steel door swung open.

Inside, an empty chamber rose to two stories. A ramp along one side led to a platform that ran along the far wall. The platform was about five feet off the floor. A simple balustrade lined the front of the platform. Mounted in the center, a rectangular podium contained bare metal levers. On either side, square openings in the floor lay beneath eyelets in the ceiling.

"Okay, there are four different ways they killed people in here," the guide began. "Obviously, the traditional way with a rope, give it slack, the doors open, breaks the neck, you're done.

"The other way was with cable or wire. Same thing, doors open, the only difference is that it would decapitate them.

"Third way was to put the rope around their neck, pull it taut, open the doors and—a couple of variations here—with the doors up, they would start a fire underneath, and the doors would get so hot that they would basically strangle themselves. They either burned their feet off or strangled themselves.

"Another way was to put acid in a tube below and slowly lower them into it as they're strangling."

The guide then demonstrated how the trap doors operate. Soldiers lifted the metal doors into place. A volunteer approached the lever.

"Is everybody clear?" he asked. "Make sure no one is below. Okay, ready?"

Lever pulled, the doors fell open with a loud clanging that echoed in the chamber and reverberated throughout the prison like a muted bell.

I realize the reasons America invaded Iraq were politically complex; I don't pretend to understand it all. My decision to enlist focused on the troops and my ability to provided trauma care. But on this day, in this particular spot, I couldn't ignore the humanity of it all.

I view my country as a force for good. The United States has a goal of spreading freedom, promoting human rights and defending democracy. In this regard, the United States has been successful here. Before the invasion, this place was filled with political prisoners, torture and random executions. Now, a tyrannical regime had been ousted, and the people of Iraq have the chance to be free. At the very least, this death house would finally be retired, and the u.s. presence here was that much more justified.

☙

Burn Boy was alive.

I forget who started calling him Burn Boy, but it stuck. Maybe it was a psychological defense, not getting used to his real name in case he died. This job was hard enough without the emotional toll of failing an innocent child.

But he wasn't dead yet.

Burn care is one of the most challenging problems a surgeon can face. People don't know. They have no idea.

Intact skin is the body's major defense against infection. When the skin is compromised, the potential for infection skyrockets. This was even worse in Iraq, where, for some reason, everything got infected.

Each day, dead and infected material needed to be debrided. The process is time consuming and, at times, extremely painful. Despite sedation and pain meds, Burn Boy suffered daily.

Full thickness burns do not heal; they require grafts. Every few days, we wheeled Burn Boy back to the OR to transplant skin from his upper torso to his legs and pelvis. His emaciated torso offered limited donor sites, and we had to use the same spots repeatedly after they healed.

Finally, despite our vigilance, we couldn't stop complications from sprouting up. Urine infection, pneumonia, failed grafts, electrolyte and nutritional problems. Every week, we had a new fire to put out.

During my tour, most patients came and went. But each day, twice or three times a day, Burn Boy demanded my complete attention. Despite my best efforts, I became emotionally attached to him.

This kid better fucking make it, I thought.

ↄ

During officer basic course, recruits were forced to wear full "battle rattle" at all times. This stuff includes the individual body armor (IBA) with neck and groin extensions, Kevlar (helmet), blast glasses, weapon and ammo. Everywhere we moved, we had to have this stuff on, including in the latrine—a challenge to say the least.

It was a real pain in the ass.

Here in Iraq, we have the same rule—full gear anywhere outside patient-care areas. This stuff weighs about 30 lbs, is very uncomfortable, and becomes unbelievably hot. Left on our own, none of us would wear this stuff every day.

And that is exactly why the rules are in place.

One morning a few weeks into my tour, I was eating lunch at

the dining facility (DFAC). I loaded my tray and sat with Goodspeed, Woletz, and VanEvry. Before I could get a bite of my sandwich, the earth shook.

As mortars began to fall, I gained a new appreciation for the rules. In an instant, my thirty pounds of hot, uncomfortable gear became vital armor.

The four of us headed for the bunker ahead of the air raid siren. More explosions followed. I had experienced the occasional incoming round, but this was different. The blasts were sporadic but relentless.

In the bunker, we waited. Long pauses assuaged the attack, but just when I thought it was over, another burst shook the ground. During a lull, the radio crackled. Tactical Operations Center (TOC) announced incoming wounded.

Shit! I thought.

The ETR lay fifty yards beyond exposed sand from the DFAC.

I keyed the mic, "What's the ETA for the wounded?"

"Ten to fifteen," replied a voice from TOC.

The rule was twenty minutes from the last mortar before we could move. The casualties would arrive before then.

"You stay right where you are," crackled the stern voice of LTC Rice. "We are under fire. Do you understand?"

"Yes ma'am," I agreed. "We are under fire."

"We'll come get you as soon as it is clear," Rice continued; "until then, the ETR will handle the wounded."

The radio went silent, and I looked at my watch. It was about five minutes since the last round.

"Whadda think?" I asked the others.

"It's not that far," Goodspeed said. It was all the encouragement I needed.

"I'm gonna make a run for it," I decided. "Who's with me?" a distant explosion punctuated my offer. I froze, glancing at them with my eyes.

"I think that was outgoing," I said with a smile.

At the main gate I saw a convoy loaded with wounded approach. I couldn't wait any longer.

"Guys, ready?" I asked.

There were nods all around.

We tore out of the DFAC, sprinting across the open space. Time slowed as I struggled against the weight of my IBA. I was back on the football field, pumping my legs like pistons, weighed down in heavy gear, headed for the goal. My derelict middle-aged body struggled to move like my brain remembered. Winded, I kept pushing, thinking of the runs I had done, the weight I lost, the pushups I could do.

Faster, faster, I thought, *get me to that door, and I promise to do better, I promise to get in better shape!*

We burst into the ETR, and I nearly collapsed out of breath.

"What the hell was that?!" Rice shouted above me.

"We ... couldn't ...." I said, bent over between gasps, "wait."

"Don't ever do that again!" Rice yelled, "This isn't some joke! This isn't a game! You get hurt, and then what do we do? Who you gonna help if you're wounded or dead?"

I knew running across an open field during an attack was, technically, the wrong thing to do. But the wounded were coming and, c'mon, what was the likelihood of getting hit during a fifty-yard dash? The odds were infinitesimal.

☙

After a month in Iraq, I finally came down from the initial adrenaline high. Fear and excitement slowly gave way to routine and familiarity. Acclimated to my new role, I befriended the staff and spent down time teaching ATLS, triage skills and procedures.

We became a real team.

During one MASCAL, five critical patients rolled into the ETR simultaneously. The staff burst into action, and we became a well-oiled machine stabilizing the wounded. I paced up and down the center, smiling, clapping my hands, saying, "I'm lovin it! I'm lovin it!"

These guys were awesome.

But when my mind wasn't occupied, I thought of my family, and become melancholy. This was the longest I had ever been away from Carmela and the kids. An excellent cell phone network rendered my satellite phone obsolete. I texted Carmela routinely, and we spoke several times a day. When there was time, I used Skype to video chat with the kids.

Never in the history of warfare has it been possible to instantly communicate with family back home. I wondered how this new ability would change the morale or discipline of the fighting forces. Was it an asset or a liability? Was it a good thing to know your wife crashed the car at home, or would it distract from wartime duties?

I found it a blessing. I missed the kids terribly, and to be able to talk with them and see them on the computer made our separation bearable.

Carmela struggled to manage at home without me. Again, I knew my deployment would be hard on her, but I didn't really know what that meant. On the phone, I heard the stress in her voice, sensed her frustration and listened to her complaints about managing without me. I would begin to feel guilty, but then I thought of the patients and their families. Yes, it was tough for us, it was hard for Carmela, and I'm sorry about that. But what about the family of a soldier who lost a leg or suffered a brain injury or was killed?

How hard was it for them?

&

"Oh, Burn Boy, my Burn Boy," I said. "What are you doing to me?"

Burn Boy didn't respond. He was busy trying to die on me again. Viewing the x-ray against fluorescent ceiling lights, I frowned at the hazy lung fields.

"What's the PEEP?" I asked.

"Ten," said the respiratory tech.

"Let's up it to fifteen," I said. "See if his sats improve."

LTC Rice looked over my shoulder.

"Pneumonia?" she asked.

"Pneumonia?" I scoffed. "He's already *had* pneumonia. My boy is moving up in the world; now he's got ARDS."

We both returned our gaze to the cachectic child.

"Have you ever seen a kid this bad before?" she asked.

My eyes glazed over at this emaciated figure lost in a sea of gauze and heating blankets. Intubated, Dobhoff, central line, arterial line, Foley catheter, sat monitor, EKG monitor, IVs hanging.

"None that lived," I conceded.

☙

On my 30th day in the Iraq Theater of Operations, I qualified for the Iraq campaign medal. I was officially a veteran.

Of all the titles and distinctions I've held over the years, I was most proud of this. I now understood why my grandfather was so dedicated to the American Legion efforts.

My role here in Iraq is supportive: I don't fight the battles, I'm not in any real danger, I'm not a grunt out there fighting the war every day. But I do live among these soldiers. I care for them, interact with them, and know them. The pride and esteem I feel for these young kids is overwhelming. I see what they are asked to do every single day. I watch them assemble outside the DFAC, readying for a night patrol, and pray I don't see them in the trauma bay that night. I tremble each time I hear a blast off the FOB, wondering if anyone was hurt. They are so young, so dedicated.

I desperately want to fit in this organization as an equal member, but I know I never will. I could never do what they do. I admire the gunner on that Humvee, exposed, vulnerable, with nothing to stop the shrapnel from tearing through his body. I do not have it in me to be like him. I want to do everything and anything to support these kids. I know my job here is important, but it seems, at times, sheltered and easy.

I think my grandfather felt the same way. He respected all veterans, especially the ones who faced danger on a regular basis. Our admiration comes from the understanding, and acceptance, of our own limitations and cowardice.

I hadn't worn my class A uniform in public since I joined the Army because I felt I had not earned the right. Now I could wear it with pride. I looked forward to spending Memorial Day with Frankie, taking him to a cemetery and laying flags on the veteran graves. I wanted him to appreciate their sacrifice as much as I did.

☙

On March 18th, I learned the true meaning of war.

So far I had been hit pretty hard: MASCALS, operating through the night, dealing with the stress of American troops and Marines near death or dying. It was what I expected, what I trained for. Duly stressed, I could still function within normal parameters.

But on the 18th, an IED with multiple secondaries caused a tsunami of wounded to flood into the ETR. One after another, they rolled in—each flanked by a bony, dark hooded figure—each a hair's breadth away from death. Blasted, shredded legs tapered to dirty, bloody, horse's tails. Bubbling guts burst from eviscerated abdomens. Pieces of nose and lips, barely recognizable, swam in a bloody mush of a mutilated faces. The ETR filled with the odor of gasoline, charred flesh, and explosive residue. The metallic smell of blood soon covered my fatigues and soaked into my boots. Anguished screams from some reassured me they were alive enough that I could focus on the near dead, silent and flaccid, halfway to the light before I somehow pulled them back to this earthly nightmare.

Every patient was critical, every one had gaping wounds and shredded amputations unlike any I have ever seen. Everyone was bleeding to death. Triage, in one way, was simple: they all needed emergent surgery. The problem remained, I was the only general surgeon. Along with the orthopedic surgeon, we could do only two cases at a time.

So who goes first? If I pick this one, that one will exsanguinate here in the ETR. Who goes first? The ones closer to the OR? What if I make the wrong decision? Am I going to be able to stop any of this bleeding?

Over the years, I have been put in these no-win situations many, many times. I can tell you that experience does nothing to help make it any easier. What I have learned, however, is that becoming paralyzed only makes the situation worse. Spending a half an hour examining each patient, looking at x-rays and polling colleagues about whom to operate on first kills your last patient. The only thing worse than making an impossible decision is not making an impossible decision. If the stakes are to kill or be killed, choose kill. If the choice is operate quickly and potentially save some lives or be indecisive and lose even more, start cutting.

I operated through the evening and into the night. Dawn came while I continued to operate. Soldiers were opened up, patched and sent out with a sterile cloth over exposed guts. The sun rose, arched over the abandoned prison and fell below the horizon. When the last life-threatening bleed was under control I started on the limbs, first with temporary shunts then proper grafts.

In my third round of operations, I cared for a patient with an ischemic leg. He had waited eight hours before I got to him. At HUP, a delay that long would be negligent. I shunted the artery as quickly as I could and spent several more hours doing the vein graft to reestablish flow. I had no regrets delaying his care. Taking him first would have certainly killed another soldier.

Well into my second night, I began to bring the first ones back for more complete repair and closure. Not until dawn of the second day was I done.

Thirty-one hours. Thirty-one grueling hours in the operating room. I was pushed to my very limit, but in the end not one soldier died and not one salvageable limb had been lost.

Emerging from the OR, I was more than exhausted—I was beaten. At first it was about coming here to help; it was about duty, honor and country; it was about camaraderie. But I felt all of this without knowing what "this" was. When I paused to catch my breath, it suddenly dawned on me like a ton of bricks.

This was war.

And it's no fucking joke.

ↄ

On May 1st, the medics wheeled Faadeen out of the CSH and loaded him into an M-997 ambulance. After spending more than six months in our hospital, he departed for long-term rehab.

Faadeen sustained severe trauma and burns to his torso and lower extremities. He suffered all of the requisite complications often seen with severe burns: sepsis, pneumonia, fungemia, even a wound infection requiring leg amputation and eventually deafness from long-term antibiotic use. He received world class care, 24 hours a day from our very skillful medics, nurses and physicians. If we could calculate the cost of his care, it would in run in the millions.

The difference was this: Faadeen was burned when his IED, being laid to kill American soldiers, accidentally detonated. Faadeen was a detainee, an enemy soldier, what you would call an insurgent. Many people ask why we provide care to people trying to kill us and destroy our nation. The answer turns out to be at the core of what we stand for and represent as Americans.

There is, foremost, a legal obligation for the United States to care for enemy soldiers. Although it may not seem intuitive, there are rules and laws that govern the conduct of war. Codified as the Geneva Convention, these rules were adopted by free nations as the generally accepted mode by which civilized war should be conducted. There are rules about what types of weapons can be used, and in what circumstances. There are also rules about how prisoners should be treated both on and off the battlefield. Within these regulations are the laws that require us to care for captured enemy soldiers injured in armed conflict. Of course, the essence of these laws is that both sides will treat prisoners and injured prisoners with the same dignity and compassion. As we have seen on CNN, this is not always true. Regardless, the U.S. military is bound by these rules.

More important, there is a moral obligation of an army to care for persons whom they have injured in conflict. This stems from understanding the goals of warfare. At first, one may think that the goal of war is to kill the entire enemy. In fact, the goal of war is to force your enemy to quit, give up his land and go home. Sun Tzu, the historic military leader and poet, was the first to define the goal of battle as the breaking of the enemy's spirit and will to fight. He went on to say, much more eloquently, that the greatest battles are those that end without a shot fired. The most skillful generals are those who can win a battle with threat and deterrent force alone.

Therefore, we are not here to kill insurgents or wipe out all jihadists; our goal is to make the insurgency unappealing and die out. We want the enemy to realize that channeling their efforts into building a new country will be more in their interest than trying to kill Americans. With that goal clearly defined, the care of persons injured in the inevitable violence of war becomes more understandable.

Lastly, we remember the experiences of war with other countries such as Japan, Germany and Vietnam. Do you hate the Japanese? Of course not. But if I asked you in 1945, the answer might be different. After the war, Japanese soldiers returned to being Japanese citizens.

After laying down their weapons, even some very evil Japanese who tortured Americans soldiers, gave up violence. Their children grew up without resentment or hatred of Americans. The Japanese are now one of the most productive and peaceful cultures in the world.

One day Iraq will be a free nation, and its people will enjoy all of the graces and blessings of peace. The insurgents will eventually put down their weapons and join society as productive members. Eventually, every single insurgent held in our custody will be released. How they were treated in our custody is how they will view the United States.

I hope that the care I gave during these few months touched one or two of these enemy soldiers. I hope my actions will make them reconsider what Americans are all about. Perhaps one or two will leave our hospital with a dulled desire to harm those who saved his life.

It is difficult to imagine the future, clouded by the emotions of the present, but we need to do that. This is the most important reason we cared for Faadeen and the reason we will continue to care for all people suffering in this war.

໑

Days and nights blurred into one long, never ending day. As a resident, I joked about every third call night leaving me out of two-thirds of the cases. I complained about the Bell Commission's restriction of resident work hours.

Well, in Iraq, there were no restrictions. I was on for every case, every problem and every patient who rolled through the ETR. I got sleep, but it was rarely more than five continuous hours. I had, at last, found something that made residency look easy.

In some ways, though, working in Iraq was easier than in the U.S.

"I need Rocephin," I would say. A minute later, Rocephin dangled above the patient. "He needs a scan"; if the scanner was working, the patient would be wheeled away before my eyes. Labs were run more quickly than I thought possible. The CSH functioned like a very small, close-knit hospital. Missing was the bureaucracy, regulations and bullshit that impeded workflow. In this regard, it was a pleasure to work in the CSH.

Meanwhile, Burn Boy had rallied.

Miraculously, his lungs cleared, and he began to gain weight.

It was touch and go for awhile, which is typical of critical patients. When he arrived, he was near dead, and the first few weeks were basically a resuscitation. Then he settled in as a critical care patient and had to endure the long haul. This is where many patients are lost. It's like a marathon. After sprinting the first mile, they run out of steam and wither. Burn Boy had hung in and managed to get through the thick of it. He still had a long way to go, but now I was more optimistic than ever.

❧

My third month progressed slowly.

Clinical demands of the hospital left little time for physical training (PT), and I was mortified when I failed my Army fitness test required for promotion. A few of the LPNs and medics became my personal trainers, forcing me to the gym whenever I was idle. LTC Rice would frequently find me sweating in my scrubs, struggling against gravity performing pushups or situps. Thanks to the encouragement of my buddies, I passed the physical fitness test.

On May 1, 2006, COL Rees presided over a small ceremony held in a plywood-enclosed conference room. Standing at attention, I listened to COL Reese commend me on my service before promoting me to the rank of Major. Other than for the births of my children, I can't recall a prouder moment in my life. At the end, I was allowed to make a few comments.

"I am so proud to be part of such a great team," I said. "I think we've done more here to spread the message of American compassion than any other medical mission in Iraq. I have been really impressed with the staff of the 344th, and I am honored to play a small part in such an outstanding combat hospital."

The room filled with applause, and there were hugs all around. Heading into my last month with these medical professionals, I was surprised at how close we had become.

❧

In the second week of May, my tour was up. It was hard to believe

I had been in Iraq for four months. Coming to Iraq was an adventure, and I believed I was helping, but fatigue and homesickness had worn me down. I felt guilty wanting to go home knowing so many soldiers were here for so much longer.

Soldiers are acutely aware of how much time they have before their tour is over. We use the designation "H" followed by the number of days left. H-10 means there are ten days left before going home.

As my final day approached, I kept a log of my final hours of this tour:

Thursday 7 a.m. H-1

The main body of the 21st CSH arrived yesterday, and I should meet the incoming general surgeon today. The plan is to spend the day together showing him around. We are supposed to bug out tomorrow night by helicopter. I'm completely packed, down to two duffels and a backpack. I mailed a footlocker of stuff, mostly souvenirs home this past weekend. We are "short," meaning we have a short time left. Lots of jokes about that: "I am so short I can't see over the berm" and "I am a single digit midget." New guys look very green. They have that stare I had when I got here—a combination of fear, despair, confusion, and anxiousness. They are H-365.

Friday 7 a.m. H-3!

Yes, we are going backwards.

As it happens with the Army, things have changed. The 21st CSH feels it needs a few more days to assimilate before taking over; our bug out is now scheduled for Monday. I will continue working until then. We will be doing a "right seat, left seat ride" over the next few days. The term is from pilots who have the student observe in the right seat and then move over to take control in the left seat when ready, being observed by the teacher. My replacement will observe me for two days and then take over on Monday morning. I will bug out with the main body Monday night. I got a full night's sleep last night, one of the best in a few weeks. Just luck. Hopefully, this keeps up until I get out of here.

Friday 11 p.m. H-3.

Long day. A few new admissions and several cases. One of my patients had a wound infection where the incision fell apart; he needed to go back to the operating room. Everything gets infected here. It's a real problem. I am beat—going to bed.

Saturday 3 a.m. H-2.

Well, I was hoping to get some sleep, but just as my head hit the pillow, I got a call that one of the sick ones in the ICU had respiratory problems. The nurse didn't hear breath sounds on one side of the chest; sure enough, he had a big pneumothorax. This wasn't totally unexpected since the lung on that side was heavily contused from a blast injury. We put a chest tube in, put in an arterial line and a central line and made some changes on the ventilator. Long day. Ready to crash.

Saturday 5 a.m. H-2.

This time, I just got to my room but didn't hit the bed yet. Two urgent transfers from the forward surgery team in Fallujah, one with an open abdomen packed and the other with a flank wound. I am taking the damage control now to the OR and getting a scan on the flank wound. This shouldn't be too bad.

Saturday 9 a.m. H-2

We finished the damage control—lots of abdominal wall necrosis, leaving a very large wound defect. Colon and small bowel resected; will have to bring him back again tomorrow; look at the muscle and bring out a colostomy. The CT of the other patient doesn't look good. A fragment had gone into the abdomen, and there is some "free air" around the colon. We are packing him up for the OR now. I have 5 ICU and 9 ward patients to see, but I can't get to that yet. I walked around and took care of immediate problems. The nurses know where to find me if they have something urgent.

Saturday 2 p.m. H-2.

We finished the second OR case around noon. He had a through and through injury to his sigmoid colon. I was able to resect and reanastamose it. So far, he's doing well. Rounds are going slow. I have ICU notes and orders done, working on the ward now. Haven't eaten today.

Saturday 6 p.m. H-2

Finished rounds and dressings. Did the burn dressing on Burn Boy. That one takes about 40 minutes every other day. Most of the other wounds look okay; a few vac changes also today. I am going to try and get to dinner. I am starving.

Saturday 11 p.m. H-2

Good dinner—chicken curry. Evening rounds went smoothly; no big problems. Patients in the ICU all going in the right direction. Lots of new people as the 21st starts taking over more and more. I don't recognize half of the ICU nurses. Watched some of a movie with the other docs, a nightly ritual, but quickly running out of steam without sleep in few days.

Sunday 2 a.m. H-1

Got a solid two hours of sleep before the nightly round of transfers. These are detainees who will be released (compassionate release). One is an old patient of mine with complex enterocutaneous fistulae. He looked great, has been gaining weight. Wrote admission notes and orders. Too easy. Headed back to bed

Sunday 5 a.m. H-1

Just as I fell into a deep sleep, the ETR called for coalition forces urgent surgical. This is unusual since the vast majority of our soldier injuries come in during the day. More information: IED explosion, one critical. *Damn,* I thought, *my last day.* He arrived along with four of his buddies. I wrote a special log about this case:

A War Surgeon's Perspective

"In other fighting, one marine was killed in the Al Anbar province after a Humvee he was riding in hit an IED." That was what I read in the AP news piece. It was one line of several paragraphs that summed up the days' casualties in Iraq during another day of the war that has gone on for three years now. These reports are so common; most people do not even read them or listen to the 30-second blurb that follows "Another day of violence in Iraq where …" on the evening news. For us, the reality is much different, a horrific drama that is played out in the field, in forward surgery tents, and combat support hospitals every single day.

Today, the warning came over the radio, "Urgent litter coming in by ground." I immediately respond to the ETR where the buzz is usually in full swing.

"IED, Marines" is all the ETR nurse said as I walked in. Damn, I thought. One day left. All I asked God for was no more Marines with one day left on my tour. The hospital staff went into full swing; these people are at the end of a year-long deployment here. They are experienced, hardened, and cool under pressure. The activity was programmed and efficient. I took my position at the head of bed number one, put my head down and waited.

Within a few minutes, the litter team burst into the ETR with the first patient. His arms dangling off the stretcher with bone exposed. I immediately knew that this was going to be a bad one. When the litter was pulled up aside the bed, I saw the full extent of what I was up against. *Driver*, I thought. Drivers always seem to get the full force of the IED. There is a pungent smell of gasoline and burned flesh. My first order of business was to remove the IBA before we move him over; to do this, we have to sit him up to pull his arms through the IBA sleeves. When we did, his arms, broken in several places on each side, flopped around like marionettes. As we moved him over, I tried to ignore the massive tissue destruction of his legs and focus on potential life-threatening injuries to chest and abdomen. He was moaning—actually a good sign—the brain was still getting blood flow. Anesthesia moved to intubate him as the emergency medicine physician started the primary survey. Nurses started lines, lab was there to bring blood, medics held pressure on bleeding wounds—all in a dance that has been repeated so many times before.

The other patients began to file in, eventually filling the ETR. One soldier in a bed next to ours called out to my patient, ignoring his own gaping wounds.

"You're going be okay, man; hang in there!"

I focused on the problem and my plan. Both legs had massive tissue destruction. The left thigh was torn apart and burned, with a tourniquet at the groin. The right leg was mangled below the knee, with a tourniquet above that. There was a neck wound that wasn't bleeding and shrapnel to the face. Both arms had multiple levels of open fractures. The pulse was weak, and the blood pressure was barely readable.

We hung blood immediately. The chest x-ray showed no thoracic injury. We shot an abdominal film to look for shrapnel in the belly. None. As we moved to the OR, the hospital commander stopped me to ask if he was going to make it. I said I was worried that once we start to resuscitate him, the bleeding would become even worse, and I didn't know if he would make it. His head dropped as he walked back to the chaos of the ETR.

In the operating room, we started by getting control of the external bleeding of the legs. Blood leaked from everywhere—bright red arterial blood, dark blue venous blood, and areas where the two swirled together in pools between the flesh. Two orthopedic surgeons and I worked frantically to get control of the bleeding, which, as predicted, became worse as we started to resuscitate him. Anesthesia struggled to keep a blood pressure, infusing unit after unit of packed red blood cells and plasma.

I had trouble finding the source of the bleeding high on the thigh. I dissected deeper and deeper into the groin to track down the source. Suddenly, my hand broke into a space, and a gush of blood burst out. I was in the retroperitoneal space; the bleeding was coming from here. This was the worst-case scenario. Bleeding from this location is the toughest area in the body to control. Packing did nothing; blood flowed from the wound in a constant stream. We opened the abdominal cavity and clamped arteries that feed the pelvis, but it didn't help. Bleeding in this area is from large veins that can't be controlled with sutures or arterial control. We packed as tight as we could and then tied a sheet around the pelvis, pulling the bones together in an attempt to tamponade the bleeding, but it was not enough. His heart began to fibrillate. We shocked him and pushed epinephrine to no avail. After a few minutes, his heart ceased all activity.

The Marine was dead.

The operating room fell silent as soon as I announced the time of death. Most of the staff had tears running down their faces; this was a long year for them with so many of these kids dying in this room. I could not physically move for several minutes. I looked at this young kid, a child, and I apologized to him for not being skillful enough to save him. As a trauma surgeon, every death I have is painful; every one takes a little out of me. Losing these kids here in Iraq rips a hole through my heart so large that it's hard for me to breathe.

After a few minutes, I collected myself and began to direct the care for his final journey home. We closed what we could of the wounds and wrapped the ones we couldn't get together. We washed all of the dirt and oil off his skin, combed his hair and washed his face. He was transferred to a litter and brought to a private enclosed room where we placed him inside a heavy black body bag. The body was draped with the American flag, and a guard was posted. The chaplain gathered some of the providers, and we said prayers over the body.

There was, and always is, a palpable grief that comes over the entire staff when we lose an American soldier. Everyone is affected, and everyone deals with it in a different way. For me, this is not a team failure; it is very, very personal. I was the surgeon who couldn't save him. For me the grief is intolerable. I became the focus of the morning for the staff—people came and gave me a hug. They asked if I was okay. They prayed for me. I appreciated it and hated it at the same time. Often, my misery turns into anger. Sometimes, I become angry with God for allowing this to happen. I just want the whole thing to be over and all of these kids to go home to their families and live long lives. I have seen so many soldiers and Marines die here. I just want it all to end.

As I made my way out of the hospital, I saw the Marine unit gathered together. Two Humvees were parked, and weapons were leaning against the vehicle. I noticed this immediately because a Marine is never without his weapon; they would never be stacked like that. These were the weapons of the Marines injured in the latest attack. I spoke with the first sergeant, the father figure of a Marine unit. I know him well. We had lost several of his Marines and had many more injured and treated here. We arranged for his buddies to come in and say goodbye, something that I cannot even bear to watch. After a time of reflection, the unit gathered the equipment and prepared to go out again that night. This is some of the raw courage I talk about, the ability to lose a friend in battle and go right back into the fight.

I love every single one of them.

The body was eventually taken to the LZ and loaded into a helicopter with some of his buddies as escorts. He was taken to BIAP, where mortuary affairs prepare the body for transport home. A friend of mine was at BIAP when the body was loaded onto the c-130. All activity on the tarmac stops when the casket is brought onto the airstrip. All personnel in the area stop what they are doing and attend a 45-minute ceremony on the airstrip. They tell me that this happens twice to three times a day, but everyone takes time out to attend the ceremonies. Soldiers manifested in these flights are going home or on R&R. As anxious they are to leave, they all take the time to honor the Marine. An honor guard then brings the flag-draped casket onto the aircraft with full military honors. The casket is situated in the center of the air-craft; nothing is placed on either side or directly in front or back. Personnel then enter the aircraft and accompany the marine to Kuwait. In Kuwait, the casket is removed first, again with a full honor guard. The Marine will be brought to Dover Air Force

Base in Delaware, and then eventually home and to his final resting place.

If I could say something to this Marine's parents, it would be this: I am so sorry that you have lost your son. We, above everyone else, know that he was a true American hero. I want you to know that the Marines, medics, doctors, and nurses of the 344th CSH did everything possible to save him. I want you to know that I personally did everything that I could and that I am sorry it wasn't enough. I want you to know that although we never knew your son, we loved him. I want you to know that although he lost his life, we preserved his dignity after death. We held his hand when he died and prayed for his soul and for God to give you strength. I want you to know that he had great friends who cared deeply for him and that they were also here when he died. He was never alone for his journey back to you. I also want you to know that I will never forget your son and that I will pray for him and all of the children lost in this war.

Exhausted and weak, I cried for hours. I was spent. My last fucking day. Worse yet, I had a full night ahead of me.

Sunday 6 p.m. H-1.

Rounds were excruciating. I'm so tired, but I want to finish strong. The new surgeon came on rounds with me, which helped a lot. We looked at every single wound, discussed plans. I really felt that he had a good grasp of everyone on the service and that there would be no surprises for him—this kind of stuff is important in surgery. Got a nap in, but that made me miss lunch. I grabbed a power bar, hoping for dinner tonight.

Sunday 11 p.m. H-1

Got dinner, finished evening rounds and watched a little of the movie. My time is now measured in hours. All I have to do is make it to 0800 hours and hand over the radio. No problem.

Monday 1 a.m. H-7 hours.

Two hours of sleep tonight before the nightly transfers.

Can't hurt me now, I thought. *It's my last night.*

Another one from the forward surgical team, again with a suspicious fragment from a flank wound. Sent him to the scanner while we dealt with the second patient, who had large soft tissue wounds. The ortho guys took this one to the OR for debridement while we determined what to do with the second patient. The scan showed a fragment in the abdominal wall, not in the abdominal cavity but directly up against it. The colon was lying just under this. Since these are high-velocity injuries, the book answer is that you should inspect the bowel for injury. In the States, I would do a laparoscopy, but here we do not have that kind of equipment. He needed a lap. I was beyond exhausted. I started to rationalize not operating so I could go to sleep. This is where weakness becomes a factor in surgery. After kicking the scanner a few times, I accepted the fact that I needed to explore him, and got him going. It was a negative lap. The only part that I tried to enjoy was that it would be my last operation in Iraq.

Monday 5 a.m. H-3 hours.

Again, I had just collapsed into my bed—this time not even taking the time to remove my clothes. The radio went off with another urgent litter on the way in, a leg injury.

Great, I thought, *ortho's problem. I'm staying right here.*

But after a minute, I decided I should get up and just see what was going on. By this point, there was physical pain to go along with my mental anguish.

The patient arrived white as a ghost. His blood pressure was in the dirt. The leg was wrapped with a mound of gauze and was completely soaked. There was a puddle of blood in the bag (they transport patients in body bags because it's a strong, easy way to move them). He was in deep shock. We started resuscitation. When I took the dressings down, there was massive bleeding from this leg below the knee. In my exhausted stupor, I read the OR report from the forward surgery team. They had taken this patient to the OR already, I assume to get control of bleeding and to do a fasciotomy.

We rushed him to the OR, slammed a large IV line into his neck vein and then got ready to intubate him. As we gave him the medicine to put him to sleep, he gasped, literally took his last breath, and coded. We tubed him, started CPR, and poured blood into him.

You've got to be kidding me, I thought. *Three hours left! This is not happening ... from a fucking leg wound!*

I was mad, exhausted and frustrated. We were able to get a pulse and blood pressure back. The leg was a mess; we found huge tears in the popliteal veins, open bleeding anterior tibia artery, and a bunch of muscle bleeders. I was confused about what exactly the forward team did, but it wasn't hemorrhage control. After fifteen units of blood and two hours in the OR, he was taken to ICU in guarded condition at 0750 hours.

Monday 8:15 a.m. H-0

The morning report was run by the 21st CSH, as it now officially has taken over clinical responsibilities. I handed the radio to CPT David Hardin at 08:15 hours and posed for a picture. I was officially off call for the first time in 90 days. I honestly think that I was on the edge at that moment, unable to physically continue any further. I walked directly from morning report to my room, took two Tylenols and fell into bed.

Before going to sleep, I raised my video camera above my face and pressed record.

"Hey. Well, it's the last day. I'm lying on my bed on May 15th, 2006. I handed in my radio this morning. I've been operating for two to three days in a row, and I'm fucking exhausted. But it's over, and I'm going home. And I'm gonna see Carm and John John and Danielle and Frankie. I gotta go to sleep now. I'll talk to you later ..."

I passed out.

God threw everything he could at me these past 90 days. Although I made it through, I lost a lot of myself in the patients I couldn't save. Of course, there were many victories as well, so in the balance, I'm willing to call it a draw.

❧

With responsibility handed over to the incoming surgeon, I focused on my next goal: getting the hell out of there. It was Tuesday. I was "scheduled" to fly out at 9 p.m. Of course, this was after my departure had already been delayed by three days.

"What d'ya think?" I asked my fellow H-0 soldiers.

"It's never the night they say," someone said. "There's always a delay."

"Probably Wednesday sometime," another said.

"I think we'll get out tonight," I said.

More opinions were offered. Finally, someone started a pool and recorded names and estimated times of departure.

"Major Pryor?"

I picked an empty time slot and handed over my cash.

"23:15 tonight," I wagered.

With their gear stowed on the "deuce" (2.5 ton-transport truck), the outgoing staff of the 344th settled in at the landing zone (LZ).

Flying into Abu Ghraib was dangerous and the pilots hated it. Two days earlier, a Blackhawk was shot down nearby. There were other reasons that made this LZ particularly treacherous, but they were classified. Pilots would use any excuse not to fly here.

I sat at the LZ watching the sun set. The sky was overcast, and twilight fell quickly. In the distance, lightning flashed against a gray background

Well, that's it, I thought. *They ain't gonna fly 'caus of weather.*

About an hour after sunset, the first sergeant from operations approached. The lounging group at the LZ became animated and quickly surrounded him.

"The mission is still a 'go' for departure tonight," he began, but then quickly added, "but currently we're on 'weather hold'…" Smiles faded, and the muttering of the crowd drowned out the last of his statement.

I let out a laugh and headed for the DFAC to get some chow.

Might as well get some eggs, I thought. *We're gonna be here all night.*

I ate quickly and headed back to the LZ. As I crossed the compound, a Marine unit geared up for nightly patrol. I hated to see it. I knew the shit they were headed for, and I knew some of them might not come back. So did the grunts. They did it night after night, without complaints and seemingly without fear. Some of them were on their second or third deployments.

Raw courage. Unbelievable stuff.

Just about 11 p.m., word got out that the storm system had moved on and the birds were airborne. I was surprised by the news and even more surprised that I had a shot at winning the pool. My optimism, however, quickly faded. The distant night sky was now aglow with reddish orange light. A half dozen battlefield lumination flares slowly made their descent.

The flares meant fighting, another good excuse not to fly.

Sure enough, word got around that the birds were grounded. The 344th resumed our waiting.

Just after midnight, the air shook with the blast of a distant IED. I had become quite adept at identifying explosions. Based on the loudness, overpressure (wind) and ground vibration, I knew this was an IED and not incoming fire.

"Just one more for the road," a voice quipped in the darkness, and the startled soldiers fell back in various states of recline.

I was tired of lying around. I got to my feet and wandered away from the LZ. The clouds had broken up to reveal a symphony of stars. Mars rose above the horizon and seemed particularly bright. I took a deep breath and took one last look at the FOB. For the first time, I almost relaxed. I began to ponder the meaning of it all, but my thoughts were soon interrupted by the sounds of an approaching helicopter.

Two double rotor Chinook helicopters descended through the gathering fog and kicked up a torrent of sand. The staff had been divided into "chalks," groups of soldiers. The crew chiefs arranged for the chalks to board each of the transport helos. Groups started to board, but when I started to move, we were stopped by the crew chief.

"WE DON'T HAVE ROOM FOR EVERYONE," he yelled over the din of the rotors. "WE'LL BE BACK TO GET YOU. TWENTY MINUTES!"

Unfazed, I thought twenty minutes was nothing. Practically on my way home, I thought, nothing could hurt me at this point. The remaining personnel resumed their waiting as silence returned to the LZ.

The second explosion was no joke.

The ground literally shook like an earthquake. It was the largest explosion I'd felt since landing in Iraq. Even in the darkness of night,

I could see rising smoke in the distance. Everyone was back on their feet. Suddenly, I had a horrific realization.

The Marines, I thought, *out on patrol.*

I paced back and forth, my heart started to race. I felt like a parent hearing of an accident and waiting for the phone call to hear if it was my child in the car.

"I hate this fucking place!" I shouted. "Twenty minutes to go, and a fucking bomb goes off!"

Despite my pleas, the first Humvees came speeding into the FOB. Disoriented drivers maneuvered vehicles in different directions. The first three drove up to the LZ and stopped. A Marine got out.

"WHERE'S THE FUCKING HOSPITAL?" he screamed, "WHERE'S THE FUCKING HOAPITAL ..."

"OVER THERE, OVER THERE ..." we shouted, pointing to the ETR entrance, "THE YELLOW LIGHTS! OVER BY THE FLASHING LIGHTS!!"

The Marine jumped back in and sped away. Just then, an up-armored troop carrier passed within a few feet of me. Time slowed, as if God made a point of displaying the spectacle. Back doors open, a flaccid Marine lay on the floor. His buddy was slapping his face, shouting at him to "Hang in there! We're almost there, man!" The Marine's legs were raw stumps in pools of blood.

In a flash, I could see it all: The HUMVEE hitting an IED, legs blown away from the body, screams of pain, the medic frantically trying to place tourniquets. I saw the Gunny directing other Marines to set up a defense perimeter. I saw the face of the surgeon, holding the radio I recently surrendered, about to experience his first Mascal. I saw the nurses and medics in the ETR, fresh from the States, about to treat victims of this war. I saw the Marine's parents, his brother, his sister gathered as they lowered the casket into the ground.

"This fucking place!" I screamed, kicking rocks at my feet. I then walked over to the rest of the unit to see if anyone else was hurt. One of the Marines was covered in blood.

"This blood is from my buddy," the Marine said.

I wanted to console the soldier. I wanted to say, "It's going to be okay," or, "They'll take good care of him." But that's not what came out of my lips.

"It's over now; you're safe," I said. "It's all over for your buddy, no more pain."

The distinctive tat-tat of the Chinook could be heard growing in the distance. I eyed the ETR entrance.

I should go back and help, I thought. *I'm abandoning them.*

The crew chief grabbed my shoulder, and I snapped out of it. My time here was over. I grabbed my bag and headed toward the center of the dust storm that was my ride home.

ɾ∽

From: **Hardin, Ronald CPT**, 21st CSH Surgeon Abu
Subject: From Hardin
Date: Mon 5/29/2006 1:24 PM EST
To: Pryor, John
CC:

John

Hope you are doing well back home. Things are going well here. The first week you were gone was the worst week of my life. It started the night you left with two Marines struck by an IED. One was dead when he came in; the other had a massive skull fracture with grey matter exposed. All four extremities had major soft tissue/vascular injuries.

He was tourniqueted on all four extremities on arrival. Getting IV access was a nightmare as bilateral groins were essentially destroyed. The subclavian wasn't available secondary to trauma, and the patient had agonal breathing without an airway. Anesthesia was trying to intubate him; we were trying to get access. It took a saphenous vein cutdown to get IV access to RSI the kid.

It was hell.

The whole time, the other Marine is lying dead on the floor staring up at us while his friends were standing there crying. I will never forget that scene as long as I live. We got him intubated, placed two chest tubes because he had decreased breath sounds, fast was negative; I placed a right IJ cordis once he was intubated, and we rushed to the OR. I packed all wounds with Heme CON, which helped all but the left groin. Wound was similar to what you described with previous Marine with pelvic fracture, except no pelvic fracture. Could place arm through and through groin to back of leg. Too much groin hematoma to get proximal control of the groin, so I had to ex lap to get left external iliac control, which successfully stopped the bleeding. I explored all other injuries. No other vascular injuries except right arm (probably brachial artery, but patient was too unstable for repair). I placed a tourniquet around right arm above the injury.

I knew secondary to the major head injury, prognosis was poor. We stopped all bleeding; By the time of transfer to Balad, patient was normotensive and warm. I had a hell of a time getting neurosurgery in Balad, which was frustrating. Finally got him sent out with one of our ICU nurses.

Everybody did pretty well. I wish I had thought about factor 7a, but it didn't enter my mind until he was gone, but bleeding seemed to have stopped. Our ICU nurse said he was stable on arrival to Balad, but there was a 3-cm defect in the top of his skull with a large amount of brain herniating.

I didn't sleep for a week because of nightmares about that resuscitation. I understand how you felt when you left. The pain of losing one of our own is something that hurts my heart. The fact that I was the quarterback calling the plays makes it worse, I think, because you are always second-guessing yourself. Nobody understands how it feels; they all pat you on the back and tell you how good it was that you "tried your best," which is BS. There's nobody calling BS telling you what you did wrong and how you could do it better.

I cried audibly every time I was alone and away from people for a long time after that. I didn't break, but sure got bent.

Things are good now. We have been knocking out cases left and right lately, and I am actually enjoying things. Thankfully, no Marines, for which I am thankful.

To make things worse, we kept getting hammered with poly trauma detainees from all around—three and four at a time. You know how it is out here—no breaks, etc.

Dave Goodspeed has been a godsend. He has been unbelievably

helpful in listening to me and encouraging everybody. I know he misses you guys terribly. I am glad he stayed behind. Yesterday, we stole a Gator and toured the guard towers. It was the coolest thing I have done since I have been in Iraq.

We got mortared a few days ago. Close call rounds—duds. They found the guys who mortared us a little while later. They died— apparently the last mortar round went off in the tube. The Marines told me there was nothing left of them but pieces. We were glad.

It has been much more manageable lately. I have been getting some sleep, which is nice. We have finished Burn Boy's legs. He is doing well, still gaining weight. We have been very liberal with his diet. He gets American DFAC food and ice cream and is getting fat, I think. No dobhoff since last trip to the OR. Haven't lost IV access in over a week either, which has been good. Just need to finish up his right arm, abdomen, and touch up the legs.

Other than that, all your other long-term players have done pretty well. Most have been transferred south or discharged.

I hope you are doing well. I greatly enjoyed having you here and appreciate everything you did to help break me in. This feels like home now almost. I am much more comfortable with our capabilities and what I can and cannot do here. I have been in close contact with the 10th CSH guys, running stuff by them from time to time.

Keep in touch. I will e-mail you as much as possible to keep you updated how Abu is doing.

Dave

From: **Pryor, John**
Subject: RE: From Hardin
Date: Mon 5/29/2006 4:32 PM EST
To: Hardin, Ronald CPT, 21st CSH Surgeon Abu
CC: Schwab, C.W.

Yes.

When I was signing out to you, I said that I had a hard week after losing a few Marines. I noticed that your expression did not change and that it really didn't register with you. I said to myself, "He has no idea of what he is in for." Now, you know what I meant. There is no way to describe the emotion in the ETR and OR when a soldier or a Marine dies. I try to convey it to friends and family, but it is impossible. Don't even try.

You and I are cut from the same stone. Every death is very, very personal—other people, and even other docs, don't get that. You are now in a very exclusive group—not only a surgeon and a military surgeon, but also a war surgeon. No one outside this small clan will fully understand what we go through.

So I will dispense with saying, "You did your best" and "the injuries were not survivable" and say this: Don't give up. When you are tired, drink coffee and keep going. If you cut corners, don't look at the wounds, don't do evening rounds, your patients will suffer.

Suck up all the emotion and reality when a soldier dies on you and use it as energy to forge ahead. The kids are relying on you —the Marines have told me the only thing that gives them strength to fight during engagements is knowing that you and I are in the ETR ready to care for them if they get hurt. You are their last line of defense. You're the wall. I know you had no idea how serious this was going to be; none of us did before we showed up. But you have the experience and the skills to get it done.

You will not fail.

I was outside waiting for the Chinook when those Marines got hit. We heard the IED—really big one—we saw the smoke. I had seen the Marines leave twenty minutes before. I knew it was them. I kept saying over and over, "Please God, not them; please God, not them." But when the Humvees started coming on the FOB at

60 miles an hour, I knew it was them. The 2.5 ton passed right in front of me. I saw the face of the lifeless Marine, yet another one with less than five minutes to go in that fucking place. I tried to calm down the other Marines. They were all covered in blood. It was pure horror there in the pitch black of the LZ. I was so angry. I was worried about you and the staff. I know how hard that was going to be for you. I was a wreck—such a long four months, such a long few weeks without sleep, and then that. I broke down and cried all the way to BIAP.

So just know that you are not alone. John Holcomb, me, and a few hundred other war surgeons who have been there know what you are going through. I am so proud of you, for your service and for your compassion.

You will help many, many people in the next few months. Try to save yourself as well.

Stay in touch

JP

PS: I told you the mortars were no joke. Remember 20 seconds in the dirt, 20 minutes in the bunker. Use the radio to call in for accountability, and wait for the Humvee to pick you up. If you try to make a run for the hospital and you get hit, there will be no one to care for the other injured.

Back Home

BOOM!

I reflectively flinched downward. Halfway to the sand, my brain intervened and I slowly stood, feeling slightly embarrassed.

The canon fire echoed from Ft. William Henry, a pivotal British stronghold sacked by the French in 1757, now a tourist attraction with colonial re-enactments.

"You okay?" Rich asked.

No one else even noticed the blast. Swimmers continued to splash in the lake, children chased around kicking up sand, adults smeared SPF 40 on squirming toddlers, and Carmela unpacked the cooler for lunch.

"Yeah," I said. "Guess I'm not really home yet."

Rich gave me a look. I'd been back for weeks, but we didn't talk about Iraq. It's hard for anyone to understand unless they've been there, so I mostly kept quiet. But at that moment, I think we realized how the tour had changed me.

While my Ivy League colleagues summered at their beach house or traveled to Europe, I returned my family to an austere vacation town

351

in the Adirondacks. As a kid, my family would spend weekends at Lake George, a twenty-six mile glacial lake an hour north of Albany.

A typical tourist trap, the village of Lake George is filled to the brim with souvenir emporiums and T-shirt shops. But to the east, Buck Mountain will give you a breathtaking two-thousand-foot vista. To the north, exclusive vacation homes give way to pristine wilderness, and to the south lay The Great Escape Amusement Park, a mecca for local children.

I liked the idea of bringing my kids to the same places I'd enjoyed at their age. That, and we couldn't afford anything else.

Rich and his kids met us at "Million Dollar Beach," the public beach at the southern tip of the lake. After a swim and lunch, we strolled the village spending the afternoon feeding arcade machines and licking ice cream cones. The kids had fun and, except for the occasional call from work, it was a perfect summer day.

At the Lake George Lodge, we checked into our rooms. After the wives and kids were settled, Rich and I retired to the hotel bar for a long overdue beer. This time, it was more than casual conversation.

"I'm in a bit of trouble," he said.

"What?" I said. "What is it this time?"

"Uhh, I sorta got fired ..." He took a quick sip of beer.

"What do you mean 'sort of'?"

"Well ..." he took a deep breath and sighed, "it's like this." He paused again to collect his thoughts.

"At Albany Med, I ran around seeing all the patients, most of the time before the residents. It was too much. I decided to work at a smaller community hospital where the volume would be less and the pay would be more. I thought it would be better.

"It turns out the environment was no less stressful. The ER is smaller, but there is only one physician, so the ratio is actually worse. I run around just as much, and it's harder to admit patients. I get the job done, but, apparently, my patient surveys were a bit uncomplimentary."

"What? Like a satisfaction survey?" I asked.

"Yeah, my scores were, let us say, sub-par for two months in a row..."

"So?"

"Right? I never knew they existed at Albany Med, but, apparently, they're important at this hospital."

"Oh ..."

"Yeah, so when my scores were low for two months, they invited me to attend 'Patient Satisfaction Academy'...'"

"What the hell is that?"

"You know, I really don't know, but I didn't want to find out. Whatever it is, it involves flying out to Ohio, and I'm certain that wouldn't improve my mood."

"Oh, come on ..."

"So the conversation with my boss went like this:

You have to go to Patient Satisfaction Academy.

Uhh, I don't think I'm going to Patient Satisfaction Academy.

You have to. It's company policy.

I'm sorry, but I really don't think I'm going.

Then we'll have to give you ninety days notice.

Okay."

"Rich ..."

"Now, I'm thinking it's a bluff. I mean they can't really fire me because they don't have enough doctors as it is. I mean, part of my attitude problem is that I asked for fewer hours, and they put me on *more*."

"So what happened?"

Rich took another swig. "So I got a certified letter saying I'm fired."

We glanced at the football game in silence.

"You know what your problem is?" I asked.

"Do tell." Rich met my gaze.

"Your problem is *you*."

"Oh, really..."

"Yeah, you need to realize your role and become more accepting of it."

"I think my problem is that I don't want to be a doctor anymore, but I'm completely stuck."

"What are you gonna do?"

"Train dolphins."

We laughed.

"How much time have you got?"

"About two months."

"Well," I said, "I can't wait to see how you get out of this one."

"Thanks."

"Glad I could help."

⁂

When I returned to Philly I received an email from CPT Hardin, the surgeon who replaced me in Iraq. The camp at Abu was being closed and handed over to the Iraqis. Hardin and the CSH would soon transfer to Camp Cropper near BIAP.

Attached photos showed a smiling, healthy young boy out of bed and walking, unassisted. Long basketball shorts partially concealed badly scarred legs, his gait bent from graft contractures. The final picture showed Najeem in the back of a flatbed truck with his father and brother, broad smiles all around, waving farewell.

Lauren entered my office as I wiped away the tears.

"You okay?" she asked.

"Yeah," I sniffled, "just happy."

Burn boy had made it home.

⁂

Shannon sat alone in the silence, tears streaming down her cheeks. Drawn shades shut out the bright vernal sun, and an empty bottle of Scotch lay tipped over on the dresser.

She was sorry.

Sorry she couldn't handle it anymore: The depression, the despair, the anxiety. There were a few good days, but it was always such a struggle.

She searched for that *something*, that elusive thing that could make her feel better. She tried going out with friends, joined an aerobics class, even took antidepressants. But the empty hopelessness remained.

Then she started drinking.

She joked to herself that it was a perfectly normal behavior considering her Irish heritage. And it worked—a little. With enough alcohol, her mood improved, and the emptiness seemed less profound.

But then the next morning dawned. She was filled with guilt, shame and defeat. It made everything worse.

Shannon slid a .38 round into the cylinder.

Today, the depression consumed her. If it had not suffused her soul, she might have thought of her husband or her sister or her niece and nephews. Instead, she thought about her parents. Both had died a few years ago, one right after the other. She thought about her brother who died when she was just a child.

And David, her brother, who committed suicide two years ago.

Shannon stared at the pistol through blurry eyes. She thumbed back the hammer.

It was all so exhausting. So much death. So much depression. She needed a way out. There was no way out.

There was one way out.

Shannon aimed the barrel at her heart. Her hand quivered, holding it in this awkward position. There was a final moment to change her mind.

Oh, fuck it, she thought.

Suddenly, her ears were ringing and sulfuric smoke tickled her nose. Surprised there was no pain, she looked down at her chest. A charred hole in her rayon blouse started oozing blood.

When Shannon arrived in my trauma bay she was alabaster white, like a China doll; her extremities were mottled and cold.

"Twenty-nine-year old female," the flight medic reported as we began the trauma dance. "Self inflicted gunshot wound to the left chest. Appears to be single-entrance wound, no exit wound."

Staff moved her over to the hospital stretcher and stripped her clothes.

"Intubated on scene, 16 gauge in each AC, about four liters normal saline, faint femoral pulse, can't get a blood pressure."

"You give any vec?" I asked.

"Didn't need any—lots of empty bottles on scene. Might want to check her blood alcohol level."

If she lives, I thought.

"No breath sounds on the left," Chovanes announced. He turned and grabbed a scalpel off the thoracotomy tray.

"I'm not getting a pulse," added a nurse.

DEATH approached the gurney. The hood looked at me, silently offering a chance to capitulate. I shook my head and stepped in to find a pulse. The monitor showed cardiac activity; but without a pulse, we'd have to crack the chest.

Or pronounce.

I steadied my hand over the femoral artery. Faint, thready pulsations vibrated my fingers.

"I got a pulse," I said. "No thoracotomy. We need blood in the rapid infusers ..."

"We're on it," said a nurse.

"And we need a right chest tube," I said.

An ER resident prepped the right chest. Chovanes punctured the intercostal muscles with a hemostat and spread. Blood erupted from the opening and poured onto the floor.

I called OR.

"Hey, it's JP," I said. "Gunshot to the chest, level one, exsanguination protocol. We're coming up right away."

The abdominal ultrasound was negative. We ran to the OR.

Chovanes and I opened the chest. Shannon got her left lung and pulmonary artery but missed her heart. I taught Chovanes how to perform a trocharectomy to find the lung bleeders, a skill I honed while in Abu Ghraib.

With the damage repaired, I left Chovanes to close and found Shannon's family in the surgical quiet room. An extended Irish Catholic family, like my dad's side, filled the room, breathlessly waiting for news.

Shannon's husband and sister, Lynn, stood front and center. Lynn had suffered the loss of two brothers already. The thought of losing Shannon was pure torture.

"She's alive and stable," I announced.

Tears of relief erupted all around.

I sat, explaining her injuries and describing how the bullet lodged in her spine.

"It's too risky to remove the bullet now," I said. "We have to see if there's spinal cord compromise when she wakes up."

I stayed until midnight checking in on Shannon. Before I left, I gave Lynn my cell number. She called throughout the night, and I was back by six the next morning. That day, we turned off the sedation, and Shannon woke up. She obeyed commands and moved all extremities.

She wasn't paralyzed.

Over the next week, Shannon's family had a constant presence in Rhoades 5 ICU. She returned to the OR, and neurosurgery extracted the bullet from her spine. A few days later, she was extubated and moved to the a floor bed.

Shannon's sister arrived one day bearing pound cake from Stocks, a local bakery.

"Just a little token to say thank you," she said.

"Stocks!" I accepted the cake. "These are the best!"

The gift meant a lot to me. I rarely get such appreciation from patients.

From then on, I became a part of Shannon's family.

ઉ

Let me tell you how I joined the FBI.

In the 1990s, the FBI realized a need to have "medical agents," special agents also trained as emergency medical service providers. The need was twofold. First, during conventional encounters a security perimeter curtailed the rescue efforts of traditional EMS responders. Second, some tactical operations became as dangerous as military operations. The FBI recognized a need to have medics ready to treat fellow operatives if needed.

The FBI calculated it was easier to take an experienced medic and train him as an agent than training agents in EMS. The Philadelphia office approached HUP for candidates, and my friend Jim McCans signed up. Jim was a flight medic for PennStar, and worked closely with the surgical fellows.

Jim realized the need to have medical directors as part of the team and recruited one ER doc and one trauma surgeon. Initially, my colleague Dr. Debrowski acted as the trauma director, but when he was called to active duty in the Navy, Jim gave me a call.

"JP," he said, "wanna join the FBI?"

How could anyone say no?

I drove out to Fort Indiantown Gap in Annville, Pennsylvania, and met the agents. Like the soldiers in Iraq, I immediately felt that same sense of camaraderie. The bureau was like a military unit, members depending on each other for survival, an exclusive club that, for most, was hard to enter.

It didn't take me but two hours to feel comfortable with these guys. I basically went on rounds, meeting the agents, asking how I could help. One agent needed an antibiotic script, another asked for a referral, others had medical questions. I gave out my card and cell number, telling them to reach me anytime. The agents tried calling me Dr. Pryor, but I insisted on being called John.

"If you call me doctor," I said, "I'd have to call you 'special agent.'"

Tactical operations mirrored military operations in Iraq. As such, the medical angle was similar. I lectured on the echelons of care, emphasizing self and buddy care while balancing the goal of accomplishing the mission.

Each month, I returned to Fort Indiangap or Fort Dix to teach and train with the SWAT team. We worked well together, and I was honored to be part of their team.

I could tell you more about what we did, but then, of course, I'd have to kill you.

&

My dreams of battle, now with experiences of combat, took on a new level of realism. In many I am back at the CSH overwhelmed with patients, surrounded by DEATH. In one dream I'm sprinting from the DFAC again, straining to outrun an incoming mortar. I can feel it tingling the back of my neck as I struggle, like running against a strong headwind, towards the ETR entrance. The more I struggle, the more slowly I move until, just before the doors, the mortar finds its target and I'm jolted awake.

So convinced I'm in Iraq, sometimes I'll be three steps to the ETR before waking up at my bedroom door.

"What is it?" Carm would ask.

"Nothing," I would say. "Just gotta pee."

"Bathroom's the other way," she'd say.

☙

Shannon continued to improve. Rarely did I see her without a member of her extended family, and the Stocks cakes started to arrive on a regular basis. She began physical therapy and regained her strength. Soon she was discharged from our service and transferred to in-patient psych. There was still the problem of her depression to tackle.

When she was discharged from psych, I saw Shannon in our clinic for follow-up appointments. At first she seemed to do well, but soon I could tell her mood had soured. I tried to be supportive and encourage her.

"You can fight this," I told her, "and you can win."

"I'm glad you think so," she said with a smile.

"No," I said. "You have to think so, too."

☙

In September 2006, Pat Riley was promoted to Vice Chief of the Division of Trauma, leaving the trauma program director position vacant. When I heard the news, I wondered who they would find to fill it.

A few days later, Lauren congratulated me as I entered the office.

"Thanks," I said. "What'd I do?"

"You're the new Trauma Program Director."

Apparently, this was decided without my input.

I had mixed feelings about my promotion. At forty, I questioned if I was experienced enough for such responsibility. But I felt honored to have the confidence and trust of my colleagues and Dr. Schwab. Like I said, sometimes you have to trust your mentors, and if Dr. Schwab thought I was ready, then the answer is, "Yes sir."

With five years on staff and my recent promotion, it was time to apply for advancement to associate professor. As an Ivy, Penn had a complicated promotional process. I needed to solicit letters from prominent trauma surgeons across the country attesting to my contributions on a national level. I also needed to submit a personal statement:

Alright, Let's Call It A Draw

Promotion to Associate Professor

Unlike other surgical specialties that revolve around the surgeon and the operative case, trauma surgery is a complex care delivery system that involves every aspect of the hospital and agencies outside the hospital. We often say that in trauma, the system is much more important than any one component, including the trauma surgeon. Patients survive and recover because the trauma system is mature, well run, and staffed with dedicated professionals. The surgeon, and the operative case, is one small part of the system that saves lives.

Excellence in trauma care depends on success at each level and during each stage of care. Thus, my goal as an educator has always been to train and support each element of the trauma system, from the prehospital setting, through the complex hospital care, to rehabilitation. Becoming the Trauma Program Director of the trauma center was a natural extension of my attempts to support trauma care as an educator, a researcher, administrator and an advocate.

As a former paramedic, it was easy for me to fill the role as an educator for prehospital care providers. I have lectured extensively at emergency medical services (EMS) meetings, including several statewide conferences. In addition to publishing several articles on prehospital care, my commitment to EMS is evidenced by my position on the editorial staff of the *Journal of Emergency Medical Services* (JEMS), the premier clinical journal for prehospital care. As an advocate for care standards, I now serve on the Pennsylvania Medical Advisory Committee that adopts standards for EMS protocols for all prehospital providers in the state.

As a member of the medical school faculty, I am dedicated to the education of medical students in surgery. My formal teaching activities include being an instructor for the Patient Based Learning (PBL) and Doctoring courses for first- and second-year students. However, most of my interaction with the students occurs in the trauma bay and on rounds with the trauma and critical care services. I have tried to stimulate students in the fields of trauma, emergency surgery and critical care, and have been lucky enough to work with several students in a more formal mentoring role. These activities led to two journal publications (Seymour, Hedrick) and one book chapter publication (Powell) with the students as authors. Recently, I was asked to be the faculty advisor for a new student organization called the Penn Association for the Surgery of Trauma (PAST) dedicated to exploring trauma as a career.

Our fellowship has completed more than 60 trauma and surgical critical care fellows in the past fifteen years. On account of their dedication and drive for perfection, mentoring them is one of the most rewarding parts of being with the trauma division. I have daily interaction with the fellows and have ongoing research projects with most of them. I attempt to guide the fellows through the entire academic process from hypothesis conception through the IRB process and data collection to presenting at national meetings and publication. I have had the pleasure to mentor more than 26 fellows. Working under my supervision, the fellows have presented a total of fifteen papers at national meetings and published ten manuscripts in journals such as the *Annals of Surgery, Critical Care,* and the *Journal of Trauma.* I was honored to be a recipient of the Fellows Teaching Award this past year. However, the greatest honor is watching former fellows leave our program to become leaders in American trauma care throughout the country.

Trauma care depends on nurses more than any other surgical field. To that end, I have striven to be a resource for nursing education within the health system and regionally. I am a regular lecturer for nursing conferences and symposia and have had the opportunity to work with nursing on a few research projects, leading to several presentations and publications. (FitzPatrick,

Sicoutris, Richmond). In addition, I am an instructor for several of the advanced nurse programs, such as the acute care nurse practitioner program. On account of my dedication to nursing education, I was pleased to receive an appointment in the School of Nursing as a Clinical Associate in the biobehavorial and health science division. Based on my work in advanced nursing education, I have developed and led the editorial team for the first surgical text specifically written for Nurse Practitioners and Physician Assistants; the Clinician's Guide to Surgical Care (McGraw-Hill, 2008).

Trauma is a collaborative science, and I have attempted to act as a liaison for physicians and surgeons in other departments to participate in trauma research. I am a co-investigator or sub-investigator for projects with the Departments of Neurology, Neurosurgery, Interventional Radiology, Emergency Medicine, and Epidemiology and private industry. In support of these activities, I have been asked to speak at a grand rounds venue for Emergency Medicine, Neurosurgery, Orthopedics and Vascular Surgery. Work from these collaborations has been presented in non-traditional journals for trauma research including the *Annals of Emergency Medicine, Clinical Orthopedics* and *Related Research and the Journal of Surgical Education.*

On September 11, 2001, I was unfortunate enough to be one of the very few surgeons helping the rescue effort at the World Trade Center site. That experience, coupled with my work as a paramedic, gave me an appreciation for the challenges of providing care during major disasters. I sublimated my feelings of profound loss from that day into teaching disaster management on small and large scales. I was asked by Sten Lenquist to write an academic summary of the disaster response in New York City for his new *International Journal of Disaster Medicine.* In the past few years, I have reached out to educate the hospital community and the region in disaster preparedness. Recently, I was tasked by the Medical Board of the Hospital to chair a committee on hospital disaster readiness. I continue to research the area with current projects involving surge capacity and the use of ultrasound in disaster triage.

I have enjoyed my position and experiences at the University of Pennsylvania immensely. However, by far the most challenging and rewarding time of my life was during my deployment to Iraq as a United States Army Reserve Surgeon. A full description of my deployment is beyond the scope of this discussion, but some of the experience was documented in essays that can be found in the *Philadelphia Inquirer, Penn Medicine* magazine, and on the Internet. While in Iraq, I attempted to bring my experience in penetrating trauma to the care of soldiers and marines. After returning, I have felt a deep obligation to share my experiences with others, highlighting the incredible people we have fighting for us in the armed services. Academically, I have tried to translate the lessons we are learning about caring for massive exsanguination injury in Iraq to the civilian trauma practice. I have received many honors for serving, but honestly they are insignificant compared to the honor deserved by the fighting men and women on the front lines every day.

I want very much to continue caring for patients, teaching, and being a leader for trauma care at the University of Pennsylvania. My goals in the next few years are to help our young faculty find their research niches, continue to teach, and above all continue to care for patients with major injury. I see my role as an advocate for trauma care growing regionally and nationally. I feel a deep responsibility to highlight the problems of inner-city violence. Last, I hope to be a role model and mentor for students, medics, nurses, staff and faculty for several years to come.

John P. Pryor, MD

❦

In October 2006, Jim McCans approached me after delivering a patient in the trauma bay.

"Hey, JP," he said, "can I talk to you?"

"Sure," I said, "what's up?"

"I'm going to Iraq," he said.

I was confused; Jim wasn't in the military.

"What do you mean?"

"I got a call from the 10th Mountain Division," he said. "They need a cadaver dog."

Cadaver dogs are essential in finding human remains, a different task than typical search and rescue dogs. Jim had completed a cadaver dog program in 2005 and was immediately deployed to New Orleans after hurricane Katrina. There was a need for cadaver dogs in Iraq and the Division found Jim through an Internet search.

"Don't go." The words rolled out before I could even think.

"What?" he was a little surprised.

"It's too dangerous," I said. "Those soldiers are dead. It's not worth risking your life."

"JP, I know it's dangerous, but ..."

"No you don't," I said. "You don't know. I thought I knew, but I was wrong. You don't know what it's like there."

"Listen, I think it's important. What if you had family in Iraq? Wouldn't you want them home?"

I looked him in the eye. If it were me, I would do the same thing.

"Listen," I said, "promise me you'll wear your flak jacket and helmet everywhere you go."

"I will," he said.

"Promise!" I said.

"Okay," he said. "I promise."

∽

I finished morning rounds, grabbed my overnight bag and waited outside the main entrance to the hospital. Presently, a silver Volkswagen Golf pulled up, and my brother jumped out.

"Ready?" he asked, opening the hatchback.

"They didn't call me 'Road-trip' for nothing," I said, tossing my bag in the boot.

We drove south, headed for the Marine Corps marathon in Washington, D.C.

During the three-hour ride, we fell into our typical conversations about patients, philosophy and politics. I told him a bit about my involvement with the FBI.

"You wouldn't believe the shit they can do," I said. "You know they can find your cell phone even if it's turned off?"

"Even if the battery is out?" he asked.

"Not sure, but I wouldn't test them. Where are we staying by the way?"

"The Ritz Carlton, just outside of D.C."

"Really?" I said. "They must be paying you pretty good at your new job."

"Not really," he said. "But, you know, if I only get to see you once a year, I'd like to go all out."

"Thanks."

"Plus," he added, "I heard they have cookies at the front desk."

We parked in a lot crowded with Mercedes, Audis, BMWs and Jaguars. The Volkswagen wouldn't be hard to find.

Inside, a plate of chocolate chip cookies beckoned at the front desk. They were warm. After checking in, we headed to the mall nearby and picked up a few things for the kids. For dinner, we settled on The Cheesecake Factory and ordered some drinks.

"How many beers are you allowed before a marathon?" I asked.

"That all depends on your training," he said with a smile.

Turns out Rich was in shape for only two. We made an early night of it, and I called home to say goodnight to Carmela and the kids.

I am standing on a road that curves in both directions around a steep mountain. The land is strange because there is no vegetation, only scattered volcanic rocks of various sizes. The dirt has a reddish hue, and I'm reminded of a Martian landscape. The deep blue sky extends to the horizon. I look out past the road. A sea of clouds floats below, stretching in all directions. I realize how high I am.

I close my eyes against the radiant sun and feel a cool breeze sweep across my body.

Suddenly, a car appears from around the bend and accelerates towards me. I am terrified, paralyzed as the car approaches. It speeds up, and I'm unable to move. Just as I prepare for impact, the car abruptly veers off. I watch as it crashes through the barrier and plummets over the cliff.

A moment later, an image rises from behind the cliff. At first, it is like a bright cloud but then begins to take shape. It moves closer becoming more solid and more defined. I realize it's a man. He's dressed in tan camouflage fatigues. I can't make out his face, but he seems familiar.

I am flooded with an intense, almost indescribable feeling of profound love. The man stands on the road now. His face is full, middle-aged. His hair is buzzed short. He smiles at me with a look of pride and admiration.

I woke up.

Rich was already up, preparing for the race. In the cab, he showed the driver a map of the start, but our exit was barricaded. We pulled over to the side of a busy highway.

"Down that way," the driver pointed, "shouldn't be too far."

With little choice, we got out and headed down a desolate exit ramp.

"There was probably a better way of getting to the start," Rich said.

"Gee, ya think?" I said.

Walking down the barren highway, we soon came upon a troop carrier surrounded by armed soldiers. A few headed to intercept us while the others covered them.

"I'll let you do the talking, *Major*," Rich said.

Luckily, I wore my fleece from Abu Ghraib, embroidered with my name and rank. I explained that our cabbie had dumped us on the highway. This got a laugh from the soldiers. I spoke to a captain about his tour in Iraq as my brother's bag was searched. Satisfied we were not terrorists, they waved us through.

We approached crowds of runners and spectators filling Jefferson Davis Highway. A large inflated arch marked the start, and bright yellow placards separated runners by pace. Marines in camouflage uniforms were everywhere.

Rich stripped off his fleece and sweatpants. The morning was cool; the sky was a great expanse of pure blue. In the distance was the Pentagon, and I couldn't help but think of 9-11. A photographer snapped a photo of us, and I took his bag.

"Good luck," I said. "What's your pace?"

"Trying for eight-minute mile," he said. "Hoping for 3:30 or better."

"I'll look for you out on the course," I said.

At 7 a.m., the gun went off, and a river of runners started to flow. I walked among the marines in military fatigues and thought about Iraq. How many of these young marines would be headed there? How many wouldn't come back?

Meandering through Arlington Cemetery, I passed each headstone with reverence and, from my experience in Iraq, a hint of understanding. I came upon the Iwo Jima Memorial and thought about the Marines I couldn't save.

I'm sorry, I whispered.

Looking at the marathon map, I headed to the first spot I might be able to see my brother. When I arrived, I could tell by the pace of the runners that I had missed him.

I walked from point to point along the course, successfully missing Rich at every turn. The sun rose, pushing the mercury into the eighties, and I started sweating. Eventually, I returned to the finish and found him. He looked a bit pallid and weak.

"I'm exhausted," I said. "You know how much I've been walking around looking for you?"

"I'm sorry." His voice was slurred from fatigue and dehydration. "Let's go back to the hotel so you can rest."

Back at the Ritz, I took a nap while Rich got a massage. We ate a late lunch and headed home.

"Thanks for coming," Rich said.

"It was fun," I said. "We need to do this more often."

"At least once a year," he said. "No wives, no kids, just the two of us doing something."

"Sounds good," I agreed.

"Next time, let's try for thirty-six hours," he said.

"I think I can do that," I said smiling.

Alright, Let's Call It A Draw

It turned out to be our last weekend together.

☙

From: **McCans, Jim**
Subject: **We got hit**
Date: Sun 11/18/2007 10:22 PM EST
To: Pryor, John
CC:

JP,

Sorry to dump on you, but I'm still shaken up and I can't talk to anyone at home about this. I think you will understand.

I got in a few weeks ago, and they've been flying me all around Iraq. I'm generally well received at the FOBs; everyone loves to see the dog. Unfortunately, we've been busy, doing our job finding lots of remains. Most are Iraqi, but there have been Americans.

Today we were south of Baghdad. Informants told some soldiers the location of the remains of some U.S. servicemen. We left our safe house and headed out into the desert.

The dog picked up a scent and led us to some caves hidden from view. Human remains were present. They turned out not to be American.

We started back to the safe house. We were almost there when a soldier about 20 meters ahead of me stepped on an IED. The blast knocked me down. When I could focus, I saw that the soldier was blown to shreds and almost everyone was hit with shrapnel. Another soldier was down close to the impact. My first impulse was to render aid, so I started to get up to help the wounded. I heard shouts but don't make them out until I heard, "GET THE FUCK DOWN!"

Then my FBI training kicked in and I thought of the secondaries. I hit the deck but can't stop thinking about the wounded man screaming a few meters from me. Eventually, the scene was secured, and Army medics tended to the wounded. Within minutes, Medevac arrived, and the victims were flown out to the CSH.

I've been shaking all day. Never been that close to an IED, wondering if the soldier died because I didn't get to him. Definitely the worst day of my life. Right now, I'm counting the days until I can get out of here.

Will write again soon.

Jim

From: **Pryor, John**
Subject: We got hit
Date: Sun 11/18/2007 11:18 PM EST
To: McCans, Jim
CC:

Jim,

I read about what happened. I am relieved you were not hurt.

You could do nothing for those wounded soldiers. If anybody could save them, it was up to the Army medics. I know you wanted to help, but that is not the role you are playing.

If you had gone up, you could have caused more casualties. You did the right thing staying put. I know this went counter to every fiber of your being. I know how difficult it must have been for you.

In war, this is the shit that happens. That bomb was meant for someone, and someone was unlucky that day. But trying to save him was not your job; that's not why you're there.

There is a system in the Army, and the system worked for those guys. The medics were there; those guys are in the system being treated at a CSH by surgeons like me.

Right now, there is a lot of emotion, a lot of anxiety—shit I tried to warn you about. You need to focus on what you're doing and concentrate on finding those soldiers if you can and getting home safe. There will be time for grieving later.

Wear your gear. Stay behind the soldiers. Keep your head low, and get home safe.

JP

☙

I saw Shannon on and off for several months, but her mood continued to deteriorate. When she showed up intoxicated, I remained nonjudgmental, but secretly I was devastated.

The physical wounds had healed, but the demons continued to torment her. I saved her body, but only Shannon could find the will to live and get her life in order.

When she failed to show for her appointments, I wondered if all our efforts were in vain.

☙

Like I've said before, trauma is the bastard child of the medical profession. Not only does it receive little attention from other doctors, but we also get little regard from the media and government.

As I watched the news coverage of the Iraqi war, I couldn't help but feel anger and frustration about the violence I was seeing every day. My role had grown in recent years from a surgeon treating individual patients to an advocate for the prevention of trauma, specifically urban violence.

A lecture I put together illustrated the problem. In 2006, 822 Americans were killed in Iraq; in Philadelphia alone 406 died from gun violence. In fact, there were more deaths per population in Philly (29/100,000) than Iraq (4.1/100,000). We lost 58,000 Americans in Vietnam; but, between 2003 and 2007, we lost 43,000 people in the streets of America.

It doesn't have to be this way.

The same problem existed with motor vehicle-related deaths. Ralph Nader advocated for increased safety standards in the 1960s. Once the problem was identified, public awareness forced an industry to improve its standards. The same needs to be done for urban violence.

Historically, federal public health support of firearm injury research has been in short supply relative to the magnitude of the problem. To enact change, there must be more public awareness and political intervention.

In July of 2007, the *New York Times* was doing a story on urban violence. I welcomed a reporter to shadow me for twenty-four hours, to experience firsthand the world of inner-city violence.

"Wow," he said after the third shooting victim came in, "this is like a war zone."

"Welcome to West Philly," I said.

The parallels between urban violence and Iraq inspired me to write an essay on the topic. *The Washington Post* printed it in August:

The War in West Philadelphia

I didn't hear the cars screech to a halt in the driveway, but one of the trauma nurses did. He ran out with two emergency department medics to find several people in a private car, all with clothes soaked with blood. The passengers in the car were screaming for someone to help the young man in the front seat, who was unresponsive. The team threw the limp victim onto a waiting gurney, one of several that lay waiting for these types of scenarios that occur almost nightly at our trauma center.

As the gurney rolled into the middle bay, I saw a lifeless young man with more gunshot wounds than I could count. I was poised to start a resuscitation effort when a loud voice behind me announced that three more were coming in. As the team started CPR and checked "quick look paddles" for any cardiac activity, the second and third victims were wheeled into the bay.

A young girl had a gunshot wound (GSW) to the abdomen that made her writhe in pain. Her movements were slow, and her mentation was impaired, signaling to me that she was in profound shock—she was dying. I caught only a passing glance of the third patient, who had a GSW to the neck and was coughing up blood. Those quick images were enough for me to sum up a desperate situation, and I pronounced the first patient dead to concentrate resources on the other critically injured.

Without the need for direction, the nursing staff rolled the deceased young man into a reserve bed and quickly readied the stall for the fourth patient, who had three GSWs to the right arm and two to the left arm. With the emergency medicine physicians, surgery residents and medics all working on the two critical patients, I assigned the fourth patient to a very capable medical student, who courageously accepted the battlefield promotion to intern.

In the swirl of screaming and moving figures, my mind drifted back to my recent experience in Iraq as an Army surgeon. There we dealt with mascals, mass-casualty situations, on a regular basis. Ironically, in Iraq, I found myself drawing on my experience as a civilian trauma surgeon each time these mascals would overrun the combat hospital. As nine or ten patients from a firefight rolled in, I caught myself saying, "Just like another Friday night in West Philadelphia." The wounds and nationalities of the patients are different, but the feelings of helplessness, despair, and loss are the same. In Iraq, soldiers die for freedom, honor, for their country and their buddies. Here in Philadelphia, they die without purpose, without honor, for no cause, for no country, for no one.

If you are a conscientious American who mourns the loss of kids dying in Iraq each day, if you feel the pain of parents who have lost a child in the war, and if you pray each day that the hostilities will end soon so all of our members of the armed forces come home, then you may wish to know a single interesting fact. More young men are killed each day on the streets of America than on the worst day of loss in Iraq. There is a war at home that rages each day, filling our trauma centers with so many wounded children that it sometimes makes Baghdad seem like a quiet street in Iowa.

You will not find this on the front page of *The Washington Post* or on CNN. You have heard of the Columbine shooting and the DC sniper, but you have not heard about the Lex Street Massacre. In

2002, ten people ages 15 to 56 were lined up and shot execution style, resulting in seven dead and three critically injured. You do not know about this tragedy because it happened to inner-city poor people in a crack house in Philadelphia. Just, for a moment, imagine the implications if this same event occurred in a suburban shopping mall or involved a Marine unit in Iraq. There would be shock, outrage, 24-hour news coverage, Senate hearings and a new color ribbon to wear. That dichotomy, that double standard, that triage of compassion and empathy is why the war on the streets continues unabated each day.

I am on call tomorrow. The statistics show that tomorrow night I will once again walk with the chaplain to a small room off the side of the emergency room. There, I will open a heavy brown door and make eye contact with a room full of people—a mother, a father, a grandmother. They will look at me with tears welling up behind their eyes, their knees weak, leaning forward watching my lips, bracing for news about their loved one who was shot and brought to our hospital. I will remain standing and reach out to hold the mother's hand. My announcement will be short and firm, the tone and intonation polished from years of practice. The words will be simple for me to say, but sharp as a sword across the throat for them to hear, "I am sorry. Your son has died."

Soon after the *Washington Post* article was published, I received a call from National Public Radio. They wanted to interview me about the story. I appeared on NPR's *Tell Me More* on August 13th, 2007:

John Pryor leads the University of Pennsylvania's trauma program and is a former combat medic in Iraq. Pryor draws parallels between his experience working in West Philadelphia Hospital emergency rooms to his work in Iraq war zones. To Pryor, urban violence is the 'war at home.'

MICHEL MARTIN, host: I'm Michel Martin. This is TELL ME MORE from NPR News.

We want to continue our conversation about violence in the inner city with Dr. John Pryor. He's experienced many combat zones—those in Iraq, where he was an Army surgeon—and those on the streets in Philadelphia. He joins us from his office at the hospital of the University of Pennsylvania in Philadelphia.

Dr. Pryor, welcome, and thanks so much for speaking with us.

Dr. JOHN PRYOR (director, Division of Traumatology and Surgical Critical Care, University of Pennsylvania): Hello, Michel. It's my pleasure.

MARTIN: Dr. Pryor, you wrote an article for The Washington Post in which you said—well, let me just read what you said, that...(Reading) "In Iraq, ironically, I found myself drawing on my experience as a civilian trauma surgeon each time MASCALs or mass-casualty situations would overrun the combat hospital. As nine or 10 patients from a firefight rolled in, I sometimes caught myself saying, 'Just like another Friday night in West Philadelphia.'It sounds like you're surprised yourself that it was so similar.

Dr. PRYOR: It is. Yeah. It's a terrible testament that, sometimes I can't tell whether I'm in Iraq or if I'm in West Philadelphia. I sometimes have to look at the ceiling and see if it's a tent above me or a solid ceiling. And, unfortunately, what we learned, how to take care of people in Iraq, we really learned on the streets of America taking care of civilian casualties over the past 20 to 30 years.

MARTIN: Now, I know that your job is to fix what's broken. But I would like to ask you why you think this is happening. This isn't the only city—Philadelphia's not the only place that's grappling with this. There've been some terrible stories out of Oakland and, of course, the Newark situation that we've just been talking about here. Why do you think this is happening? Do you have any idea?

Dr. PRYOR: It's—the first thing is that's been going on for a long time. The epidemic of interpersonal violence has gone through the '90s and now into the 2000 to 2007 period. It gets worse, and it gets better. Right now, we're on a kind of a trend of getting worse again. And it's always there in the background. There are always thousands and thousands of kids being killed every year. But, of course, we get used to that fact. And we have a lot of other things that we need to worry about—international events—and sometimes it gets off our radar screen. But now, the violence seems to be getting worse again. And that's why I think it's back again.

MARTIN: But why do you think—and again—I understand this is not your area of expertise. Your area of expertise is to try to keep these kids alive, to save their lives. But, I've been following the discussion in Philadelphia. People are just outraged and disgusted as one would hope they would be. But you're saying, well, it's the parents. Well, there are dysfunctional parents in lots of situation. People say it's guns. Well, there have always been guns in the United States. What is it that leads to these—I don't know. It's almost like a virus, like some virus that breaks out.

Dr. PRYOR: Yeah. And, of course, the problem is it's an extremely complex problem. We just heard from Mr. Harvey, who emotionally told us how he did everything he could to keep his son out of trouble. And he did. And his son wasn't in trouble. He was an innocent victim of the violence that's going on in the cities. And obviously, when you look at this problem, it's very multi-factorial. It has a lot to do with economics. It has to do with social situations. It has to do with, basically with how people interact with each other. And when you put all that together, there's no quick, easy fix. And I think that's the thing that frustrates people. People want an easy answer like, 'Let's do this and this and this; then it'll go away.' And, obviously, it's not. And it has a lot to do with the whole structure of the city, the whole way we interact with each other. And I think that's the difficulty right now.

MARTIN: Well, I also read your piece as a cry for attention. I think part of what I thought you were saying is that this matters and that we can't just act as if it doesn't happen to me; it's not happening. And I'm just wondering why you think it is that we have vanquished other diseases in this country and we pretty much wiped out tuberculosis—although it does sort of surface again from time to time— we wiped out polio. Do you think it is possible to wipe out urban violence if we address it as a disease that has to be fought?

Dr. PRYOR: That's very insightful, Michel. What we're trying to do at the University of Pennsylvania with the Firearm Injury Center here, and others, is to look at this interpersonal violence as a disease.

And when you do that, there are ways you can use public health type of techniques to address the problem.

Let me give you an example. Back in the '50s and '60s, automobiles were deathtraps. They were horrendously bad instruments, and people were getting killed. And the government, along with researchers, was able to address that as a health problem—not as a economic problem, not as a political problem—but as a health problem. And over the past 20 or 30 years, we've been able to do amazing things to try to stem the death from motor-vehicle crashes. We need to do the same thing with interpersonal violence. We need to adapt these techniques in learning research to interpersonal violence.

MARTIN: But what would that mean?

Dr. PRYOR: Well, it means, like, a good example here in Pennsylvania, Pennsylvania obviously recognized the problem and established, back in 2005, what's called a PIRIS Program, which is the Pennsylvania Injury Reporting and Intervention System. And what this is basically taking every gun-shooting that happens in the city and try to put it into a database, try to understand what happened with that shooting—not only the physical shooting, but also what happened with the victim and with the shooter, and then try to have some type of intervention to make sure that that type of interaction doesn't happen again. And using data and using scientific methods could really look at the problem as a scientific and public health problem, not as a political problem or a socioeconomic problem.

MARTIN: To see what the triggers are. And finally, doctor, I don't mean to intrude, but—and I know you're a professional and your job requires a lot of emotional discipline, but I wonder if this ever gets to you.

Dr. PRYOR: Absolutely. And let me tell you, Michel, that what—listening to Mr. Harvey—is what drives me and my nine partners who work every single day to try to get these kids through their injuries. That is exactly why we do it, because, 50 or 60 times a year, I have to walk into the emergency room and tell somebody that their son is dead. And that is the motivation for us to work harder.

MARTIN: You ever think about getting out or doing something else?

Dr. PRYOR: No, we say you're born a trauma surgeon; there's not much else you can do. And, I think someday it might all get to you. But right now, we're trying to do the best we can to get these kids saved.

MARTIN: What can the rest of us do?

Dr. PRYOR: I think one thing is to realize that there's a problem and push our political leaders to make this a national agenda item. We're in the midst of a campaign, and I have not heard interpersonal violence come up on the radar screen of our national leaders very often in the early debates. And that's something we can probably push, because this is clearly a national problem. It affects every city in the country.

MARTIN: Dr. John Pryor is the director of the Trauma Center at the University of Pennsylvania Hospital. He joined us from his office.

Dr. Pryor, thank you so much for speaking with us.

Dr. PRYOR: Thank you for having me, Michel.

⌘

In the Fall of 2007, the presidential election fever was in full swing, a year before the election. My conversations and email with Rich frequently settled on politics and our thoughts about the next president.

"It's gonna be a long year," Rich said.

"Who are you liberals gonna choose?" I asked.

"You know, it drives me nuts how the Democrats don't know how to win elections. Of all the people in the world, they have to offer Hillary Clinton. That would be Bush, Clinton, Bush, Clinton. What would be next, another Bush? I don't think the country is gonna go for it."

"What about Obama?"

"I don't think the country would vote for a black president. New York would. California would. But I'm not so sure about the rest of the country. That's what I hate: Bush has given the Republicans such a bad name that the Democrats just need to put any white male on the ballot, and they'll win. But no, that would be too easy. So they'll try for the first woman president or the first black president, and they'll lose."

"Listen," I said sarcastically. "I'll have you know Bush has been a terrific president …"

"Cheney," he interrupted, "you mean President Cheney, and the word you're looking for is *maleficent*."

"Anyway, we'll do better in the next term …"

"HA! Who are the Republicans going to nominate, McCain?"

"McCain's the man," I said.

"McCain *was* the man." Rich became animated. "I would've voted for him in 2000. He was exactly the kind of candidate I was hoping for, an independent thinker who had political courage. Then the party fucked him over, and for the past seven years, he's been their lapdog, keeping his mouth shut, agreeing with Bush nonsense. He's been a faithful soldier of the party, falling in step, biding his time. It's like the powers that be struck a deal with him: shut up and tow the party line, and you'll have the nomination next time. The only problem is that he lost all credibility along the way. And now he's too old."

"He's still better than the Democrats," I said.

"No, but it'll be McCain and Clinton or McCain and Obama, and he'll win because the county doesn't have the courage to vote for a woman or black man. Then, we'll have four more years of Republican leadership. I wonder which country we'll invade next."

❧

Months passed and still no word from Shannon. Then, one day I was surprised by her smiling face in the clinic. I gave her a big hug, and she handed me a Stocks cake.

"It's so great to see you," I said.

"I've been sober for four months," she said.

"That's awesome! You're doing it," I said. "You're winning. You've got to keep it up."

I was so proud of her.

My life was hectic. Teaching, writing, lecturing, family, kids—all while trying to operate and save lives. Sometimes you lose track of what's it's all about.

Shannon reminded me why I do what I do.

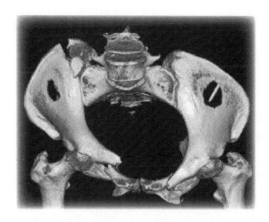

Trauma at Home

Kennedy assassination. September 11. Space shuttle Challenger explosion. Indelible dates, burned in your mind, freezing the memory of where you were, what you were doing.

You have more. We all do. Good dates and bad. The birth of a child. A wedding. The death of a parent or sibling. Some are expected; others strike like lightning—a mundane day interrupted by a seemingly routine phone call.

That irrevocably changes your life.

My turn came in the early afternoon on Thursday, January 3, 2008. While rounding with Ben Braslow, a fellow, and Kate Fitzpatrick, our trauma program manager, my cell rang. I noticed Carmela's number and excused myself from the conversation.

"Hey," I said. "What's up?"

"JOHN!" a frantic voice—not Carmela's—with screams filling the background, "John, it's Peg. Carm's been hurt ..."

Peg? I thought. *Peg's a nurse who works with Carmela.*

"Where are you?" I asked. "What happened?"

"She was getting out of the van, and it rolled." More screams mixed with crying in the background. "John, *it ran over her!*"

At first, I imaged a tire running over my wife's foot.

I'm trying to get shit done at work, I thought, *and now my wife has to break her leg.*

"Is she able to get up?" I asked.

"What?" Peg was shocked. "No! John, her leg is rotated and shortened, and her …"

There was a pause.

"…John there's a tire mark across her abdomen."

"What?" *That can't be right.* "Let me talk to her."

I expected her to be pissed or swearing that she got hurt. But she wasn't angry. She was *scared*, and that sent a chill down my back.

"I feel something sticking in my chest," she said. "It's getting hard to breathe … John I can't breathe …"

Reality detonated. This was much more than a broken foot.

"Okay, okay," I said. "Put Peg back on the phone."

"John," Peg said.

"Okay," I said.

My role snapped from perturbed husband to trauma surgeon.

"Is her airway okay? Nothing blocking her breathing?"

"No," Peg said.

"Her neck? Any injury there?"

"No, her neck is fine.

I guided Peg through the primary and secondary survey. Walking in circles, head down, I completely focused on the other end of the connection. Kate and Ben listened intently, trying to figure out what was going on.

Peg dialed 911 before calling me, and a first responder arrived. I was relieved to hear the EMT assessing Carmela.

"Tell them to start an IV," I said.

There were muffled voices before she spoke again.

"He doesn't start IVs. I said I would do it, but they don't have the equipment."

They were first responders, not paramedics.

"What's her pressure?" I asked.

More muffled voices. "He doesn't have a cuff," Peg said.

Great, I thought.

My mind sped through a half dozen possibilities before settling on one unacceptable outcome. Carmela was across the Delaware River in New Jersey. The ambulance would take her to Cooper Hospital in Camden. Cooper was a decent hospital, but we were better at trauma.

She needs to come here, I thought.

"Peg, I'm gonna get a helicopter out to you," I said. "Tell them she's going to HUP."

I hung up and dialed Jim McCans at PennStar. As I paced, more staff noticed the change in my demeanor and watched in silence.

"Jim" I said, "it's JP. I need your help." I gave a quick rundown of the situation.

"She's in Jersey?" he said.

"Yeah."

"We'll get her here," he said. "Let me make some calls."

I hung up and took a breath. Fraught expressions met my gaze.

"Carm's been hurt," I said. "Minivan rolled and ran her over."

"Is she coming here?" Kate asked.

"I don't know yet," I said. "Do me a favor and call Schwab and let him know."

I waited breathlessly for Jim to call back. The uncertainty was torture. Was she coming here, or should I start driving to Cooper? I almost headed to the garage in case she was going to Camden. I could turn around and come back if she wasn't.

My phone rang.

"Jim?"

"SouthStar's been dispatched to get her," he said.

Trauma centers, EMS organizations and Med Flight programs are like big families. Like any family, there is bickering and infighting, but during a crisis everyone pulls together. When word got around that my wife was hurt, the system went into overdrive.

PennStar could have been sent, but SouthStar was closer to the scene and could respond more quickly. The difference between Cooper and Penn by helicopter was only a matter of seconds. Flying across state lines was a breach in protocol, but professional courtesy won out.

"So she's coming here?" I nodded to Mary Kate and Ben.

"She'll be landing here," Jimmy said.

"Thanks, Jim." I hung up.

"I'll get the team ready," Braslow headed for the ER. Kate and I took the elevator to the helipad. On the roof, I called my dad and told him what was happening.

A dot appeared in the frigid, blue sky. The distant sound of rotors soon thundered closer. Flashbacks to the Chinooks in Iraq intruded my thoughts. I shook away the memory.

Focus, I thought.

SouthStar slowly approached and touched down. It performed a hot unload, meaning the rotors were still spinning as the patient disembarked.

Hot unloads were reserved for critical patients.

As they lifted her to the hospital gurney, she screamed out in pain. I couldn't believe this was Carmela. I couldn't believe she was hurt bad enough to scream like that. I still thought she was overreacting.

"Oh no," I said. "We're not going to have any of *that.*"

The trauma team waited in the ER. A dozen surgeons, fellows and nurses dressed in blue gowns, masks and gloves stood silently as the gurney wheeled in. The trauma dance began. IVs were hung, clothes were cut, electrodes placed.

"Thirty-nine-year-old female," the flight medic began, "knocked down and run over by a minivan. No loss of consciousness. Airway remained patent. Decreased breath sounds on the right, flail segment and crepitus to the right chest…"

DEATH appeared next to my wife.

What is the ultimate test of a surgeon? His skills? The lives he has saved? For me, the ultimate test is not what I have done or could do. It is the performance of those I trained, like the success of a child is a reflection of his parents. On January 3, I was given the ultimate test. I was forced to stand back and observe my team—the doctors and nurses I had trained—work on the most important person in my life.

I should have felt fear. I should have worried about DEATH next to her gurney. I should have wanted to jump in and treat her myself. Instead, I felt pride. I worked with these guys every day, and I pushed them to be the best. Now I observed the fruit of my labor. Years of sleepless nights, thousands of cases, countless lectures and teaching rounds culminating in this moment. Unknowingly, I had prepared myself and my team for this. You practice medicine as if the patient is your family.

Now the patient was my family.

"You want blood?" I heard in the mêlée.

"What's her pressure?" asked Ben.

"70s systolic after four liters."

"Yeah, start two units on the rapid infuser," he said.

"X-RAY!!" shouted the tech.

Ben walked over to me. "We're gonna have to put in a chest tube," he said.

"I know."

"Look, it's probably better if we put her down."

I thought for a moment, trying to accept how badly she was injured. There's a point in any trauma resuscitation where a decision has to be made: Is the patient in control, or are we in control?

We had our survey. We knew she had normal neurologic function. There was no reason to keep her awake and in pain.

"She'll be better off intubated," I said.

I thought of her injuries. Her pelvis was crushed, and her right chest was fucked up. There's no way the tire could've missed her liver; the only question was how bad. You can't stitch a liver. I've had patients present exactly like this only to bleed to death from an uncontrollable liver laceration.

"Twenty of etomidate," I heard as I approached her left side, "then one of vec, then a hundred of sux."

Chovanes circled betadine onto her exposed breast. Another resident prepared the laryngosope and tube.

Holding her hand, I kissed her forehead. I tried not to think this might be the last time we would speak. Tears streamed down her face.

"I'm sorry," she said.

"Don't be silly," I said. "It's going to be okay."

"I thought I was going to die out there."

"You're not going to die. Everything's gonna to be fine."

"I love you," she said.

"I love you so much," I said, and kissed her again.

Carmela fell unconscious as the medications took effect. I let go of her flaccid hand and returned to my role as observer.

Scalpel met skin; flesh parted. There was a pause before the blood oozed from the incision. Another cut deeper, deeper, down to the muscle.

The laryngoscope was inserted and lifted. My wife's throat bulged like a bullfrog.

"Tube!"

The endotracheal tube was passed. The respiratory tech stood by with the ventilator.

A hemostat forced through the intercostals with an audible "pop." Muscles were spread with a ripping sound, and bloody air farted out the opening. Chovanes inserted the tube. It immediately filled with blood.

A grim-faced resident handed Ben a picture from the bedside ultrasound. It showed blood in her belly.

"Okay," said Ben. "Let's get her to CT."

On the way to CT, I called my brother. I never called him during the work day, so he immediately knew something was wrong.

"Carm's been hurt," I said, and detailed the injuries we knew about.

"What's in her belly?" he asked.

"We're getting her in the scanner now," I said.

My parents were in Florida. Carm's parents were in Brooklyn, but they didn't drive. Her sister was in Staten Island, but she wouldn't be able to come. Rich was the only person I could rely on right now, and he was in Albany.

"I'm on my way," he said.

"Really?" I was so relieved. "You can leave work?"

"Fuck work," he said. "I'm leaving the hospital now. I'll be there in four hours depending on traffic."

I felt a wave of emotion and relief.

"Thanks, Rich."

Husbands like to think they are in control of their family. In reality, most of us fail to appreciate the tasks our wives perform each day. This is especially true with the children. I tried to think of how I could possibly assume her role. I came up with a complete blank.

Pacing nervously, they began the scan, and I thought of life without her ...

"This can't be happening, Ben," I said. "She's gotta be okay."

"John, it's going to be okay." He tried to reassure me. "She's going to be okay."

"No, you don't understand," I said. "I don't even know where my *kids go to school!*"

Nervous laughter filled the control room.

Watching that scan was the worst moment of my life. I imagined the worst, a large blush of white where the liver should be. Holding my breath, the tech slowly scrolled through the images. Each new screen was a relief; there was injury, but no major devastation. Finally, we were through. Grade 2, at worst Grade 3, laceration. It could be handled in vascular interventional radiology (VIR).

There were positive comments and sighs of relief all around. Then images of her pelvis started to appear, and silence returned.

The right sacroilliac joint was fractured and splayed wide. Her superior and inferior rami were in pieces, on both sides.

"Rich," I said into my cell.

"What'd the scan show?"

"Grade 2 or 3 liver lac," I said. "We'll take her to VIR and coil the bleeders."

"Thank God. What about her pelvis?"

"Her pelvis is fucked up," I said with a sigh. "But, the good news is her acetabulum is intact, and there is no spinal injury. She really got lucky."

"That's good. I'm halfway to your house. I'll call when I get there."

"Thanks," I said. "Dad got a flight for tomorrow. Carm's parents are arranging for a car. If you could just hold down the fort until tomorrow ..."

"No problem..."

"Listen," I said, "I told Danielle that she broke her leg. She doesn't know how bad she's been hurt."

"Okay, I'll handle it."

"I'll stop by in the morning to see them and take a shower."

"Okay."

"Rich," I said.

"Yeah?"

"Thanks."

One thing that medicine has taught me is this: There's always worse. Carmela suffered life-threatening injuries, and I was *grateful*. Grateful she was flown to my trauma center. Grateful she didn't have a brain injury or a spinal injury. Even the sparing of her acetabulum was a blessing. True, she had a complex pelvis fracture, but even here she was lucky. One of our orthopods recently completed a fellowship in complex pelvis fractures. Of all the hospitals in the country to have such an injury, Carmela was in the perfect place.

From CT, Carm was taken to VIR and then Rhoades 5. I couldn't believe she was in my ICU. Unconscious, intubated, NG tube, IVs, arterial line, Foley, pleurovac bubbling, monitor beeping and lower extremities in traction. I sat for a moment holding her hand, staring at her face half obscured by the tube holder.

In just a few hours, my life had turned upside down. In my business, it's impossible to ignore tragedy. Every day, I treat victims of circumstance or bad luck. I never doubted someday it would be my turn. Even so, it was hard to accept.

Fortuna had found me.

In a flash, I realized how much I had taken my wife for granted. All the meals, all the shopping, the laundry, getting the kids to karate or scouts or soccer, helping with their homework—Carmela did it all. She managed ninety percent of the household tasks. I tried to imagine how I could survive the next few months.

After a few days in the ICU, her condition stabilized, and repeat scans showed no further bleeding. I knew her condition was stable when staff began their banter.

"Hell of a way to spend time with your wife," they said. "Next time, you should just go on vacation."

Rich stayed a few days but needed to return to his family. The night before he left, we sat at the kitchen table with my parents.

"John," he said, "I need to say something."

He looked serious.

"Up until now, you have given a hundred percent to your career.

I understand it's important to you. But I think this whole episode is a wake-up call. Carmela nearly died. It's time to stop for a moment and reflect on what is really important in your life. You're extremely dedicated to your profession, but you need to examine the priorities in your life—your wife, your kids, your health. These things need more of your attention. Your job is important, but so is your family."

"I know," I said. "I hear what you're saying."

"I hope so," he said.

Within a week, she was stable for the OR. Ortho placed two plates along the anterior sacroilliac joint, and a percutaneous upper sacral segment screw was placed to stabilize the posterior ring. Finally, a supra acetabular external fixator was screwed into place.

It looked like a robot stuck to her hip.

After the operation, she was finally extubated. I was so relieved to finally hear her voice, hoarse as it was.

I took a moment to email my colleagues:

From: **Pryor, John**
Subject: Thank You
Date: Wednesday, January 09, 2008 9:24 PM EST
To: <Staff>
CC: Michael Rotondo

Consider this my feeble attempt to thank you for everything you did for my wife Carmela, our children, and me during this unfortunate event.

When you work in a hospital or a business or a restaurant, you often tout your shop as the best—you call your partners the best, and you lavish praise on the product, regardless of how seriously you believe it to be true. When faced with a medical emergency with a family member as I was, the immediate reaction was to mobilize the best medical team possible. All thoughts of being polite or having people involved because it is courtesy or appropriate because you work with them go straight out the window. Your mind immediately makes an assessment, and you decide who the very best medical professionals you want to care for the most important person in your life, no matter if they are in your division, hospital or even specialty.

On Thursday, without hesitation, I wanted my wife brought directly to HUP and cared for by you. To be completely honest, I made a quick list of whom I wanted in that trauma bay, and it was every single one of you. There were no gaps, no adjustments needed to the system, no resource human or other that I needed to mobilize other than getting her here. Standing in the trauma bay as a husband and an observer, I felt no fear. I was completely at rest, and I believed that she could not die because she was in your hands.

Curiously, the overwhelming emotion I had during the first day was pride. I looked at Dustin, Munish, Pat Kim, Adam, Jose running the code, and it suddenly dawned on me that I had a hand in training this entire team. Without the ability to do anything, I was forced to just watch with such emotion as you all went on the same way you do 3,000 times a year, this time under the added pressure of the unusual situation. I love every single one you guys.

In the subsequent days, I realized something else. We all have family, and we are all colleagues. Over the past days I felt that you were my family and are as dear to me as anyone with whom I share a name. I could not have made it without you, and I will not make it through the next few months without you.

Words will never be able to convey my gratitude—instead, I promise to continue to work as hard as I can every single day to hold the torch ignited by Dr. Schwab and carried by Mike Rotondo and Pat Reilly, and continue to make this the best trauma center in the United States of America. I pray to God none of you will ever need the services we needed, but if anything like that is in the cards, I will make sure we (and the system) are all here for you.

JP

❦

After a week in the ICU, Carm was transferred to the floor. Eventually, the chest tube was pulled, and we could take her home. A hospital bed with ortho trapeze replaced the living room couch. A bedside commode, walker and other equipment filled the space. The coffee table became littered with thermometers, medication bottles, wound care dressing and a blood pressure cuff.

Franco, Pauleta and my parents all moved in. It took four of them to manage what Carmela did single handedly. Pauleta performed most of the nursing care, washing Carmela and taking care of the urine catheter and bedpan. My dad did most of the driving.

I continued my work schedule.

In February, I had planned to fly to Pittsburgh for a lecture. Carmela didn't want me to go. She had a fever.

"Why," I said, "what am I going to do here?"

"John," she said, "I have a fever; there's pus coming from one of the pins, and it hurts like hell. Could you please stay home?"

"Carm, there's no one else to give the lecture. I have to go."

Rich called the next day.

"I think you should stay home this weekend," he said.

"Rich, you don't understand. There's nobody else to do this lecture."

"Then they can cancel it."

"What? They can't *cancel* it! People are already signed up and coming ..."

"Yes, you can," he said. "You say, 'My wife nearly died when she was run over by a car, and I need to be with her.' You say, 'I'm sorry, but my wife is more important than the lecture.'"

"You don't understand ..."

"John, remember my little talk about priorities? Remember how I said your family deserves more of your attention? Well, this is exactly what I was talking about."

"I know what you're saying, but you don't get it. We can't cancel the lecture, and there's no one else, so I'm going."

"Well, I think you're making a mistake."

"Well, I don't think you know what you're talking about."

⌘

Before Carmela's accident, I had started to think seriously about my future. I had accomplished nearly all of my medical goals and, although I was happy where I was, I needed to plan for the future.

I have been enamored with political office since Binghamton.

Meeting Senator Lugar, Bob Dole and Vice President Bush at an early age affected me. When I conceived of the next chapter in my life, I could not rule out the possibility of political office.

My plan was to make the first steps for an eventual run for the House of Representatives. It would be several years away, but I needed to make connections and get involved.

I contacted Michael Warner, the chair of Burlington County Republicans. The upcoming presidential election offered an opportunity to make a name for myself:

> ... I feel it is time for me to get back in the game. I especially have strong feelings about the 2008 campaign, and would like to get involved in helping a particular Republican candidate in a presidential run. I know the place to get involved is with my county party, so I am contacting you today. Perhaps you can plug me into the communication tree and let me know if there are any events coming up where I could meet up with the team.

In February, I received an email to join the McCain's Healthcare Professionals Coalition. After a series of conference calls I volunteered to be the Pennsylvania state chair of the coalition. When the regional officer failed to return emails, I was promoted to regional coordinator.

In addition to weekly meetings, phone recruitment and fundraising, I wrote about my views on where healthcare should be headed in the u.s.:

> There will be a great deal of discussion about healthcare reform over the next few months. One of the central issues in the debate will be access to care. Although virtually everyone agrees that all Americans should have access to healthcare, it is less clear how much should be under governmental control versus private industry in an open-market system. A move towards government-controlled healthcare will greatly affect the way medicine is delivered in the future. We can catch a glimpse of what such a scenario may look like by examining other government-controlled services.

Take the Department of Motor Vehicles (DMV). Chances are good that I have never been to your home-town or ever stepped foot in your local DMV. However, I feel somewhat confident that I could describe your last experience there. The office was not well located, and the hours of operation were inconvenient and strictly enforced. Almost immediately upon entering the facility, you are confronted with a maze of confusing instructions and regulations that leave you wandering from line A to line B and then back to the hard metal chairs to fill out additional forms. The personnel are aloof and annoyed at best, hostile and confrontational at the worst. Because of the militant atmosphere, you avoid asking the questions that you really want to ask and feel convicted when you make any mistakes during the administrative obstacle course. The frustration builds as you determine that in addition to the stress you are enduring, you have spent the better part of the afternoon there, neglecting the many other tasks you have to get accomplished for the day.

I may be wrong, of course. But for all of you who agree with what I said, just imagine now what a government-controlled healthcare system would look like. Can you imagine showing up to a government clinic feeling ill and having to go through a similar process? Do you think the doctors and nurses forced to work in such a system will be more like a businessman running their own company with pride and determination or more like the government employee forced to work under inflexible policies and procedures?

In almost every respect, healthcare is the most important service that we will ever use. Before we surrender that service to governmental control, it would be wise to consider the potential consequences. If you enjoy reheated food and burnt coffee at high prices, maybe you will be satisfied with state run medicine. If you feel you get great service from dedicated personnel at the DMV, then you will love the service at government clinics. If you are a fan of cost containment and regulations, you may be happy to be issued a foil packet of 'mix, drink, powder, lemon flavor' with instructions in government-speak for you to make your own lemonade. As for me, I think I will stick with the free-market system, private industry, and quality service.

John P. Pryor, MD, FACS

Member, John McCain Healthcare Professionals Coalition

☙

For six weeks, Carm remained essentially bed bound, requiring a Hoyer to transfer to wheelchair or commode. After six weeks, it was time to remove the Robot.

"Awww," I teased. "Are you gonna miss your Robot?"

Carmela had a perfect look of disgust whenever I pissed her off.

"You think this is fun?" she said. "This left pin has been killing me for weeks. I can't wait to get this thing out."

I knew she was exaggerating. Once the pins are screwed in, they don't cause any pain.

We returned to HUP, and she had the Robot removed. When the orthopod came out, he spoke to me.

"That left pin was hardly in at all."

"Uh… really?" I said.

"That must've hurt like hell." He shook his head.

"Oh."

☙

With the Robot removed, Carmela could start physical therapy. Using crutches, she slowly increased weight bearing on the right side. We couldn't rush the process. It still hurt, and her bones remained delicate; the last thing she needed was a fall.

Through March and April, she slowly weaned off the crutches. Finally, in May she started to walk independently. I couldn't avoid telling her any longer.

"WHAT?" she said.

"I'm going back to Iraq," I repeated.

"When?" Her eyes bore through me.

"Probably November or December ..."

"November? November?!" Now she was yelling, "and, what, you'll be gone over Christmas?"

"I know," I said, "but I need to be back in April for site survey; and the sooner I deploy, the sooner I'll be back."

"John," she rubbed her forehead. "It's been such a crappy year with my accident—I've been through so much. Can't we just finish the year together and have a nice Christmas? Can't you put it off until next year?"

"I think it'll be better if I just get it over with."

She didn't understand. I was the trauma program director now. Our site survey for trauma accreditation came up in April, and I needed to be there. If I didn't go sooner, then I would have to wait until after April. I just wanted to get my second tour over with.

I contacted the Boots on the Ground Program director. He sent me a list of current open rotations:

Id No	Mission	Start Date
6005 61J - 345 MC HSP CMBT SPT IRAQ		3/27/2008
7840 61J - 848 IRAQ 3		12/20/2008
6130 61J -1MC DET SURG (FWD) IRAQ 3		12/6/2008
6146 61J - 945 MC DET SURG (FWD) IRAQ 3		11/8/2008

The tempo in Iraq had changed since my last deployment. The surge Bush had ordered in January of 2007 had paid off. Violence was down, and casualties had plummeted. Conditions in Afghanistan, however, appeared to be heating up, and I wanted to go where I would be needed the most.

I put in a request for an Afghanistan CSH rotation that mobilized on November 5, but it was no longer available. I couldn't help feeling disappointed. With hostilities winding down in Iraq, I feared I would arrive after the party was over.

Stuck with another deployment in Iraq, I chose to mobilize on December 6. This allowed me Thanksgiving with my family and a return in time for site survey. I emailed Carmela my decision. She wrote back:

John,

Thanksgiving is Nov. 27. You can visit all you want with your parents up until that holiday weekend, Sunday Nov 30. But the last week before your deployment is our time as a family alone.

Carmela

Carm,

No problem.

Will have them come on 21st, leave 29th - OK?

JP

John,

Sounds good. I don't mean to be difficult. I appreciate your parents, but I'm very protective of our time together before you leave. The kids need you to themselves.

I love you sooo much. This is killing me.

Carmela

Carm,

I love you even more.

I know you do not understand why I need to do this. But this is part of my mental disease. I have internal scorecards, and I have to get all of the boxes filled.

Nothing means more to me than you and the kids. I have no more real professional goals. The rest of my life is all about you and them. This means home for homework time more often, supporting you in your fellowship, maximizing weekends home and vacations. This is the last big hump to get over, and then we are free and clear.

Last, I have a better understanding of what to expect than last time. I promise to stay safe—no hero work. Lay low and take no chances. I know how important it is to come home quickly and safely.

JP

In July, my request was approved. I emailed my colleagues at work to let them know it was official:

From: **Pryor, John**
Subject: WARNO
Date: Monday, July 07, 2008 3:08 PM EST
To: Schwab, C.W.; Reilly, Patrick; Mullen, Angela; Sarani, Babak;
CC: Calvo, Carmela

Mobilization report date (Ft. Benning) 6-Dec. Anticipate return from active duty (HUP) 6-April

See attached letter. Lauren, can you print up hard copies for LRK and those cc'd? I will sign.

Sue/AMP, we will need to move Mock to April...will discuss dates.

Angela, FYI. Formal orders are not cut until 30 days prior.....

Carmela, I love you more than life itself.

Thanks all.

JP

❧

The Republican National Convention was scheduled September 1-4 in St. Paul, Minnesota. I had my plane ticket, hotel reservation and car rental, but as hurricane Gustav threatened the Gulf Coast, convention plans were thrown into disarray.

My Republican contact failed to confirm my credentials for the convention. With an estimated 45,000 people vying for 20,000 seats in the convention center, I feared I wouldn't make it inside.

Also, the first night was being cancelled with a distinct chance that the entire convention would be a washout. This, along with the thought of spending an entire week away from the kids, including missing their first day at school, added up to a no-go for me. I lost about $1,300 by cancelling the trip.

I mention this because missing the convention put me years behind schedule. I planned to make a real effort in networking, find RNC leaders and political machine people to help find me a campaign in New Jersey. The only saving grace is that Pennsylvania was in play for the general election, so I was included in campaign activities in the following eight weeks.

The setback delayed my plans for the House from 2010 to 2012.

McCain announced his running mate on August 29th. During the convention, we were introduced to Sarah Palin. Personally, I didn't really care who she was; the vice presidential candidate doesn't matter. My brother felt differently, and it wasn't long before I heard from him.

"Palin?" he said. "Really, John, that's the best you guys can do?"

"Come on, Rich, who cares about the vice president?"

"HA!" he laughed. "*I can see Russia from my house?* Really, John? McCain's been arguing Obama is too young, has no experience, then he comes up with Palin? He just shot himself in the foot with that argument. And now, she's turning out so stupid she makes Bush look smart."

"It's not going to matter," I said. "People vote for the presidential candidate."

"Normally, I'd agree with you, but McCain is what, 70? with a history of skin cancer? I hate to say it, but there's fairly good odds he won't make it through the next four years. Can you seriously tell me you'd be comfortable with Palin as president?"

"He'll be fine," I said.

"Whatever. It's all over. McCain just handed the presidency to Obama. I was worried, but now I'm feeling pretty good. Thanks to George Bush and John McCain, the country will have its first black president."

"We'll see," I said.

"Either that, or I'm leaving the country," he added. "You can stay when Palin takes office and invades Canada."

☙

I made plans a year earlier to bring my family to the American Association for the Surgery of Trauma (AAST) conference held the last week of September. The conference was held in Hawaii. Carmela's accident had put our plans in jeopardy, but by August she had recuperated and wanted to go.

We arrived at The Grand Wailea Resort in Maui, and I literally thought I had died and gone to heaven. The weather was perfect, warm and sunny with clear blue skies. The resort was eloquent and lavish without being ostentatious. A palm-lined veranda opened to a crystal blue fountain. A short path led to the beach and pools.

I attended the conference during the day while Carm and the kids enjoyed the resort. One of the pools had a rope swing. John John, four years old and barely able to swim, spent hours swinging out, falling into the pool and doggy paddling back to do it again.

One afternoon, we drove out to Haleakala National Park and scaled the mostly dormant volcano. As we ascended Haleakala Highway, vegetation gave way to a barren landscape cluttered with volcanic rock.

At 10,000 feet, we reached the summit just below the observatory. The kids pulled their jackets tight against brisk altitude winds. Above us was clear blue sky, but just below the horizon, a sea of clouds reached in all directions.

"Look, John John," I said. "We're above the clouds."

We approached the overlook. Frankie and Danielle raced ahead and fought over a coin-operated telescope.

I paused a moment to take in the scenery. The rocky landscape couldn't be much different on Mars—rust-colored rocks scattered along the lifeless mountainside.

Déjà vu.

I walked back to the road, slowly turning; blue sky, sea of clouds, rocky landscape. When it hit me, my knees went weak.

This is the place in my dream, I thought.

Half expecting the car crash and rising figure to play out in front of me, I shook it off and returned to my family. I tried not to give it any more thought.

We spent eight days in Hawaii, and it was the best vacation of my life. Danielle loved the food, Frankie loved the beach and John John couldn't get enough of that rope swing. Carmela relaxed, grateful to be healed after her accident.

We promised to return someday without the inconvenience of the conference.

∾

Discussions about my return to Iraq had excluded the children. I didn't want to upset them, and there was no reason for them to know until everything was set. In October, it was time to break the news. The conversation was my first blog of my second tour:

Back Again

I had been dreading the conversation for weeks. I finally found the right time while my four-year-old was being captivated by a episode of Wonder-Pets on *Noggin*. I called the older two kids into our sun-room far enough away from John John so that he wouldn't hear our conversation. I didn't know how to begin. With my initial stuttering and delay, the kids began to get concerned. As a trauma surgeon, I knew from years of breaking bad news to families that often the best way to start is with the painful facts.

"Daddy is going back to Iraq," I said.

The words had an immediate impact, and Danielle, my 10 year-old daughter, began to cry. Along with her, Frankie, who is now eight, got up from the chair he was sitting in and came to the couch. We all collapsed into one big sobbing hug. My plan to contain the scene worked as far as John John did not hear the commotion in the sunroom. Forty-five seconds and only a few words to deliver, the message clearly changed the kids' world in a deep way.

My first deployment as an Army Reserve surgeon was a blur. The two years from the time I took the oath of office to become a reservist to the day I left for the first deployment seemed like a time warp. The only recollection I have of that time are the daily torrents from my wife Carmela about my decision to join the Army and her ongoing disbelief that I could intentionally put her and the children through this ordeal.

Less emotional, but still personal, was the effect my leaving had on my colleagues at the Trauma Center at the University of Pennsylvania. The surgeons I work with are more than colleagues; they are my extended family. My leaving meant they would have to cover my responsibilities—which in many cases meant more time for them apart from their families. Some had to curtail vacations and give up some professional opportunities.

In retrospect, I balanced all of these sacrifices with an overwhelming feeling of service and duty. I felt, and still do feel to an extent, that I had a skill set in trauma surgery that would help the soldiers, the Army and by extension, the mission in Iraq. I have always had a great sense of patriotism and felt that it was an obligation for me to serve, especially during a time of war. Without any real military experience to temper my altruism, I was excited to serve. I even felt a sense of adventure peppered with a healthy dose of male bravado. I wanted to go to war.

This time is much different. Although I will never regret serving and I am fully volunteering for this next deployment, I have been having deep reservations. Although with the same sense of patriotism, I now feel that I am dragging my family into a commitment that they never agreed to. Since returning from Iraq, I have come to realize that there are two types of Americans: those who understand duty, honor, country and those who do not. It is not a measure of how good of a person you are or even how good a citizen you are. It is just that some people understand sacrifice for one's country, and some do not. My wife does not see the honor in serving. She sees three children who need their father. My children may understand why there is a war, but they do not understand why I need to go to the war. By signing up to do this,

I inadvertently drafted the people I love the most into a very serious commitment that they did not want to make. It was unfair, and I now regret that I am putting them through this for so long.

Likewise, my professional colleagues have become fatigued and impatient with military deployments. I am one of several surgeons in my division who has been called into service. This has created significant hardships for our Division of Surgery and for the Trauma Center as a whole. With the unprecedented role of reserve units in all aspects of the war on terror, the continued call-up of citizen soldiers is straining relationships in many workplaces. Although my team is always supportive and gracious externally, I know that there are feelings of frustration and anger under the surface.

In the center of the swirling emotions I have about going back to Iraq is the cold hard realization that I need to go back to Iraq. Although the combat tempo continues to improve monthly, Iraq and Afghanistan remain extremely dangerous places. Perhaps being blinded by excitement, I completely underestimated the danger of working in Iraq during my first tour. There is no safe haven in the country, no "behind the lines." The war is everywhere, all of the time. And beyond the actual threat of IEDs, mortars and snipers, there are thousands of ways to get hurt by accident. Helicopters crash, cars roll over in ditches, young soldiers accidentally discharge their weapons, buildings collapse, there are friendly fire mishaps. It is an endless OSHA nightmare.

The culmination of all this is a deep depression about leaving in December. I also feel a great deal of anger—anger that the war is still going on, frustration that young kids are still getting hurt and killed and that the brunt of suffering of the Iraqi people continues. Unlike the first time, when everything seemed clear and precise, I feel this tour is pushing my family, my colleagues and my luck over the edge.

I concluded our talk in the sunroom with many hugs and kisses. My message to them and to my wife, to my mom and dad, and to everyone I work with is this: I am sorry that I have to go back to Iraq. I am sorry that you were all dragged into this commitment. To my colleagues, I know you have my back, and I will find a way to return the favor somehow in the future. To Danielle, Frankie and John, I pray that someday you understand why I joined the Army, why I had to go to Iraq. To Carmela, I love you more than anything in the world, and I am sorry I have put you through so much. To everyone, I hope that you forgive me for making you unwilling compatriots in this seemingly unending saga.

❦

On November 4th, I put in my vote for John McCain. The polls had Obama ahead, but I remained optimistic.

That night, I stood in front of the television, pensive, closely following the returns. More states turned blue, but I still thought it would be close.

"I think we're going to win," I said.

"Are you out of your mind?" Carmela said getting up from the couch. "I'm going to bed."

The next day, I emailed my brother:

From: **Pryor, John**
Subject:
Date: November 5, 2008 3:55 PM EST
To: Pryor, MD Richard J
CC:

I do not have your new cell number

Call me when you get a chance

I had this terrible dream that the Dems took over control of Government.....

❦

I broke the news to my parents and Rich about returning to Iraq.

It didn't give Rich much time to plan a weekend together. We compared schedules, but he didn't have a free weekend until November 22.

"That's the weekend before Thanksgiving," Rich said, "and we'll be coming that Thursday anyway."

"Yeah," I said. "Want to just forget about it?"

"No, why don't I come down by myself for the 22nd and then I'll come back with the family on Thanksgiving?"

"You sure? That's a lot of driving."

"It's not a problem, besides I didn't get to see you at all this year."

Rich came down on Friday. That night, a protracted discussion about what to do finally proved fruitless, and we surrendered in front of the television with the kids. The next morning, I made rounds at 6 a.m. and was home by nine.

Rich was at the breakfast table when I kicked off my Reeboks.

"So," he said. "What do you want to do today?"

"Let's go into Philly," I said. "I want to get some Christmas presents."

Rich climbed in my Honda Pilot and scanned the CDs in the visor CD holder. I had Dylan, Phish, The Dead, and half dozen Arabic discs.

"What is this crap?" he asked, pulling out *Sunset Boulevard* and *Les Miserables*.

"That's *culture*," I said.

"Right. That's weird is what that is," Rich said, putting the CD back. "Don't you have that Rush CD I sent you?"

"You sent me a Rush CD?" I said.

He ignored me and turned on the radio.

I drove into Philly and found a pay lot. We zipped up against a frigid wind and walked along Walnut Street, stopping occasionally to look in the windows.

"Get your Christmas shopping done yet?" I asked.

"Nah," he said. "I figure I'll wait until 9 p.m. on Christmas eve, that way I don't have to make any decisions. I just buy whatever's left on the shelf."

"That's actually not a bad idea," I said.

A few blocks down, we found an Irish pub. Glad to be out of the cold, we sat at a small table in the middle of the nearly empty establishment. The waitress came, and I ordered a Sam Adams; Rich ordered a Guinness.

The conversation was mundane. Work, family, kids. Much of the discussion focused on Obama's election. We didn't discuss my deployment.

Lunch came, and we ate.

"What'd you get?" I looked over.

"Shepherd's pie," Rich said, "but there's no shepherd in it."

I smiled. "Ders no meeet in a meat pie!" I said.

"One eye is *winking*," he said; "two eyes is *blinking*."

Inside jokes from a bygone era.

There was nothing special about that lunch. Nothing memorable or noteworthy. Nothing to indicate that it would be our last meal alone together. It was simply another moment for two brothers. A time together, increasingly rare, that was like a relaxed sigh, a pause in the cacophony of life, a break from the stressors of work, and chaos of family, where we could just sit and talk and relax for a moment.

And then, all too soon, lunch was over.

Across the street, we entered a store called 10,000 villages.

"You know about this store?" I asked. "They buy handmade crafts from Third World villages and sell them in the u.s. ..."

"Wow, talk about profit ..." Rich said.

"No, really," I said. "They use the money to help out the local economy."

Rich stopped and looked at me. "Who are you, and what have you done with my brother?"

"No, really..." I said.

"No really," Rich interrupted, "now who's the bleeding heart liberal?"

"Just tryin' to save the world ...." I smiled.

"Right."

We perused the store, examining intricate wood carvings from Kenya, handbags from Nepal, and woven baskets from Uganda. The craftsmanship was impressive.

I found a glass vase for Carmela. Rich was drawn to a Vietnamese calligraphy brush set. We paid and slowly continued down Walnut.

"Hey, I want to go in here," I said, at a store that sold exquisite shaving gear. As staff helped other customer, I inspected different brushes, soaps and handles. They even had straight razors for sale.

"What are we doing?" Rich asked. "Are you really getting something?"

"It's for Franco," I said. "He uses a brush and shaving soap."

I picked out a razor handle, mug and soap combination.

"This is great," I said. "I've got most of my Christmas shopping done, and it's not even Thanksgiving. I'm psyched I found something for Franco; he's the hardest to shop for."

We left Philly and stopped at the mall before returning home. At the music store, we tried out expensive guitars, and I purchased some strings. We stopped at Eastern Mountain Sports. I needed a few more items for my "camping trip" to the sandbox. We were home by late afternoon.

The rest of the day was spent playing with the kids and jamming in the basement. Rich took turns on backup guitar and drums. John John howled into the microphone while I strummed a Phish tune. Very loud and obnoxious, but fun.

On Sunday, I walked Rich out to his car.

"Sorry it wasn't a good weekend alone together," I said.

"Wasting time with you isn't wasting time at all," he said.

"What's that, from a song?"

"Sort of. I'll see you in a couple of days."

Three days later, Rich returned with his family. My parents had flown in the day before, and soon Carmela's sister would arrive. The house quickly became a hive of activity. The aroma of Italian cooking escaped the kitchen. Screaming children ran wild before we corralled them into the basement.

For a few moments, everyone crowded around the dining room table. Plates loaded with food were passed around. Danielle looked over a dozen different platters and complained, "There's nothing good to eat." John John bubbled in his seat, crying that we denied him soda.

Then, like a compressed spring straining against holiday entropy, the family burst from the table. Children resumed their games, the wives began to clean up and I tried to spend time with my parents.

Sunday came. and I suggested we go to the "Please Touch" Children's Museum in Philly. Carmela and my mom stayed home. I drove my dad and kids in one van; Rich drove his family in another. They planned on leaving for home after the museum.

We walked through Fairmont Park and approached Memorial Hall, an impressive granite structure with an iron and glass dome.

"Wow, this is really nice," Rich said.

"Yeah, it was built for the World's Fair in 1876," I said. "It was neglected and derelict, but they restored it recently. I've been meaning to bring the kids here."

The museum was packed. An enormous rotunda filled with bright sunlight and the echoes of laughing children running amuck. I couldn't believe such a beautiful and ornate building was allowed to rot for so many years.

John John, fearless as always, disappeared among the water exhibit. My dad was charged with finding him. Rich followed the girls into the Alice in Wonderland exhibit, and I stayed with Frankie.

Slowly, we made our way through all the exhibits: a space station with flying machines, a city bus and cars to play in, a centennial exhibit and a little village.

The kids enjoyed the museum. Rich and I spent more time together, not alone, but it was good nonetheless. We walked outside and paused at the base of one of the large bronze horses for a group photo.

Back at the cars, Rich said goodbye. It was easy to forget the significance of the moment. The kids were getting antsy, Rich had a long drive home, we had been together for nearly the past week. It was hard to remember this was the goodbye for Iraq as well.

"Alright ... well, I'll see ya," I said, avoiding certain words.

"Yeah, you be careful over there," Rich said. "Hurry back so we can put this Army stuff behind us, okay?"

"Yeah, okay."

I walked to my minivan and made sure the kids were secured. I climbed in and closed the door. After a minute, I got out and walked back to Rich's car.

Rich was settling his children and pulled the sliding door shut. He was about to get in when I approached him.

"What?" he asked.

I answered by embracing my little brother.

It was very uncharacteristic of me.

☙

I am standing on a road that curves in both directions around a steep mountain. The land is strange because there is no vegetation, only scattered volcanic rocks of various sizes. The dirt has a reddish hue, and I'm reminded of a Martian landscape. The deep blue sky extends to the horizon. I look out past the road. A sea of clouds floats below, stretching in all directions. I realize how high I am.

I close my eyes against the radiant sun and feel a cool breeze sweep across my body.

Suddenly a car appears from around the bend and accelerates towards me. I am terrified, paralyzed as the car approaches. It speeds up, and I'm unable to move. Just as I prepare for impact, the car abruptly veers off. I watch as it crashes through the barrier and plummets over the cliff.

A moment later, an image rises from behind the cliff. At first it is like a bright cloud but then begins to take shape. It moves closer, becoming more solid and more defined. I realize it's a man. He's dressed in tan camouflage fatigues. I can't make out his face, but he seems familiar.

I am flooded with an intense, almost indescribable feeling of profound love. The man stands on the road now. His face is full, middle aged. His hair is buzzed short. He smiles at me with a look of pride and admiration.

He walks towards me, and I reach out to touch him, but he walks past without regard. I wanted so much to grasp his hand.

I have a sudden epiphany of recognition, but when I turn to face him, he's gone.

The man was me.

I awoke crying, trembling in a cold sweat.

The dream.

It never made sense; but now, a week before deployment, I knew what it meant.

All my life I had dreams of dying in battle, premonitions about my own death. Finally, this recurring dream had revealed itself, and I felt my life coming to a close. I had the sensation I was looking out of a plane window right before the crash.

Carmela awoke and saw me sitting up in tears.

"What?" she said. "John, what is it?"

I wiped my face and looked at my wife.

"I'm not coming back from Iraq," I said.

Mosul, Iraq

As much as we deny it, we know DEATH will one day find us. We hope it occurs in bed, at a ripe age, surrounded by loving family and friends. After a thousand trauma codes, 9-11 and a combat deployment, I knew differently.

For some reason, since the end of residency, I've been preparing myself. The constant presence of DEATH at work, dreams of battle, experience on 9-11, premonitions—it all forced me to confront my own mortality.

So I have. And I was ready—whether he came for me or not. I achieved most of my life goals, had a great wife, beautiful children and prided myself on helping others. I lived my life without regrets and could die with a clear conscience.

I just never guessed it would be in Mosul.

ఴ

On Saturday, December 6th, I hugged my family goodbye, hoping it would be easier since I'd done this once before. If anything, it was worse.

Much worse.

We huddled together, crying as if it were the last time we'd be together. Finally, I forced myself away and grabbed my bags. I left through the garage, ducking under the automatic door as it closed behind me.

Later that night, I arrived at a hotel in Columbus, Georgia. Again, I wanted to document my tour with a video diary. Pulling out my camera, I pointed it at the full- length closet mirror and began recording:

"So here we are again. I am... beat, emotionally, absolutely drained... It was the longest day... saying goodbye to the kids. I don't know, this time uhhh, just emotionally much more... difficult than it was before, I don't know why.

So, I'm in my room. Here it is." I panned around the room. "This is my last night, six o'clock at night; tomorrow morning, I get on the transport bus and go to CRC and do it all over again." I managed a forced smile. "I'm ready, cause I... Carmela said I have to focus... Look at my eyes from crying so much—freaking believe that shit?

I love those kids more than anything else. All right, Hoo-Rah."

I gave a thumbs up and turned off the camera.

☙

Transitioning from the civilian world to the military realm is truly crossing a border into the sublime. It is, in every sense, a complete parallel universe with its own language, customs, expectations and social norms. When first faced with military life, I was overwhelmed with the apparent complexity and intricacy. However, it turns out to be a very logical and regimented life; in many ways, much more easy to navigate than civilian life. I am not saying I love military life, but the structure does resonate with my obsessive-compulsive personality.

So, returning to CRC at Fort Benning was a bit easier. I had been through the process before; I knew what to expect. But also, this time I would have a friend.

Mosul, Iraq

A fellow Committee on Trauma member, Dr. Simon, had a colleague at Bellevue who would be deployed with me.

"His name is Omar," Ron wrote, "real solid surgeon and great guy; you two should hit it off well."

In November, I cc'd Omar in an email to introduce myself:

From: **Pryor, John P MAJ RES USAMEDCOM**
Subject: 1st FST MOB
Date: Tuesday, November 6, 2008 16:13 EST
To: nelson.rosen
CC: omar.bholat

Sir-

Tried to call you at work but seems you have already bugged out.

I received notice about MRE training. I will attend.

Are you going through CRC?

Let me know if I can be of any assistance to you as the team prepares to mob...my cell is 958-555-0112 and home phone is 958-555-0136.

I have a good idea of the mission from some friends in theater—sounds like we will be busy and productive. Looking forward to working with you and your team.

Dr. Bholat, I see that you keep Dr. Simon out of trouble at Bellevue. Looking forward to meeting you. Perhaps we can talk some time and get acquainted. Feel free to call me whenever you have some spare time.

John P. Pryor, MD, FACS

MAJ, MC, USAR

General Surgeon

A few days later, Omar called, and we spoke for about a half hour, exchanging anecdotes and floating ideas for the upcoming deployment. I followed up with an email:

From: **Pryor, John P MAJ RES USAMEDCOM**
Subject: 1st FST MOB
  Date: Thursday, November 8, 2008 21:27 EST
    To: omar.bholat
  CC:

Omar

Great speaking with you. Sounds like we will have a great time no matter what mission we get. Let me know if you hear anything about CRC...I will call the LNO at CRC next week.

Take care

JP

John P. Pryor, MD, FACS

MAJ, MC, USAR

General Surgeon

I found Omar at the billeting office waiting for in-processing and bunk assignment. All smiles, we were glad to have a companion in the crowded milieu. Despite an ethnic sounding name, Omar was Caucasian, in his thirties with black hair and glasses. A runner, he appeared rather fit for a surgeon. In a way, he reminded me of Rich.

"You psyched?" said Omar.

"You bet!" I said.

I suppressed my negative thoughts, herding them into a dark recess of my brain and closing the door. The premonitions, the separation from Carm and kids, colleagues covering my call schedule—worrying was pointless and counterproductive. I had a job to do and needed to focus my energy towards completing the mission.

The next few days were a rerun of my first CRC processing. Routine tasks performed with military automation: hurry up, wait, stand in line, fill out forms, repeat.

Stuck in a line, advancing at a glacial pace, our conversation turned to family.

"What's your wife do?" I asked Omar.

"Lizzy's a colorectal surgeon," he said, "How about yours?"

"Carmela's a pediatrician," I said. "She's been working part time in the ER since residency. It works out with the shifts."

"Where'd she go to medical school?"

"Well, we both started in Grenada," I said, "but she finished at New York Medical College…"

"Really?" he said. "When did she go to New York med? My wife went there."

"'93, '94…" I said.

"No shit? My wife graduated in '94!"

A bizarre coincidence; our wives graduated in the same class.

"I wonder if they knew each other," I said.

"I have a friend who went to Grenada," Omar continued. "Did you know John Degliuomini?"

"I knew John," I said with a squint. "I think he was after Carmela before we started dating."

"John and I were chief residents together," Omar said.

The parallels were uncanny: Two surgeons, both in the military, whose wives graduated medical school together. I was amazed we hadn't met before.

In the medical building, we made our way through the various stations. I remained relatively healthy over the years and never had time for routine physicals. Being on the other side of the needle, as it were, was a rare event for me.

"I feel like a patient," I said to Omar.

"Is this what it's like?"

"Although to be one of my patients, I need to be drunk and have at least one bullet hole …"

Omar smiled, "and mind your own business …"

"Oh, they come to New York too?" I said.

"I think they're everywhere."

Directed toward a scale, I initially resisted. For my first deployment, I worked hard to lose weight but gained most of it back. This time I only had a few months to prepare and wasn't able to get into the shape I wanted.

"I think I'm 190," I said to the nurse, "couldn't you just take my word for it?"

She tilted her head with a little smile of empathy, "Sorry."

I stood on the scale: 210.

Shit!

Omar gave me a consoling pat on the shoulder. "Don't worry," he said, "you got four months of the best diet plan ahead—think of it—you'll be too busy to eat."

We migrated through the physical stations. A stethoscope was placed on my chest, a hammer tapped my reflexes, a needle stung a vein, and my teeth were prodded with a sharp metal pick. As a final gift, I was given a flu shot and boosters for Yellow Fever, Menigoccocus and Anthrax.

Wednesday, we woke at zero dark thirty (before sunrise) for Army Warrior Training and TSIRT Training. Thursday included PMI, Weapons Qualification and Familiarization Fire. Most soldiers were scheduled to depart Friday, but our flight left that night. Exhausted from a long day of military training, I boarded my plane at 10 p.m. and took off for Kuwait. Through the night, I caught bits of sleep over Atlantic. After a short layover in Shannon, Ireland, we landed in the Mesopotamian desert.

Omar and I disembarked into the barren, lifeless sandpit. On the tarmac we met the other members of our advanced medical party, MAJ Poraygalski, CRNA, and 1st Lieutenant Baker, one of the administrators. Presently a short, camouflage-painted school bus pulled up. The driver got out and found us.

"I'm Staff Sergeant Rowe," he said. "I'll be your transport here in Kuwait."

My ninety days had begun when I hit the ground in Kuwait, and the military was eager to get us imbedded as soon as possible. Rowe was there to move us quickly through the process. Anytime we needed to move, Rowe would be waiting with the engine running.

"I feel *special*," I said, implying the double entendre of those who ride a short bus to school.

"Team Window-licker," Omar saluted before boarding, "reporting for duty."

"We should get a patch for that," I said.

Rowe drove us to Camp Virginia for final preparations. The arid expanse of sand scrolled by, camels lumbered in the distance and my thoughts returned to the first tour: DEATH, fatigue, mortars, family separation. I began to feel apprehensive, tense and a bit fearful.

I just want to get this over, I thought, *and go home.*

☙

At Camp Virginia, I stowed my gear and called to let Carmela know I arrived safely in Kuwait. After hanging up, I noticed I missed a call from my brother and called him back.

"Hey, what's up?" he answered.

"Did you call me?" I asked.

"Yeah," he said. "I guess your phone must've called my phone while it was in your pocket. All I heard was muffled sounds…"

"Really?"

"Yeah, I got nervous at first. I thought you were trying to say "Tell… Carmela… I… love… her…""

We both laughed.

"Sorry about that…" I said. "No, things are good. I'm here in Kuwait; will be shipping over to Iraq in a couple of days."

"Okay, I don't want to keep you. Give me a call when you can."

"I'll call when I get settled in Mosul."

☙

In Kuwait, we linked up with the 1st Forward Surgical Team. They arrived a few days before and, given their deployment for a full year, passed through at a slower pace while Rowe helped expedite our processing. During downtime, I practiced drawing my Beretta from its holster. It gave me something to do, and when I got good, I felt like a cowboy. In a few days, Omar and I were issued our ammunition and packed up for the final leg of our journey.

We buckled in the c-17 and lifted off just before midnight. Full battle rattle made the seating cramped and the trip feel long. Still, the enthusiasm was palpable, and I was grateful for one thing: No convoy.

The precipitous drop from the heavens didn't disappoint my memory, but this time I was prepared for the ride. Forgetting for the moment it was done to avoid enemy fire and ignoring how close we came to performing a face plant into the tarmac, I almost enjoyed it.

"Hooah!" I joined the others as we bounced along the runway.

༄

Ltc Nancy McLaughlin, the commander of Task Force 345 Mosul, escorted us from PAX terminal to the CSH. We were assigned accommodations well after midnight. Rather than the tents I had come to expect, we were housed in containerized housing units (CHU). A city of CHUs had been created around the hospital. They were warm and clean, with both TV and Internet access.

So, here's the deal with Mosul.

I was assigned to the 1st Forward Surgical Team (FST). A FST is a twenty-person unit that usually moves out with the forward edge of the battlefield (FEBA)—the front lines. As the battlefield advances or moves, the FST remains active and mobile, providing the second echelon of care to the wounded.

During my first deployment, I received wounded from FSTs operating near the front lines. Now it was my turn to be out front.

But when the operational tempo is slow and the FEBA is static, the FST folds back into a CSH to augment their capabilities. This is FST doctrine.

In Mosul, however, the CSH was split into three groups among Mosul, Al Asad, and Tikrit. The segment assigned to Mosul lacked surgical assets, so it was staffed with surgeons from the 1st FST.

Currently, the 86th CSH was assigned in Mosul, but when I arrived the 345th CSH was beginning to replace them.

Our base, Camp Diamondback, was situated next to Mosul International airport. The airport had initially been taken over by the 101st airborne but now housed the 1st Squadron / 9th Cavalry. It functioned as a logistics hub in the fight against Iraqi insurgents.

Individual CHUs measure 22 × 8 feet, a little bigger than a commercial shipping container, making them easy to transport. Each CHU has a door, a blast shield-covered window, a top vent, power cabling, and an air conditioner. Some housed two soldiers with a bunk, but I had one all to myself.

My CHU included free-standing closets on the right and a single bed against the back left wall. A small bedside table with drawers flanked the bed. A window in the back remained sealed, facing the back of another CHU. A silent air-conditioner protruded from the far wall, and a desk fit just inside the door on the left.

Around 2 a.m., I unloaded my duffle, glad to be inside from the chill desert night. The bed was a big step up from the cot I had at Abu.

If this tour is anything like the last, I thought, *I won't be seeing it much anyway.*

I pulled off my fatigues and crawled into bed.

H-85, I thought, *too long to even think about.*

ℝ

After a few hours sleep, I headed to the showers in the pre-dawn twilight. December in Mosul was similar to winter in the southwest United States. Despite being a desert, temperatures could dip towards freezing, and the annual rainfall was on par with Colorado. During the rainy season, the sandy desert transformed into a cold, muddy, sloppy mess.

In the light of day, I could clearly see the Logistical Support Area (LSA). I lived on Scalpel Lane, a row of CHUs that housed physicians and surgeons. Midline between two rows of facing units lay stacks of sandbags and concrete bunkers. Only a narrow walkway remained between barracks and fortifications. During an attack, soldiers had only a dozen steps to shelter. Roofs were lined with sandbags, and twenty-foot concrete T-walls enclosed the base.

It couldn't be any more secure against attack.

ℝ

After breakfast, Omar and I met up with the doctors we were to replace: Nicole Papas, fresh out of general surgery residency; Anne Naclerio, a pediatric intensivist in charge of the ICU; and Chris Newton, a pediatric surgeon.

Dr. Papas led us on a tour of the facilities.

Everything in the military is the same but different. Familiar equipment and facilities made me feel as if I were in Abu, but the people and setup were unique. It was an odd feeling. We moved through the hospital, then the ICU and finally peeked into the ORs.

"It's all pretty much what you're used to," Papas concluded.

Off the ICU, we sat in a small staff lounge. Naclerio poured coffee as we discussed the call schedule.

"I've been on odd days, which usually gives me an extra day each month," Papas said. "It means two days in a row if the month ends on the 31st."

I looked at Omar but didn't give him time to answer.

"Sure," I said. "I'll take the odd days."

Papas noted it on the schedule.

"The other thing is, Dr. Rosen will be Deputy Commander of Clinical Services (DCCS), so he won't have much time for clinical work."

Omar looked at the schedule.

"We could probably cover it without him," I said.

"This isn't Abu, John," Omar said. "You've got other surgeons."

"I know, but if he's DCCS, when is he gonna see a patient?" I said, "and even if he does, who's gonna be really be taking care of them anyway?"

We arranged the schedule between the two of us and put Rosen on backup call.

In the lounge, we addressed a litany of details needed to get up and running: Passwords and access codes, charting and orders, mascals protocols and transport procedures. We also reviewed the doomsday stuff, plans in case the base was attacked.

I was impressed with the facility and the degree of organization. The only thing lacking was patients—the hospital appeared only sparsely filled.

"How's it been lately?" I asked.

"Actually," Naclerio said, "it's been rather quiet."

Disappointed by so few patients, I wondered again if my skills wouldn't be wasted while casualties mounted in Afghanistan.

ভ

After lunch, Omar and I joined a conference with a dozen other newbies for a briefing on the current status of the war. Throughout the country, the insurgency had been largely suppressed. The exception was Mosul, now reputed to be the most dangerous place in Iraq.

"Al Qaeda is making a stand in Mosul," the commander said. "We're sitting in the middle of it."

The airfield adjacent to the hospital housed predator drones used to patrol Mosul and Nineveh Province. Instrumental in monitoring the city and finding the bad guys, these drones didn't carry ordnance but were vital in guiding special forces to their targets. Insurgents loathed them, and the airfield remained a constant target for mortar and rocket attacks.

"The base is protected with Counter Rocket Artillery and Mortar (C-RAM)," he continued, "but it won't stop rockets flying below radar. The base gets hit sporadically, but there's been little damage."

"Who puts a hospital next to a military target?" Omar whispered. I just shrugged.

The commander reviewed procedures for attack. "Remember," he concluded, "twenty seconds on the ground, twenty minutes in the bunker and call in."

⁄

Over the next few days, I acclimated while the 86th played left-seat-right-seat with the 345th. Sporadic explosions occasionally forced me into a bunker, but after twenty minutes I continued on with my day.

My first week, I treated few American combat injuries, mostly insurgents on the wrong side of our patrols. That's not to say I wasn't operating on Americans.

"Seven," I said to Omar. "Seeh-vuuhn," I repeated, holding up five and two fingers.

"I hear ya. I hear ya," Omar said.

"I've never seen so many appys in one week," I said.

"I don't know what to say," Omar continued; "maybe it's the food."

"We need to do a study," I said. "Do we have an epidemiologist?"

"Don't worry," Omar said. "We're bound to get some trauma soon."

⁄

Fashad, an insurgent specialized in IED production, had the misfortune of being ratted out by his neighbors. Special forces kicked in his front door and emptied four rounds into his chest when he reached for a weapon. After refusing to die, he was transferred to the 86th CSH. Three operations later, it was still not clear whether he would survive; but his time with us was over. He was to be transferred out.

I rounded on Fashad earlier in the morning and okayed the transfer. Since then, a few things had happened: A pile of transfer papers had been filed, arrangements for a helicopter had been called and Fashad started to crap out.

"How long has he been like this?" I asked.

"Like what?" the nurse feigned ignorance.

"Like tachycardia and hypotensive?" I reviewed the ICU flow sheet. Vital signs were conspicuously absent for the past three hours.

A few staff lingered around Fashad's bed, avoiding my gaze.

He's a terrorist, they thought. *We're on the verge of kicking his ass out of here. Let's just transport him out, and he'll be someone else's problem.*

"But he's all set to go." she said.

"His pressure's 80," I said. "Open the saline and start some Levophed." The nurse hesitated. I knew what this was about, but it wasn't the way I worked.

"And cancel the helicopter," I added.

"What?" The staff became animated. "But they're en route!"

"And he's unstable; check your protocol." I wrote new orders in the chart starting with bold letters, "CANCEL TRANSFER IMMEDIATELY!!"

The nurse stormed off, fuming.

Omar appeared at my side.

"What's up?" he asked.

"They want me to ship out a guy who's hypotensive."

"That's not good," he said. "Is he the prisoner?"

"Doesn't fucking matter."

෴

Connecting the Ethernet cable into my Powerbook, I logged in to the network. Skype booted up. Within minutes, my family waved to me across six-thousand miles and seven time zones.

"Hi, Daddy!" the kids smiled and waved at the camera. Carmela, sitting with a look of relief, held John John on her lap. It was so good to see them.

"Hey, guys!" I smiled. "Isn't this great? We can see each other any time you want."

Frankie and John John asked me questions about the base, and I panned the laptop to show them my room.

"This is where I live," I said. "I have the whole place to myself."

The conversation turned to Christmas—what Santa would bring and whether he came to Iraq.

After a while, Carmela sent the kids upstairs so we could talk privately. I started to talk but stopped.

"What?" Carmela asked.

She didn't need to hear what I was going to say. Carmela was under enough stress taking care of the kids without me. But I've always been open and honest with her. I've never held back my feelings. Through good and bad, I've shared my worries, hopes and aspirations. Carmela was my soulmate, and I never kept my feelings from her. I couldn't keep this to myself.

"I'm sorry," I said, "I just... I can't shake this feeling, Carm, like something bad is about to happen ..."

"John ..."

"I can't help it; I feel like I'm not coming back alive, Carm ..."

"John, don't do this. Don't be ridiculous..."

"I just want you to know how much I love you and the kids." I started to tear up.

"I know. We know. We love you. Just don't think about it. Concentrate on the job, and it'll be okay..."

"Alright, I know."

She doesn't believe me, I thought.

&

Two days before Christmas, we gathered for another briefing. This time the conference room was packed with personnel. While we waited for the commander to speak, I asked Omar about the incoming fire.

"Why do they attack with only one rocket every so often?" I said.

"Sending a volley every now and then doesn't cause any real damage, but it has an effect on morale. The attacks force us to gear up, they interrupt our work and there's the occasional casualty. But these recent attacks are different. It's not an attack; they're bracketing."

"Bracketing?" I said.

"It's a primitive targeting maneuver. They set parameters and shoot one rocket far to one side. Then they do the same far to the other side. Based on that information, they can adjust to strike dead center. They do the same for near and far."

"Great," I said. "So we've been a targeting range for the last week?"

The briefing began. Intelligence reports concluded Al Qaeda was gearing up for an attack on Christmas day. I wasn't surprised.

All's fair in love and war, I thought.

The commander explained we should prepare for a rocket attack followed by a ground assault

"Expect a suicide bomber either at the main gate or along the perimeter," he said. "A ground attack could follow. We're not going to give them the chance. Throughout the night, we will aggressively patrol the city and thwart any neutralized organized activity, essentially taking the fight into the city."

"Won't that leave us vulnerable?" I whispered to Omar.

"You got a gun," he whispered. "What're you worried about?"

After the briefing, I returned to my CHU to inspect my doomsday rifle. The M-16 was like any other, but this was my M-16, and if a surgeon is ever called upon to use his weapon, it means doomsday is certainly upon us.

෴

As the sun set on Christmas Eve, Diamondback became a hive of activity. In the dimming twilight, I paused to watch soldiers gear up for the preemptive attack.

My pulse quickened, and I felt a cold sweat break out. I'd seen this before, the last day of my first tour, youthful faces mounting up and riding out only to return bloody and broken, screaming in pain or, deadly silent.

I forced a smile and returned a thumbs up as a sergeant fired up his HUMVEE. The gunner swiveled in his turret, and the HUMVEE rumbled for the gate.

They're just kids, I thought, *when will this shit be over?*

In my CHU, I loaded my M-16 and laid it next to my bunk, muzzle towards the door. Anxiety and worry from a possible attack and troops on patrol precluded sleep. Vehicle ignitions and soldiers test firing their weapons startled me upright.

Is this it? I thought, *is this the assault?*

I spent a fitful night anticipating the call for incoming wounded. But the call never came.

❧

Christmas morning I started rounds at 6 a.m. By 10:00 a.m., I was done with no new cases to keep me busy. I met up with Omar, and it started to rain as we walked back to Scalpel Lane.

"You going to mass?" I asked.

"Nah," he smiled. "I don't go unless my wife makes me."

"I promised my mom I would go," I said. "It shouldn't be more than an hour. Want to meet for chow later?"

"Sounds good," he said. "I have some stuff to do but should be done by then." Omar headed for the hospital.

At 10:30, I met up with COL Giulitto, the commander of the outgoing 86th CSH. LTC Anne Naclerio joined us as we walked across the muddy compound to Diamondback Chapel.

The Shiites and Sunnis grabbed all the headline, so it was easy to forget a large minority of Christians living in Iraq. Interestingly, the largest population of Catholics reside in and around Mosul. It might appear the best place to celebrate Christmas except that the bishop had been kidnapped and killed on Easter a year earlier.

Inside, the chapel was packed. Most of the parishioners were military, but many were contractors and "third country nationals"—workers from outside the U.S. Anne and I found a seat halfway down the crowded pews. COL Giulitto continued up toward the front.

Father Michael Albano spoke with a thick Philippine accent. He reminded me of the Spanish priest I struggled to understand during

Danielle's baptism. Throughout the sermon I had flashbacks, thinking about Rich and me as children, failing to stifle our snickering in church.

Corpus Christi, I thought, *sugar coated Jesus' that walk on milk.*

I smiled at the memory.

After mass, COL Giulitto rejoined me and Anne and we trudged through the sloppy mess back to the compound.

"I'm meeting Omar for chow if anyone's interested," I said.

"I need to check on some patients, but then I'm free," said Anne.

"I gotta pick up some laundry," said Giulitto. "Maybe I'll meet you there."

Anne and I continued to the LSA as Giulitto headed for the laundry. We came to the end of a row of CHUS and stopped. Anne walked away from me to chat with Nicole Papas. I turned and headed for the latrine and shower units.

BANG !!

The noise stopped me in my tracks. It sounded like a large metal container dropped off the back of a truck, but it came from outside the concrete barricade.

Was that an explosion? I thought.

I listened for the C-RAM siren, but there was only silence.

As I searched the sky, a loud shriek shot directly towards me.

It'd been a long time since I experienced a rocket attack. Maybe if I had another week, my reflexes would've been quicker. Instead of hitting the deck, I hesitated—frozen in a second's indecision.

It's hard to say,

if it would've made a difference.

The explosion,

was so goddamn close.

Last Call

I laid the pen and flipped through the pages from the beginning.

All I had been through, all the ambulance calls, college, the fight to get into medical school, the years of sleepless residency, marriage, kids, lectures, 9-11, Iraq. None of it was easy, every day a struggle.

But the Journal was not even a third filled; I began flipping through the empty pages. So much more could be written. How many birthdays, vacations, Christmases? How many patients I could help, fellows I could train? Who would teach my kids to drive? Take Frankie and John John Camping? Escort Danielle down the aisle on her wedding day? Blank page after blank page flipped by.

"Hey, what's that?"

Rich stood above me holding two pints. What was he doing here? My heart sank—was he dead too?

"What?..."

I looked around. DEATH had gone. I sat in a dimly lit bar, the walls filled with dust covered photos and memorabilia. Behind the bar stood a wooden icebox carved with the phrase, "Be good or be gone."

"Are we at... McSorley's?" I said.

"It's my dream," Rich said. "I get to choose."

"So..." I said tentatively, "you're not dead."

"No, John," he sighed, flipping casually through the journal. "You're dead. What's this?"

I took a long draught of dark beer.

"DEATH was here, he asked what led me to Iraq. I said I'd have to tell him my life story, so he gave me this journal to write it."

"What, like a final exam?"

"I don't know, you can ask if he comes back."

Rich took a sip of beer.

"You write about where you fucked up and joined the Army?"

"Rich..." I sighed, "why do you have to say that?"

"Cause I was right, Carmela was right. I said it wasn't worth it; we told you it was a bad idea; she told you not to go..."

"What do you mean you were right?"

"What do I mean? What do I mean? You're fucking dead!!"

"Rich, a bad outcome doesn't mean a wrong decision, you should know that. It happens in medicine all the time."

"Oh no, I'm not going to hear this bullshit about you were right all along. Typical Republican, never wrong until you're really wrong. Then you say, 'But it was the right decision at the time.'"

"You still don't understand... "

"I'm sick of hearing how I don't understand. Carmela asked you not to go and you went, and now you're dead..."

"Rich, I could have died in a car accident. I could've been in a plane crash. I could have gotten cancer; there's a hundred ways to die and I would still be dead."

"John, most people drive, most people fly. These are acceptable risks of

modern society. Joining the military and re-locating to a combat zone is not a normal risk. When you did that you put your life in danger above and beyond..."

"Yeah, but what is acceptable risk? What is acceptable risk for an airline pilot? What about a firefighter? A mountain climber? People have passions, careers, interests. This is what life is about, pursuing your life purpose. It's not existing, it's living. The cost of living is risk, risk of failure, risk of injury or DEATH. *It's the risk that separates the men from the boys. It's the risk that makes success so rewarding."*

I took a breath.

"I'm a trauma surgeon. It's who I am; you know that better than anyone. Like it or not, politically rational or not, risky or not, the place for a trained trauma surgeon during war is in combat. Otherwise what good am I? It's like a firefighter not going to a fire because its risky. Right? That would be insane, right?

"It's not the same..."

"Why? Why not?"

"Because you had an obligation to your family and your children..."

"What, and firefighters don't have children?"

"No, it's that you're drawing the wrong analogy. Firefighters are trained for the risks they take, their families know what they're getting into. What you did went beyond the normal risks of your profession and you acted without regard to your family."

"Like when the off duty firefighters responded to 9-11 and died in the collapse?"

Pause.

"Sort of..."

"What, you expected them to stay home?"

"Okay, we're getting off subject..."

"Rich, if you were working at St. Vincent's on 9-11 where would you be?"

I'd be halfway up the tower, I thought instantly.

John read my thoughts.

"That's right, and would having a family have stopped you?"

Pause.

"No," I conceded in a whisper.

"If I had to do it all over again," he said, "I would make the same decision."

I realized there was no way around it. The decision John made to go to Iraq was the same determination that made him a paramedic, the same that made him a surgeon, the same that made him jump in his car on 9-11. It was part of who he was. Asking him not to make these decisions would be like asking him to be somebody else.

If I could go back in time and change him, what would I rather have—my brother alive, as some lesser person, or dead, as the man he wanted to be?

I didn't like the choice.

"Where does that leave your family?" I asked him.

"Rich, I'm not happy about this. I didn't want to die; I wouldn't choose this outcome. But we all die. The best we can do is prepare for DEATH, *live life so that when* DEATH *comes there are no regrets. I lived to the best of my ability, I took advantage of opportunities available to me. I can't be blamed for things beyond my control."*

McSorley's began to fade, the dream dissolved around me. I fought to keep it in place.

NO! I screamed, Wait! There's more I need to say!

John smiled at me and raised his beer.

WAIT! I reached out to him…

⁊

I woke in pitch blackness—blackness around me and blackness in my mind. Memory of a dream lingered, but the more I struggled to remember the quicker it slipped away. I opened my eyes wondering where I was.

Carmela's weeping echoed from downstairs and the day's events rushed back in a flood of painful images. Reality hit, like a hot dagger thrust into my belly. Doubling over, I began to sob.

Oh god, I thought, *this is real, he's really dead!*

My first instance of waking into a nightmare.

Requiem

From: **Rich Pryor**
Subject: What Happened
Date: June 26, 2010 3:50:16 PM EDT
To: Pryor, John <johnpryor@elysianfields.com>
CC:

John,

It's taken over a year of research to fully understand the events of that day. The details are important to me. True, I want to know the exact circumstances, your final thoughts and actions, but there's more. I find it difficult to accept you died so far away, in a strange and hostile land. When I know what happened, I can imagine myself with you and pretend you were not alone.

While events played out in Mosul, the rest of us were sleeping; visions of sugar-plums danced in our heads, as it were. All except Carmela, who remained as restless and as fitful as you were anticipating the attack.

Around 9 a.m. local time, insurgents set to work three miles to the east, across the Tigris. In a roofless, half-constructed cinderblock structure, surrounded by open field, they lowered fifty-six rockets into large aluminum tubes. Stacks of cinder blocks and sand bags aimed the launchers west.

Wires, strung from a central station, connected the rockets to an electronic launcher powered by car batteries. With timers activated, the insurgents absconded.

The rockets, like everything else in the world, were made in China. Not specifically Katyusha, which are Russian, but close enough. Six feet long and 107 mm in girth, they remain the preferred armament of Hamas and other discerning Middle East terrorists.

The rocket consisted of three parts: an engine with propellant; a high-grade explosive primer; and forty pounds of low-grade ordnance, usually ammonia nitrate.

With conditions set, the fate of each rocket led to one of several possibilities. Of fifty-six, only twenty-five successfully launched. Of these, ten landed harmlessly while thirteen triggered just the primary explosive. Only three detonated fully.

The trajectory placed them under the C-RAM radar, so you had no warning. The first rocket, an impacting dud just outside the perimeter, caught your attention. The second one was yours.

You didn't know Sergeant Darin Elkins. In theater for more than a year, Darin had become accustomed to the explosions. While lounging in his PTs, he heard the first impact and jumped off his bunk, expecting a routine trip to the bunker.

Opening the door to his CHU, Darin was slammed to the ground by an earth-shattering blast. Stunned, his eardrums felt ruptured, and he looked down to see if he was still intact.

Sirens began to wail, soldiers yelled, "BUNKERS! BUNKERS! BUNKERS!" as smoke clouds bloomed in the distance. Darin got up and ran.

The scene unfolded like a dream—running felt like wading through water, the chaos tuned out, only the sound of his breathing remained. COL Shen leaned up against the rear of Darin's CHU, leg ripped open— a hand, swallowed by flesh, stemming the hemorrhage. CPT Tanner arrived at his side, so Darin kept moving.

A shrapnel-pierced fire extinguisher vented thick white powder, obscuring the impact site. Through the fog, Darin made out a pair of boots and ran forward. Acrid phosphorous burned his nose and blurred his eyes as he passed a concrete-imbedded rocket tail.

Darin knelt at your side and read the name tape: PRYOR. He looked at your head as you exhaled your final breath.

I won't lie, John; you were a mess.

The right side of your face was pulp, and your eyes were blown back so only the whites showed. Your scalp, open in the back, fed an expanding pool of blood surrounding your head.

Darin hesitated. As bad as it was, he didn't want to cause any more harm. But a second later, he was joined by a corpsman, and they lifted you toward the hospital. Blood flowed along Darin's arms, soaking his PT shorts and dripping down his legs.

Halfway to the entrance Darin was met by more corpsmen. They laid you on a wheeled litter and ran you to the ER.

Moments earlier, your friend Omar sat in the emergency room, engaged in casual conversation. Through open doors, he noticed soldiers returning from Christmas mass, one heading for laundry another coming to the hospital. Your group stopped; after a moment, you continued on, alone.

The concrete-reinforced building rocked like an earthquake; Omar nearly fell to the ground.

"Holy shit!" Omar said.

Several soldiers rolled out of the soft OR section. Omar and CPT O'Bannon rushed over to check for injured, but there were none. Reversing direction, they headed to triage where staff had sprinted into action.

Omar sent O'Bannon to page you when the ER doors burst open. Two corpsmen carried in Dr. Dwight Shen, the DCCS, covered in blood.

Jesus Christ, he thought, *they hit us!*

COL Shen, placed on a gurney, was immediately surrounded by a medical team. With bleeding controlled, his wound was deemed non life-threatening. Omar moved him to triage three and headed back to the entrance.

The second patient wheeled in, and Omar noted his eyes and

exposed brain matter. He rushed you to Trauma Bay One. The team assembled and slid you over to the hospital gurney.

In the commotion, Omar felt something odd. He looked over his shoulder and thought, *Where the hell is Pryor?*

You know what happened next. You played this game since high school, through medical school, residency and a thousand times at HUP: The trauma dance.

One final time.

In your honor.

This time, it was largely symbolic—the nonsurvivable brain trauma inescapable, the resuscitation futile. But, just as you would have done, they did not give up: CPR started, tube placed, lines inserted, blood hung.

Cutting your pants to expose the groin, Omar came close enough to finally recognize you. He stood paralyzed. The room fell away, and sounds of the resuscitation muted. He felt as if he would pass out.

"Come on, Omar." MAJ Papas snapped him out of it. "Let's get going."

After twenty minutes, CPR was suspended and an ultrasound probe was placed on your chest. Your heart remained motionless.

"Omar," CPT Nolan said quietly, "I think it's over."

The team knew you two were friends and waited for Omar to make the final call. He was a surgeon for ten years and knew you had a nonsurvivable injury. Still, his voice cracked and could barely speak above a whisper.

"Stop CPR," Omar said.

The team stood in stunned silence. Omar turned away and almost gasped at the sight. Nearly the entire CSH stood behind him—many crying, most too stunned to speak.

They had been watching the whole time.

At five a.m. Carmela gave up on sleep. She and the kids had come to Staten Island to spend the holidays with Nella and her parents. Dressed in pajamas and a bathrobe, she put on a pot of coffee and picked up her cell phone. You exchanged texts daily, so she found the blank screen extremely disquieting.

Christmas morning, and he doesn't text? she thought.

Carmela began rationalizing. You must be operating or busy with patients or...?

She texted you: John, merry xmas. Call me when u can. Luv u, Carm.

Omar forced himself to carry on; there was still work to do. Priority was given to the other casualties. Dwight Shen required a fasciotomy, and Anne Naclerio needed a frag removed from her face.

With the wounded tended to, he headed for the morgue. A military technicality, but you needed to be officially identified. Omar filled out some paperwork and left the morticians to their work.

At Scalpel Lane, he passed the rocket tail and blood-soaked deck. Omar entered your room, recovered your weapons and secured your valuables. Before leaving, he paused, unable to break his gaze from the pictures of Carmela and the kids pinned to your wall.

Too early, as usual for Christmas, my kids ran downstairs to tear open their gifts. The adults followed, a little more groggy, first groping for a cup of coffee before sitting by the tree.

For once, I was happy to be home on Christmas. Traditionally, we traveled to Kingston and gathered with Deidre's sister from NYC, but this year we hosted. Deidre's family arrived Christmas Eve and stayed over.

When the excitement died down I sat at the computer. We hadn't communicated since you left Kuwait, so I sent an email. I wanted to call, but I never knew how busy you would be.

From: **Rich Pryor**
Subject: **Merry Christmas**
Date: **December 25, 2008 6:45:23 AM EST**
To: **Pryor, John**
CC:

John,

Dad said you were available via this email address. So I'll give it a try.

Merry Christmas. Did Santa make it to Islam central?

I'll keep the Skype program on if you want to try to connect some-time.

Let me know if you get this.

Rich

I sent the message and returned to my family. Sophia and Olivia played quietly with three-year-old cousin Nolan. I sat and put my feet up, looking forward to three days off, sans holiday travel.

Finally, I thought, *a Christmas at home.*

Carmela sat at her sister's computer and sipped her coffee. She navigated to CNN and read a report from Iraq:

Car bomb kills 4 in Baghdad

December 25, 2008

A car bomb exploded in northwestern Baghdad Thursday morning, killing four people and wounding 26 others, an Interior Ministry official said.

The attack took place in the Shula neighborhood and targeted a popular restaurant, according to the official.

The U.S. military issued a statement on the incident and reported different numbers—one local citizen dead and at least 21 wounded.

It said a police officer was among the injured.

Also Thursday, a U.S. soldier died of wounds sustained in an indirect fire attack near the northern Iraqi city of Mosul, the military said.

The last paragraph resonated. She read it again and again, trying to reason why that soldier could not possibly be you.

Major Charles Causey, a twenty-year reserve chaplain and Iraq combat veteran, held one of the most unenviable positions in the service. Military advertisements promise adventure, entice young people with training, extol discipline and honor.

It's funny how they never mention death.

Among soldiers, families and friends, there's a collective denial, a refusal to consider military service may have a lethal outcome. I suppose I shared in this denial. Sure, I thought, people die in war.

Other people.

As a casualty notification officer, Causey could not participate in the delusion. Charged with the ultimate burden, he delivered the cold, stark, undeniable reality of war.

The call came as he prepared for dinner with relatives. Causey came downstairs in his dress blues, deflating the Christmas spirit. He kissed his wife and four children goodbye and headed for your house.

Unable to reach you throughout the afternoon, Carmela became increasingly anxious. Your silence was very uncharacteristic, and she perseverated on the one u.s. casualty. Likewise, I checked my email throughout the day, disappointed you had not responded.

Causey and his partner rang the bell again, but the midday porch light was a telltale sign. Next door, Cara Mueller knew Carmela had gone to her parents' house. She looked up the address on the Internet and wrote it down for Causey. More than an hour later, they arrived in Brooklyn only to discover another empty house. A neighbor supplied Nella's phone number.

"Hello?" Nella answered the phone. "Yes, yes he is… *Who* is this?" she handed the phone to Franco, "It's for you."

Franco gave her a quizzical look and raised the receiver to his ear. "Hello?" he said.

Carmela remained in another room, but she heard Franco on the phone.

"Yes… no… What's this about? Why are… yes. It's in Staten

Island. Address? Tompkins Avenue… yes, that's right. What's this… okay." Franco hung up. Nella and Pauleta met his gaze.

"Who was that?" asked Pauleta.

Franco looked around. In a hushed voice, he said, "It was the Army; they're looking for Carmela."

"Why?"

"They wouldn't say," he shrugged. "They say they're coming right over."

Carmela appeared in the doorway of the dining room.

"Who was on the phone?" she asked.

Nobody answered.

Causey found the house, eager to conclude his Christmas goose chase. He closed his eyes for a minute and mentally reviewed his speech:

The Secretary of the Army has asked me to express his deep regret that your husband, Major John Pryor, was killed in action in Mosul, Iraq, on December 25th from injuries sustained in a rocket attack. The Secretary extends his deepest sympathy to you and your family in your tragic loss.

He knocked on the door.

There was a knock at the door.

Carmela sat on the couch, her back to the front door. She heard the knock but refused to turn around. Nella opened the door.

"Carm," Nella said, "there is someone here for you."

Carmela turned to see two soldiers in full dress uniform.

She screamed.

"HE'S THE ONE?" she yelled. "HE'S THE ONE SOLDIER KILLED IN MOSUL?!"

Stunned by her foreknowledge, Causey floundered. Instead of the prepared speech, all he could muster was, "How did you know?"

I remember standing near the tree when the phone rang. Deidre walked into the living room and answered, "Merry Christmas." She froze; her expression turned to horror.

"Carmela, NO!"

It came out like a primordial scream, a guttural anguish disguised as English. I've never heard anything like it. Deidre doubled over, and I ran to grab the phone.

"Carm..?"

"HE'S DEAD! THEY KILLED HIM," she screamed between sobs. HE'S DEAD!"

"Carmela…"

This can't be right, I thought, *how can you be dead? You just got there! You're on a secure base. There must be some mistake.*

"Carmela…?" Her cries became distant as she dropped the phone. The call disconnected.

Carmela collapsed to the ground, weeping. Nella and Franco helped her back to the couch. The cell phone rang in her hand.

"Carm, what happened?" I said. "What did they say?"

I struggled with disbelief, but Carmela had two uniformed men standing above her.

"Don't call your parents." She composed herself enough to relay the message from the officers. "They're sending someone there now."

"Where are you?" I asked. "What do you want me to do?"

"I'm at my sister's," she said. "Francesco will drive us home."

"Do you want me to come down?"

"Yes."

Then, John, it got worse.

I sat alone in my bedroom, phone cradled in my palm, and waited. I waited for a pair of uniformed men to knock on Mom and Dad's door in Florida and inform them of your death. I waited for them to pick up the phone and call me. Then I had to sit, alone, without your help for the first time and listen to their reaction. I will absolve you of almost every hardship I have endured related to your decision to join the army.

But not this.

Walking into the gas station was surreal. My face puffy from crying, I moved through the space like a zombie, barely aware of my surroundings. A nuclear bomb had gone off in my life; the worst possible thing that could happen had come true. While in line for coffee, my despondent stare observed the scene like a dream, and a curious thought crossed my mind.

It's still Christmas for these people.

I returned to my car and began the four-hour drive to your house, not completely confident I would make it. I struggled to see in the darkness, to make out the road through blurry tears, trying to breathe through the suffocating grief.

All my life, I looked to you for support. A few supportive words from you were all I needed to lift my depression or self-doubt. I could handle any crisis or a problem because I knew you had my back.

Now, when I needed you the most …

It was the longest, loneliest, darkest drive of my life.

Your front door unlocked, I let myself in. Carmela sat at the kitchen table surrounded by a dozen nurses, neighbors and friends. A heavy silence hung in the air. The children remained next door for the night.

I hugged Carmela, and she broke down sobbing, "What am I going to do? What am I going to do? The kids have no father. What am I going to do?"

The visitors slowly filed out, leaving me alone with Carm and her parents. There was no rest that night. Carm never approached her bed, remaining instead on the small leather couch, weeping and grieving as I never knew was possible.

In Frankie's room, I tried to sleep. I fell under for about an hour, but at four in the morning I woke with a start. For a moment, I had no idea where I was. Then Carmela's crying echoed from downstairs, and the day's events came rushing back.

I realized this was my nightmare. A strange paradoxical experience where sleep provided comfort and the waking world contained the terror. The reality was suffocating; it was physically hard to breathe. I cried, trying to wrap my mind around the fact you were dead. I couldn't do it. I still couldn't believe it.

I composed myself and descended to the living room. I passed the darkened Christmas tree, presents strewn about its base like tombstones in a ransacked cemetery. Carm is on the couch with Pauleta. I sit on the ottoman, across from Carmela, and say nothing. There's nothing to say. She is quiet, then weeps, and then tries to compose herself.

The cycle repeats all night.

Friday, December 26

In the morning I wanted to let my friends know what happened, but I wasn't composed enough to call anyone. Instead, I sent out a notice on Facebook:

Dr. John P. Pryor is dead.
Friday, December 26, 2008, at 8:59 a.m.
My brother, Dr. John Paul Pryor, was killed Christmas morning in Mosul, Iraq, from a mortar fired into the air force base he was stationed at. John was in Iraq as a surgeon treating American and Iraqi casualties.

I forced myself downstairs to face the day. Carm said the Army would be coming around 11:30. I found your doomsday binder. It contained instructions, insurance information, music CDs and the obituary you wrote. Tears blurred my vision, and my chest physically ached, but I forced myself to read the document:

To be read only upon the death of John P. Pryor

This is a document to provide my final instructions upon my death. I have thought these things out for a long time, and I would like the instructions followed as best you can. This information can be shared freely with all those involved in making the appropriate arrangements.

I. Supervision
    A. I appoint my brother Richard J. Pryor, MD the supervisor of these instructions. I expect he will work with my wife Carmela V. Calvo, MD and my father Richard C. Pryor as needed.

B. If Richard J. Pryor is not able to perform the tasks, Richard C. Pryor should be the supervisor.

II. Documents.

    A. Carmela and I have arranged a somewhat complex trust fund system for our life insurances. The originals of all documents are in a safe at Archer and Greiner attorneys in Haddonfield, NJ. (One centennial square 958-555-0144). Copies can be found in the safe in our house. This is a fireproof safe that is located in my office near the window. If the house is destroyed, the safe may be recovered; but again, the originals are not there, so don't go crazy looking for it.

    B. In brief, I have Wills, family trusts, irrevocable trust, health care proxy and durable power of attorney in this package. I tried forever to figure all of this stuff out, but it goes in one ear and out the other. Get a lawyer to help you weed through it all. I will attach a spreadsheet with all the insurances and the contact info for each. I would not wait to contact the lawyer and the insurance companies, *I command you to do this the day after the funeral.*

    C. Make a package of all my documents such as drivers licenses, wallet contents, hospital IDs, etc., and keep them together. You may need these during insurance procedures.

       1. When you are done with all of these documents, eventually give them to Frankie.

III.   Funeral Arrangements

    A. Funeral plans have already been arranged by me at the Lankenau Funeral home, 334 Chester Avenue, Moorestown. 856-555-007. All of the paper work is completed the best we could.

       1. Specific casket has not been picked—I have stated generally what type—Batesville mahogany, half door.

       2. I respectfully request transfer out of any military provided casket into the one above, unless the original casket meets my specifications and has no military markers or insignia of any kind.

B. I have written the obituary—copy enclosed here—electronic copy on the computer under "John's dead" folder

C. Questions or additional decisions should be handled by Richard J. Pryor and Richard C. Pryor, in consultation with Carmela.

D. I would like a traditional Christian mass and burial at Our Lady of Good Council in Moorestown, New Jersey
  1. I would like the following songs included in the ceremony; there is a CD with all of the songs on it. I charge Rich with figuring out how to play then during the mass—you will have to get an audio system worked out and arrange with the priest. Keep the order:
     a) Wonderful World (For Dad)
     b) Ave Maria (For Mom)
     c) Nessen Dorma (For Carmela)
     d) Amazing Grace (For Danielle)
     e) Bid You Good Night (For Frankie)
     f) Bring Him Home (For Baby John)
  2. I will prepare a eulogy to be read…this should be read by someone NOT close to me…can't get too emotional, like I did when I fucked up papa's eulogy…up to you to pick someone.

E. I want a traditional wake. Wake is two days only; more is excessive; less will be unfair to people's schedules.
  1. *I absolutely refuse to use a funeral home in Brooklyn.* If the Moorestown Funeral Home cannot be used for some reason, only locations I will except are Philadelphia, Moorestown/Cherry Hill or Clifton Park.
  2. During the wake, I would like lots of pictures of all those close to me. Mom, this is your job… Fill the whole place with the great memories we all had. Also, I want to play videos of the kids. Rich, you are in charge of this. Set it up the best you can.
  3. Play good music in background. Required bands are
     a) Grateful dead
     b) Bob Dylan

     c) Pink Floyd

     d) Elvis (for mom)

     e) Phish

     f) *Les Mes* soundtrack

     g) *Camelot* Soundtrack

4. I want open casket if possible—half open, not all the way open. Obviously, depends on the mode of death. If head is involved, no open casket. This is at discretion of Dad and Rich.

5. I like flowers. Some say, give the money to a charity. Screw that... I want everything coming to me...

6. If there is an open casket wake, thus minimal facial damage, Danielle and Frank should attend the wake. I know this is a hard decision, and that is why I am making it for you. John John should not attend—and specifically, I do not want him brought to the funeral home and kept outside—this would be a worse situation for him. Carm– be honest with them and tell them exactly what is going on... I do not want Danielle and Frankie to regret not getting to say goodbye.

F. Artifacts

1. I have assembled artifacts from my life that I would like to be buried with me. These are located in my office on the wall shelves. All of the items on the third shelve are to be put into the casket with me. They all have special meanings for me—and most represent the people who I have known and loved throughout my life. No substitutions, and no exclusions please.

G. Internment

This is a little sticky, but I have thought about it a long time.

1. I request a ground burial at the Pryor/Dalton plot in Yonkers.

2. I absolutely refuse burial in Brooklyn or Staten Island.

3. Last option is St. Mary's Cemetery in Clifton Park.

4. I considered cremation and decided against it.

5. *If a second family member dies at the same time,* I instruct

the supervisor to purchase a new Pryor family plot (ground plot) for both/all deceased. This plot should have at least 10 positions. It should then be offered to any other family members in the future.

   a) *In this specific case* of a second family member dying at the same time, the plot can be in the Staten Island Cemetery. This is so everyone can visit the other member more easily.

   b) This should be a ground plot.

H. Military honors

This section pertains if I die in combat and/or on active duty. Carmela never understood duty, honor and country, so if I die this way, she will be pissed. Thus, try to minimize the military aspects.

   1. I respectfully refuse to be buried in a military uniform.

   2. I respectfully refuse a military casket. If it is necessary for partial preparation of the body to be done in the military, I understand and give permission. But I want to be transferred to a civilian casket asap.

   3. I respectfully refuse burial in a national cemetery.

   4. I respectfully refuse a military honor guard or gun salute.

   5. I *will* accept a flag on the casket to be given to my daughter Danielle.

IV. Organ donation

   A. I am a full organ donor, if this affects funeral arrangements, too bad—donating is more important.

      1. I do not want you to ever contact the family or patients I donate to. I want this to stay anonymous.

      2. I thought about donating for anatomy class but decided against it. So after donation, go right to burial.

      3. I am all for warm heart donation—the doctors will understand what that means.

V. Memorial

I am sure work will want to have some type of memorial. That is fine with me. As far as a lasting memorial, I direct that a sum of money go to a fund to support a lecture series in trauma/emergency surgery with an emphasis on humanity, professionalism and dedication to the care of the indigent, poor and abused. The details of how much, I leave to the discretion of Carmela and Dr. William Schwab. It will need to be enough to support travel, honoraria, and a faculty dinner.

VI.   Obituary
Electronic copy in folder "John's Dead"

I initiated the first steps for your arrangements. Steve Lankenau, the funeral home director, remembered you fondly and expressed disbelief. He cautioned about military bureaucracy and advised we prepare for a long delay before you returned home.

Father McElvoy explained a funeral was not possible in the week following Christmas. Considering we didn't know when you would arrive home, this was not a problem.

The children came home in the morning. Danielle cried. John John appeared frightened. Frankie cried and gave me this look. This *look*, John, I'll never forget. It was angry, accusing, but also like he saw a ghost. Maybe he saw you in me?

During the day I began my ordeal, notifying friends and family. Dozens of painful, heart-wrenching phone calls: Chris Sheridan and Brian McClintock from high school, Brent Steuerwald your football coach, Ed Dickenson from work, our Scoutmasters Jerry Burr and Mike Lonczak, who broke down like he lost a son.

I left a message on Mike McEvoy's phone, "John died, please call me back." When he returned the call, I walked out and sat on your front stoop.

"Mike," I cried, "oh, Mike, he loved you Mike; he loved you so much."

Mike maintained his composure.

I made many calls, reaching people from our past—most I hadn't spoken to in years. They had no idea you were in the military, and your death was a complete surprise.

Lieutenant Colonel Stuart Gillard, our casualty assistance officer (CAO), arrived in the afternoon. A binder entitled, "The Days Ahead," lay on the kitchen table as Carmela and I sat in silence. Stu pulled out various forms and paperwork.

"Okay," he began, "You get a check for $100,000. Did you want that direct deposit?"

Carmela and I looked at each other, too stunned to speak.

Money? I thought. *My brother's dead, and you want to give us* MONEY?

Carmela graciously voided a check for Stu, and we moved on to other items.

Military policy dictates the CAO be a higher rank than the deceased. You were a Major, so our CAO had to be at least a Lieutenant Colonel. Officers of your rank held the lowest risk of death in Iraq and Afghanistan. Stu had been called to this task only once or twice previously. He meant well, but lacked experience in these matters. Mostly he responded, "I don't know, but I'll find out right away."

Late afternoon, Mom and Dad arrived. Dad began helping me with your arrangements.

Early evening, your story began to break. Local television affiliates learned of your death and sent reporters to the house. Dad's first instinct was to ignore the media and send them away. I felt differently.

The world should know about you. If any good could come of this nightmare, it lay in the inspirational force you possessed. Even in death, you have the ability to influence others in a positive way.

I also had a more selfish reason for letting them in.

During your first tour, it was unavoidable to imagine this present scenario. I imagined what it would be like if you died. Devastated, outraged, infuriated, I would not settle for some minuscule obituary buried deep in the local paper. I would want to announce it to the world and scream, "Wait a minute! My brother died! You don't understand; this is not any ordinary person, not some nameless casualty. This was my brother!" I would take out a full-page advertisement in the *New York Times* just to tell people about the loss that this country had suffered.

But I didn't need to take out an ad or write an op-ed piece. I made no calls to the paper or television affiliates. Somehow, the world already had an idea of how special you were, and they came to find out more.

The doorbell rang. I led a reporter and videographer to the sunroom. Bright lights, lapel microphone and camera rolling, I spoke about you, about your belief in duty, honor, country, about your inability to remain idle when your skills were desperately needed. Somehow I managed without tearing up.

One by one, each affiliate appeared in the sunroom, and I repeated my ordeal before the camera. Then newspaper reporters began calling. *Albany Times Union, The New York Post, The New York Daily News, The Philadelphia Inquirer*; over the next few days, I gave dozens of interviews. Radio stations called asking for on-air interviews. Within a week, professional journals and alumni organizations started calling. American Academy of Surgery, British Medical Journal, Grenada, Binghamton, JEMS, General Surgery News, Buffalo,—the list was long.

You would have never expected this John, but when you died, the world took note.

Sat / Sun, December 27-28

Friends, neighbors and relatives began to fill your house. Well-meaning neighbors and caterers delivered a continuous flow of platters, sandwiches, salads and dinners. Even with the crowds, your refrigerators quickly filled to capacity.

Throughout the day, I heard your laugh or saw you in my periphery, only to be disappointed by Francesco or some other relative. It was my first experience with your ghost, like the afterimage from a camera flash. You were there, in your house, where you should be.

But of course, you weren't.

Dr. Schwab, with expert political finesse, inserted himself into the arrangement plans. The church you preferred in Moorestown, he argued, was much too small. A more appropriate venue would the Basilica of St. Peter and St. Paul in Philadelphia. He also advocated for full military honors. It made sense, and I agreed.

Aunt Marguerite arrived with cousin Michael. Uncle Lou remained at home. At one point, Marguerite handed me her cell phone.

"It's Lou," she said, "he wants to say hi."

Great, I thought, *now I have to talk to Lou.*

"Hello?" I said.

"Hey Richie," Lou said, "I'm sorry to hear about your brother. Say, did you talk to Geraldo Rivera yet?"

"*What?*" I said.

"Geraldo loves the troops," Lou continued. "He's always talking about the troops on his show. I'll bet he would do a whole show on your brother if you talk to him."

This is what you left me to deal with. You're dead, your kids are fatherless, we're all devastated and I've got Lou on the phone who wants to be on Geraldo.

I bet you didn't see that one coming.

Monday, December 29

On Monday, Dr. Schwab and Fr. McElvoy secured a date for the Basilica. This took a bit of Catholic political finagling involving the Camden diocese bishop and the Archbishop of Philadelphia.

Stu called. "Let me tell ya," he said, "I've been in the service twenty years; I've never seen things move so fast." He said you would arrive at Dover Air Force Base (AFB) on Wednesday.

That was the good news. The bad news concerned your "remains." The Army officially recommended a closed casket funeral.

Not encouraging.

Let me digress for a minute here. In addition to the fear, anxiety, depression and utter grief shredding our souls, another thought weighed heavily on our minds. Details about the incident remained murky. Something exploded very close to you; that's all we knew.

The fact that soldiers who die from explosions are frequently returned *in pieces* was not lost on us. The unspoken possibility that you were not completely intact lurked in the back of our minds. The recommendation for a closed casket only added to our distress.

Monday night, I drove home to my wife and children. We would return on Wednesday. In the meantime, I prepared for your closed casket wake.

Searching through your iPhoto library, I settled on twelve photographs and sent them to a printer for enlargement. I then created a slide show including music from Dylan, Grateful Dead, Phish, Pink Floyd and Dave Matthews. I skipped *Camelot* and *Les Mis*.

At the printer, I inspected your poster-sized photos: A nice one of you in scrubs sitting in the ER, your family posing in front of Lake George, you and the kids on a boat in Cape Cod, your family in front of the Lincoln Memorial, Danielle wearing a helicopter helmet, one of just you and Carmela on vacation.

"Is this the guy I read about in the paper?" the cashier asked.

"Yeah," I said. "he's my brother."

Was, I still couldn't say it.

"It's on the house," he said, closing the cash register.

Tuesday, December 30

Tuesday evening, while completing errands, NPR forced me to the side of the road. Tears streamed as I listened:

Friends and family are mourning the death of a prominent Pennsylvania doctor in Iraq. Maj. John Pryor served in the Army Reserve and was the head of the trauma team at the Hospital of the University of Pennsylvania. He was killed on Christmas Day.

MELISSA BLOCK, host:

Now we're going to hear about a trauma surgeon who was killed in Iraq on Christmas Day. Major John Pryor wrote and spoke eloquently about his work in Iraq and in Philadelphia. He was killed near Mosul, where he was stationed with an army medical detachment. From Philadelphia, Joel Rose reports.

JOEL ROSE: John Pryor wasn't one to hide from a tough job. On September 11, he rushed from Philadelphia to Manhattan to help treat the injured. A major in the army reserves, Pryor was serving his second tour of duty with a surgical unit in Iraq when he was killed by shrapnel from a mortar round. As he told NPR's Michel Martin last year, Pryor saw clear parallels between saving lives in Iraq and on a different battlefield.(Sound bite of phone call)

Doctor **JOHN PRYOR** (Major, U.S. Army Reserves): Sometimes I can't tell whether I'm in Iraq or if I'm in West Philadelphia. Listen, I have to look at the ceiling and see if it's a tent above me or a solid ceiling. And, you know, unfortunately, what we've learned on how to take care of people in Iraq, we really learned on the streets of

America taking care of the civilian casualties over the past 20 or 30 years.

ROSE: As trauma program director at the hospital of the University of Pennsylvania,, Pryor treated hundreds of gunshot victims, and it troubled him that those casualties never got as much attention as Americans killed in Iraq.

Dr. PRYOR: There's always thousands and thousands of kids being killed every year. But of course, we get used to that fact, and we have, you know, a lot of other things that we need to worry about—international events—and sometimes it gets off our radar screen. But now the violence seems to be getting worse again, and that's why I think it's back again.

ROSE: John Pryor did everything he could to put the violence at home back on the national radar screen, contributing op-ed articles to the Washington Post and the Philadelphia Inquirer. 'There's a war at home raging every day,' he wrote in an article last year 'for the Post, filling our trauma centers with so many wounded children that it sometimes makes Baghdad seem like a quiet city in Iowa.'

Doctor **BILL SCHWAB** (Chief, Division of Traumatology and Surgical Critical Care, University of Pennsylvania): This guy has lived and breathed this creed of service and honor and duty. It just - all over his life, no matter what phase of his life you look at.

ROSE: Bill Schwab is chief of trauma care at the University of Pennsylvania, where he was Pryor's teacher and mentor. He says Pryor was a brilliant surgeon with big, gentle hands and tremendous devotion to his patients.

Dr. SCHWAB: My sadness is that we don't have John personally, but we don't have John as the next generation of leaders in American medicine. I think we've lost a great, great contributor for the future.

ROSE: Pryor also served as chief medical adviser to the Red Cross of Southeastern Pennsylvania. CEO Tom Foley says Pryor knew he was signing up for a dangerous assignment in Iraq.

Mr. TOM FOLEY (CEO, Southeastern Pennsylvania Chapter, Red Cross): He was very aware that he was in harm's way. That just is the way this guy was from the time he was a young teenager.

ROSE: Pryor was certified in CPR by the time he was 14. He leaves behind a wife and three young children. As Pryor told NPR in 2007, he'd seen many families try to cope with the loss of a loved one from the other side.

(Sound bite of phone call)

Dr. PRYOR: It's 50 or 60 times a year I have to walk into that emergency room and tell somebody that their son is dead, and that is the motivation for us to work harder.

ROSE: Funeral services for John Pryor are scheduled for Monday at the Cathedral Basilica of Saints Peter and Paul in downtown Philadelphia, which has hosted funerals for some of the city's most revered citizens. For NPR News, I'm Joel Rose in Philadelphia.

Wednesday, December 31

I returned to your house with just enough time to change before driving to the funeral home.

You were heading home from Dover AFB.

Carmela, Dad and I waited on the front porch. Presently, a motorcade of police cruisers commandeered the street, lights flashing for a full block. Your hearse turned into the driveway, and we entered the funeral home.

When you were ready, Steve retrieved us from the anteroom. Parlor doors opened, revealing a mirrored mahogany coffin bearing a folded triangle of the American flag.

Chills.

Asphyxiation.

Time dilation.

Like a movie, the room blurred with only the coffin in focus. I could see how people pass out at times like this.

We reached the coffin, and Carmela's legs gave out. She collapsed over the coffin, crying, grieving, angry, frightened. If you only knew, John—oh, if you had a clue that this would happen …

When we returned home, Steve's wife arrived with a big book of floral arrangements. One by one, each family member sat with her to select a standing spray or bouquet.

I was last and picked an arrangement at random.

"What would you like it to say?" she asked.

I thought for a moment.

"Liberal ass brother," I said.

"Pardon me," she said. "What did you say?"

"Liberal. Ass. Brother."

Thursday, January 1

We dropped off your suit and placed your posters around the parlor. The one of you in scrubs would be next to the casket. Laptops were placed where people would see them while in line. The rooms were filled with flowers.

Arrangements were set for the private family wake on Friday, followed by the public wake on Saturday and Sunday.

Friday, January 2

Friday morning, Dad approached me saying he wanted to "talk to Steve" about something before the family wake. I knew what this was about—I was thinking the same thing.

We had to see you.

Good or bad or horrible—I needed to confront your "remains" or regret it the rest of my life. I needed to see you. I needed to see the extent of your trauma, because from my experience in the ER, I can imagine some pretty messed-up shit.

Steve understood the look in our eyes, having seen it countless times in relatives of traumatic deaths. I was relieved to hear Steve explain you were intact and appeared remarkably good.

"In fact," he said, "I would be amenable to an open casket if you decide." He left us behind closed doors.

We waited.

The parlor doors opened, and we approached the open casket.

It was you. No doubts. They worked hard on your face but couldn't achieve symmetry. Your right orbit drooped, and your cheek sagged. Your hair, buzzed short, revealed sutures in your scalp.

I required no autopsy report or further explanation; clearly, you experienced instant traumatic brain death.

I was glad.

One minute, you were walking—the next, lights out, gone before you hit the ground. No pain. No time to rehash your life. No time to mourn. No guilt. No regrets. I could only hope to be so lucky when I die.

When the rest of me dies.

Steve closed the coffin. Dad and I returned home to retrieve the family.

A few hours later, we all arrived in separate cars. Carm collapsed on the coffin and wept. Danielle cried. Frankie appeared stunned and was crying. I wasn't convinced John John was able to understand. I think he observed the grown ups' emotions and tried to mimic them.

Sophia and Olivia clung to Deidre in another room. We offered them a chance to view the coffin, but both refused to look.

Near the end of our allotted time, Carmela approached me. She wanted to see you, too. I expected it. I spoke with Steve, and he agreed. When everyone left, Carmela and I waited behind closed doors while Steve opened the casket again.

So it was the three of us one final time—me, the consummate third wheel. The dress uniform gloves remained on your hands. It upset Carm because she wanted to touch your hands one last time. She felt you were not presentable for an open casket or for the children.

"Definitely not," she said.

She kissed her fingers and laid them on your forehead.

Saturday / Sunday, January 3-4

Flashing police cruisers filled the street again. A line of mourners had already formed, patiently waiting. Carmela clung to my arm as we stepped past solemn faces and entered the funeral home.

Bouquets surrounded your coffin, lined the walls and spilled over into the other rooms. The sweet smell of fresh flowers, so scarce in my life that their fragrance reminds me of funerals, overwhelmed the senses.

You got your flowers.

Facing the casket, a line would emerge from the adjacent room to the right with a family receiving line to the left. FBI agents stood guard at the entrances and patrolled the grounds outside.

For two days, morning and afternoon, a continuous line of mourners slowly paid respects. I greeted each one, accepted condolences and warmly thanked them for taking the time to come.

Hundreds.

Surgical colleagues, hospital physicians, fellows, students, nurses, staff, neighbors—the line stretched outside onto the sidewalk. Officers in full military dress stood at attention and saluted your coffin. One, an Asian man, paused for a minute and slowly bowed before you.

Former patients, failing to control the tears, explained how you had helped them, saved them, or sustained their family through times of tragedy. One man guided his adult son through the line. Uncoordinated gait, tracheostomy scar, and dysphasia, the residual evidence of some horrible trauma he'd suffered.

"Your brother saved my son's life," the man said, choking back tears.

Strangers, hearing your story in the news, felt compelled to come. Combat veterans from Vietnam, Korea, even World War II, would not neglect a fallen comrade.

New Jersey Governor Jon Corzine arrived to convey his condolences. The New Jersey State flag, as well as the New York State flag, would fly at half mast on Monday.

Sunday evening, a full house lingered for the final goodbye. Father Frank recited a sermon and blessing. Then he invited guests to share memories of you. Shawn Brimhall and Paul Lonczak described you throwing Joe Fox off the cliff at Tupper Lake. They placed a Troop 30 patch on your coffin to be buried with you.

Finally, I stood before the crowd, in front of your coffin.

"Before there was Carmela," I said, "before he was a doctor and before he was on the football team, there was simply my brother John.

"When we moved to Clifton Park, we didn't have any friends, so we just played with each other. I think we invented one-on-one football. In the front yard of our corner lot, we faced off against each other. There'd be a kick-off, and enough hang time would allow a tackle just after the catch.

"We'd line up along the scrimmage, hike the ball and begin the count: one-Mississippi, two-Mississippi, three-Mississippi, while scrambling back and forth. By tossing the ball in a steep incline, we learned how to pass to ourselves.

"Back and forth, up and down the yard, running, tackling, laughing. The score never mattered. We accumulated grass stains and bruises, playing until the sun set and twilight enveloped us, until we barely made out the white laces in the darkness.

"Finally, when it was too dark to see, the final punt would land, invisible, with the distinctive sound of a football bouncing on asphalt.

"It was time to go home."

Remaining friends and family filed out and, for a moment, I was alone with you. I placed my hand on the mirrored mahogany, turning my head away, fighting back the tears.

Obscured by his cloak, an unearthly figure stood hidden in the shadows; boney hands and a glint off the sickle betrayed his concealment.

DEATH had come to pay his respects.

Monday, January 5

Four limousines and a full police escort idled outside the funeral home. When the family arrived we began our procession from Moorestown to the Basilica in Philadelphia. Police stopped traffic at every intersection, standing at attention and saluting as we drove past.

The display tore my heart.

Outside the Basilica, a horde of reporters gathered, aiming cameras as you were lifted past an honor guard, up the stairs and into the church. Chris Sheridan, Brian McClintock, Ben Braslow, Francesco and cousin Michael, among others, served as your pallbearers. Carmela and the kids followed and then me and my family.

I stepped inside the cathedral, stunned and vertiginous at the scene. Absolute and complete silence, save nothing—neither cough nor whisper—belied the sight of thousands crowded in the pews and lining the walls. I advanced up the aisle, recognizing sorrowful faces in the crowd, struggling to maintain my composure.

Katie Fitzpatrick spoke, as did Dr. Schwab, then Father McElvoy, who delivered your eulogy. John John squirmed like a four-year-old in church, finally forcing Nella to remove him to the foyer.

McElvoy spoke about God and how he should comfort us in times of tragedy. I tried not to think of God, tried not to imagine how a compassionate God might allow you a few seconds leeway, in any direction, that would spare your life. I tried not to think that the odds of a rocket hitting you were so inconceivably small that it took an act of God to have a hand in it.

I tried.

The procession rolled into Colestown Cemetery, your new home. Carmela, Mom, Dad and your kids were given roses to lay on the coffin; the rest of us received red carnations.

Presiding over the burial was General Erik Schoonmaker, Surgeon General of the United States Army. Reciting propaganda that lost any meaning long ago, he praised your effort in the global war on terror and the operation in Iraq. Seven rifles were raised into the air and fired off three volleys for a twenty-one gun salute. Helicopters from PennStar, SouthStar and the state flew over in formation before one veered off, representing the "missing man."

The color guard removed your coffin flag and began to fold it. Without enough slack at the end, they were forced to unfold it and try again. As they faltered a second time, your ghost appeared next to me.

"We could do better in the Scouts," you whispered.

I know, right? I thought, *maybe we fucked around, but at least we could fold a flag.*

Schoonmaker knelt before Mom, Carmela and the kids, presenting each with a flag and duplicates of the meaningless medals you won. Roses were laid, then the carnations. Carmela led Danielle and Frankie away, clutching the triangular flag, sobbing, her face twisted in misery.

Out the rear window of the limousine, your coffin remained, alone, waiting to be lowered into the cold earth. The image will never fade—that moment we left you, in that box, in that grave. Even now, I can't help avoid the image of you laying in the dark, in silence, under the ground.

At least, I'll always know where you are.

☙

Eleven days elapsed from notification to burial. Time slowed, and it literally felt like a month had passed. The burden of it all—your "remains," the wake, the service and your burial—had finally lifted. But this, like a college commencement, was not the end, but a beginning.

We set forth along a new timeline, one in which you no longer exist. I became bitter and resentful of that alternate reality, the one where you stopped to tie your shoelace, or the rocket failed to detonate, and you called me on Christmas, shaken by such a close call with DEATH.

The Saturday following your burial, I held a memorial in Clifton Park. Several hundred neighbors, Scouts, friends and ambulance members all came to remember you. I presented a slide show, detailing your life after high school. Few knew about your success in surgery, and no one knew about your military service. You would have loved to have seen everyone.

I returned to work the following Monday. In retrospect, I should have taken more time, but I get my work ethic from you. I wondered, if I had died, how much time you would take from work. Not two weeks—I know that much.

A few weeks later, John Chovanes liaised with the military to return your personal effects. I unwrapped your camera, screen shattered from the blast, and removed the memory card. I powered up the iPhone, only a few weeks old, and checked your voicemail.

"Oh, Lord, oh, Lord Jesus," an urban black-sounding grandmother wailed. "Oh, Lord, Dr. Pryor, why did the good Lord have to take you?"

Many others were the same; older inner city black women lamenting your death.

Who are these people? I thought. *How did they get your number?*

I tried to get down to see Carmela and the kids as much as possible. I even interviewed for a job in Pennsylvania, entertaining the possibility of moving closer to your family, but they chose someone else.

Omar returned from active duty in April and brought his family to your house. I met his wife, Lizzy, children and their newborn son, John Paul.

Named after you.

In the basement, Omar pulled out a laptop, shared unclassified photos of the base and explained the attack.

"Special forces went out hunting," he said. "They got the bastards responsible."

Really? I thought. *They got Cheney and Bush?*

A string of memorials, awards and honors lasted the entire year. Penn held a memorial. Jems and east each created an award in your honor. Fort Dix named their reserve center after you, and *Philadelphia* magazine named you "Best Philadelphian" of 2009. Binghamton, Shenendehowa, a park in Moorestown, a fire department in Delran—every month there was something else. We appreciate the sentiment, but it became very taxing after a while.

And, oh, you were finally promoted to Associate Professor. Posthumously.

Good job.

Now I need to wrap this up and say goodbye.

I often wonder what I would say to you in person if I had the chance. I like to think that words are not necessary—that, in death, you know my thoughts: you know how much you meant to me, how much I lived just to sit with you and talk, how much I tried to be like you, how much I loved you.

How much of me died with you.

I would hope I could be spared the embarrassment of having to say it out loud.

I also hope you've been watching Carmela and your children, that you understand their daily struggle, burdened with grief, anger and despair. Carmela, the woman you wed, mother of your children, promised a life together, now raising three children alone. How you left her holding the motorcycle.

If not, then all I can say is that we miss you, John.

We miss you so much.

Your Liberal Ass Brother,

Rich

What the hell is this? A book isn't supposed to end this way! Sure, the protagonist gets pummeled; obstacles befall him, failure plagues him. But he forges ahead, against insurmountable odds, to claim redemption, success, victory!

He doesn't *die*.

Americans are accustomed to a Hollywood ending. We expect a happily ever after.

Not this crap.

But wait, all is not lost. There is still hope for a Hollywood ending. You may think it's a cop-out, but it's really not.

Honest.

Okay, it's a cop-out for me, but not necessarily for you.

John Pryor thought in very broad terms. He viewed his life as one thread in the fabric of the universe. His motivation was not only to improve his own life but to lift humanity as a whole.

Had he lived, John would have continued to teach and inspire but in a limited realm of influence, restricted to his immediate space and time.

And this book never would have been written.

But now, John Pryor has the potential to reach across time and space, crossing boundaries and transcending generations.

The Hollywood ending is still possible with you. He never met you, but he cared about you. He'd be the first to pull over if you crashed your car. He'd lose sleep treating your illness or injury. He cared about you because he cared about his fellow man, and saw the good in everyone.

As I survey American society, it's easy to feel despair. Hypocrisy spews from our politicians; bombastic commentators pull nonsense out of their asses and broadcast it as journalism; millionaire celebrities lament about exhausting photo shoots; reality television shows abound, filled with the dregs of society, both criminal and surgically augmented; and financial predators, believing they're entitled to million-dollar bonuses, hide their thievery behind legal technicalities.

Isn't there anyone genuine out there? Just one example of an honest man not looking to feed his ego, get on television or make unscrupulous wealth? Is there a single example I can respect? Who might inspire me to improve my life instead of thinking, "Look at them; they're not working, so why should I?"

Is there no one who lives for the principles of helping their fellow man instead of worshiping the almighty dollar? Is there anyone I can admire who encourages me to work harder, who leads me forward, toward a positive life?

There was one.

He was my inspiration, my mentor, my brother.

If you learn one lesson from his life, then he has not died. If his story inspires you to serve others, to join an ambulance, to apply to medical school, to serve your country … if you hear a little voice telling you to *go help* and you found the inspiration in these pages to act on that voice, then he has not died. If you read this book and feel a sense of humanity, then he has not died.

If you listen to that inner voice, you may find yourself joining the ranks of those like John Pryor, the unsung heroes of life. You won't find them on television or in the movies. Their lives are not glamorous. They don't generate much revenue, and they're not the center of attention. But, they are the keepers of the very core of who we are.

They guard our humanity.

If you pick up the flag and carry it forward, you can help ensure the survival of qualities sorely missing: integrity, honesty, altruism and humanity.

The final chapter of John's life does not end with his death.

It ends with you holding this book.

STOP!

You have reached the end.

What follows is intended for new members of *The Grief Club*.

If you are asking, "What's the Grief Club?"
then you're probably not in it.

If you're not in The Grief Club, you'll want to skip this part.

Really.

Go browse the appendix or, if it's late, this would be
a good time to turn off the light and hit the hay.

The Grief Club

The word "Doctor" comes from the Latin verb, *Docere*, to teach. John Pryor epitomized this definition by teaching clinical skills, writing papers, lecturing and sharing his experiences both on 9-11 and in Iraq.

So, to write a book about John Pryor without sharing what I have learned since his death is pure negligence. The purpose of this chapter is to provide, at least another perspective, if not actual support, to those in similar circumstances of grief and loss. I am not qualified to provide psychological counseling, so my words should be viewed as opinion, not therapy.

છ

To understand grief, one must first understand loss. To understand loss, we require a language to communicate that loss. If the language is correct, the impact and meaning become clear.

A plane travels from New York to Los Angeles with two hundred aboard. Mid-flight, one person suffers a heart attack and, unfortunately, dies.

The above paragraph may or may not elicit an emotional response. But let me change the language a bit.

A plane travels from New York to Los Angeles with two hundred aboard. Mid-flight, the *pilot* suffers a heart attack and, unfortunately, dies. There is no co-pilot, and no one else can fly the plane.

Now you may be thinking, "Oh, shit!"

Person. Pilot.

The same is true when we try to articulate loss. I crashed my car—no response. I crashed my Ferrari 308GTS—oh, crap! My computer was stolen—meh; my computer, with four years of Doctoral thesis data, was stolen—oh, shit! My cat died—no response; the cat I've had for eighteen years died—still, no response.

You get the idea.

Unless you knew the relationship I had with my brother, you will not understand my loss when he died. We all have friends and family members who die, but our language fails to differentiate routine deaths from tragic ones.

Our language lacks a word to describe that special person in our lives, that *Most Important Person* who stands above all others. Not everyone has a Most Important Person—those of you who don't won't fully appreciate what I'm getting at.

For the rest, you know who I mean. The Most Important Person is the one you look to for guidance, the one who gets you through tough times, the first person you call when you get a new job, the one who *listens to you* when you're sad. He or she is the person you can't possibly live without, the one you want to go through life with.

To define this person, I've broadened the term "Talisman" to include the Most Important Person. With the added meaning, we can imagine a conversation in the future:

"My grandmother died."

"That's too bad." She was probably old, probably no big deal.

"She was my Talisman."

"Oh, god, I'm so sorry!"

When your Talisman dies, you will embark on a long, tempestuous, process into a new realm without him or her. Following the initial shock, you may find yourself indoctrinated by members of The Grief Club. Grief, despair and anger will persist; the length of time is different for everyone, but it ultimately becomes very fatiguing. Recovery is slow, and reaching a "new normal" is difficult.

Initial Shock

What do you do when your Talisman dies?

What do you do when a nuclear bomb explodes in Manhattan?

This is the analogy. This is the personal equivalent of a nuclear bomb in NYC. You never thought it possible, couldn't even consider such a scenario. But now it's happened. The absolute worst thing has happened.

The adrenergic fight and flight response kick you into survival mode. The immediate crisis demands all of your attention, and there are pressing tasks at hand: funeral arrangement, financial demands, managing the children, rescheduling work—life will not stop for you.

Fortunately, during this initial period, you will have help. Empathy abounds with the tragedy fresh in the minds of friends, family, coworkers, and, possibly, parishioners. Sincere offers are spoken, usually phrased like, "If there's anything I can do to help, anything, call me, okay?"

During this time, confusion may arise between what you actually need and what people think you need. Friends may want to provide meals when you really need them to pick up the kids. You will appreciate the help, but be assertive in explaining what you really need.

Take it one day at a time. This is a hard phase, but it passes quickly.

Indoctrination

When I returned to work, some colleagues welcomed me into The Grief Club. Coworkers, acquaintances, even strangers approached me, retelling tragic stories of loss. People I've known for years suddenly felt comfortable confiding in me about a loss they had kept secret.

"I lost a brother in Vietnam."

"My son was killed in a shooting."

"My father died of cancer."

"When my step-mother died, I cried for a year."

These are not deaths. These are tragedies. Stories retold in breaking voices and tearing eyes, as if the loss had just occurred. They are shared in confidence because you will understand, because you are now a member of The Grief Club.

This indoctrination taught me two things. First, only people who experience grief will understand grief. Second, some wounds never heal. Tragic loss is never resolved. It may remain cocooned and hidden, suppressed daily. But it remains there, waiting for the right trigger, an image, a smell, a video, to make an unexpected and unwelcome recurrence.

A Word About Condolences

Accepting condolences was very hard for me. My brother and I spent our lives rescuing and helping others. I found it very difficult to be on the receiving end.

In attempt to provide comfort, people will say some really dumb ass things. You may infer some comments as insulting. Opinions about what happened, afterlife predictions, and justification for a deity's actions might instigate anger or distress.

Let it pass.

This is no time to be petty. Be gracious, smile, say "Thank You" while thinking, *what a twit*. Allow the comments to roll over you. People generally mean well, even if what they say seems offensive.

Grief, Despair and Anger

In days to weeks after the initial shock, friends and most family members will return to their lives. For them, the loss is unfortunate, but they quickly "get over it." But for you, it is far from over. While everyone else resumes normalcy, you will enter a miasma of Grief, Despair and Anger.

Grief entails waking up crying, crying during the day and going to bed crying. It will collapse you, hitting you out of nowhere and double you over. Everyone is different. For me, this lasted about a year and a half.

I define Despair as any decrease in the will to live. I imagine my will to live decreased 80 percent. Everyone is different. Some will experience less; some may contemplate suicide. I never thought of suicide, but if diagnosed with cancer, I wouldn't be interested in treating it.

Anger is normal. I was angry at John for joining the Army, which led to his death, but I would be angry regardless of how he died. Anger that he's dead, that he left us, that I'm forced to live my life without him.

The period of Grief, Despair and Anger is very difficult. These are rough waters beyond the initial attention and support and the eventual "healing" stage that comes later.

Helping you through this difficult time is your existing support network of friends, family and coworkers. Know that there will be people who help—just not the people you thought.

What happened to my friends?

Few will understand what this means for you. Even if they do, *they really won't know what it means for you.* Even members of The Grief Club have had time to resolve much of their pain and grief. So:

Rule One: Don't expect anyone to understand how you feel.

Rule Two: Relationships will change.

Hidden within the pages of your address book are members of The Grief Club. They may not be your closest friends, but they will have a better understanding of your tragedy. As such, close friends may fade while casual acquaintances will begin to call regularly.

What I'm saying is that some will "get it," and some will not. You will not be able to predict who.

A few friends won't be able to cope with your grief, like you suddenly took on too much baggage. Also, if the worst-case scenario can happen to you, it can happen to them. This uncomfortable possibility may drive some away.

Frustration may force other friends away. Grief is very draining, not only for you but also for your relationships. The inability for others to help may cause fatigue and exasperation, causing them to distance themselves.

Finally, most will "get over it" more quickly than you. To everyone else, this is a death, not a tragedy. This was not their Talisman. Viewed as a routine death, they might wonder why you still mourn.

Fatigue

Grief, Despair and Anger may last months to years. You will get sick of it. Your wife will get sick of it. Your friends will get sick of it. Your kids will … you get the idea. After a while, you'll wonder if there will ever be relief, peace.

When will it end?

Through it all, you are forced to confront routine stressors of life: sick children, a busted water heater, a car accident, coworkers calling in. The grief you bear will exacerbate routine stressors. Life becomes that much harder.

It's like you're the pilot of a plane that loses a wing. While you struggle, fighting desperately to keep the aircraft alight, passengers may remain blissfully ignorant of the problem. Likewise, your co-workers may be unaware you cried all the way to work that morning.

When you have cried your eyes dry and beat your fists numb, you may be forced with a horrible decision: "forget about them," or the grief will consume you.

You may feel this is a "Sophie's Choice" problem. Allow the grief to destroy you or forget about them.

What'll it be?

Luckily, you don't have to choose.

Rule Three: Discarding grief is not discarding your Talisman.

Recovery

Things will *change* over time. I'm reluctant to say "better." In a way, you won't want to get better. You may feel getting better means the loss isn't important anymore. You might fear getting over it means forgetting your Talisman or that others will forget them.

As my grief diminished, it was replaced with yearning. I can't comprehend John's death. All I know is that he's missing. My family spends a weekend with Carmela and the kids at Ocean City, and he's not there. We have dinner, and he's not there. There's a laugh or a birthday or an ER visit, and he's not there.

He's not dead; *he's missing.*

The other feeling I experience is sadness. It pervades my life. Every laugh with my children is tempered by sadness, sadness that John will never laugh like this with his children. Every birthday, movie or vacation is another event my brother won't share with his family.

New Normal

I cannot imagine a more loathsome phrase than *The New Normal*. I may be forced to live in this alternate universe where John is dead, but I refuse to call it normal. The loss of your Talisman is an emotional wound that will never "heal."

Tempus sanat omnia vulnera. Time heals all wounds.

This is not entirely true; ask any paraplegic.

Some wounds heal. Some do not. Some wounds will change you into a different person. Burns to your face will change the way you look forever. The loss of a limb will change your ability to function forever.

The "new normal" might never be as good as the old normal.

After two years, I entered a stage of utter fatigue. It's a feeling of "Okay, I give up; where is he? No, really, I don't want to play anymore. I want to have a beer with my brother now." If I had this feeling at my job, I would quit and look for a new job. If it was my marriage, I would seek a divorce. It's the feeling of "okay, I put up with this as long as I could, but now things have to change, or I'm going to lose it."

This is my new normal.

What to Do

I can't tell you what to do. I don't know you. Even if I did know you, I wouldn't tell you what to do. I will say that you will find a way to get through it. You may not want to get through it; you may want to lie down and die or let someone else take care of life, but if you are like me, these are not options.

Time marches on, and it will drag you along, kicking and screaming.

I can tell you what I did or how I stumbled through life without losing my sanity. It wasn't easy.

There are probably resources at your disposal that I didn't utilize. Hundreds of grief books line bookshelves, attentive grief counselors will sit and listen and discussion groups abound on the Internet. You may have a religious community to provide support.

As with anything in life, I encourage you to try what interests you; use what works, and discard what doesn't.

I read only one book.

I've always been a fan of the rock band Rush. The drummer, Neil Peart, suffered a terrible loss of both his daughter and wife. Surely, this man knew about grief. Seeking guidance, reassurance, maybe a word of support, I read his book *Ghost Rider: Travels on the Healing Road*.

Neil's response to grief entailed quitting the band, embarking on a motorcycle tour of North America while lodging at five-star resorts, sipping brandy and smoking cigars. He took a year.

A physician acquaintance shared his experiences in The Grief Club. An eight-month sabbatical was enough for him to get his head together. He advised me to do the same. Another friend lost his brother and left work for a year. A third acquaintance suffered the death of her twin sister. She claimed disability for clinical depression.

Unfortunately, I didn't have a million dollars to spend on a cross-country therapy ride; I couldn't afford to leave work, and hitting the dole wasn't an option.

That left one final option: Suck It Up and get back to work.

So that's what I did. And it may be what you have to do. It's hard, but you can do it. Here's how.

Grief

Cry. A lot. Don't fight the tears. When it hits, find a solitary place and let it out. For the first few months, I cried all the way to work and all the way home. At work, when the grief struck, I found a secluded conference room to collapse and sob.

Get it out. Wipe your face, and get back to work.

Do not burden friends with your grief. You'll just ruin their day, and they won't be able to improve yours.

Friends will call and ask, "How are you doing?"

The answer is, "Good."

Anything else, they won't understand or want to hear. Expressing grief months after a loss is an invitation for disaster. This is when friends will provide comments like, "You need to {insert dumb-ass statement here}." It doesn't help.

There will be good days and bad days. Speak to your friends only on the good days.

Despair

Recognize your reduction in the will to live. This may be defined as depression or grief or both. I fully expected to share my entire life with John, well into old age. He was the person who kept me going. With his death, I wondered what I had to live for.

Fight despair with activity. This is very difficult because you will lack motivation. As a runner, I literally had to force myself out the door. Absent any motivation or joy, I viewed my running as a means of survival. Without it, I would spiral into an irretrievable abyss.

Force yourself to continue activities you performed before the death. Again, there will be no joy, no happiness, but you need function. Think of it as distasteful medicine you need to swallow to remain healthy.

Rule Five: When it's sink or swim, keep swimming.

Remember, others are depending on you. The loss of your life or functionality will be an exponential burden on the ones you love. There's already been one loss. If you check out, it will be that much worse. You may not realize it now, *but you are a Talisman to others.*

Anger

The anger can be overwhelming, especially at times of increased stress. I recommend screaming at the top of your lungs while alone in the car.

Another outlet I found cathartic is writing. Write the lost Talisman every day: tell him/her what a bastard they are and how stupid they were. Explain, in writing, how bad things have been since the death. Write your feelings, list your grievances, and explain your perspective.

You may want to visit the grave and admonish the loved one in person. I haven't done this personally, but I can see the benefits.

Sanity

Each of us has a baseline capacity for handling stress. With the death of your Talisman, this capacity will be diminished. Our normal reserve to handle increased stressors is quickly depleted. A flat tire, a problem at work, a sick child, stressful events that could routinely be handled may cause acute panic or anxiety.

Rule Six: You will feel as if you've lost control.

Four months after John died, my job was eliminated. Faced with possible unemployment, I felt pushed to the edge. I now understood the term "nervous breakdown.'" I experienced panic attacks, wondering how I was going to survive.

I can see how people snap. Start with the death of a Talisman, lose the will to live, add in some overwhelming stressors—voilà! Next thing you know, you're atop a bell tower, gambling your life savings in Vegas or lying shit-faced in a gutter.

Nobody talks about how close they came to the edge. We only hear about those who snapped, who went postal, who fell into the abyss. It's not a happy place to be, and no one is proud of it.

When your nerves are rattled, when you feel sanity slipping from your grasp, realize what is happening. Stop and say, "I'm losing it. I need to get back in control."

Take a break—a few minutes, an hour, a day. Call in a favor from a "Really, anything I can do to help" friend and ask them to watch the kids. Call in sick. Go see a movie. Take stock in your assets. Formulate a plan. Laugh, and shake your fist, shouting, "Is this all you can do to me?" Call up your support network. Talk to your counselor.

Don't give in to the insanity.

Hold tight, and weather the storm. The skies will clear.

The skies will clear.

Pain

You are experiencing horrible, emotional pain. Ordinarily, our first response to pain is to find ways of relieving it.

Many seek counseling; others take antidepressants. Many people turn to alcohol or drugs to ease their pain. Some will change their behavior, move, run away, quit their job, obsessively engage in some activity.

My problem with these measures is that, in the end, John would still be dead. No amount of counseling or antidepressants would bring him back.

There is another option.

Instead of trying to rid the pain, you can accept it, embrace it.

When the dog bites your arm and won't let go, don't fight him, pet him, name him. Wear your pain like an uncomfortable pair of shoes.

If you learn to live with the pain, it becomes bearable. It slowly fatigues, dissolving into the background like a bad smell.

It Could Be Worse

As bad as things are you need to keep in mind that it can get worse. Things can always get worse.

Obviously, some circumstances are beyond your control. How you respond to those circumstances are within your control. Better or worse, depends on your response to the stressors that arise.

Quitting your job will make it worse. Being drunk will make it worse. Leaving your family will make it worse. Not taking care of yourself and getting sick will make it worse. Trying to hurt yourself will make it worse. Giving up will make it worse.

Rule Seven: Don't make it worse.

Redemption

My mentor, Richie Cantor, occasionally provides expert testimony for physicians in malpractice cases. Lawyers frequently try to discredit him.

"Are you getting paid to provide your testimony today, Dr. Cantor?"

"Yes," he would say, "but I donate it to the children's hospital."

"You donate your fee to the children's hospital?"

"Yes."

"Why do you do that?"

"Because it's the only good that can come of this."

Your loss is tragic. It's horrible. It is, in every sense, a nightmare.

But can any good come of it? Is there any redemption? Could your tragedy teach others, could it prevent future tragedies? If yes, then it is your responsibility to make it happen.

Some people form foundations, volunteer organizations, support groups. Some write books. It's your job to see what good can come of this and make it happen.

Final Thoughts

The Talisman is meant to be lost. In mythology, the Mentor or teacher must die so the Hero can be born.

In your life, you thought your Talisman was the hero, but you're wrong. That person was here to help you, guide you and teach you. But now that he is gone, you are the hero. You have become the Talisman.

So I will dispense with saying, "You'll get over it" or "You'll find someone else someday," and say this:

Don't give up.

When you're tired, drink coffee and keep going. When the grief hits, close the door and let it out. Cry, scream, beat your head; then wipe away the tears and get back to work.

Suck up all the emotion and reality when your Talisman dies and use it as energy to forge ahead. The kids are relying on you. You are their last line of defense—you're the wall. I know you had no idea how serious this was going to be; none of us did before it happened. But you have the experience and the skills to get it done.

You will not fail.

Appendix

A Hero in Scrubs
by Christine M. Flowers
Philadelphia Daily News

John Pryor would have frowned at all the attention.

Like so many truly good men, he was humble. While so many athletes and movie stars give little and claim much, he gave life with his hands and claimed nothing in return.

This was a person you encounter once or twice in a lifetime if you're lucky. Fortunately, many Philadelphians were.

And because they had the privilege of knowing him, they gathered at the cathedral this week to mourn. But, mostly, they were there to celebrate a luminous soul that burned brightly among them all too briefly.

We all know the sad, skeletal facts of a life made public on the front pages over the last few days. Pryor was the leader of the trauma team at the Hospital of the University of Pennsylvania, where he'd worked since 1999.

He was married to Carmela, a pediatrician, and they had three young children. He was from Albany, N.Y., a Boy Scout, a Catholic, a teacher, a soldier. A healer. A man who would have laughed at the idea of being thought special, but who was clearly better than most of us will ever be.

After the Twin Towers crashed on 9/11, he rushed to New York and worked through the night at Ground Zero. He wanted to be in the thick of it, healing wounds and grieving for those he couldn't save.

He wasn't a mere observer but the most compassionate of participants. He was also angered by the carnage in Philadelphia, having watched too many young men die "without honor, without purpose, for no country, for no one," as he wrote in a poignant essay in the Washington Post.

He joined the Army Reserve Medical Corps and went to Iraq in 2006, and then again on Dec. 6, to care for those who, contrary to the fallen in our own streets, did have honor, purpose and country.

He was killed by an enemy mortar on Christmas Day. He was 42.

When people die, we often say, "What a pity," or "What a shame." We cry, we shake our heads or, in those cases where death is a welcome relief because it ends a long Calvary of pain, we say, "It's a blessing."

But when someone like Pryor loses his life, none of those fit. Priests can try to find some meaning in Scripture to comfort us, and loved ones can look back and try to seek solace in memories, but the loss of a person of this caliber is something that simply can't be rationalized.

Sad to say, but the vast majority of deaths are painful for only a small circle, those who had close contact with the deceased. In other cases, such as when one of the world's bad guys draws his last breath, death can be a source of celebration.

But there's no joy anywhere in the passing of Pryor. In a world where evil abounds and bad people roam freely to prey on the innocent, he was a hope for the future. As a very wise person once wrote, hope sees the invisible, feels the intangible and achieves the impossible.

Pryor saw the invisible, the slim but real possibility that the killing in this, his adopted city, might one day end.

He felt the intangible, the pain that his brothers and sisters experienced when they were wounded on the battlefield, and made it his own. He achieved the impossible: complete and total devotion to something other than self. He was his brother's keeper, when so many of those brothers only care about the reflection in the mirror.

It's easy to canonize someone who dies under such tragic circumstances. But Pryor was the kind of guy who'd be the first to rip off the halo and say, I'm just a human, lady, stop with the melodrama.

And that's why he deserves the accolades and the front-page tributes, the endless line of mourners and the endless trail of tears.

He was an exceptional man who never acknowledged just how exceptional he was.

He was a father who loved his wife and kids, but also cared for the bleeding strangers brought to him in the emergency rooms and on the battlefield. He took himself out of himself, and reached out toward humanity.

How many of us do that, especially those who have so much to lose?

Some lives are expendable. This one was not.

Philadelphia mourns you, Dr. Pryor.

Manifesto
by John Pryor

On My Future as a Person

There comes a time in life when we re-evaluate who we are, why we are here, and who we want to be. For most of us, this 'midlife crisis' comes in the mid-thirties. I had a midlife crisis about ten years ago, and I got over it very well. At that time, my concerns were about succeeding in life, making major choices in my private and professional life and coming to grips with my own mortality. In retrospect, I am confident that I made the right choices, have succeeded in my career and am now comfortable with the inevitability of death. After finishing fellowship and starting at Penn, I suddenly found myself at the top of the proverbial hill that I have been climbing for the last 35 years. I look around, see the nice view and now feel a sense of emptiness about what to do next. My day-to-day life is very enjoyable, especially my family and the extra time I get to spend with them. However, my future, which has always been so structured and clear, is now muddled. I feel more lost now then I ever did in my life. After years of reflection, I have come to realize that the remaining years of my life can be spent in a finite number of ways.

I can continue to practice surgery, move up the academic ladder, take a new academic position every five years, become a division head, hopefully someday chairman, have a portrait done and if all goes right, have a lecture series named after me when I die.

I can quit academics, go into private practice, get to know my patients well, work a lot, miss my kids soccer games, try to make it up with stereo systems and cars, retire in the Caribbean and leave my kids plenty of money to fight over when I die.

I can change careers altogether, go to law school, cause my family great financial pain, start the new career as a forty year old rookie, consult a lot, write a book, and retire early. Frankly, none of these sound appealing.

Since these are the 'traditional', 'accepted' and 'normal' paths of pursuit, any alternative to them will be considered 'radical' or 'stupid'. I understand that any choices I make will profoundly effect my family, especially my wife and children. However, I have made countless sacrifices in pursuing a"traditional" path in life, specifically because of my family. I am ready now to make the choices that allow me to justify my life. In short, I have decided to dedicate a significant portion of my remaining life to improving the equality of health care to people throughout this country and the world. What this means specifically will be outlined later in this treatise. First, I will try to give a candid portrayal of my thoughts and feelings which ultimately led me to some profound, but not unique conclusions about my life. This is necessary because the question everyone will eventually ask me is, "Why?" It has taken me a lifetime to answer that question and I will try to summarize those thoughts here.

My Relationship to the Universe

Many of the foundations for understanding my role in the "Big Picture" comes from an appreciation of my relationship with the rest of the world and universe. The scale of the universe is incomprehensible, in both directions, from the point on the scale that our world resides. We live on a small planet, next to a small star in a small planetary system on the outskirts of a common, spiral galaxy, expanding amongst billions of galaxies. Recently the Hubble Telescope was pointed to a small section of the sky where there was no known objects. This "deep space" observation revealed an image of thousands of previously unseen galaxies, scattered across the field like salt spilled on the table. When I look at this endlessness—this proof that time and the universe are boundless—our world, all of our known existence seems completely irrelevant. Even more, the immensity of mass and energy of the universe is dwarfed by the nothingness that separates these objects. Distances are incomprehensible, and light from some very distant stars takes millions of years to reach Earth. When we look out to the night sky, we are literally seeing into the past, as light from those distant stars finally reaches our speck of a planet. Some stars that we see now have exploded into dust thousands of years ago, unbeknown to us until the light from the supernova one day finds its way here.

Looking down the scale of our world is even more disturbing. All of the mass we experience is made up of atoms that are specks of mass dispersed in vast nothingness. Even the atoms themselves are 99% empty space and 1% mass. When the subatomic particles that make up the atom are broken down further and further, it is realized that there is really is no mass at all, only manipulations of energy. We are made from nothingness and live in a vacuum of a universe.

Our whole existence is a quirk of physics caught between these extremes of scale. Some would argue that this is the miracle of human experience—that among all this impossibility, there is life. Perhaps, pathologically, this is always on my mind. The most devastating weather storm or colossal earthquake is barely a ripple compared to the collision of galaxies or the compression of matter to singularity in a black hole. I see all of my life within this context. Sometimes when faced with life events, I can not help but hear the words of that great poet, John Belushi, chanting, "It just doesn't matter."

All Humans as One Entity

I think one of the biggest mistakes we have made as a species is identifying the individual human being as a distinct entity. It has become clear to me that all human beings are really a single entity—each human person being a piece of the whole organism. This is easy to prove to yourself—sit on the couch and ask someone to get a drink of water for you. Without moving you would not be able to get the water, but with the ability to speak, and to be understood, another human being becomes part of your volition. For this period of time the two of you are connected, performing a single task. The signaling between the two humans is no different than hormonal signaling within an individual human being. Humans live in proximity of each other for the benefit of sharing tasks, not unlike the evolution of organ systems in animals. One could even consider the development of a monetary system a Darwinian adaptation of the human organism to perform specific tasks and at the same time benefit from all human effort.

In addition, knowledge and experience is accumulated as a species, not unlike an individual human brain during development. If humans were not all one organism, why would some humans sacrifice themselves for all the others, such as in war? If we are not all one organism, why do we mourn the death of another? Why would we ever need the ability to communicate? I now consider the aggregate human species as really one single organism. As part of that organism, my attention is now drawn to what my role should be for this being. I can not be separated from other individuals, suffering by one is eventually suffering by all. September 11 showed this to all of us.

Opportunity, Fairness, and Equality

I have no illusions of how I got where I am in life. I was born in an affluent state in the wealthiest nation of the world. I had loving, caring, intelligent and hard working parents and grandparents. I was allowed to go to school, and I was never hungry a day in my life. The only time I lived under inadequate shelter is when I did it for fun in the Boy Scouts. I worked, but never had to support myself or anyone else when I was young. I had my college education payed for by my parents, and they continued to support me through medical school. I wanted for nothing in my life growing up.

I am a tall, white male who speaks fluent English. I have never in my life been discriminated against or had my race, or my color used against me. As a physician I am respected immediately without having to earn that respect. I have a job at a prestigious university, a new home and a beautiful wife and children. My cup truly does runneth over.

In the past few years I have come to realize how unfair my life has been. With minimal effort, I have had everything thrown in my lap. I worked hard to succeed, yes—but the barriers were a joke. I started so close to the top, all I had to do was roll over into security and accomplishment.

Everyday I deal with people whose lives are also unfair, but at the opposite pole. Born poor, without supportive parents, without the means to succeed even if they had the ability, these individuals have practically no chance of being successful. The ones that break loose of the cycle of poverty and disadvantage are the truly strong and able. Even with those with a support system, many still have to deal with prejudice, racism, and financial disadvantage. And with all this considered, the most disadvantaged person in this country is still far better off than many people throughout the world. If you are homeless and penniless in this country, and you are hit by a car, you receive medical care without cost. Although far from perfect, there is an entire social service structure to assist everyone in this country, even if you are here illegally! Those without means in many countries simply die from treatable disease, or malnutrition—I understand why people risk their lives to immigrate to our country—being destitute here is far better then surviving in many countries around the world. A Haitian immigrant said once about why he risked his life to come to the u.s., "I want to live in a country where the poor people are fat."

There is no equality in the world. Everyone starts out with a different amount of tokens and on different playing fields. Simply saying that, "this is a free country, anyone can succeed if they work hard enough" is bullshit. In a different circumstance, I wouldn't have made it anywhere in my life. I realize this now, and I need to repay this debt that I owe to the world for the opportunities, and unfair advantage, I had growing up.

The Role of God

I have struggled with my relationship with God for many years. I am not overtly religious—I hardly go to church. Like many scientists, I see God's presence in strange places, like that "deep space" image or looking at a human brain and contemplating the miracle of consciousness. I believe creation and evolution co-exist in the big bang theory, with the 'beginning' at singularity. I am comfortable with accepting some beliefs without evidence, realizing that our capacity to understand the universe is severely limited by our incapacity to understand the universe. I never had any 'visions' or any delusional experiences with God, but I do have very strong dreams that center on a very intense feeling that is hard to describe, I would call it 'love'. The feeling is not directed at anyone, it just consumes me in the dream. The image of Christ has been in these dreams, but the images never speak. One dream that was particularly disturbing had me standing on a mountain top road. A car passed me and flew over the embankment. Soon an image rose from behind the cliff and came to rest in front of me. It was a man dressed in a military uniform. A flood of emotion came over me, with that intense feeling of profound love. The image started towards me and I reached out to touch it, but the image walked past me without touching. I wanted so much to grasp his hand. That dream was several years ago and I still think about it.

I often communicate with an inner consciousness that guides many of my decisions, but I do not feel that this is spiritual. The best religious explanation I can fit this into the presence of the Holy Spirit, which I feel is always waiting somewhere just out of my daily thoughts (I keep it out, actively). The intensity of the dreams is nothing new for me, I have always had very vivid and complex dreams. However, these specific dreams of this intense love are vividly remembered by me in long-term memory.

I do recognize that this part of my person, whether religious or psychological, does affect my decision making. This part of my mind is pushing me towards the ultimate resolution stated below, and is constantly at odds with my pragmatic side (which is very weak).

The Role of My Ancestry

Our family is not only important on a social level, but also in a historical one. Genetically similar humans who are raised within similar environments will obviously develop in a similar manner. Thus looking at ancestry gives insight into how your life may develop. I am not excluding self determination, but trends are more than apparent. My ancestors include several priests, a Christian brother who devoted his life to service in the Philippines, a writer who died in service in WWI, and many others who made significant sacrifices to those less fortunate than themselves. My father dedicated his career to child abuse as a social worker and after retirement became part of the National Red Cross. My mother has shown true compassion for people who are suffering.

Lineage does not obligate me into service, but it does exemplify the fact that my genetic makeup is somehow commensurate with selfless service to others. I have always had a special appreciation for my great uncle who became a Christian Brother. John Pryor took the name Cornelius Luke Pryor when he joined the order at 12 years old. He was an extremely intelligent and dedicated brother. He gave up prestigious positions in desirable locations to serve the "poorest of the poor" in Manila. He was an active teacher until his 90s. This life of dedicated teaching and service has always been attractive to me. Of course, I never had a true religious calling, and I could not imagine my life without my wife and kids—not withstanding, his life has always been an inspiration to me.

I was blessed by two wonderful sets of grandparents. The Italian side taught me about family and *[SIC]*

My Experience in Grenada

My 'punishment' for not putting in any effort in college was banishment to a third world medical school in 1990. As my father once said, "John was rejected from some of the most prestigious medical schools in the country." Actually, it was virtually every medical school, including the University of Buffalo where I eventually graduated from in 1994 (becoming a student that graduated in a class that I was rejected admission to). This punishment turned out to be an educational experience far beyond that of preclinical medicine. I will never forget arriving at the Point Salines airport and getting off the plane. The humid air hit you like a smothering towel. We got into rusted out buses and clanked away to the campus. The bus stopped in the middle of a clearing in the forrest. I asked why we stopped, and the driver said, "We're here."

I said, "We're where?"

"Campus, man."

I was floored. The buildings were remnants of the brick and mortar slapped together when they were built twenty years ago. There were ox and cattle rooming around everywhere. The smell of burning garbage permeated the air—a distinctive smell that reminded me of burning corn. I truly felt like I feel off the face of the earth, and all I could keep saying is that this was the biggest mistake of my life. I mean, there was no TV here, except for the one in the Sugar Shack that we could catch 30 minutes of CNN every night...there was NOT ONE pizza place on the whole island, what the hell was I doing there?

Those first few weeks were very hard, but eventually I started to enjoy life in Grenada, and the love of the island grew over the next two years. I now look back at those years as the best in my life. Why? Well first, and foremost, it is where I met Carmela. We really started together with nothing…our 'kitchen' was a trunk on two chairs with a hotplate on top. We would cook in stages—first the water for the noodles, then hotdogs, then boil water for coffee. Dinner took two hours. We have lots of great memories like that. But what I learned most in the West Indies was how the MAJORITY of people in this world live. Life is slow and simple. Without the many distractions of 'modern' life, life becomes much more enjoyable. For example, we had movie night on Saturday night, in the lecture hall. Everyone showed up every week. No one ever knew or asked what movie was playing, it didn't matter. Without TV or any choices, we all gathered, and appreciated any form of entertainment. I miss that.

Of course the most profound lesson was how medical care is delivered in countries such as Grenada. We had a student in the first year who overdosed on alcohol and drugs—he was found unresponsive in his room and the roommates called an 'ambulance'. Two guys showed up in a van, no medical equipment, and obviously with no medical training. They said, "He's dead." The roommate quickly corrected them by saying he is not breathing but has a pulse. The attendants then lifted him into the van, both got in the front seat and drove off. We got the news that he was dead that morning at lecture.

Another time the bus we used to shuttle between campuses ran over a motorcyclist who lost control around a curve. I hesitated to even get involved, but as a medic I was the only one around with any training. He had a open pelvic fracture, chest injury and dislocated arm (badly). This guy was in a world of hurt. Police arrived and said that there is no ambulance today (something you get used to…no water today, no electricity today…whatever). So we lifted him into a reggae bus—a modified VW bus that functions as a taxi. Another student and I tried to hold immobilization and keep his airway open best we could as the clearly intoxicated driver negotiated the narrow hilltop streets with all the accuracy of a blind man. I knew the patient was going to die, and I was starting to worry about the rest of us as well.

We arrived at the 'hospital'—a shack on a hill top overlooking St. George's. We took him into the accident room where a practitioner looked at him, listened to his chest and said quite definitively, "He is stable." I actually laughed out loud. As I looked around I saw some amazing things. A pair of rubber gloves in a soap solution—these are THE gloves—they are used over and over again. I saw an EKG machine right from the Smithsonian (actually eventually saw the same one several years later at the Buffalo VA—funny). I later heard that he died after having respiratory trouble, not surprising since there are no ventilators on the Island.

And you know what makes medical care on the Island of Grenada different than many other third world countries? It is one of the most modern and competent! For the rest of my career I can not help but be haunted by the massive rift in the level of medical care around the world. When I am in the ICU, adjusting drips and vent settings on a 92 year old who has been on dialysis for ten years who has just had palliative surgery for metastatic cancer, all I can think of is how that student could have been saved with the most basic life support, or how that motorcyclist never had a fucking chance. There needs to be a basic level of medical care afforded to all human beings in all countries, and if that means taking some resources from our system, where blatant excess is allowed to continue, so be it.

My Experience on September 11, 2001

Everything about 9-11 sucked. Every minute of that day is burned into my brain, and I am sure I will go to my grave with memories from everything that happened. As I look back on that day, I realize that the main emotion I was feeling while standing on that pile of ruble, was not anger, but deep sadness. Not only for those involved, and the rescuers who were missing, but for all the soldiers, families, civilians, and others who would die and be hurt in the upcoming response to what happened there. I knew that this was the start of a long war, with many more casualties to come.

After leaving New York, it took a few days to come off the adrenalin. Then a deep and protracted depression came on that lasted weeks. I was a mess. I still have trouble talking about that day, or seeing images of it on TV. However, what I do not have is regrets. I take solace in believing that, however useless, I did everything I possibly could to help that day. I risked my job, my career and at times my life to be there—I have no regrets. That was an important lesson for me. I want to be able to lie in my bed when I get the news that I have aggressive cancer, or when I am having crushing chest pain on way to the cath lab, or am lying bleeding from a RUQ gunshot wound, that I have no regrets from life. That I was a faithful and loving husband. That I raised my kids the best I could. That I loved Danielle, Frankie, and John as much as a human heart could. That I prepared our finances, insurances, trust funds so that they all will be cared for. And that I have completed, to the best of my ability, my life 'to do' list. Without regrets, I will be able to accept death and go gently into that good night. When it becomes my turn to burn alive or jump from 100 stories, I pray for the strength to jump and face death straight on.

That is what I learned from 9-11.

[John's writing ends at this point. I never learned what he was alluding to in the first paragraph but I believe he was thinking of running for politcal office. –RP]

Obituary
John P. Pryor, MD

Dr. John P. Pryor was born in Mount Vernon, New York on January 23, 1966. He lived in Westchester County until his family relocated to Clifton Park, New York at the age of eight. For many years, he was an active member of Boy Scout Troop 30 under the leadership of Michael Lonczak and George Heffelfinger. He attended Shenendehowa high School and was a member of Brent Stuerwald's football program from his freshman year until graduation in 1984.

Dr. Pryor attended the State University of New York at Binghamton where he majored in biochemistry. During that time, he was a member of the Sigma Nu fraternity, played club lacrosse and was the chairman of the local chapter of the college republicans. After college, Dr. Pryor spent a year performing biomedical research in the lab of Dr. Richard Deckelbaum at the Columbia College of Physicians and Surgeons in New York City. He returned to the Albany area in 1989 to take a position as director of the Albany Medical Center remote central monitoring station.

Since an early age, Dr. Pryor was involved in the care of the sick and injured. He was certified in CPR when he was 14 years old, joined the Clifton Park-Halfmoon Ambulance Corp at 17, and became a NY State Emergency Medical Technician at 18. During college he took courses at night to become certified as a prehospital critical care technician and was a member of the Union Volunteer Emergency Squad. Later, upon returning to Albany in 1989, he completed his certification as a full paramedic. He lists Mike McEvoy, Dwight Pakan, Jeff Gotro and Kevin Krause as some of the influential mentors that he had during his EMS career.

Dr. Pryor spent two years at the St. George's University School of Medicine in Grenada, West Indies, an experience that would shape his view of the world, and his privileged station in it, for many years to come. Most importantly, it was here that he met his best friend, and ultimately his wife, Carmela Calvo. He ultimately transferred to the University of Buffalo and completed medical School in 1994. Dr. Pryor was elected into the prestigious Alpha Omega Alpha medical honor society in 1999. He remained in Buffalo to complete general surgery training under the supervision of Ralph Doerr, Jim Hassett, John Ricotta, Roger Seibel, and Eddie Hoover, among many others. After residency, was accepted into a fellowship in trauma and critical care surgery at the University of Pennsylvania. Under the mentorship of C. William Schwab, Donald R. Kauder and Patrick M. Reilly, he completed training and joined the staff as an Assistant Professor of Surgery where he remained until his untimely death.

John and Carmela V. Calvo were Married in April 1996 in Brooklyn New York. His princess, Danielle Nicole was born in 1998, his best little buddy Francis Xavier, was born in 2000, and his namesake and precious little man, baby John, was born in 2004. He is also survived by his mother, Victoria Geraldine and father Richard Christopher Pryor; the two people for which he owes all of his success and happiness. John had one brother, best friend and confidant, Richard Joseph.

Major Pryor joined the United States Army Reserve in Oct 2004, completed Officer Basic Course in 2005 and volunteered for service in Operation Iraqi Freedom. His awards include the …

As a surgeon, and as a citizen, Major Pryor felt very strongly about his duty to serve, especially during wartime. His decision was not supported by those close to him, and it was emotionally very challenging to balance his dedication to his duty and hurting those he loved. He hopes and prays for forgiveness from his family and colleagues.

Appendix

Home
by Major John Pryor

I am on the flight from Dallas Texas to Philadelphia on 25 May, 2006. The trip from Iraq was a blur of long plane rides, endless waiting, torturous out-processing, Army red tape and more waiting. I now have in my hand the DD 214, the Army's get out of jail free card that says I am REFRAD—returned from active duty. It is time to look back on the last four months, tie things up in a big bow, and tuck the entire experience away forever.

Although I look forward to seeing my friends and colleagues, I am anxious about how to handle the conversations. Everyone who has gone through a re-deployment back home has had difficulty speaking to people about the experience. The problem is that there is no short, concise answer to questions like, "How was it over there," or " What was the war like?" If you read my essays, you can see how difficult it would be to summate all of that into a casual sentence or two. Col. Rees, who has gone through several tours, had the best answer when asked about the experience, he just says, "It's nice to be home." I think I will stick with that one.

If you want some other tips about how to handle vets coming back, I have a few. First, thank them for their service. Some people feel awkward about this, but all you have to say is literally, "Thank you for your service." That alone goes a long way to make the vet feel welcome. Secondly, do not ask too many questions. Stick with comments like, "It's nice to see you," or, "Glad you are home." There will be time for stories and questions after the vet has adjusted, and in specific venues like a pub or at home. For combat veterans there are some questions and topics that should never be broached. The biggest one is what we call the million-dollar question, "Did you kill anyone?" That topic is completely off-limits. Corollaries to that are any topics specifically about the violence, "Did you see anyone die? Did you see bodies? Did you know anyone who got killed?" Just don't go there; even with the best intentions, these topics are off limits to anyone who has not been in theater. The vet needs space and time to adjust. It will not be something that happens overnight. Patience and support are the most important things you can do to support those just back from theater.

Obviously, I have been thinking a great deal about this war, why we are fighting it, and what the goal in Iraq should be. As I said in the first article, this is not a political forum, and as an Officer in the U.S. Army, I am not going to make political comments. I realize that I am not really sure how I feel about things right now. I will need a few months to mill things over. I know that my perspective is different. The question that I am going to have to answer, as well as all of us as Americans, is was all of this worth it. Was this war worth the 2,455 dead young men and women? Was it worth it to the Iraqi people who have lost nearly 50,000 men, women and children? Was it worth me leaving my family, and the suffering I caused to my wife, children and colleagues at Penn? It is a question that we just cannot answer right now. I hope that by the time my sons reach the age where they may be called into service, the Middle East has become a peaceful region, without war or terrorism. I hope that the world is a better place on account of the sacrifices these young kids are making today.

I hope one day we can say it was worth the sacrifices.

About the Authors

- **John Pryor** had a magical ability to make you feel good about yourself and boost your self esteem. His avuncular personality and comforting smile lifted your spirits no matter what trouble befell you.

  He's still dead.

- **Rich Pryor** is a retired emergency room physician, currently training dolphins in Australia.

GRATIAS TIBI AGO

This book could not have been completed without the generous support and encouragement of Carmela Calvo. Special thanks to my editor, Mary Jane Dittmar, and proofreaders: Jill Adams, Amy Hughart, Mike McEvoy, Diane Rapp and Elizabeth Sherman.

In addition the author would like to extend his thanks to the following who helped make this work possible:

Omar Bholat ∘ John Chovanes ∘ Maureen Coath ∘ Darin Elkins ∘ Kate Fitzpatrick ∘ Laura Floge ∘ Steve Foster ∘ Dean R Giulitto ∘ Dave Hardin ∘ Todd Kesselman ∘ Gayle Krebs ∘ Jim McCans ∘ Peg Moran ∘ Lauren Platt ∘ Danielle Pryor ∘ Brian Rees ∘ Leslie Rice ∘ Dwight Shen ∘ Chris & Nancy Sheridan ∘ Colleen Williams

18669055R00296

Made in the USA
Lexington, KY
17 November 2012